Tim Rus

0152

£10

COMPLETE
LAKELAND
FELLS

BCA

LONDON   NEW YORK   SYDNEY   TORONTO

COMPLETE
LAKELAND
FELLS

BILL BIRKETT

To the free spirits of the fells.

This edition published in 1994 by BCA
by arrangement with
HarperCollins*Publishers*

CN 2801

© Bill Birkett 1994

The Author asserts the moral right
to be identified as the author of this work

**A CIP catalogue record for this book
is available from the British Library**

All photographs by Bill Birkett Photo Library
(tel: 05394 37420)

Printed and bound in Italy

Additional photographs:
Half-title page: View down Borrowdale from Robin Hood.
Title page: Grey Crag (foreground) and High Crag above
the depths of Birkness Combe.
This page: Scafell Pike, the summit cairn.
page 13: Great Gable above Wasdale Head.
page 107: Robinson above Newlands Hause.
page 133: Skiddaw Massif and Derwent Water.
page 161: East face of the Helvellyn Massif.
page 191: Hartsop Dodd (left of picture).
page 235: Coniston Old Man and Wetherlam.

AUTHOR'S DISCLAIMER

Although the author encountered no difficulty of access
on the routes described, and while considerable effort has
been made to avoid so doing, the inclusion of a walk in
this book does not imply that a right of way exists in every
case. Readers are also advised that changes can occur to
the landscape which may effect the contents of this book.
The author welcomes notification of any such changes.

CONTENTS

ACKNOWLEDGEMENTS

It should be made clear from the start that a project such as this is very much a team effort. It draws on all guidebooks and reference works that have gone before, particularly the genius of A.Wainwright; the photographic inspiration of W.A. Poucher; and for guidance and tuition in the field, John Cleare.

Thanks must go to the Ordnance Survey for their field maps, which serve the public admirably; to family and friends who assisted and supported me during the long preparation of this book, particularly Susan Birkett, my wife, who fastidiously read and corrected copy; and friends who accompanied me on many of the walks, notably John Hargreaves and Eric Stephenson.

I would also like to thank the publishers for their patience and commitment, especially Tom Whiting, Rachel Smyth, Michael Doggart and Ray Barnett; Martin Bagness for his excellent maps; the resident working community of Cumbria, who lend a unique character to the region and make the national park into something more than an outdoor museum; the bodies who keep a careful watch over the area and do their best to preserve its beauty and character – The National Parks' Authority, The National Trust, The Countryside Commission, The Friends of the Lake District; and those who hold the best interests of the hill walker and mountaineer to heart – The Ramblers' Association, The British Mountaineering Council and the Open Spaces Society.

Excellent outdoor equipment from Karrimor International has assisted me faithfully and reliably over many years. Finally, due acknowledgement should be made to my father, Jim Birkett, for showing me the crags and wild places, which he knew better than anyone.

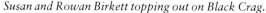

Susan and Rowan Birkett topping out on Black Crag.

INTRODUCTION

The English Lake District is one of the most spectacular and popular regions of the British Isles. Its legendary beauty, unique character and ease of accessibility combine with a breathtaking subtlety of scale to make for an outstanding quality of landscape. Here is a deliciously balanced blend of lakes, rivers, woodlands, dales, farms and villages; and, rising above them all, crowned by Scafell Pike, the magnificent Lakeland Fells.

Compared with the Alps, the Himalayas and even the Scottish Hills, the Lakeland Fells are moderate in altitude. For the hill walker, this has its advantages. For while the challenge remains, with experiences as extreme as one could wish for, at the end of the day a return can be made to the comforts of the valley; to the traditional Lakeland Inn with a warm fire and good beer; or to a club hut, Youth Hostel, even family and home. No need here to suffer endless days of depravation or cold bivouacs (though if you have a mind to, then these options exist).

All these things, of course, are well known and have been written about extensively for centuries. So what makes this book different from the rest? After all, there are many books on the Central Fells, Northern Fells, Lakeland Peaks, Low Fells, High Fells, Classic Walks, Scrambles, and so on; why write another?

When I was a child, a local Langdalian bred and born, I listened in wonder to our 'visitors' talk about their favourite peaks and their intended routes. Following in the footsteps of my father (in his day one of Britain's leading rock climbers and a great naturalist) I developed an overwhelming fascination for the fells both for the very act of scaling them and exploring all they had to offer, and also for reading everything I could on the subject. I longed for that book that listed all the fells and gave the overall picture of what I knew surrounded me. A work that was comprehensive yet detailed – the whole story.

Mysteriously it never appeared and, after giving up a perfectly good career as a civil engineer to enter the 'outdoors' arena, I realised no one else was going to write this book. How could they, for this project, large, real and vivid was something in my head alone. So, finally, I decided to take up the challenge and accept the responsibility for yet another book on the Lake District.

The completed work is designed to be the most comprehensive and detailed route reference guide to the Lakeland Fells available in a single volume. It covers all the fell tops over 1000ft in the English Lake District National Park, which with an area of more than 880 square miles is the largest of its kind in Britain. Some 129 circular walks are described, encompassing in total 541 fell tops. To achieve this, the book divides the region into six geographical areas, within which it identifies the separate chains, or groups, of fells, e.g. The Scafells, Great Gable Group. These groups contain, on average, four walks.

I have always intended that this book should be used for reference and inspiration at home or base. To this end, it has been painstakingly structured. Areas, groups and walks are all carefully defined and accurately described. A series of maps delineate the areas, and show the individual walks within each group. These are to be used in conjunction with Ordnance Survey maps, preferably the 1:25000 Pathfinder and Outdoor Leisure Maps of which seven sheets in total are required to cover the fells described. Using these maps, you have a means by which to select instantly both your base and your route, and preplan your day, weekend or holiday.

Too bulky to be a practical fieldbook, *Complete Lakeland Fells* is a work to be enjoyed as an appreciation of the fells. Descriptions are concise and succinct. I have highlighted points of interest and tried to bring alive the unique flavour of the landscape. Furthermore, the colour photography has been carefully chosen not only to reveal the topography of this outstanding region but also to capture its special magic throughout all the four seasons.

The walks have been selected for their character, quality and practicability. They range from established classics to those that are virtually unknown. Though comprehensive as this work is, it must be realised that every book is finite; the ultimate aim is to give routes that ascend all the tops. Within 880 square miles of national park there are obviously many possible walks that simply cannot be included. Therefore, the author aims to follow this work with guidebooks (which will also serve as practical fieldbooks to be carried for reference en route) reviewing further walks and scrambles of particular quality.

On a personal note, I must admit that this book was always a labour of love. There is solace, wonder, and inspiration in these fells; and in living, working and walking among them, I know that I am privileged. Above all else, I want the book to reflect this and hope that by applying my highest standards of accuracy and craftsmanship this project imparts some of that enjoyment and fulfilment to you.

Bill Birkett

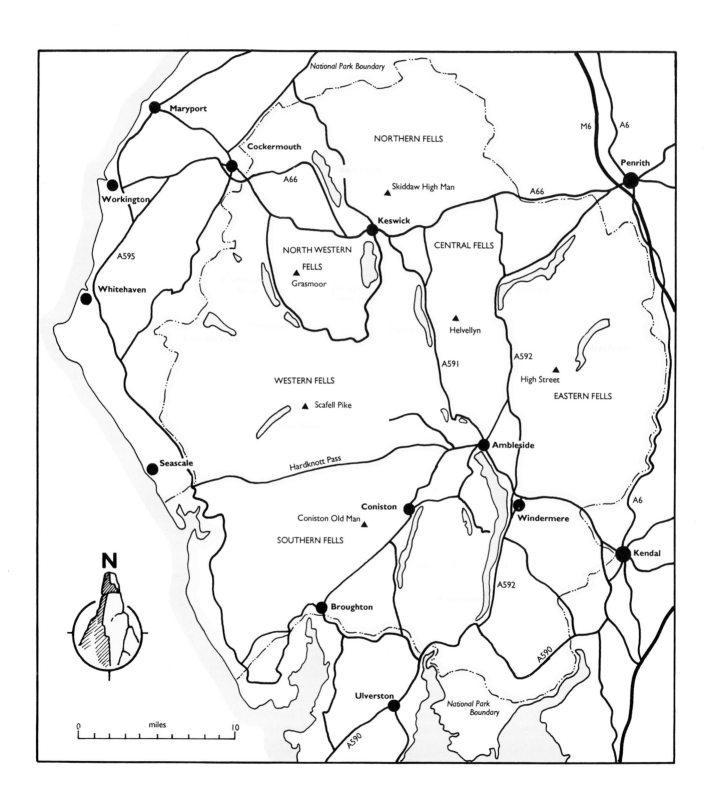

USING THIS BOOK

This book has been structured in modular form to provide a quick and simple system of reference. The six areas are covered in clockwise fashion around The Lake District National Park, starting with the Western Fells. Likewise, within these areas the groups and walks have been ordered clockwise. In all cases, an Area Introduction and Area Fact Sheet are located opposite the map for that area. This is followed by a Group Introduction and map, which are sited opposite a photograph selected to best capture the intimate qualities of that group.

At the back of the book paginated tables list the tops both in altitude order and, for quick reference, alphabetical order. Both provide the area and group in which the top may be found. A further table lists, in altitude order, each top to be found in any particular group, with a six-figure map reference for rapid location on the OS maps. A reference work such as this would be incomplete without an index; accordingly a comprehensive general index also can be found at the back of the book.

Areas

As a result of both geological formation and physical erosion, particularly glacial action, the valleys and fells of the Lake District can be thought of in simple terms as roughly radiating outwards from a central point. From this pattern of landscape, using the main lines of communication (roads) through the region, I have divided the Lakeland Fells into six distinct areas. My decision was based on the particular character of the fells to be found within each area as well as their geographical position. In clockwise order, beginning with the largest concentration and highest of the fells:

WESTERN FELLS cover 205 square miles and consist of 13 groups in which 43 walks and 2 supplementary walks are described over 188 tops;

NORTH WESTERN FELLS cover 80 square miles and consist of 4 groups in which 12 walks are described over 56 tops;

NORTHERN FELLS cover 85 square miles and consist of 4 groups in which 14 walks and 1 supplementary walk are described over 58 tops;

CENTRAL FELLS cover 90 square miles and consist of 4 groups in which 16 walks are described over 66 tops;

EASTERN FELLS cover 140 square miles consisting of 6 groups in which 23 walks are described over 95 tops; and finally

SOUTHERN FELLS cover the largest geographical area of 280 square miles and consist of 6 groups in which 18 walks are described over 78 tops.

Groups

Again these are physically delineated, as far as practicable, by roads or mountain passes – the logical access points from which all walks within the group must start. The composition of any single group is based both on the topography and the general character of the fells within it. Taking into consideration the diversity and remote nature of much of the region I have assumed that the starting point will be reached most commonly by car/private transport. There are a few walks, however, which begin from the Centres.

Tops

The logical objective of the hill walker is, at some stage, to gain the highest point of the fell/mountain/hill/peak over which he or she is walking. I have referred to these high points, summits if you like, as *tops*. In deciding just what to classify as a top I have applied various criteria both to the 1:25 000 OS maps and to the actual physical form on the ground. In so doing I have identified 541 separate tops equal to or over 1000ft in altitude.

Altitude

Based on the good work of the Ordnance Survey the altitude of each top is given as accurately as possible. However, this should be regarded as a guide rather than an absolute value. The heights awarded are based on the 1989 1:25 000 OS maps. Since earlier editions, aerial survey and computer techniques have ensured greater accuracy, which means spot heights given refer more specifically to the actual top of the fell. Similarly the contours, given at 10 metre intervals, are drawn to a higher standard of accuracy than previously. Where tops have not been awarded specific spot heights, I have made a mathematical extrapolation from the contours to estimate the height.

However, minor complications arise in a number of respects. Some heights given on the 1989 OS maps have been obtained from ground survey information. Usually, these are the height of the ground at a trig point, not necessarily sited at the top of the fell. Historically, these heights have always been regarded by hill walkers as the altitude of the top – accordingly I have let these heights stand.

Moreover, while the latest aerial survey information is more accurate, the heights are given in *metres*. This is fine until they are converted back into feet. Put simply, this cannot be done to an absolute accuracy because a metre is a substantially larger unit than a foot (3.2808 feet = 1 metre). Whilst spot heights are given to the full metre, say 10m (32.808ft), in practice the actual heights of fells are not precisely packaged in whole metres; they are a slightly under or over. To make them precise metres, a system of either rounding up or down is employed. Given that the 10m spot height may represent an actual height of 9.5m (31ft) or 10.4m (34ft) it can be seen that exact mathematical conversion from the larger to the smaller unit can induce error. For those seasoned hill walkers who know for certain that the top of Scafell

Pike is 3210ft based on a perfectly good land survey, a figure enshrined on all imperial maps and all previous guidebooks, so be it. I do not intend to change this. Where, historically, an imperial height has been given within the mathematical range explained above, I have kept that imperial height and not simply done a straight mathematical conversion from whole metres to feet. In cases where a new spot height obviously supersedes the original land survey, and straight mathematical conversion of metres to feet is the most accurate technique, I have taken this course.

It could be argued that feet should be dropped and the tops referred to only in metres. While this would have made my job considerably easier, many would find it quite unacceptable. Understandably so, for it is feet that carry us to the tops and a quick look down serves as an instant reference to just how far a good old foot really is!

Walks

All the walks described in this book start from and return to the same point and are circular in concept. This is the most practical form of walking, avoiding pick-up points, forced overnight stays etc, and allows you to travel light and enjoy the walk to a maximum. There are 126 main walks and 3 supplements. The latter, although outings in their own right, branch off a main walk and return to it at a later stage. They involve scrambling or easy climbing, i.e. Broad Stand on Scafell, Pillar Rock and Sharp Edge on Blencathra. The walks are my personal choice and they range from long established classics like the Fairfield or Kentmere Horseshoes to lesser-known outings such as the Ullscarf Round.

Each walk is uniquely referenced to the group in which it lies and appears on the Group Map, i.e. NOS 1 refers to Walk 1 within the North O'Skiddaw Group (NOS). The fell tops are listed in the order in which they are encountered on the walk. A fact sheet of data enables you to easily select your base, map and starting point. It also details the vital statistics of the walk, in order that you may accurately assess the magnitude of the undertaking and plan accordingly. The fact sheet

provides the following information:

Valley Base and Town Base: These are the most convenient to the walk. Details on each base will be found within each Area Fact Sheet at the start of the section.

Maps: Reference has been made solely to the Ordnance Survey publications, which are the most up to date and accurate available. For using in the field and for planning purposes, the detail of the 1:25 000 (2.5 inches to the mile) series is unbeatable. Within the Outdoor Leisure series, four maps, Nos. 4, 5, 6 and 7, (labelled OD4, OD5, OD6 and OD7 in this book) cover most of the Lake District. However, at the same scale, Pathfinder Nos. 576, 625 and 626 are also required to cover all the fells within the national park boundary. One disturbing feature of the 1989 series of maps are the dotted green lines which supposedly represent public paths. Over the fells these are often drawn where there are no paths on the ground, and occasionally head straight over cliffs or dangerous ground. As a tip, look for the thin dotted black lines which are part of the original survey; these were located when surveyors actually walked the terrain (as opposed to a computer plotting the information from aerial survey). On a lesser scale the 1:50 000 (1.25 inches to the mile) Landranger series is also useful, each map covering a larger area but with less detail. Four of these maps, Nos. 89, 90, 96 and 97 (labelled L89, L90, L96 and L97 in this book) cover the area. The 1:63 360 (1 inch to 1 mile) Tourist Map shows the area as a whole.

Length and Ascent: This is a vital combination of information which, used together, is the best overall means of assessing the difficulty of the walk and which allows the application of Naismith's Rule ('A reasonably fit walker will average 3mph/5km/h plus 0.5 hour for every 1000ft/300m of ascent').

Approx Time: This is a realistic time based on my personal experience (as opposed to a purely theoretical one devised from Naismith's Rule) for a walker of average ability. On the longer walks it takes into account a short stop for a snack. Nevertheless, it should be used as

a relative guide only, not as an absolute value.

Start & Finish: Includes a unique six-figure national grid reference.

Difficulty: This applies to good conditions in summer only and takes the form of a salient note as opposed to a technical grading. It should be read in conjunction with all the above information.

Photography

All the photography in this book is my own. It has been specially selected to show both the topography and to bring out the magic of the Lakeland fells. It is 35mm taken on colour transparency film.

Maps

The 44 maps within the book have all been drawn exclusively for this project by cartographer Martin Bagness. The following provides a key to the symbols used:

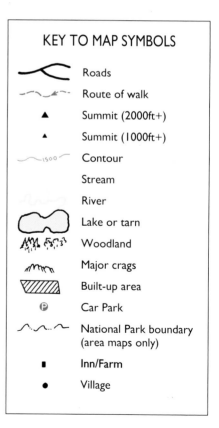

KEY TO MAP SYMBOLS

	Roads
	Route of walk
▲	Summit (2000ft+)
▲	Summit (1000ft+)
1500	Contour
	Stream
	River
	Lake or tarn
	Woodland
	Major crags
	Built-up area
Ⓟ	Car Park
	National Park boundary (area maps only)
■	Inn/Farm
●	Village

Terminology

There are certain words/expressions which, because they are used extensively within the text, have either been abbreviated or left unexplained.

fell wall – the stone wall boundary which separates open fell from cultivated pasture below.

left/right – the direction defined by the walker as he/she is facing at the time of description.

true left/right – the direction looking downstream with the flow of the beck (stream or river).

trig point – triangulation station used by the Ordnance Survey. Usually, this is a pillar built of stone or concrete. Occasionally, it takes the form of a 'concrete ring'. It is taken to be the highest point of the fell, although on occasions it is not so located, e.g., when a jagged rocky knoll unsuitable for pillar construction assumes the highest point.

Local names, spellings and pronunciation – An extensive glossary on the meanings and correct pronunciation of the local names is beyond the scope of this book. However, the word 'fell' is so central that it deserves an explanation. It comes from the Norse *fjall*, meaning hill. However, the Viking settlers named the hillsides on which they grazed their sheep with little consideration for hill walkers. Often their names refer to the flanks of a peak/hill rather than any particular top. Spellings for the most part agree with Ordnance Survey information. On occasions where a spelling may differ, the version I have given is the one I prefer and may be found in various other sources of reference.

Safety on The Hills

It is assumed that everyone using this book will have some mountain walking experience and be familiar with all techniques (survival and navigation) and equipment vital for safe hill walking. The decision to go on a certain walk and, for the prevailing conditions, to choose the correct equipment and adopt the right techniques is the personal responsibility of the individual. Make no mistake, especially so in winter, the Lakeland Fells can be dangerous. For those seeking further detailed information I recommend the *Hillwalker's Manual* (Cicerone Press, 1993). It covers in detail the modern-day essential elements of hill/mountain walking terrain, equipment, navigation, techniques, survival and includes a chapter on the fundamentals and priciples of hill walking photography.

Fell Management

Remarkably free access exists on the Lakeland Fells. Whilst many of us regard the fells as 'god given' and maintain we have a moral 'right' to roam, it should be appreciated that to a large extent this happy state of access is due to the goodwill of private landowners, local farmers, and careful management by The National Parks' Authority and The National Trust. We as hill walkers should respect this and, as individuals, do our utmost to maintain the environment. The ideal we should adopt is to take only photographs and leave as little trace of our passing as possible. It is assumed that every reader of this book will be familiar with and adhere rigidly to the *Country Code*.

Erosion is a problem and for the wider good of the fells one should comply with any upland management schemes that are in progress. The National Parks' Authority and The National Trust have done much excellent work in restoring footpaths and preventing further erosion. They do this for our benefit as hill lovers and they deserve every assistance we can give them.

The jagged rocks of Swirl How with Wetherlam beyond.

WESTERN FELLS

Derwent Water/Thirlmere Fells DER (28 tops) • Langdale Fells LAN (22 tops)
Bowfell Group BOW (20 tops) • Borrowdale Fells BOR (12 tops)
Eskdale Fells ESK (13 tops) • Scafells SCA (8 tops) • Screes SCR (4 tops)
Great Gable Group GRG (10 tops) • Pillar Group PIL (18 tops)
Lank Rigg Group LAK (12 tops) • High Stile Group HIG (13 tops)
Loweswater Fells LOW (21 tops) • Fellbarrow Group FEL (7 tops)

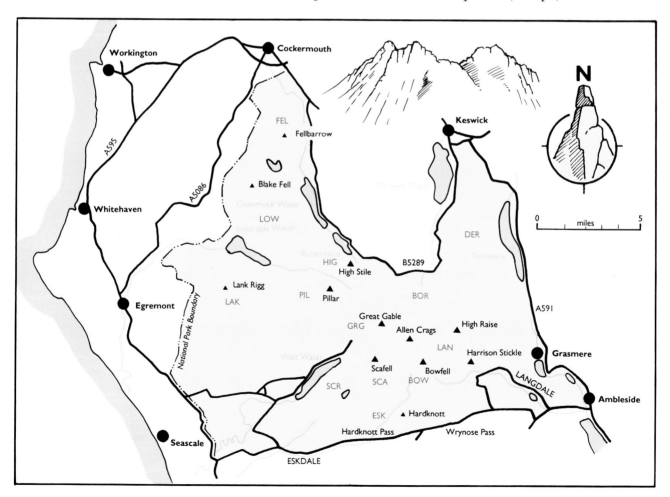

While physically this area may form the western boundary of the Lake District, for many it represents the spiritual heartland. From lakeshore to meadow, these fells offer unparalleled elegance and drama: Scafell Pike, the highest mountain in England; Great Gable, an evocative name for an equally enchanting mountain; the Langdale Pikes; the majestic reclining lion's profile of Pike O'Stickle and Pavey Ark seen across Windermere Lake; and Pillar Mountain together with the sheer Pillar Rock, romantically immortalised by Wordsworth in his poem *The Brothers*.

Within the 205 square miles that make up this area lies the greatest concentration of tops in the district: thirteen groups of fells containing 188 separate tops. Defined to the north by Lorton Vale and the Buttermere and Borrowdale valleys, the area is outlined to the east by the A591 Ambleside to Keswick road. To the south, the Little Langdale to Eskdale road scales the passes of Wrynose and Hardknott to delineate a natural boundary; while the Cumbrian coastal plains' national park boundary follows the western flanks, beyond which England tumbles into the Irish Sea. Within these defined boundaries lies a concentrated area of mountain upland penetrated by the narrow valleys of Langdale, Wasdale, Ennerdale and Loweswater – the glacially eroded western spokes of an imaginary wheel.

It was from Wasdale Head in the mid-1800s that the first recorded hill walking and climbing began in the Lake District. Despite the timeless appeal and savage beauty of this hamlet sheltered beneath Great Gable and the Scafells, it seems puzzling that this secluded and remote place, still relatively difficult to reach by car, should have been the centre of popularity in those bygone days.

The reason is quite simple. In the absence of motor cars the industrial west coast was served by rail, with Drigg Railway Station providing a convenient access point for Wasdale. Today the situation is somewhat reversed. The valleys of Langdale and Borrowdale provide the easiest access points and this has made the eastern half of the massif the most popular. The northern region of the far western fells, including the Ennerdale, Lamplugh and Loweswater groups, requires a few hours further travel from the M6, so remain relatively quiet.

From east to west, north to south, the area offers tremendous variety: sharp featured, defiant and magnificent as formed from mountain rhyolite and Borrowdale volcanics; subtle and elegantly rounded when created from the ancient Skiddaw slates; and slab-like, bold and gregarious when fashioned from Eskdale granite. Here can be found some of the most easily approachable summits of the region as well as many of the most difficult and demanding.

AREA FACT SHEET

THE VALLEY BASES

Borrowdale
Camping: Seathwaite Farm, Thornythwaite Farm, Borrowdale Village, Stonethwaite, Ashness Farm, Dalt Wood – Grange.
Youth Hostels: Longthwaite, Barrow House.
Inns: The Scafell Hotel.
Bus Services: Keswick to Seatoller.

Buttermere
Camping: Gatesgarth Farm.
Youth Hostels: Buttermere, Honister Hause.
Inns: The Fish.
Bus Services: None.

Ennerdale
Camping: None.
Youth Hostels: High Gillerthwaite, Black Sail Hut.
Inns: Ennerdale Bridge.
Bus Services: None.

Eskdale
Camping: Boot, Fisherground Farm.
Youth Hostel: Eskdale.

Inns: Burnmoor, Woolpack.
Bus Services: Mountain Goat Mini Bus.

Great Langdale
Camping: Head of Valley, Baysbrown Farm at Chapel Stile, Neaum Crag above Skelwith Bridge.
Youth Hostels: Elterwater, High Close.
Inns: Old Dungeon Ghyll, New Dungeon Ghyll.
Bus Services: Ambleside to Old Dungeon Ghyll.

Little Langdale
Camping: None.
Youth Hostels: None.
Inn: The Three Shires.
Bus Services: The Mountain Goat Mini Bus.

Thirlmere
Camping: Dale Bottom, Bridge End Farm.
Youth Hostel: Thirlmere.
Inn: Thirlspot/King's Head.
Bus Services: Ambleside to Keswick.

THE TOWN BASES

Ambleside
Camping: None.
Youth Hostel: Ambleside (Waterhead).
All facilities except railway station.

Cockermouth
All facilities.
Youth Hostel: Double Mills.

Egremont
Limited facilities, no camping, no Youth Hostel.

Grasmere
Limited facilities, no camping.
Youth Hostels: Butterlip How and Thorney How.

Keswick
Camping: The Headlands, Derwent Water, Castlerigg Hall and Castlerigg Farm.
Youth Hostel: Keswick.
All facilities except railway station.

The prospect north over the Group from Low White Stones, High Raise.

DERWENT WATER THIRLMERE FELLS

•DER•

Stretching between the valleys of Borrowdale and Thirlmere, this extensive upland tongue of fells forms the watershed feeding Derwent Water to the west and Thirlmere Reservoir to the east.

From the highest top, High Raise in the south, to Bleaberry Fell above Castlerigg and Derwent Water in the north, the walks savour many of the charms of the two contrasting valleys. For instance, ramblers can explore the delights of Borrowdale, arguably the most romantically beautiful of all the lakeland valleys with her sylvan splendour and open craggy aspect; or alternatively liberate, from the secretive shroud of conifers, the attributes of quiet Thirlmere.

With a proliferation of heather and bilberry the often gentle, rounded tops and slopes below offer an area of considerable variety, from the impressive rock precipices of Eagle and Raven Crag to the sad remnants of the drowned community of Armboth; the magic of Dock Tarn, cradled amongst a blaze of purple in August, to the breathtaking scene along the length of Borrowdale from King's How.

Providing a visual exploration of the intricacies of the hidden valleys of Watendlath, Greenup, Langstrath and Wythburn, the Derwent Water/Thirlmere Fells represent an area of quiet beauty.

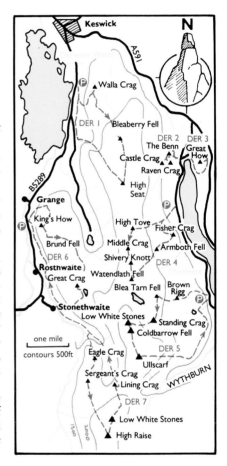

·DER 1·

GREAT WOOD TO HIGH SEAT

Walla Crag 1243ft/379m
Bleaberry Fell 1935ft/590m
High Seat 1995ft/608m

Valley Base: Borrowdale.
Maps: OS OD4, The English Lakes –
North West. L90 Penrith & Keswick.
Length: 6.25miles/10km.
Approx Time: 4hrs.
Start & Finish: Great Wood Car Park
(NY 272212).
Ascent: 2000ft/610m.
Difficulty: The initial section of ascent is
quite steep but generally the walking is
easy and route finding straightforward.
Entirely on well trodden paths, there are
nevertheless a couple of short boggy
sections.

The great vegetated dome of Bleaberry Fell and the higher summit of High Seat effectively form the northern tip of this upland tongue which I have labelled the Derwent Water/Thirlmere Fells. Walla Crag, famous for its excellent views, is popularly regarded as a summit in its own right and provides an invigorating approach to the higher fells rising beyond. On the latter section of the walk, the vague tops of Ashness Fell and Dodd cannot really be classified as anything other than protrusions on the flanks of High Seat. Descent into Borrowdale is enlightened first by Ashness Gill and then later by inspirational views across the expanse of Derwent Water.

Leave the car park by the stile and follow the track forking right to Cat Gill. Follow the path steeply up the north bank of the gill to emerge through pines, then bear left up the open shoulder. A wooden stile, through a gap in the stone wall on the left, leads to a charming path following the quieter side of the wall with occasional views through the trees. Soon the trees disappear, the main path is rejoined and you reach the open bare rock top of Walla Crag .

Retrace your steps for a short way to the first break in the stone wall, from where you follow the well-defined path traversing the upper reaches of Cat Gill to Bleaberry Fell.

With a number of minor variations possible, the path stretches along the broad ridge to High Seat. A post and wire fence marks most of the route though inevitably, whichever route is followed, bog will have been encountered before the curiously named rocky mounds of Threefooted Brandreth are crossed to gain the summit and triangulation point.

Descend to a little hollow and more bog. A well-defined path crosses a ruined stone wall before descending into the upper regions of Ashness Gill. To visit the whimsically cairned rocky outcrops marking the possible top of Ashness Fell it is necessary to make a detour left. The

Walla Crag (right of centre) looks over Derwent Water and Keswick.

bulge in the shoulder below these is known simply as Dodd.

A steep descent leads back to the path. After the initial section of gill, at the head of a sizeable waterfall, bear left. Move down the flanks of the gill past rock, bracken, trees and everything that makes Borrowdale so magnificent.

A photograph of stone-arched Ashness Bridge, over to Derwent Water with Skiddaw floating beyond is hard to resist, though it may have appeared on every Lakeland calendar. It makes for a scene of timeless beauty that captures much of the addictively oriental charm of this locality.

Descend a short section of road until a track, signposted 'Great Wood and Keswick', bears right to climb a stile. The lower track follows the contours of the hillside beneath Falcon Crags to regain Great Wood. From here, a footbridge crosses over Cat Gill to the original track.

Raven Crag and the Benn as seen from Thirlmere Dam.

ABOVE THIRLMERE DAM

Raven Crag 1512ft/461m
Castle Crag 1381ft/421m
The Benn 1463ft/446m
Great How 1100ft/335m

Valley Base: Thirlmere.
Maps: OS OD4, The English Lakes – North West. L90 Penrith & Keswick.
Length: DER 2: 2miles/3.5km.
DER 3: 3miles/5km.
Approx Time: DER 2: 2hrs.
DER 3: 1.5hrs.
Start & Finish: For both walks, this is the car park at the western end of Thirlmere Dam (NY 307189).
Ascent: DER 2: 425ft/128m.
DER 3: 430ft/130m.
Difficulty: These two walks can either be treated separately, and as such are highly suitable for a part day/evening outing, or can be combined with a break and sandwich stop at the car park.

The common starting point of these two walks offers the energetic rambler the possibility of combining them into one. DER 2 climbs to the summit of Raven Crag, whose east face is seen as a sheer

rock precipice from the A591 and from the road over the dam (from where it is often photographed). The walk continues to the more secluded Castle Crag Fort and The Benn. DER 3, taking in the top of Great How, may be slightly easier yet is nonetheless a walk of undeniable quality.

For DER 2, leave the car park and walk north along the road until after about 100m a sign 'Castle Crag Ancient Monument' directs you left through a little gate. Steep going up a rough path leads through pines to a forest track. This loops up the hillside, taking you directly beneath the sheer north east face of Raven Crag then back again into the pines. As the dark pines begin to change to friendlier larch, a diagonal path joins the track from the left. Follow this as it rises rapidly, with beech taking over from conifer, to reach a shoulder and another wide forest track. Bear left on this and almost immediately leave it on the left to find a path leading up a tiny valley to the top of Raven Crag. Despite the encroaching pines, the view over Thirlmere, which can be enhanced by descending to a lower grassy platform, is splendid. Take great care for the unguarded vertical rock face lies directly below.

Retrace your steps to the track. A sign points to the curious rocky protuberance of Castle Crag Fort. Ascent in a clockwise direction reveals a level platform guarded

by remnants of a boundary wall and strange earthworks. A short scramble gains the summit of the final rocky knoll. Guarded by steep rocks on most sides, its defensive position is easy to appreciate. Over to the west, the formidable buttress of Iron Crag presents an impressive profile. Descent from the summit is straightforward. Walk north to find a path leading back to the original point of ascent.

Return to the main forest track and follow this north for a few hundred metres until a slight path bears off to the right. This follows roughly the crest of the shoulder through the pines, until the steep slopes that mark the top of The Benn are reached. The path runs up to the right, bypassing the steep scree, to the hollow summit cone. Raven Crag offers a bold profile when seen from here.

Descend to the north, following a narrow path and occasional marker post. Soon this intercepts a forestry track which on further descent will be found to be the original track followed. Retrace your steps to the car park.

DER 3 leads across the dam to find steps and the 'Permissive Path: Dalehead Swirls' on the right. This is a delightful and secluded walk through mixed woodland just above the waters of Thirlmere Reservoir. Proceed along the bank of the reservoir until the path breaks away from the water's edge. Follow the contours of

Great How as viewed across Thirlmere.

the hillside to find a track bearing up to the left. As this becomes overgrown a sign 'Great How Summit' marks a path which leads up to the right. In a short while the rocky top is reached. Descend to the base of the How from where a return can be made in the same direction. Alternatively, strike an anticlockwise course along the track until the road is reached.

•DER 4•

ARMBOTH HIGH TOVE ROUND

High Tove 1689ft/515m
Middle Crag 1587ft/484m
Shivery Knott 1610ft/491m
Watendlath Fell 1689ft/515m
Armboth Fell 1570ft/479m
Fisher Crag 1381ft/421m

Valley Base: Thirlmere.
Maps: OS OD4, The English Lakes – North West. L90 Penrith & Keswick.
Length: 5miles/8km.
Approx Time: 3.5hrs.
Start & Finish: Armboth Car Park (NY 306172).
Ascent: 1340ft/425m.
Difficulty: Extensive boggy areas prevail around High Tove and a fair proportion of the walk traverses rough heather with no definite path. Nevertheless, apart from a steepish start, the walk is fairly mild-natured. Wet feet guaranteed.

Once a thriving community before Thirlmere was dammed and flooded, Armboth is now a North West Water Authority car park. This walk begins here and takes a well trodden path to the summit of High Tove. It then traverses the watershed of the Derwent Fells as far as Watendlath Fell (unnamed on the OS map) before heading through heather down to Armboth Fell and on to the fine viewpoint of Fisher Crag. Although High Tove and Armboth Fell may never truthfully be described as individual gems of Lakeland, this walk should not be under-estimated. It is an outing of wild character, exploring long guarded aspects of Thirlmere.

Across the road from the car park a sign reads 'Public Footpath Watendlath'. Leading over a bridge to open fellside, a path takes a pleasant rift through the otherwise tightly ranked conifers. Passing some interesting boulders, presumably fallen from the rocky Cockrigg Crags to the right, the path rises steeply. With Fisher Gill tumbling through the conifer plantation to the left, it is best to break right and follow the constructed zigzags of the old packhorse track. At the top of the rise, right of the gill and plantation, the path leads to a gap through a stone wall. Beyond this, a vague path continues to the summit cairn of High Tove.

The hamlet of Watendlath lies directly below, but grit the teeth and bear left along the flat and boggy watershed. At least the post and wire fence line does offer some possibility to wire-walk the wettest sections before the rocky knoll of Middle Fell rises to its right. It is necessary to scale the fence to reach the knoll.

Move on to the next rocky outcrop. It may be better to avoid the bogs and re-cross the fence line to follow its eastern side. Old iron posts of an abandoned fence lead to the top of Shivery Knott.

The next substantial rocky plateau is Watendlath Fell, from where excellent views extend north to the distinct Reecastle Crag. Clamber over the fence to a cairn on its west spur for views of Blea Tarn.

From here, head north east for Armboth Fell over thick heather, then descend into a small basin and cross the stream. Rising from the stream an ancient cairn stands to the right, covered in green lichen and balanced on a boulder (presumably built by shepherds before Thirlmere was flooded). The summit of Armboth Fell is marked by a tiny cairn and can be found on the most northerly outcrop of rock, on the left edge of the upland mass now appearing before you.

Strike east. Heather, rock, tarns and pines, with Helvellyn rising beyond, give the scene a strong Scottish flavour. Take care not to fall over the small but precipitous crags on the descent towards Fisher Crag. In the heathery hollow at the base of the shoulder walk around the right side

of the tarn. To reach the top of Fisher Crag, scale the wire fence and probe the perimeter conifers to cross a broken stone wall, before climbing to find the rocky knoll swathed in vegetation.

Return the same way before taking a course due west that rises to a rocky knoll. An easy gully breaks down to the left, after which a circular traverse can be made. Keep reasonably high, to cross the main source of Fisher Gill. The wooded gill above here is sunk into the flanks of the hillside. It emerges by a lone holly where a crossing can be made. Continue on to cross the second source of the gill and regain the original path at the head of the plantation.

Following this path, a steepish descent leads back to the shores of Thirlmere.

The grassy top of High Tove.

Down Greenup Edge to Ullscarf.

·DER 5·

ULLSCARF ROUND

Brown Rigg 1519ft/463m
Blea Tarn Fell 1830ft/558m
Standing Crag 2005ft/611m
Coldbarrow Fell – Low Saddle 2152ft/656m
Coldbarrow Fell – High Saddle 2215ft/675m
Ullscarf 2382ft/726m
Wythburn Fell 1667ft/508m

Valley Base: Thirlmere.
Maps: OS OD4, The English Lakes –
North West. L90 Penrith & Keswick.
Length: 6miles/10km.
Approx Time: 4hrs.
Start & Finish: Dobgill Car Park
(NY 316140).
Ascent: 2230ft/680m.
Difficulty: While there is no distinct path
covering some sections of this walk, in
contrast to the Derwent Fells immediately
north, grassland prevails and the walking
is generally amiable. However, the altitude
and remoteness of Ullscarf, with few
places to find shelter, should not be
underestimated. Not a walk to be tackled
in poor weather.

High Ullscarf, a broad upland shoulder
formed by the deeply cut valleys of
Greenup, Wythburn and Thirlmere, is the
ultimate objective of this walk. Despite
presenting a formidable array of crags
when viewed from below, the extensive
summit area is rather gentle and rolling.
The route described offers an interesting
and varied journey, ascending numerous
tops and offering superlative views in all
directions. The walk itself descends over
Black Knott and the stark curving ridge
that dominates the Wythburn valley, to
end at secluded Harrop Tarn.

A short stroll down the road reveals
another parking place, should Dobgill be
full, and beyond this a large rift devoid of
conifers. This presents a pleasant opening
up the fell. Take the stile leading over the
fence and enter a walled but now redun-
dant lane. Leave it by a breach in the wall
and continue up the hillside to find a tight
ring of iron railings protecting what was
once perhaps a well. Gain the track and
bear right, crossing an embankment
bridge to find a small gate above to the

left. Climb steeply and find the remnants
of an old zigzagging path. The angle
slackens beyond the top of Bank Crags to
the right and soon an old building is
passed before a leftward traverse above
the forestry gains the balanced stone and
summit of Brown Rigg. Look for grazing
deer in the basin beyond.

Descend to Stone Hause then begin
climbing Blea Tarn Fell by the broad rake
on the left. Soon it becomes easier to
avoid the short rocky buttresses by cir-
cumnavigating them to the right. The
summit of Blea Tarn Fell (unnamed on
the OS map) reveals a trig point and, on
its most northerly point, a naturally
curved rock seat from which to admire
the tarn and the view stretching to the Solway Firth. Ancient quarry buildings lie
below. The ascent to the rocky bastion of
Standing Crag is steep but is a worthy
prize after which a traverse across to the
distinct low saddle top of Coldbarrow
Fell is easily made. This airy perch of
rough, colour-banded volcanic rock
topped by a cairn offers incredible views.

The boulder cluster of High Saddle
follows. A gentle walk, eventually guided
by old iron posts (useful in the mist), leads
to the summit cairn of Ullscarf, with a
vista across the entire length of the Lake
District, over Windermere, south to
Morecambe Bay and north to the Solway.
The route (no definite path) lies east in the

direction of Seat Sandal and Fairfield.
Skirt Black Knott to gain the long curving
ridge situated above Wythburn valley.
Descend the ridge, keeping near its edge
to pass a shepherd's cairn situated on an
indefinite top. Below, a rocky outcrop
(conveniently given a spot height on the
1:25 000 OS map) stands proud, its out-
line traced by a steep sweeping gully to the
south west. The top of Wythburn Fell is a
positive marker offering uninterrupted
views down Wythburn to Steel End Farm.

Ahead lies the beacon marked on the
map; care should be taken not to fall over
one of the many rocky knolls. Although
an obvious landmark seen from the A591
below, on closer inspection it is just a
short section of stone wall balanced on
the rocky ridge. Below, a long forgotten
grass track leads through a gap in the
wall. From here, follow the deer fence.
Inside the compound, conifers have been
cleared and an uninterrupted sighting of
Harrop Tarn is once more available.

Beyond stand the rocky heights of
Tarn Crags. By the corner in the fence a
subsidiary fence is crossed to gain and follow the line of the old wall. A gate gives
access through the deer fence to the tarn.
Take the track, cross the exit stream and
immediately turn right to follow the constructed path above Dob Gill. This
descends steeply through the conifers
back to the car park.

•DER 6•

GRANGE FELL TO GREAT CRAG

King's How – Grange Fell 1286ft/392m
Brund Fell 1363ft/415m
Great Crag 1444ft/440m

Valley Base: Borrowdale.
Maps: OS OD4, The English Lakes – North West. L90 Penrith & Keswick.
Length: 6.5miles/10.5km.
Approx Time: 4hrs.
Start & Finish: The Bowderstone car park (NY 253168).
Ascent: 1625ft/495m.
Difficulty: Apart from the final section of ascent to the summit of Great Crag, this route lies entirely on well-defined paths. Even so, a few boggy sections exist, some of which cannot be circumnavigated.

This is a fine walk, contrasting the woods of rowan, silver birch and oak with the open heather and bilberry-clad heights of King's How, Brund Fell and Great Crag. Watendlath hamlet lies to the east, while out below to the west stretches the whole of Borrowdale. Located centrally, the craggy heights of King's How combine with Castle Crag on the opposite bank of the River Derwent to form the 'Jaws of Borrowdale'; while among the upland craggy folds nestles the idyllic Dock Tarn.

From the top corner of the Bowderstone car park take the stile over the wire fence. A well-defined path crosses a small stream and proceeds gently at first past some old quarry workings, then a steady pull leads to an open shoulder. To the right lies a distinctive boulder. Higher up, a sheer rock face known as Greatend Crag forms the Borrowdale face of our first objective – King's How. Straight ahead, above the Troutdale Valley, looms the huge precipice of Black Crag.

Dropping from the shoulder through the stone wall, the path enters the thickly wooded head of Troutdale. Bearing right, it soon begins to climb steeply through the trees – via stone steps – to emerge onto an open shoulder. From here, continue to a wire fence and bear right along it. Climb to gain a small boggy valley between rocky hummocks, then bear right across the end of the valley. A stout yew tree on the left marks the way before the path follows the contours of the hillside.

Backtrack to the Borrowdale face of the fell. Pass a slate plaque and dedication (which reads, 'In Loving Memory of King Edward VII. Grange Fell is dedicated by his Sister Louise') and rise to the summit cairn of King's How.

The path proceeds along the fell to the end of the shoulder of Brund Fell. Descend and cross the path, noting the fine open panorama to the right. On the shoulder of Brund Fell bear left to pass through the rock outcrops. Finally, climb

The view down to King's How and the Jaws of Borrowdale.

to the cairned highest point, another rock tower, immediately above the path.

Descend to a wall and follow it down on the Watendlath side (where it is boggy in places) to cross the main Rosthwaite/Watendlath track in the hollow. Opposite lies a kissing gate and beyond a path continues, aiming ultimately for an obvious valley weakness in the next section of raised fell. Before this is reached, a detour sign will be found directing you left to circumnavigate the approaching bog, thereby protecting the environmentally sensitive wetlands.

A kissing gate through the stone wall gives access to the weakness in the hillside from where the ascent is made. At the top of the slope, where the cairned main path levels, leave it and strike up to the right through thick heather and rough ground to find the summit of Great Crag (there is no real path). Herein lies a dilemma –

three cairns mark the tops, but which is the summit? The most northerly spur, marked by two cairns, feels higher than the separate southern summit. Just to make sure, visit the latter before locating the best way to descend to the main cairned path seen below.

Further on, and surrounded by thick heather, lies the tranquil Dock Tarn with a tiny rocky island bearing a rowan. The purple heather is best viewed in late August. Beyond a boggy section midway along the tarn, the unmistakable path leads over the edge of the fell. An uneven rock staircase descends through the woods, the angle easing before the main track along the valley floor. A pleasant, level walk leads to Rosthwaite.

Our route continues to the right. Initially, follow the track to Watendlath. Pass a raised walkway, which may have to be used if the stream is in flood. The

track emerges from the trees and begins to rise up the hillside. Leave it and bear left, beneath the bows of an oak and along by the post and wire fence. Pass through a small gate and cross a stream. Eventually, the road is joined at a small car park. Walk along the pavement on the left of the road until, with an open section of grass leading to the River Derwent on the left, a stile/wooden gate gives access to a rocky track on the right. This leads past two cottages, now climbing club huts, to the huge Bowderstone. This great rock, weighing some 1500 tons, appears to balance precariously on a knife edge. You can shake hands through a hole underneath it. Make a suitable wish. A fixed wooden stairway takes you to its summit.

The track continues past a small rock face to the right and then a large slate quarry, before reaching the car park and starting point.

The Bowderstone (top) and Dock Tarn (bottom).

◆ D E R 7 ◆

STONETHWAITE TO HIGH RAISE

Eagle Crag 1709ft/521m
Sergeant's Crag 1873ft/571m
High Raise 2500ft/762m
Low White Stones 2398ft/731m
Lining Crag 1778ft/542m

Valley Base: Borrowdale.
Maps: OS OD4, The English Lakes – North West. L90 Penrith & Keswick.
Length: 7miles/11.5km.
Approx Time: 4.5hrs.
Start & Finish: Stonethwaite (NY 262137). Limited car parking in the centre of the hamlet by the telephone kiosk.
Ascent: 2500ft/762m.
Difficulty: Quite a stiff outing, with a section of steep ascent. The path is vague in places and sheer rocky crags abound – not a walk for poor visibility or bad weather. Sections approaching and descending from High Raise are inevitably wet and boggy.

The traditional red telephone kiosk in Stonethwaite emphasizes that little has changed in this quiet mountain hamlet. From here, the ultimate goal of this quite

The mighty head of Eagle Crag above the confluence of Greenup Gill and Langstrath Beck.

demanding circular walk is High Raise, the highest and most southerly top of the Derwent Water Fells. Yet it is the precipitous end of the upland spur between Greenup and Langstrath, the great rock bastion of Eagle Crag, that dominates the Stonethwaite Valley. Along with Sergeant's Crag, the higher top behind Eagle Crag which peeps over its shoulder, their ascent provides an invigorating approach to the summit of High Raise.

Follow the track over Stonethwaite Bridge and make a right turn at the junction. Lining the track are stone walls and green fields, above which the flanks of the valley rise in mixed woodlands and bracken, while the tumbling waterfalls of Stonethwaite Beck sound to the right.

The beck turns and divides into Greenup Gill and Langstrath Beck. Cross the bridge and find a small stile over the post and wire fence on the left. Continue along a path passing through two stone walls. At the second wall turn right, making a strenuous ascent directly up the hill-side. At the top of the wall bear left, until the higher wall of the enclosure can be crossed where it meets the crag on the left. Move right onto the shoulder to find a short gully through the craggy ground above. Climb this to the shoulder until it is possible to traverse right under a rock face. The path continues through easier terrain to reach the angled rock slab and cairn that marks the summit of mighty Eagle Crag. Descent of this section is not advised without prior knowledge, for steep and dangerous crags lie directly beneath the summit of this famous rock climbing face. For this reason the walk is not recommended in the reverse direction to that described.

Aiming for Sergeant's Crag, move down to the corner of the wall. Continue along this, eventually deviating right to gain the summit of Sergeant's Crag. The route is now straightforward, leading across the final section of the spur to join the flanks of High Raise. Keep Long Crag to your left but gain the shoulder above, then bear easily right to the summit of High Raise – the highest point of the fell and of the boulder field named High White Stones.

A veritable dual carriageway leads back along to the cairned hump of Low White Stones and down Greenup Edge. Although this descent is quite steep, water defies gravity and bogs proliferate. In the hollow, bear left and follow the cairned path to the narrow top of Lining Crag. Take care here, for a cliff lies directly below. Turn right to find a paved staircase spiralling safely down the north side of the crag. The path continues through an interesting area of moraine in the narrow valley of Greenup Gill. The stream tumbles over numerous small waterfalls and pools, with the steep-sided slopes and crags (Eagle Crag to the left, Lining Crag high above to the right) heightening the drama of this wild landscape.

Soon the original track is rejoined. Easy walking past the ruined barn and ancient yews leads back to Stonethwaite.

The Langdale Pikes seen over Elterwater.

LANGDALE FELLS

•LAN•

Cutting deep into the south eastern corner of the Western Fells, the valley of Great Langdale provides a natural gateway to an exceptional area highlighted by The Langdale Pikes, rising 2000ft from the valley floor to crown the rugged northern skyline.

From the remote head of Mickleden, the Langdale Fells stretch down the S-shaped Great Langdale Valley with the rocky cluster of Pike O' Stickle, Harrison Stickle and Pavey Ark forming the magnificent centrepiece. Beyond, the distinct rocky cone of Sergeant Man heads both the Langdale Edge, which leads down to Silver How and the Helm Crag to Steel Fell Horseshoe. Both shape the skyline above Easedale and Grasmere, before the Langdale Edge makes a natural continuation along Loughrigg, stopping just short of Ambleside and the head of Lake Windermere.

Five walks have been selected to crest all 22 tops of the group. Above Grasmere, the distinctive summit of Helm Crag, famed for its 'Lion And The Lamb', leads onto a natural horseshoe rounding Greenburn Bottom and ending with Steel Fell. Helm Crag offers a Lakeland summit that can only be reached by simple rock climbing while Loughrigg, a delightful fell full of interest, offers a remarkable view to the higher tops. The walk chosen here starts from Ambleside and returns along Loughrigg Terrace above Rydal in the heart of Wordsworth country.

The multi-knolled Langdale Edge from Silver How is situated between the charms of Grasmere and the wilder influence of Langdale. With splendid views of the former, it sports four mountain tarns: Youdell ('Seagull'), Easedale, Codale and Stickle. Ascending the east ridge of Tarn Crag allows exploration of Easedale, a Victorian favourite, before topping out onto Codale Head and Sergeant Man.

Of course, it is the central cluster of fells, particularly Harrison Stickle (the highest of this group) and Pike O' Stickle – known collectively as The Langdale Pikes – which is the focal point of interest. In all, this is a group of excellence.

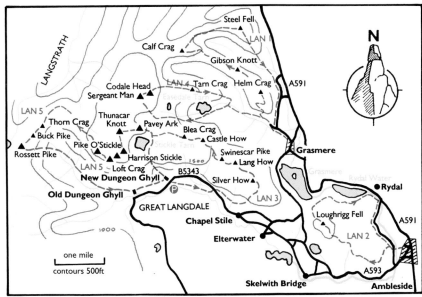

• L A N 1 •

HELM CRAG TO STEEL FELL HORSESHOE

Helm Crag 1329ft/405m
Gibson Knott 1384ft/422m
Calf Crag 1762ft/537m
Dead Pike – Steel Fell 1812ft/553m

Valley Base: Grasmere.
Maps: OS OD7, The English Lakes –
South East and OD4, The English Lakes –
North West. L90 Penrith & Keswick.
Length: 7miles/11.5km.
Ascent: 2035ft/620m.
Approx Time: 4.5hrs.
Start & Finish: Car park on the Easedale
Road above Grasmere (NY 334080).
Difficulty: Ascent of The Lion and The
Lamb, forming the summit point of Helm
Crag, requires a short rock climb of mod-
erate difficulty. Overall, ascent of Helm
Crag and descent of Steel Fell is strenuous
yet straightforward. The path is generally
in good condition although a few boggy
sections will be found.

The rocky cock's comb of Helm Crag stands loftily above Grasmere and the pass of Dunmail Raise. It may appear independent from below, but Helm Crag is actually the final spur of a ridge that extends above Far Easedale.

The eye-catching summit of Helm Crag is famed for its 'Lion And The Lamb' rock configuration. In fact, there are two Lions and two Lambs – two rock pinnacle formations placed at either end of the summit ridge. The one on the south east point takes on its popularly recognized form when viewed from the Swan Hotel at Grasmere; that on the north west point is the highest point of the mountain. Its appearance changes depending on your viewpoint. When sighted from Dunmail Raise on the A591 it appears as the famous 'Lion And The Lamb' or 'Howitzer'. Below this position, a subsidiary finger of rock to its right becomes more prominent, and it then becomes known as 'The Old Lady Playing The Organ'.

An iron gate takes the road through sweet hay meadows to the last hamlet of Easedale. As the road becomes rocky,

follow it through a further gate before taking the right lane leading onto open fellside and the site of some old quarries. Buildings constructed from the most attractive purple (iron) stained slate – once extracted here – abound in the nearby hamlet and in Grasmere below. The path has been re-routed and no longer traverses right to ascend the nose of Helm Crag directly. Instead it winds left, zigzagging above Jackdaw Crag before returning to the original path at an open shoulder, above the rocky knoll of White Crag. A steepish ascent leads to the first rocky pinnacle at the south east end of the summit ridge.

As the traverse continues towards the actual summit, the pinnacle or 'Howitzer', the unique nature of this special Lakeland top will become apparent. The ridge itself is a rugged crown falling steeply to a deep rocky hollow to the west. This hollow is formed by a secondary ridge to its west.

On reaching the summit rock outcrop on the north west end of the ridge, a problem presents itself: how to reach the top?

Helm Crag above Grasmere.

Helm Crag and the 'Lion and the Lamb' seen in silhouette above Dunmail Raise.

LOUGHRIGG

Loughrigg 1101ft/335m

Town Base: Ambleside.
Maps: OS OD7, The English Lakes –
South East. L90 Penrith & Keswick.
Length: 6miles/9.5km.
Ascent: 985ft/300m.
Approx Time: 3hrs.
Start & Finish: Central car park,
Ambleside (NY 376047).
Difficulty: On well-defined paths, track
and road the going is straightforward if a
little boggy in places. A proliferation of
paths makes route finding rather tricky
along the top.

Unique to Lakeland, it can only be reached by rock climbing. (Pillar Rock is a magnificent top but not actually the summit of a mountain.) Take heart, for it is only 25ft and very moderate as rock climbs go. When the rocks are dry most of firm limb will have little problem making the ascent. If in doubt, or if the rocks are greasy, little will be lost in terms of view or pleasantness of surroundings by not tackling those final few feet.

A steep descent leads to the col of Bracken Hause above Far Easedale. The path mostly traverses below the bumpy crest, yet do not miss the cairned top of Gibson Knott to the right. At the far end, passing the shapely Pike of Carrs to the left, the rocky summit of Calf Crag is reached. A gentle descent leads towards the tarn on Brownrigg Moss, swinging right after a short way to gain the remnants of an old iron fence – the old county boundary between Westmorland to the south and Cumberland to the north. The great upland plateau of Ullscarf looms to the north. As you follow the fence line, notice a fine little tarn to the left.

An easy ascent leads to the summit of Steel Fell (marked as Dead Pike on the OS map). Tremendous views down Thirlmere are your reward; this is a fine exposed top with a commanding position high above Dunmail Pass.

Three paths lead from the summit. Bear right and take that which descends Cotra Breast. Take care, for this can be slippery when wet. The path returns to the road just below the large house of Helmside. Follow it back beneath Helm Crag to pass Underhelm Farm, joining the Easedale Road just above Goody Bridge.

From small fells great views are often revealed. When tackled end-on from Ambleside with a return along The Terraces above Rydal Water, Loughrigg provides a delightful outing, one suitable for all seasons and markedly different in each. Not only is the mild mannered walking of the route a treat in itself, the views afforded from this modest fell, placed centrally in Wordsworth country, are quite exceptional.

The proliferation of paths along the broad top of Loughrigg Fell, with its many undulations and rocky knolls, may cause some confusion. The actual summit, with concrete trig point, does not distinguish itself until you stand upon it. As a piece of general advice follow the path taking in most of the high ground without making a descent to the left or deviating too far to the right.

From the car park in Ambleside take the road towards Grasmere, passing the fire and police stations. Bear left on the lane through the houses to find the path along the banks of Stock Ghyll to its confluence with the River Rothay. Take slate-arched Miller Bridge across the river, then bear right over the cattle grid. Almost immediately, a surfaced lane leads steeply up to the left. Follow this, through a gate past a converted farm. At a bend, a small iron ladder will be found on the left. This leads to a path between Miller How Wood above and Loughrigg Brow Wood below. A squeeze stile

Loughrigg rising above Loughrigg Tarn.

through a stone wall leads to open fell. Rising steeply, take the left branch in the path to reach a rocky outcrop. Now follow the path right to pass the bank of Lily Tarn and continue over the undulations, passing a rocky tarn on the right before making a descent into a broad valley. Continue straight across this to take the path rising steeply up the hill on its far side. Move through more undulations, past tiny tarns, until reaching the summit. The views across Grasmere are superb.

A steep descent leads to the end of Loughrigg Terrace, where a high-level track runs way above Rydal Water to the great open slate quarry of Rydal Cave. Beyond this, it descends to another track leading through a gate and woods to the surfaced road. Bear right at the bottom of the road by Pelter Bridge and follow the road back to Miller Bridge. Either return to the car park or bear right through Rothay Park, passing Ambleside Church before bearing left on the main road.

◆ LAN 3 ◆

SILVER HOW AND THE LANGDALE EDGE

Silver How 1294ft/395m
Lang How 1358ft/414m
Swinescar Pike 1348ft/411m
Castle How 1640ft/500m
Blea Rigg 1776ft/541m

Valley Base: Great Langdale.
Maps: OS OD6, The English Lakes – South West. L90 Penrith & Keswick.
Length: 6.25miles/10km.
Ascent: 1475ft/450m.
Approx Time: 3.5hrs.
Start & Finish: Small parking space by road beneath Robinson Place Farm (NY 312062). Alternatively, there is the car park in front of The New Dungeon Ghyll Hotel (NY 296064).
Difficulty: Straightforward in clear weather.

The broad-backed Langdale Edge, traversed from Silver How, offers a chance to view and contrast the delicate charms

Beneath Lang How, heading for Silver How.

of Grasmere and Easedale Tarn on the one side, with the rugged grandeur of Great Langdale on the other. This excursion alternates between grass slope and rocky knoll and takes in five tops. Described here as contouring across Megs Gill to gain Silver How and ending beneath the great rock face of Pavey Ark, it could easily be extended to include Sergeant Man if desired. The tarns viewed on this route – Youdell below Lang How (unnamed on OS map), Easedale, Codale and Stickle – all have a remote mountain feel about them.

The old road up the valley cuts loose from its new section beneath Robinson Place and this is a good place to begin. Follow the new road until just past Harry Place Farm. Opposite the barn, a path leads up left under two trees. At the wall find a gate leading to open fellside and an excellent path. Cutting effortlessly through bracken, with steep ground above and below, it follows a natural line behind the rocky knoll of Thrang Crag to gain Megs Gill. Crossing the steep scree-filled gill at this point is straightforward and soon the path rises steeply to reach

the cairned top of a grassy mound. To appreciate the commanding position of Silver How, traverse right to find the cairned summit, offering a suitably authoritative panorama over Grasmere.

Bear left to regain the main path towards the apparently sharp mound of Lang How. Pass the first unnamed tarn, then steeply ascend its flanks. The second larger tarn is called Youdell Tarn, but is known locally as 'Seagull Tarn' for reasons which become obvious in the nesting season. Long How is seen to be aptly named, for in effect it is a surprisingly long ridge. Descend from here, bearing left to a rocky knoll. Beyond this lies the curious mound of Swinescar Pike and a commanding view over Great Langdale.

After completing the circuit of the bog, find a path rising diagonally right across rocky scree to crest Little Castle How just below its summit. On its ascent, note the curious natural stone shelter that exists beneath a huge tilted boulder. It lies just above the path, hidden among the bouldery scree. A slight descent leads to the hollow area between the three summits of Castle How. The highest, according to

the OS, is that on the left, Castle How. However, the most interesting is the small distinct rock summit over to the right, Great Castle How, offering fine views of upper Easedale and Sergeant Man.

On the rise to Blea Rigg notice another natural stone shelter on the left. From the summit, admire Easedale Tarn and above this the perfect view of a mountain tarn: the remote and exposed Codale Tarn. Soon a good path bears left and descends to Stickle Tarn and, particularly if the evening light begins to set in, the awe-inspiring precipice of Pavey Ark. A masonry dam contains the tarn, offering a viewpoint.

Descent down the true left bank of Stickle Ghyll involves a short section of easy scrambling by the side of Tarn Crag but is thereafter on constructed paths and quite straightforward. Nearing the base of the ghyll, cross the footbridge and continue descending to the New Dungeon Ghyll Hotel. Continue down the front drive, crossing the main road into a car park to find the old road. A pleasant, tree-lined track leads back across the fields to your starting point.

•LAN4•

TARN CRAG EAST RIDGE TO SERGEANT MAN

Tarn Crag 1807ft/551m
Codale Head 2401ft/732m
Sergeant Man 2414ft/736m

Valley Base: Grasmere.
Maps: OS OD7, The English Lakes –
South East. OS OD6, The English Lakes –
South West. L90 Penrith & Keswick.
Length: 7miles/11km.
Ascent: 2165ft/660m.
Approx Time: 4hrs.
Start & Finish: Car park on the Easedale
Road above Grasmere (NY 334080).
Difficulty: Fairly steep ascent and
descent with some easy scrambling. The
path is vague in places. Crossing Sourmilk
Gill below Easedale Tarn may be impossi-
ble in spate conditions. If so, a path leads
to the foot of the East Ridge from just
above a small wooden footbridge in Far
Easedale (marked Stythwaite Steps on the
OS map).

While the ultimate objective of this outing
is the famous rocky knoll of Sergeant
Man, its progression through and above
Easedale is scenically magnificent. From
quiet Easedale by the white falls of Sourmilk Gill, the route enters the hidden
hanging valley of upper Easedale beneath
the tarn. It then follows the east ridge of
Tarn Crag to gain its rock summit. Proceeding over little frequented Codale
Head, it is only a short stroll to Sergeant
Man. For those with time and energy to
spare, the summit of High Raise lies only
a little further and may seem a worthwhile objective before returning to the
route described here.

At the bend in the road, opposite a
postbox set in the stone wall, enter the
wood on the far side of Easedale Beck.
Cross the wooden footbridge. Exit the
wood by an iron gate and follow the
rocky track which in turn follows the
bank of the beck. Fine views to the tumbling waterfalls of Sourmilk Gill soon
come into view. The track bears left and
rises beside the gill.

Above the falls, ringed by juniper and
holly, as the path begins to steepen bear
right to cross the stream using the step-

ping stones. In spate this will be impossible; in normal conditions it is a relatively
simple affair. A small path rises up the
fine open east ridge of Tarn Crag. After
passing beneath a rock tor there are fine
views left to Easdale Tarn and right to the
top of Deer Bield Crag.

The steep bastion straight ahead looks
difficult enough, but a rake cuts easily up
its centre, after which a move right brings
you to the elevated rocky top of Tarn Crag.

The edge now broadens and the path
becomes a little vague. No problems
should be encountered in finding the line
of the old iron fence posts leading to the
right up to Codale Head. This summit
marks a corner in the old boundary
between Cumberland to the north and
Westmorland. It is a top in its own right
but one often bypassed by those intent on
the more obvious attraction of Sergeant
Man, now only a short stroll away.
Although following the old boundary
will lead to the summit of High Raise,
crossing the rocky outcrops will lead to
the real objective of this walk: the high-
profile cone of Sergeant Man.

On descent from the summit cairn, a
prominent path traverses a boggy area in

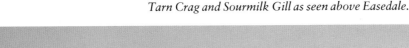

Tarn Crag and Sourmilk Gill as seen above Easedale.

front of Sergeant Man before heading down the ridge towards Blea Rigg. A long but easily tackled rock slab is followed by a hollow and a view to Codale Tarn. Numerous cairns mark this spot, an important crossroads. Nevertheless, it is easy to pass it by and continue down the ridge leading to Blea Rigg. Take great care not to do this, but bear left immediately before descending steeply. The path levels out before a further steep section with rocky steps. Caution should be exercised before the path levels again in the bottom of the basin which contains Easedale Tarn. Behind you, above the second steep section Belles Knott ('The Matterhorn of Easedale') takes on an unmistakable prominence .

Easedale Tarn is a site of tranquil beauty, a place to linger before passing the large boulder and ruined remains of a Victorian refreshment hut that heads the path as it descends by Sourmilk Gill. Brimmer Head Farm comes into view as the route begins retracing its steps.

•LAN 5•

LANGDALE PIKES – THE GREATER TRAVERSE

Pavey Ark 2288ft/697m
Thunacar Knott 2372ft/723m
Harrison Stickle 2414ft/736m
Thorn Crag 2106ft/642m
Loft Crag 2238ft/682m
Pike O'Stickle 2324ft/709m
Black Crag 1929ft/588m
Buck Pike 1988ft/606m
Rossett Pike 2136ft/651m

Valley Base: Great Langdale.
Maps: OS OD6, The English Lakes – South West. L90 Penrith & Keswick.
Length: 9miles/14.5km.
Ascent: 3460ft/1055m.
Approx Time: 5.5hrs.
Start & Finish: Car park beside The Stickle Barn/New Dungeon Ghyll Hotel (NY 295064).
Difficulty: Steep ascent and fairly arduous going make this a reasonably tough proposition. However, there are numerous escape paths.

For many The Langdale Pikes represent the throne of the Lakeland Fells. Seen across Windermere or from the valley, they appear like a majestic, reclining lion. Harrison Stickle, the proud head, Pavey Ark the thick dark body and Loft Crag with Pike O'Stickle behind the paw – towering 2000ft above the floor of the Langdale valley they present a dramatic and magnificent aspect.

Opinions range as to just how many of the tops constitute 'The Pikes'. In the author's opinion only Harrison Stickle, the highest point, and the distinct cone of Pike O'Stickle fit the classification. However, this should not detract from the other lesser tops, for they all individually fashion the rugged skyline above the Great Langdale Valley.

The Greater Traverse of the northern skyline visits them all. After negotiating 'The Pikes' and nearby Thunacar Knott it continues across Martcrag Moor, rounding Stake Pass to top Rossett Pike. Descent down Rossett Ghyll leads to the green swathe of the valley and return along Mickleden.

The large car park alongside the Stickle Barn provides the starting point. A recently reconstructed path leads up Stickle Ghyll (the name on the OS maps, elsewhere it is referred to as Mill Gill) to pass under Tarn Crag and arrive at Stickle Tarn on the east end of the dam. Looking over the tarn to the huge cliff of Pavey Ark is one of Lakeland's finest sights. Traverse above the eastern shore until, bearing left, the path crosses its main feeder stream, Bright Beck. A little further on, follow the good path up the easy eastern shoulder of Pavey Ark. Cross a little wall on the left to reach the rock summit.

A sense of satisfaction is justified, as the bulk of the ascent lies below. The edge of the huge cliff lies just beyond – do not attempt to get closer. (Note that the easiest escape route back to Stickle Tarn lies roughly at the lowest point between this summit and that of Harrison Stickle. If an early return is planned, either take this or the route just ascended. Attempt no other without prior knowledge.)

Head west towards Thunacar Knott and pick up a path before moving left to the highest point south of the little tarn. (North of the tarn there is also a cairned top, sometimes regarded as *the* top although it is a lower point.) A path heads

directly across to make the slight ascent to Harrison Stickle. A cairn on the northern end of a rocky ridge marks the summit and highest point of The Langdale Pikes.

Descend into the hollow above the deep-cut, rocky ravine of Dungeon Ghyll. Rising from the stream the cairned head of Thorn Crag presents no problems before the path bears west up to Loft Crag. Directly below, unseen from here but plainly visible from Pike O'Stickle beyond, lies Gimmer Crag – one of the finest and most exposed rock climbing crags in the Great Langdale Valley.

The path continues to skirt the top of

Over the head of Langdale to the Langdale Pikes.

the Stickle Stone Shoot before climbing steeply up the rocky summit cone of Pike O'Stickle. This is a marvellous top, exposed and independent even from the High Raise plateau to its north.

Leave Pike O'Stickle only by the same route taken in ascent. A scree-run descent of the Stickle Stone Shoot provides a rapid trip virtually to the floor of the valley. However, the top section of this stone shoot is now severely eroded and cannot be recommended. Beside the stone shoot, a small cave marks the site of a neolithic stone axe factory, one of the most important in Europe – any stone axes found here or elsewhere should be left in situ. They are limited in number and can provide important archeological information on the history of the region.

Our path continues across Martcrag Moor to round the hidden hollow of Stake Pass. This and Rossett Pass beyond effectively define the craggy head of Mickleden as an independent mass. Ascent up and left leads to the rocky top of Black Crag, which in turn provides access to Buck Pike and lofty Rossett Pike, the highest point of the group.

From here, descend the grassy back of the Pike before aiming down the red scree of Rossett Gill. Notorious for its steep and eroded nature, the recent attentions of the National Park footpath repair team have improved the situation, though it still requires caution.

Levelling out, the path passes over a little footbridge before following the bank of Mickleden Beck. Soon, the grassy greensward of Mickleden valley is followed by a rocky lane to the Old Dungeon Ghyll Hotel. By skirting above the buildings to the left by a signposted route, the lane can be regained and followed back to Stickle Barn/New Dungeon Ghyll car park.

By Red Tarn with Crinkle Crags and Bowfell beyond.

BOWFELL GROUP

·BOW·

Mighty Bowfell, although falling just short of the 3000ft mark, crowns one of the finest mountain ranges of the region. From Esk Pike in the north west to Lingmoor at its south eastern tip, extends a rugged upland arm of striking proportions. Esk Hause, a strategic crossroads of mountain passes, defines its northern limit, Wrynose Pass and the Three Shires Stone its southern boundary. To the west lie the desolate and deserted heads of Mosedale, Ling Cove and Upper Eskdale; and to the east Great and Little Langdale.

Esk Pike, beyond Bowfell, is best appreciated when seen from the Eskdale side. The distinctively light-coloured summit rocks of Esk Pike form the end of the curving ridge rising from Lingcove Beck through High Gait Crags and Pike de Bield. Of course, it is the Langdale face of the group that is the most famous. Seen as a dramatic skyline, the rocky turrets of the Crinkle Crags and looming hulk of Bowfell dominate the head of the Great Langdale Valley. Above Oxendale, Pike O'Blisco gives way to craggy Blake Rigg standing abruptly above Blea Tarn, dark and serene. The clenched fist of the arm, formed by the cluster of tops above Wrynose Pass, adds another dimension to the group. Finally, the continuation of the range, Side Pike and Lingmoor, form the divide between the two Langdales. While not possessing the same rocky grandeur as their higher neighbours, these tops lack nothing either in charm or aestheticism.

The choice of walks are many, the points of interest vast. I have selected four walks, all of which are circular and collectively visit the twenty tops of the group. Lingmoor and Side Pike are explored from Blea Tarn and the Little Langdale side; the craggy fist of the group is visited starting from Wrynose Bridge; from the Old Dungeon Ghyll, we cross the Crinkles to crest Bowfell; and from Cockley Beck up Mosedale we ascend Esk Pike, returning over The Crinkles and, finally, Little Stand.

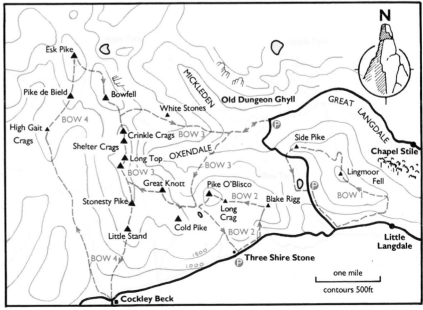

•BOW1•

LINGMOOR AND SIDE PIKE

Brown Howe – Lingmoor Fell 1538ft/469m
Side Pike 1187ft/362m

Valley Base: Little Langdale.
Maps: OS OD6, The English Lakes –
South West. L90 Penrith & Keswick.
Length: 5.25miles/8.5km.
Ascent: 1410ft/430m.
Approx Time: 3hrs.
Start & Finish: Blea Tarn car park
(NY 296043).
Difficulty: Generally the going is straight-
forward, if a little damp along the top. There
is no safe direct ascent/descent between
the summit of Side Pike and the western
shoulder of Lingmoor. Despite appear-
ances, beware, for the cliff is continuous.

The hump of Lingmoor separates the valleys of Great Langdale and Little Langdale. It is an enchanting and secluded fell,
its nature influenced more by Little Langdale than by Great Langdale. Despite the
close proximity of its higher and grander
neighbours it remains an unruffled,
peaceful place in the fells. From below,
protected by its sprawling flanks, the
independence of its summit ridge goes
unnoticed, the charms of Lingmoor Tarn
unseen. Only Blea Tarn – over which the
view to The Langdale Pikes is one of the
all-time greats – and the plucky isolation
of Side Pike hint at what lies above.

The walk starts opposite Blea Tarn
and takes an anticlockwise route, first
descending Little Langdale before traversing the flanks of the fell above the fell
wall. As it nears the southern end of Lingmoor, it climbs steeply via an old quarry
track. This gains the spine of the fell.

Follow this to the highest point, Brown
Howe. Finally, make an easy ascent of
Side Pike, which is a fine rock tower.

Take the road to cross the cattle grid
and descend the hill, passing extensive
juniper, gorse and holly, with the open
expanse of Blea Moss Common below to
the right and the open fellside above. A little way above the lower cattle grid, a
grassy track leads off to the right (a low
barrier prevents vehicular access). This
climbs to a flat area (there is a gate in the
wall on the left), descends slightly then
rises again to a gate in the fence. Cross the
gill just above the wall and trees. A rocky
step leads to a well-defined, undulating
path contouring the flanks of Lingmoor
above the fell wall.

Pass beneath Busk Pike and Bield Crag
(the buildings of High and Low Bield lie
just below). Then rise to a point where a
meandering track leads steeply upwards.

Looking to Lingmoor above Little Langdale.

Side Pike above Bleatarn House, the latter also known as 'Solitary'.

This is the old quarry track and the modern path often shortcuts it, taking a more direct line. As the gradient eases, the path veers left to a cairn.

At this point the old packhorse roads, which once served the numerous slate quarries, intersect to cross the shoulder from Little to Great Langdale and also to traverse the length of the fell. Beyond, the well-defined path divides. The higher variant to the right generally hugs the summit ridge, following a stone wall. Take this to gain an occasional peep over Great Langdale.

The rocky knoll of Brown Howe is reached and a path taken to cross a stile to the summit of Lingmoor. From here, there is a classic view down the ridge over Side Pike to The Langdale Pikes beyond. Secluded Lingmoor Tarn nestles amid the rock and heather down to the right.

Moving on, the path descends along the side of a stone wall. Crossing this, the going steepens before you emerge abruptly onto the gentle shoulder beneath Side Pike. Do not be fooled here: there is no

easy ascent directly onto the summit. A stile leads over to a smaller path which ascends to the foot of the cliff, before bearing left behind a large rock and on around the summit cone of Side Pike to its easier southern flanks. A short ascent leads to a ridge, then the summit.

Descend the same ridge, following the main path to join the road north of the cattle grid. Cross the road in front of the cattle grid to take the path leading down to the delightful little wood behind Blea Tarn. Cutting through the wood, thick with rhododendrons and pine, an excursion left should be made from the path to a rocky viewpoint above the tarn.

The tarn itself is quite enchanting. In late May or early June the sweet scent of the reddish-pink rhododendron blooms mixes with that of the pungent pine needles to provide an intoxicating fragrance.

Continue along the path to a footbridge that crosses the stream on the left. The wood is left again, via a stile. From here, a track leads to the road and back to the car park.

•BOW 2•

PIKE O'BLISCO AND WRYNOSE FELL CIRCUIT

Blake Rigg 1755ft/535m
Long Crag – Wrynose Fell 1788ft/545m
Pike O'Blisco 2313ft/705m
Great Knott 2283ft/696m
Cold Pike 2300ft/701m

Valley Base: Little Langdale.
Maps: OS OD6, The English Lakes – South West. L90 Penrith & Keswick.
Length: 5miles/8km.
Ascent: 2165ft/660m.
Approx Time: 3hrs.
Start & Finish: Wrynose Bridge (NY 285033). Limited parking here and in spaces just above the bend. Alternatively, continue up the road to find further extensive parking over the crest of Wrynose to the left and descend the road on foot to the bridge.
Difficulty: Initially steepish ascent with no definite path. Boggy in places throughout.

The top of Cold Pike, the Langdale Pikes (left), with Pike O'Blisco (right) beyond.

Wrynose Fell is the name given to this upland mass. It forms a clenched fist at the south eastern end of the long arm of Bowfell and Crinkle Crags. Its highest knuckle, the bell-shaped Pike O'Blisco, dominates Oxendale at the head of Great Langdale, while precipitous Blake Rigg does the same for Little Langdale. Viewed from Wrynose pass, its most pronounced digit, the rocky thumb of Cold Pike rises from the Three Shires Stone.

Three of the tops rise over 2000ft, the other two falling only a little short. The summit of Pike O'Blisco offers a famous view of the Crinkles. In addition, there are commanding views north to The Pikes and west, over lower Langdale, to the Central Fells. South of Wrynose Pass, the prospect is dramatically curtailed by Wetherlam and its rocky horseshoe.

Beginning around the 1000ft contour of Wrynose Bridge, the circuit is it a very attractive proposition. From any other starting point, it is notably more arduous. Above the bridge, a vague path rises into the basin containing the finger streams

feeding the beck. Cross these to the right and traverse above Little Horse Crag onto the shoulder of Blake Rigg. Ascend its rocky top; it is a worthy summit and viewpoint. Beneath stands a dark, vegetated and complex cliff, one from which, as a local cragsman, I am often called to rescue crag fast sheep and foxhounds.

The plateau between here and the cairned rocky outcrop of Long Crag, the top of Wrynose Fell, is boggy but with prudence can be negotiated dry. There is no path. Long Crag is a fine rock outcrop with a steep face between it and Pike O'Blisco. It is better to descend the same way as you came up, then skirt around its northern end to gain access to the hollow beneath the slopes of Blisco. A straightforward march up grass, rock and scree leads to the rocky knoll of Blisco, its most northerly cairned top constituting the highest point of this excursion. The Pikes, mighty Bowfell and the Crinkles are all paraded to magnificent effect.

Continue on. A well-trodden path drops steeply towards Red Tarn. Cross

the Browney Gill trod rising from Langdale and ascend gently towards the Crinkles. The slight, domed summit of Great Knott is reached by bearing right from the main trod as it levels. It occupies an exposed position over the steeply plunging basin of Oxendale.

Contour around to the shoulder of Cold Pike and ascend to the summit, a crown of bare rock rising in a dignified manner above the grassy slopes below. The most northerly rocky outcrop is the highest point, only fractionally higher than its partner to the south. It sports a precariously balanced cairn.

Red Tarn can be admired in detail from here. The slopes above, traversed by the path, reveal the origin of the name. The ground is coloured red by a rich vein of haematite and this site as well as that of Browney Gill was once an important source of the mineral. Traditionally, locals dug here for 'Schmitt', the red dye used to mark the fell sheep (the name possibly originating from a German miner who brought his expertise to Lakeland in

Elizabethan times). Make a sweeping return to the path rising from Red Tarn.

An old packhorse road that fed the mine can be followed down to the Three Shires Stone. Standing near the summit of Wrynose Pass this stone – the meeting point of the three old counties Cumberland, Westmorland and Lancashire – serves as a popular starting point for Pike O'Blisco or a traverse of the Crinkles. A short descent down the road completes our route.

◆ BOW 3 ◆

CRINKLE CRAGS AND BOWFELL FROM GREAT LANGDALE

Great Knott 2283ft/696m
First Crinkle 2733ft/833m
Long Top – Second Crinkle 2816ft/859m
Third Crinkle 2754ft/840m
Fourth Crinkle 2730ft/832m
Gunson Knott – Fifth Crinkle 2674ft/815m
Shelter Crags 2674ft/815m
Bowfell 2960ft/902m
White Stones – The Band 1863ft/568m

Valley Base: Great Langdale.
Maps: OS OD6, The English Lakes – South West. L90 Penrith & Keswick.
Length: 8miles/13km.
Ascent: 3280ft/1000m.
Approx Time: 4.5hrs.
Start & Finish: The Old Dungeon Ghyll car park (NY 286062).
Difficulty: A long and rugged walk, taking an exposed rocky ridge located high in a mountain setting. The Bad Step on the south end of Long Top – Second Crinkle requires careful negotiation. This route takes it in ascent and although it involves a short scramble (using hands as well as feet) it is not exposed and should not present undue difficulty. Off the path, rocky steps abound and many who have strayed in bad weather (poor visibility or when ice/snow conditions prevail) have suffered tragic consequences.

Stretching south to north and silhouetted against the western sky, the rocky ramparts of the Crinkle Crags, culminating in the towering hulk of Bowfell, dominate the head of the Great Langdale Valley. Tackling them makes for a classic mountain outing. Many expeditions are possible – my choice climbs steeply from the deep bowl of Oxendale and utilizes the natural ramp of the Band in descent.

Cars must be left at the Old Dungeon Ghyll even though a good track leads to Stool End Farm nestling at the toe of the Band. Through the farmyard, a tiny gate beside the farmhouse gives access to the fell. Take the left track at the fork, that rising to the right being the path up the Band, our subsequent line of descent. Stiles lead over stone walls and a sheepfold is bypassed to the right before Oxendale beck is joined and a footbridge taken to cross it. Oxendale is remarkable for its deeply cut gills.

Lying dead ahead, Crinkle Gill leads directly to Mickle Door and the highest Crinkle, Long Top. It is much deeper and more impressive than when viewed from below. To its right, Hell Gill is famous for its waterfall, Whorneyside Force. However, our way lies to the left of the basin and proceeds from the footbridge to rise steeply, via stone steps and a constructed footpath over Brown Howe, to join the upper section of Browney Gill.

This last section is steepest of all, with old mine levels piercing the hillside at the head of the gill. It soon falls back to reveal the hollow, between Pike O'Blisco and Cold Pike, cradling Red Tarn. At the unmistakable junction of paths, bear right to rise again. Just off the path to the right, Great Knott may be visited. Soon

Wintry conditions across the Crinkles towards Bowfell.

the first all-rock outcrop, elongated and multi-cairned, is encountered: this is the First Crinkle. Follow a dip to the highest of them all, Long Top, the Second Crinkle. Its linear shape stretches towards Ling Cove in the west, crossing the main ridge at right angles. This explains why its appearance from the Langdale side of the range does not do it justice as 'The Crinkle'. The cairn at its south eastern corner represents the highest point.

Reaching this cairn from the dip requires negotiation of the Bad Step. This is a short gully blocked by chockstones which can be bypassed by steepish rocks to the right. It is only a short scramble and most will not give it a second thought. However, an easier grassy rake can be found to the left (west) of the dip. This leads to the summit cairn.

From Long Top, the main path bypasses the tops of the other Crinkles. Visiting them requires a detour. The conical Third Crinkle lies about 50 yards east above the path. The cairned Fourth Crinkle is sited about 10 yards east of the path directly above steep cliffs. Gunson Knott – Fifth Crinkle, a lower but distinctively formed triangulated buttress of rock, is reached about 20 yards east of the path.

The path continues to cross the summit of Shelter Crags. An interesting descent, with a view to the sphinx-like head of Bowfell and its furrowed western flanks (Bowfell Links), leads to the col of the Three Tarns.

Beyond some steep rocky scree lies a level plateau beneath the mighty head of Bowfell. Follow the path around the cone on its east before bearing back south and taking the path to the summit.

Return to the Three Tarns and bear left down the Band. Where the path passes a little tarn and extensive peat bogs, a detour left leads to the summit of White Stones. There is no real path, or top for that matter, but there is a position with a good view missed by the main path.

Retrieve the main path, and traverse the flanks of White Stones. Do not attempt to continue down the crest of the ridge, for a steep crag intervenes. A junction with the original course is reached at the toe of the Band. It is easy going from here on, with the track through the farm, over the bridge and across the meadows leading back to the road. The Old Dungeon Ghyll Hotel lies just beyond.

• B O W 4 •

ESK PIKE, BOWFELL AND CRINKLE CRAGS FROM COCKLEY BECK

High Gait Crags 1877ft/572m
Pike de Bield 2657ft/810m
Esk Pike 2903ft/885m
Bowfell 2960ft/902m
Shelter Crags 2674ft/815m
Gunson Knott – Fifth Crinkle 2674ft/815m
Fourth Crinkle 2730ft/832m
Third Crinkle 2754ft/840m
Long Top – Second Crinkle 2816ft/859m
First Crinkle 2733ft/833m
Stonesty Pike 2510ft/765m
Little Stand 2428ft/740m

Valley Base: The Duddon.
Maps: OS OD6, The English Lakes – South West. L90 Penrith & Keswick.
Length: 8.5miles/14km.
Ascent: 3345ft/1020m.
Approx Time: 5.5hrs.
Start & Finish: Cockley Beck. Above the bridge by the side of the Hardknott Pass Road. Limited pull-off parking space (NY244018).
Difficulty: This is a long, arduous outing covering remote ground. For sections of the way there is no path, the going is often rough and in the early stages boggy ground prevails. It crests numerous peaks and traverses an exposed rocky ridge located in a high mountain setting. The Bad Step, found on the south end of Long Top – the Second Crinkle – is taken in descent. It involves a short steep scramble (using hands as well as feet) though should not present undue difficulty. Below the path, steep cliffs abound and it is important to keep to the route in poor visibility or winter conditions.

The nature of Esk Pike, Bowfell and The Crinkles on their western (Eskdale) flank is quite different to that observed on their Langdale side. Not quite so rugged or as precipitous perhaps, but rising from a barren landscape they invoke an air of impressive solitude. Across the Great Moss of Upper Eskdale, the Scafell massif casts a powerful spell over the scene. Indeed, there are no better views of the

'back o'Scafell' than from this walk. As a testimony to its wild appeal, this was the area chosen by the Golden Eagle when it first returned to nest in the Lake District.

The walk strikes up the long, curving ridge which drops from Esk Pike into Upper Eskdale. Having reached the heights it takes in the greater traverse of the Bowfell group – comprising Esk Pike, Bowfell, The Crinkles and Stonesty Pike – before dropping over the end of Little Stand to return to Cockley Beck.

Leave the road and follow a track along the bank above Mosedale Beck. In the far distance, the distinctive, light-coloured rock of Esk Pike, the peak that begins the high-level route, stands apart from the darker thumb of Pike de Bield.

After the track enters the upper basin of Mosedale and levels out, a path veers up to the left. Take this and make a high circuitous traverse around the head of the basin. The track which crossed the moss to emerge onto the col at its head has now disappeared into the bog. Whichever route is chosen, you will be lucky to emerge onto the col with dry feet (it would be wise to carry dry socks).

On reaching the col the view across to the Scafells and Esk Buttress (the climber's crag variously marked on the OS 1:25000 as Dow Crag and Central Pillar, neither of which is correct) is magnificent. Above the col to the right Adam-a-Cove hangs below Long Top, the highest of The Crinkles. Floating aloof at the head of Ling Cove is Bowfell, its craggy flanks seamed by a series of parallel gullies, The Bowfell Links; to its right the col of the Three Tarns and to its left Ore Gap.

Our way lies up the curving shoulder to the left. Its Eskdale flanks follow a series of crags – Pianet Knott, Long Crag, Low Gait Crags and High Gait Crags – before it swings back east with Greenhole Crags and Yeastrigg Crags defining the edge above Upper Ling Cove.

Cross the crystal clear waters of Lingcove Beck and leave the path for the rough fell. With selective judgment the walking is not difficult. After the initial pull to Pianet Knott the grade eases and most will skirt the rocky outcrops of Long Crag and Low Gait Crags to make a beeline for High Gait Crags. The furthest protrusion, a cairned rock outcrop, is the highest point and gives a gripping view of Esk Buttress – around 400ft of clean rhyolite

Looking north across the white rocks of Esk Pike.

and one of the finest rock climbing crags in the region.

Veer right to skirt the edge of Pike de Bield Moss and climb the Ling Cove edge of the ridge. The rare Mountain Ringlet Butterfly (only found in the Lake District and parts of Scotland) inhabits these slopes. Yeastrigg Crags are best tackled on the right edge, where the distinctive white rock is broken and presents no difficulty. Above, a vague path can be picked out moving left to skirt beneath a rocky outcrop. Immediately above to the left opposite the outcrop is the separate thumb of Pike de Bield. This is a worthy top with a memorable view along the 'back o'Scafell' and up into the rocky domain of Little Narrowcove.

Behind this it is possible to see the ancient Roman Port of Ravenglass on the West Coast, while ahead stand the startling white/pink rocks of Esk Pike. Skirt the rocks to the right to join the main path

and follow it to the summit. From here, the view to the West Coast, the Solway and down along Windermere Lake is simply breathtaking.

We now begin the high-level traverse of this mighty Bowfell group. Take the main path into Ore Gap. Not only is it stained red but actual flakes of heamatite (iron ore) litter the path. A long haul leads to the sphinx-like upper shoulder of Bowfell and a steeper path to its head. The great arm of The Crinkles stretches out beyond. After skirting the top of the Great Slab to the left, a well-defined footpath descends to the Three Tarns. The path across The Crinkles is now reversed (see Walk BOW 3). On descending from the summit of Long Top keep left, taking the Bad Step to avoid the steep chockstone-capped gully. This involves a short but straightforward scramble.

After descending from the multicairned First Crinkle bear right to strike a

central line across the moss to Stonesty Pike. Beyond, a rake descending beneath a long low wall of rock leads to the col in the shadow of Little Stand. A short climb from here leads to the summit. Note a number of tiny tarns, which although permanent during most summers are not shown on the OS map.

A natural corridor descends from the summit rocks until a broad gully breaks off to the right. There is a vague path but the going is rough and a number of small rock outcrops must be negotiated. Aim for a stone wall which can easily be seen from high on the fell. On closer acquaintance a wire fence will be encountered before the wall. Bear right along this until a gate leads to a track. This descends by Clemety Sike down towards the arched, stone bridge of Cockley Beck.

A stile near the corner of the field, then a footbridge, lead to the Hardknott Road. Teas may be enjoyed at the farm.

Looking over the high Borrowdale Fells, Glaramara left and Allen Crags right.

BORROWDALE FELLS

·BOR·

A group of fells cap the Borrowdale Valley as it divides to become Langstrath to the east and Seathwaite to the west. Forming a natural horseshoe around the hanging basin of The Combe, the fells rise in a continuous spine over Glaramara to Allen Crags, the highest point. They then sweep around the head of Grains Gill, in another horseshoe, to Seathwaite Fell. While some may consider them to be an extension of the Scafell range, they are markedly separated by the high-level pass between Styhead and Tongue Head. Quite distinct in character, they are rightly known as the Borrowdale Fells.

Twelve tops are ascended by two walks. The character of the first horseshoe around the hidden hanging valley of The Combe is influenced by nearby Borrowdale. It is a wild and grand outing. Yet the sylvan character and rustic idyll of Borrowdale always seems close to hand. The upper horseshoe, by contrast, revels in the ambience of a higher mountain world. Here we have the huge black cliff of Great End staring down menacingly while Great Gable and the Langdale Pikes add spice to the view.

Combe Head forms the highest point of the lower horseshoe, yet there is much of interest on the walk. Thornythwaite Fell, Rosthwaite Cam, Tarn at Leaves and Bessyboot will not disappoint.

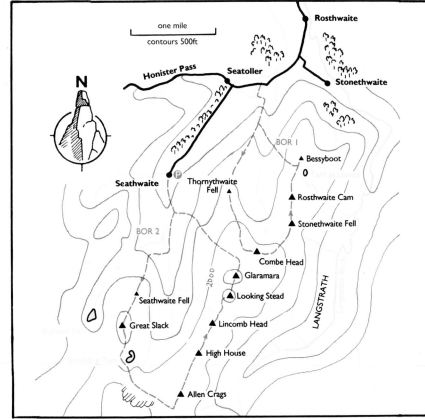

•BOR 1•

COMBE GILL HORSESHOE – BORROWDALE FELLS

Thornythwaite Fell 1883ft/574m
Combe Head 2405ft/733m
Stonethwaite Fell 2073ft/632m
Rosthwaite Cam – Rosthwaite Fell
2008ft/612m
Bessyboot – Rosthwaite Fell 1807ft/550m

Valley Base: Borrowdale.
Maps: OS OD4, The English Lakes –
North West. L90 Penrith & Keswick.
Length: 5miles/8km.
Ascent: 2395ft/730m.
Approx Time: 3.5hrs.
Start & Finish: Immediately below
Strands Bridge on the Borrowdale Road
opposite the cottages of Mountain View, a
narrow road leads to Thornythwaite.
Follow this for approximately 400 metres
until, rounding a bend, a large-ish grass
area on the right provides parking space –
do not block the gate (NY 249135).
Difficulty: Rough and slightly boggy, with
the path vague in places. Although generally straightforward in good visibility, it is
important not to lose the route. Craggy
outcrops must be negotiated en route and
steep cliffs litter the rim of the horseshoe
below.

Despite their position at the head of Borrowdale, this cluster of fells does not present a highly visual profile to observers in
the valley below. Quite the opposite.
Much is hidden from view and the only
real way to appreciate their quality is to
lace up your boots and walk. The horseshoe of Combe Gill combines the logical
linking of five summits with a thorough
exploration of the area.

Along the road, in the direction of
Strands Bridge, a gate/stile gives access to
the wooded field on the right. A track
leads directly to the path (the path itself
begins at another stile placed nearer
Strands Bridge) which sweeps to the right
through the woods to a kissing gate in a
stone wall. Notice the waterfall tumbling
into Blackmoss Pot below to the left.
Open fellside follows and the desolate
hanging valley of the combe unfolds to
the left. The path splits and we take the
right fork. Initially, it rises steeply taking
a sharp rib but soon the gradient slackens
as it ambles gently onto the shoulder of
Thornythwaite Fell.

The summit of Thornythwaite Fell is a
rock knoll standing above the path and
protruding only slightly from the general
run of the shoulder. It offers an open view
across the head of the combe to the rocky
pinnacle of Rosthwaite Cam opposite
and Stonethwaite Fell to the right. Bessyboot stands over to the left. Beneath Rosthwaite Cam notice the massively frac-
tured Dovenest Crag, famed for its caves

Over Combe Gill to Rosthwaite Cam (left) and Stonethwaite Fell (right).

and passages. Its open face is also a popular haunt of the rock climber who traditionally combines his trip with an exploration underground.

The path continues across a rift, passing an area where the rocks resemble a
heap of paving stones. At this point it
bears right, aiming for Glaramara. We,
however, leave it left to take rougher and
steeper ground rising to Combe Head.
There is no real path here.

Combe Head is a distinct summit
dominating the combe below. Descend
slightly right of the edge, taking a line into
the great natural corridor of Combe

Golden light over Stonethwaite Fell (in front) and Rosthwaite Cam (beyond).

Door. Follow the contours around the rocky outcrop forming the eastern 'doorpost' to find an indistinct path leading to the hollow below. On the far side take a grassy break rising up the rocky incline over a stone wall. The vague path bears right over the shoulder but first climb up left to the largest top overlooking the combe – the summit of Stonethwaite Fell. A rocky finger to its right may be equal in altitude yet is not as significant in size.

Bear right and descend to Great Hollow, taking the vague path on its right side. The cube-shaped summit of Rosthwaite Cam lies to the left on leaving the

hollow. On first acquaintance it looks more than a little daunting, resembling the rocky 'Howitzer' summit of Helm Crag above Grasmere. Fortunately, it can be gained by an easy scramble via a route starting from its southern end, and should present no problems to the average hill walker with a cool head.

Descend by the same route and continue along the flanks above the delightfully named Tarn at Leaves. Interestingly, there is not a tree in sight. Behind, over the combe enjoy an excellent view of Raven Crag. Catching the eye, a vertical gully splits the right side of the crag; this makes

for a classic rock climb first made directly by the legendary climber O.G. Jones ('Only Genuine' Jones) in 1897.

Do not miss the nose of Bessyboot, cairned with a well worn path. Retrace your steps down the nose before heading straight towards the combe to gain the wide head of an easy gully, from which flows a small stream. A vague path leads down and left. Cross the stream to descend a curious wedge-shaped grassy ramp leading directly to a sheepfold above the beck. The beck is narrow and in normal conditions there are plenty of boulders from which to select a stepping stone for a dry crossing.

Retrace your earlier steps through the hazels and oaks as the evening shadows fall and the wood smoke rises peacefully from the chimneys of the nearby Mountain View Cottages.

Alternatively, if the beck is in spate descent above its east bank soon picks up a path. In due course, this crosses the beck by a small bridge to finally emerge on the Borrowdale Road just below Strands Bridge, your original starting point.

is a mountain world. Great End, the huge north facing cliff that marks the end of the Scafell Group, looms menacingly above the head of the walk while the shapely head of Great Gable looks on to the west and monolithic Pike O'Stickle stands to the east.

Take a direct line up the nose of Seathwaite Fell, then walk along its rocky back to Great Slack before dropping slightly past Sprinkling Tarn. Rising to Esk Hause, the route turns again to follow the

undulating ridge along Allen Crags to Glaramara. Finally, a steep descent along the impressive rift of Hind Gill leads back to Seathwaite.

Walk through the farm and follow the track over Stockley Bridge, before rising up the fell away from Grains Gill. The path continues through a gate in the fell wall after which the old packhorse route will be found to bear left (the modern path to Styhead bears right). Follow this until it is necessary to move left again past

Sunset over Allen Crags (top) and the view from Allen Crags to Glaramara (bottom).

•BOR 2•

SEATHWAITE FELL, ALLEN CRAGS AND GLARAMARA

Seathwaite Fell 1970ft/601m
Great Slack – Seathwaite Fell 2073ft/632m
Allen Crags 2574ft/785m
High House – Allen Crags 2244ft/684m
Lincomb Head – Glaramara 2365ft/721m
Looking Stead – Glaramara 2543ft/775m
Glaramara 2568ft/783m

Valley Base: Borrowdale.
Maps: OS OD4, The English Lakes – North West. OS OD6 The English Lakes – South West. L90 Penrith & Keswick.
Length: 7miles/11km.
Ascent: 2950ft/900m.
Approx Time: 4.5hrs.
Start & Finish: The head of the Seathwaite valley, by the side of the road beneath the farm – do not block any field entrances or the road (NY 236123).
Difficulty: A high-level route through mountain terrain. The going is both rough and strenuous in places. A short section of descent, although on a well-worn path, includes a moderate rock scramble (hands and feet need to be employed). Not a walk for poor weather.
Note: Teas available at Seathwaite Farm.

This route starts from Seathwaite, the most westerly arm of the Borrowdale valley, and takes a high-level horseshoe around Grains Gill. Its prize is that champion of the Borrowdale Fells, the evocatively named Glaramara. Paradoxically, Borrowdale exerts little influence for this

Over Sprinkling Tarn to Seathwaite Fell (left) and Glaramara (right).

the end of Black Waugh to gain slacker ground above. Aim for the right of Aaron Crags, bearing left over a stream to pass a sizeable boulder. A copper rain gauge sunk into the ground is strategically placed here.

A gully will be found rising to the right of Aaron Crags. Although, it is grassy in nature and quite straightforward. Pass a fallen wall on a rocky nose above the crag to reach the cairned summit of Seathwaite Fell, a rocky knoll standing just above a little tarn. The position is sublime; beyond lies Great Gable,while below stretches secluded Seathwaite.

Take the next two tarns in anticlockwise manner. Views down Wasdale to the West Coast suddenly materialize, until you reach a cylindrical cairn standing above a third tarn. Numerous little tarns follow before the rocky top of Great Slack. Beyond and below a larger tarn (unnamed on the OS map) lies hidden in a

rocky hollow. Pause here to view the reflection of Great End before continuing on above Sprinkling Tarn. This is the princess of mountain tarns: dark and serene, and on a still summer evening rippled only by the rings of jumping trout.

At the main track bear left and ascend to Esk Hause, thereafter branching left to the summit of Allen Crags. A rough, broad ridge falls easily to the gap holding High House and Lincomb Tarns. Detouring from the well-blazoned path is necessary to reach the little rocky knoll of High House above.

Beyond the two tarns the shoulder climbs to Glaramara, the main path traversing to the right of its most northerly top, Lincomb Head. Move back up and left to reach it. Next to be ascended and lying dead ahead is the middle top of Glaramara – Looking Steads. Two rocky points rise above the summit; the north easterly of these is the Glaramara summit.

Descend to move right across the plateau. A steep, well-worn rocky runnel leads down through the craggy north face that crowns the fell. Although a scramble is necessary here, the distance is short and it should not cause any problems. Easier boggy ground follows before a line of cairns can be seen leading away to the left. Follow them until the head of Hind Gill can be identified, then take the left bank in descent. Care must be exercised not to lose the route for the gill is deep and precipitous – stay out of it.

At its base the open fellside levels before a gate through the stone wall leads easily down towards the main track traversing the valley floor. It is best to stride the fence at the left corner of the field to join the track. Bear right, following its stony course back to the cobbled yard and distinctive aroma of a working Lakeland hill farm which mark an end to this mountain outing.

Over Brotherilkeld into Upper Eskdale with Border End standing to the right.

ESKDALE FELLS

·ESK·

Flowing west from the foot of the Scafells to the Irish Sea and the ancient Roman port of Ravenglass, the River Esk cuts a fine trace through the landscape. From the wilderness of Great Moss and Ling Cove through the savage grandeur of Upper Eskdale to the subtle features of Eskdale granite and its carpet of meadow, oak, rowan and silver birch, Eskdale is a matchless valley that forms a natural southern boundary to the Western Fells.

Although now one of the quieter Lakeland valleys, Eskdale has not always been so. The dramatic Hard Knott Fort suggests that Roman legions once marched its length, while the prehistoric stone circles reflect the presence of long forgotten communities. Today, even the iron mines that once flourished in the haematite-rich granite have gone. Only the plucky whistle of the 'La'al Ratty' (the Eskdale to Ravenglass Railway) reminds us of their past importance. These Eskdale hills, with their hidden tarns, great crags, crystal clear waters and tumbling waterfalls are now the sole province of the shepherd and hill lover.

East of Upper Eskdale and effectively forming the head of the main body of the valley, the Hard Knott cluster of fells are the highest. The rest to the west, and generally north of the valley, bathe in the shadow of the Scafells and to a lesser extent Illgill Head. These heights, from Great How and the summit of Eskdale Fell to lowly Goat Crag, occupy a hidden middle kingdom between the highest mountain of England and quintessential Eskdale.

Three diverse walks have been detailed, in total claiming thirteen tops. The first takes a high mantel around Upper Eskdale. Another walk explores the hidden fells behind the Woolpack Inn to circle the elusive Stony Tarn.

Beginning at Boot, a third expedition takes in Brats Moss to Boat How above Eskdale Moor and Burnmoor Tarn (the latter one of the largest mountain tarns in Lakeland) to scale Eskdale Fell and its summit Great How.

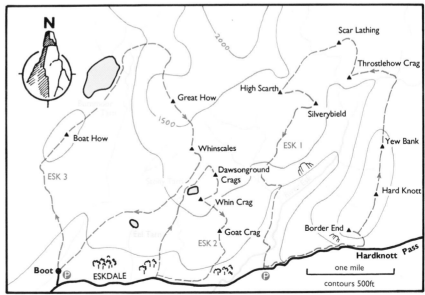

•ESK I•

UPPER ESKDALE ROUND

Border End 1713ft/522m
Hard Knott 1803ft/549m
Yew Bank 1637ft/499m
Throstlehow Crag 1325ft/404m
Scar Lathing 1440ft/439m
High Scarth 1598ft/487m
Silverybield 1296ft/395m

Valley Base: Eskdale.
Maps: OS OD6, The English Lakes –
South West. L90 Penrith & Keswick.
Length: 7.25miles/11.5km.
Ascent: 1575ft/480m.
Approx Time: 5hrs.
Start: Top of Hardknott Pass
(NY 232015). There are limited parking
spaces either side of the summit, but do
not block any passing places on this
narrow yet busy mountain pass.
Finish: Brotherilkeld (NY 211011) by the
telephone kiosk. There is parking here or
further (west) down the road on a large
grassy pull-off.
Difficulty: There are no particularly
tricky sections on this walk though it covers a remote area, sometimes without
paths, and there are boggy sections. Quite
arduous due to the many undulations and
overall length. Two becks have to be
crossed, Lingcove and the Esk; this may be
impossible in spate conditions. Those
wishing to make it into a circular walk may
ascend Hardknott Pass from
Brotherilkeld, returning to their starting
point in a further 0.5 hr.

Scar Lathing above the River Esk.

Uninhabited save for the hardy Herdwick, beguiling Upper Eskdale penetrates
deep into mountain terrain. Steep crag,
scree and bracken form its flanks, while
the crystal clear waters of the River Esk
flow along its base.

Striking a line north, this valley head is
overlooked by Hardknott Fort to the east
– surely the most dramatic mountain
encampment in Britain – and the crags of
Border End and Hard Knott. Directly
below Hard Knott perches the 50ft high,
free-standing Eskdale Needle. The west
flank of the valley is hardly less daunting,
with a succession of rocky crags culminating in the unbroken 150ft rocky bastion of Heron Crag. Feeding the River Esk

through a succession of tumbling waterfalls and deep rock pools, are the desolate
basins of Great Moss and Lingcove Beck.
Above them all, to the north west, the
mighty Scafell Group casts an
inescapably powerful spell.

Starting from the summit of Hardknott Pass above the Roman fort of
Mediobogdvm, this long and satisfying
upland horseshoe traverses the rim of the
valley. Commencing over Border End
and Hard Knott the walk descends the
shoulder of Yew Bank to cross Lingcove
Beck, going on to explore the rocky summits of Throstlehow Crag and Scar Lathing before crossing the young River Esk
beneath Great Moss. Rising to High
Scarth Crag, it crosses the main path to
gain the top of Silverybield before returning and following it sedately back to Scale
Bridge beneath Scale Force waterfall. The
track leads to Taw House Farm, crosses
the Esk by footbridge and finishes at the
telephone kiosk of Brotherilkeld.

Just east of the summit pass a path
leads up a natural grass rake to a boggy
hollow in the ridge above. Bear left, rising
to a cairned rocky outcrop. Continue to
the next upstanding area on the edge
overlooking Eskdale, the OS accredited
summit of Border End.

Returning to the hollow, strike north
across the bog, following cairns to rise
slightly, then pass through the large knots
of rock on the shoulder. In front of you
lies the biggest of the rock pyramids.
Ascent from here bearing first left then
right gives access to the summit cairn of
Hard Knott. A grand scene of high peaks
and desolation fills the entire panorama.
Being the highest point of this walk, it is a
tempting place to linger though there is
still far to go.

Descend from the summit, heading
due north with a mountain tarn
(unnamed on OS) to your right. On the
left is a craggy top but a more prominent
feature lies on the lower shoulder – an
ancient cairn. On the older OS maps it is
the cairn that is marked as the top of Yew
Bank with a height of 1570ft/478m. Of
course, the crag above is higher and the
new OS maps, from aerial survey, give
this as 1637ft/499m. Continue easily
down the grassy highway to the top of
Mosedale and then on to Lingcove Beck.

Boulder hopping gives a dry crossing
and above a path contours left. Follow
this, moving across the hillside. When it
begins to ascend, leave it to continue the
traverse left across a boggy section to an
old broken stone wall rising up the hill-

side. Follow this stone wall and continue upwards to the grassy, domed summit of Throstlehow Crag.

Head north from here, descending to cross the path. Pass a short, squat row of stones (the ancient remnants of a ruined stone wall or building) and pass to the right of the bog beyond. Rise steeply to the grassy neck leading to the top of Scar Lathing. Between you and the meandering River Esk below, and almost hidden from view, is an 80ft high cliff. Beyond to the north west across the flat, boggy tract of Great Moss, stands the cliff of Cam Spout, some 500ft high. To its right lies How Beck waterfall and a well-trodden path ascending to Mickledore – the rugged neck between Scafell and Scafell Pike. Right again sees the impressive, clean-sweeping pillar of Esk Buttress (marked Dow Crag and Central Pillar on the 1:25000 OS map).

Descend to the west, bearing slightly right but staying left of the bog and reeds above the river. There is a large boulder on the opposite bank; head for this, crossing the river just above the rocky rapids (in normal conditions it is possible to cross dry footed; in spate a crossing will

be impossible). Cross the main footpath, pass the boulder and continue to rise, bearing left to the vague summit of High Scarth Crag.

Circumnavigate a rocky knoll to the left, where a grass corridor leads down to the main track. Cross it and pass the bog to the left beneath some little crags, then rise to the rocky knott of Silverybield. An enticing view down to the rock pools of the River Esk is your reward.

Round the southern end of Silverybield bog to return to the main path. Follow this until it swings right at the junction of the mires of Damas Dubs and Cowcove. It is best to keep high and right until the path crosses the narrowest point, taking the little stream by a rusty corrugated iron 'bridge'. A good track zigzags down to the valley floor, reaching Scale Bridge beneath a lovely waterfall. It continues to run down left through the fields to Taw House Farm.

A wooden stile leads to a corridor down the edge of the field and a wooden footbridge across the River Esk. From here the track skirts Brotherilkeld Farm and continues to the road and original telephone kiosk.

• ESK 2 •

A ROUND OF STONY TARN

Dawsonground Crags 1302ft/397m
Whin Crag 1158ft/353m
Goat Crag 1024ft/312m

Valley Base: Eskdale.
Maps: OS OD6, The English Lakes – South West. L90 Penrith & Keswick.
Length: 3.75miles/6km.
Ascent: 1200ft/365m.
Approx Time: 2hrs.
Start & Finish: The car park to the right of the Woolpack Inn (NY 190010).
Difficulty: A straightforward outing although beyond the tarn there is no definite path and the going can be rough and heathery.

Rounding hidden and secretive Stony Tarn, this walk uses its 1200ft of ascent to top three craggy summits: sprawling Dawsonground Crags, the shapely Whin

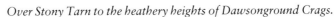

Over Stony Tarn to the heathery heights of Dawsonground Crags.

Crag and finally the bare pink granite dome of Goat Crag. Rising from the Eskdale Granite above the Woolpack Inn the crags surrounding the tarn itself are dark grey-blue mountain rhyolite of the same type as the Scafell massif beyond. Above the tarn the track disappears and much of the going is over heather and craggy outcrop before Goat Crag, again constructed of Eskdale Granite, is reached. Descend to the road running along the floor of this special Lakeland vale above Wha House farm.

Round the left side of the building and take a small gate behind, as the track rises from the Woolpack Inn. The larch plantation can be exited by another small gate and the track.

Ignore the fork left and continue straight ahead into the rocky hummocks. Again ignore a track swinging off left, (invisible in any case when the bracken grows high). A vista opens to the right from where a view of the final objective – the naked pink/white rocks of Goat Crag – is possible. The path traverses to rise yet again, with a view to the shapely cairned summit of Whin Crag.

Gloriously named Peelplace Noddle is crossed before an ascent is made to the left. Cross a stream and make a final pull to gain the shoulder. Secluded Stony Tarn lies to the right, with its cirque of heathery crags above.

Skirt the end of the tarn, re-crossing the stream before rising up left to a ruined building. Contour right under a craggy outcrop and climb to the heathery plateau. The view beyond is capped by Slight Side and Scafell. Bear right to find the top of Dawsonground Crags and follow the ridge running out above the tarn. The cairned top at its end is the summit of Whin Crag.

Pick a careful line back east heading for the light granite dome of Goat Crag. Descend through craggy outcrops, to a grassy hollow and cross this over bog and stream to pass the granite cliff of Bull How. From here, ascend to gain the top of Goat Crag.

Moving down from here, a natural narrow corridor leads between the rocks before a traverse right, beneath a steep slab wall, leads easily down to a well-defined path (a popular route from Wha House to the Slight Side shoulder of Scafell) and the road.

◆ ESK 3 ◆

BURNMOOR AND ESKDALE FELL

Boat How 1105ft/337m
Great How – Eskdale Fell 1713ft/522m
Whinscales – Eskdale Fell 1394ft/425m

Valley Base: Eskdale.
Maps: OS OD6, The English Lakes – South West. L90 Penrith & Keswick.
Length: 7miles/11km.
Ascent: 1800ft/550m.
Approx Time: 3.5hrs.
Start & Finish: Boot (NY 176011). Parking within the hamlet is very limited – it may be necessary to park by the narrow road just outside. The Burnmoor Inn has a large car park and the landlord does allow walkers who use his services to park here (do not park and walk – ask permission first).
Difficulty: Save its length, this walk is generally straightforward. However, the ascent into Oliver Gill is quite steep and the traverse of Great How is without a well-defined path. The section traversing the head of Burnmoor Tarn is unavoidably boggy.

Starting from the granite hamlet of Boot this walk explores a wonderfully wild upland countryside. Beneath the Slight Side edge of Scafell and the Eskdale Flanks of Illgill Head, observe the fascinating remnants of the past such as the five stone circles on the shoulder of Boat How. From the top the view extends over isolated Burnmoor Tarn, across unseen Wasdale, to the Pillar Group, Kirk Fell and Great Gable. A steep climb to Great How, the summit of Eskdale Fell, is followed by a descent taking in the top of Whinscales and the wonderful Stony Tarn and Eel Tarn, before return to Boot.

Boot was once the busy centre of industry. Its mill ground locally produced wheat, while the red rift up on the hillside above was an iron mine of sufficient size to justify the construction of a narrow-gauge railway in 1875. The mill has now been restored as a museum and the Eskdale to Ravenglass Railway ('La'al Ratty') now operates throughout the year from Dalegarth Station just below Boot.

Our way lies over the stone arched bridge, past the mill and onto the stone-walled bridleway leading in the direction of Brat's Moss.

Zigzagging steeply at first, the bridleway is lined with walls constructed from hefty boulders of Eskdale Granite. Within their confines the broad track is edged with bracken, frequent patches of gorse and the occasional rowan.

As open moor is encountered, a cluster of interesting stone buildings are encountered. Their design is very specific. Built into the hillside, a level track feeds a wide opening in the back top of the building. The height of the masonry then takes in the fall of the hill and a narrow front doorway allows access into the base of the building. Only one slate roof remains in situ at the time of writing, though otherwise these rugged structures remain in a reasonable state of repair.

What was their purpose? It is said that they were peat houses used to store and dry the peat cut from the moor. This was then transported to the valley to be burnt as fuel. Perhaps this explains the origin of the name Burnmoor.

In front of the last building the track bears right, up onto Brat's Moss. As the track levels to cross Brat's Hill a grass mound, which presents itself as an obvious vantage point, stands to the left. Leave the track to surmount this mound to find immediately below on the other side a stone circle with around thirty standing and fallen stones. Inside, there are five circular burial chambers with indented tops. Beyond, lie another two circles. Pass these and climb onto the shoulder of Low Loughrigg to discover two smaller circles, then ascend the easy shoulder towards Boat How, climbing the side of a rocky rampart onto a flat area. The rocky knoll summit of Boat How lies further along to the left.

Burnmoor Lodge appears on the left along with numerous slightly raised circles of earth and rock (they may be burial chambers or hut circles; but they are not marked on the map). An easy descent leads down the broad spur to Burnmoor Tarn. The lodge indicates that this sizeable stretch of water was once fished for trout and the moor shot for game.

A line of shooting butts rises up the south flank of Boat How. The tarn is cradled in a hollow that once served as an

Eskdale Fell stands in the distance beyond the ruins of the peat house.

important pass between Wasdale and Eskdale. It is popularly remembered as the Coffin Road over which the dead from Wasdale were brought to be buried in Eskdale. The path crosses over Whillan Beck on a bridge made from wooden sleepers, before the track bears right across the bog.

Cross the stream (no problem in normal conditions) just above the confluence of Hardrigg and Oliver Gills. Ascend the steep, rough hillside directly above to find a hidden path that has crossed the hillside from distant Lambford Bridge. Continue along the path to the side of Oliver Gill,

then follow the gill up until it enters a little ravine cutting through the end of Bleaberry How. Keep to the south bank, traversing its steep sides before it is best advised to climb right, up the northern shoulder of Eskdale Fell. Pass the little tarns, located closer to the edge over to the right, and rise to the rocky summit of Eskdale Fell – Great How.

A cleft in the rocks will be found to the west. Descend through this to find a crescent-shaped spur leading to the top of Whinscales. From this point, the shoulder continues to fall towards Stony Tarn before bearing right. Intermittent paths

disappear and reappear; but by carefully picking a sensible course through the rock and heather you can descend fairly easily to Eel Tarn.

The path leads above the north shore, descending from the tarn to a good track. Follow this to an escape route formed by stone walls, providing an exit from the open fellside. A curious umbrella-shaped monkey puzzle tree stands in a field to the right before our signposted 'Bridleway To Boot' proceeds through a gate. This becomes surfaced and descends pleasantly through gorse and trees before emerging on Boot's main street by the bridge.

The Scafells above Wast Water.

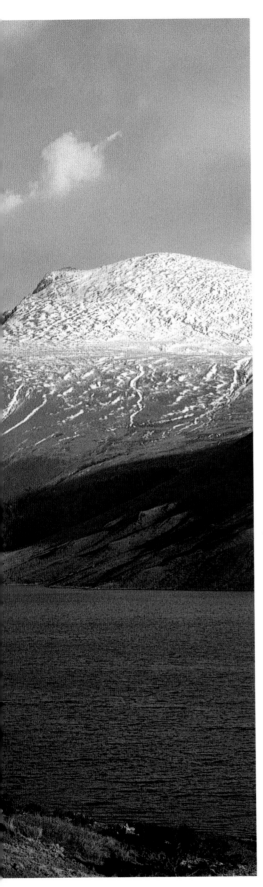

SCAFELLS

•SCA•

The mighty Scafells, the roof of England, form the highest mountain massif in the country. This rough and stony high mountain crest, for the most part devoid of vegetation, stretches uninterrupted from Great End to Scafell Pike, with the deep gap of Mickledore separating Scafell Pike from Scafell. Lying either side of this northern spine, Ill Crag and Broad Crag offer two further independent summits. Beyond, Lingmell stands prominently above Wasdale and the little shapely rock pyramid of Pen above the Great Moss of Upper Eskdale. Finally, Slight Side forms the last top as the great hulking shoulder of Scafell falls to the south.

While Scafell Pike is the highest point in England it is the rock climbing mecca of Scafell, guarded by the huge precipitous cliffs crowning its northern and eastern flanks, which remains the most inaccessible. Apart from the Wasdale approach, which is short and steep, distances are great and an ascent of the Scafells requires a certain degree of walking fitness. Nevertheless, with the exception of Pen ascent of all the tops in this group need not be unduly difficult.

On a clear day, the view from Scafell looks out to the distant peaks of Scotland, Wales, the Isle of Man, and the emerald hills of Ireland. Climbing any one of these summits is a worthy accomplishment. A

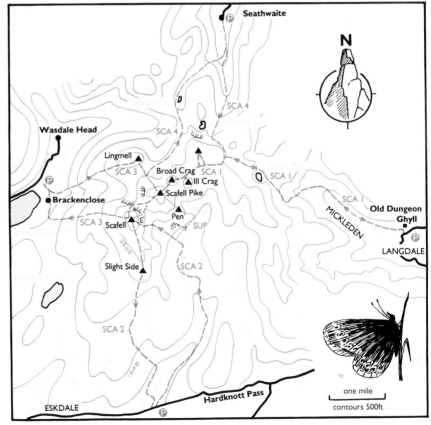

one mile

contours 500ft

complete traverse of the group would be a considerable feather in anyone's cap.

Four walks have been selected, exploring the range from the main glacial valleys that emanate from its heights: Great Langdale, Eskdale, Wasdale and Seathwaite in Borrowdale. A supplement includes the route from Great Moss in Upper Eskdale to Scafell Pike, visiting the independent top of Pen. This should be considered a mild scramble.

Logically, the supplement goes on to tackle the notorious Broad Stand route from Mickledore to Scafell. Although a much frequented course, it should be considered as a difficult scramble or as an easy rock climb rather than a walk. It is after all very exposed – a slip would be disastrous. The regular walk from Eskdale ascends Scafell via Fox's Tarn, the simplest and safest route from the Mickledore end of Scafell. The Wasdale walk takes in Lingmell and Scafell Pike before descending to Mickledore and then ascending Scafell's great northern cliffs by Lord's Rake.

The classic route from Great Langdale is long and is terminated at Scafell Pike, as is that from Seathwaite via Sty Head and the Corridor Route. Those wishing to extend these trips by ascending Scafell from Mickledore should refer to the walks from Eskdale and Wasdale. No routes up the cliffs between Mickledore and Scafell are described other than Fox's Tarn (the best way for walkers), Lord's Rake and Broad Stand (only for those with climbing ability). Without detailed knowledge and climbing ability, all other routes should be avoided.

Inevitably, walking the Scafells means long but great days in the hills.

Over Esk Hause below Great End.

•SCA1•

GREAT LANGDALE TO SCAFELL PIKE

Great End 2984ft/910m
Ill Crag 3067ft/935m
Broad Crag 3054ft/931m
Scafell Pike 3210ft/978m

Valley Base: Great Langdale.
Maps: OS OD6, The English Lakes – South West. L90 Penrith and Keswick.
Length: 11 miles/18km.
Ascent: 3775ft/1150m.
Approx Time: 7hrs.
Start & Finish: Old Dungeon Ghyll Hotel car park (NY 286062).
Difficulty: Despite its lack of technical difficulty this remains an arduous walk of some considerable length. The path, for the most part, is well defined although the going is principally over rough stony ground.

Naturally, an ascent of England's highest mountain, Scafell Pike, is a considerable attraction in itself. Rising from Great Langdale to explore the Scafell range from its most northerly point, Great End, this walk visits the tops of Ill Crag and Broad Crag before culminating in the ascent of Scafell Pike. Taken overall, the generally gradual nature of ascent, lack of technical difficulty and unparalleled mountain panoramas make this one of Lakeland's classic outings.

The walk being linear in concept, those with tiring legs on the approach should bear in mind the equal distance of return. The route home, however, does bypass the tops to strike a central line along the main path. That and the fact that it is mostly in descent makes the return somewhat easier than the approach. Those with doubts may note that this was once a favourite route for pioneer rock climbers visiting the great north face of Scafell Crag. A day on the cliff would end with their return to the Old Dungeon Ghyll Hotel, this walk forming only a part of their mountain day in the Lake District.

From the the Old Dungeon Ghyll the walled stony track soon gives way to the openness of Mickleden. Towering high to

The moon rises above Broad Crag on the return to Langdale.

SCAFELL FROM ESKDALE

Scafell 3162ft/964m
Slight Side 2499ft/762m

Valley Base: Eskdale.
Maps: OS OD6, The English Lakes –
South West. L90 Penrith and Keswick.
Length: 8.25miles/13.5km.
Ascent: 2950ft/900m.
Approx Time: 5hrs.
Start & Finish: Car park by the side of
Hardknott Pass just above the cattle grid
at Brotherilkeld (NY 214011).
Difficulty: This long walk covers remote
high ground and although good paths prevail the going varies from rough and stony,
to wet and boggy. The River Esk must be
crossed in the Great Moss. It is a strenuous pull from Great Moss to the summit
of Scafell. Also note, because they cannot
be seen from the summit of Scafell, that a
great horseshoe of cliffs separate Scafell
from Mickledore and Scafell Pike. There is
no direct easy access down to Mickledore
from Scafell.

the right, Gimmer Crag and Pike O'Stickle set the mood for this impressive high
mountain walk.

Rossett Gill presents the first steep
climb. It has a rather notorious reputation, although path construction has
made it more accessible. Alternatively, an
old packhorse track zigzags more sedately up to its left, joining the gill at its head.
The demanding ascent is worthwhile for
a little way ahead lies Angle Tarn,
nestling in a secluded hollow beneath
Hanging Knotts.

The gentle ascent from the tarn leads
to the stony shoulder of Esk Hause and
the stone-walled shelter formed in a cross.
In any prevailing wind you should be able
to seek cover here. Rough, stony ground
devoid of vegetation stretches ahead. Proceed along the stone path until it is possible to move right to the broad summit of
Great End. A cairn and trig point stand
among a sprawl of rocks.

The whole upland range the Scafells
lies ahead. The shoulder first descends
then rises, and you should bear left off the
main path to gain the peak of Ill Crag.
Latest OS data puts this as second in altitude to Scafell Pike. Those unfamiliar
with the topography may easily have mistaken this top when viewing it from Esk
Hause below for that of Scafell Pike. All
will now be revealed, with the true roof of
the Lake District and England lying ahead

over the depths of Little Narrowcove.

Descend to the main path situated in a
deep gap below the rocky shoulder of
Broad Crag. Photographers should note
the definitive view of Great Gable to the
north – a magnificent sight. The main
path rises to pass the top of Broad Crag on
its southern flank before dropping to the
gap beneath Scafell Pike. To reach the
summit of Broad Crag bear right at the
highest point and make a rough scramble
over awkward boulder and scree.

Return to the main path and descend
into the gap ahead. This forms the head of
Little Narrowcove to the south east and
Piers Gill to the north west. Take heart
and rise steeply up the other side. Soon,
effort rewarded, the angle slackens and
the path leads easily over the summit
dome to a large circular chambered cairn.
This is the top of Scafell Pike. Beneath lies
the concrete trig point, a broad rock
strewn plateau with breathtaking views
of the rest of England.

The hardy may wish to continue down
to Mickledore and up to Scafell (see SCA
2, SCA 2A and SCA 3 for details). Those
wishing to return to Langdale should
retrace their steps though remain on the
main well-defined path, which takes a
central route beneath the tops of Broad
Crag and Ill Crag to Esk Hause without
taking in Great End. From this point,
descend to the welcome flat of Mickleden.

Pre-eminent as the mightiest Lakeland
Fell, Scafell is separated from Scafell Pike
by a tremendous cirque of cliffs. To the
south its huge shoulder falls over Slight
Side to dominate Eskdale Fell and Burnmoor, and becomes the most prominent
feature of the group when viewed from
the south and the west. Its great bulk
marks the southern end of the Scafell
range. To the south, lesser hills tumble
toward the flat plains of the west coast to
Ravenglass and the Irish Sea. Immediately to the north, east and west stand the
great mountains of The Lake District:
Scafell Pike, Bowfell, Great Gable and
last, but not least, Pillar.

The attraction of the Eskdale
approach to the summit of Scafell, even
above that of its considerable aesthetic
beauty, lies in the way it bypasses the cliffs
along Fox's Tarn to provide a safe ascent.
Starting from above Brotherilkeld, it proceeds along Upper Eskdale, crosses Lingcove Bridge and climbs to Great Moss
before ascending towards Mickledore via
the waterfall north of Cam Spout Crag.
Bearing left beneath the East Buttress, it

The formidable East Buttress with Mickledore to the right.

reaches the shoulder to top the Scafell summit. Descending over the independent top of Slight Side, it traverses Cowcove and Catcove to Taw House before it crosses the River Esk and returns to the starting point above Brotherilkeld.

From the sloping car park opposite the plantation, find the path running above the plantation to enter the fields above Brotherilkeld Farm. The well-defined path leads into the wilds of Upper Eskdale with Eskdale Needle visible to the right and Heron Crag to the left. The clear, deep rock pools of the River Esk are most inviting, but the heights of Scafell beckon. Press on over Lingcove Bridge and begin climbing towards Great Moss.

The path flattens, passes beneath Scar Lathing and continues to follow the true left bank of the River Esk in the shadow of the impressive precipice of Cam Spout Crag. The bog here is known as Great Moss. To the left, How Beck makes an impressive waterfall, and a valley leads up to Mickledore. Above the confluence where How Beck joins the Esk, make a crossing. Usually this can be made dry by boulder hopping.

Take the steep path rising impressively just right of the waterfall (scrambling may be necessary). Continue up the steep hanging valley above until, some 100 yards below the rocky bastion of the East

Buttress a stream issues from a stony gully to the left. Climb the gully (rough but not difficult) which leads directly to Fox's Tarn, the smallest tarn in the Lake District. (Note, if the gully is missed a well-defined traverse takes a higher route to the tarn.) The way ahead lies directly up to the shoulder, then left to the summit cairn situated on a slight rise. The remains of a ruined shelter lie just beyond.

The summit cairn stands back from the cliffs, which from here lay undetected. To the north, above the rocky ridge of Mickledore connecting Scafell to Scafell Pike, they sweep west as Scafell Crag, approaching 500ft in height, and east as East Buttress. Beware, for there is danger here – few safe links to Mickledore exist for the walker. Lord's Rake (see Walk SCA 3) to the west is one, Broad Stand (see Walk SCA 2A) sited centrally is another, though this latter route is only for those with a some rock climbing ability and a cool head for heights.

A fine panorama unfolds from this broad, stony top extending to all of Britain's five kingdoms: Scotland, the Isle of Man, Ireland, England and Wales. The descent along the shoulder and down Long Green to Slight Side seems a long way. The summit cairn lies on top of the sloping rock outcrop (known to some as Horn Crag). A rough scramble leads

through the rocks down to the right, to gain the path leading down the flanks of Scafell. Rapid progress can be made until the going levels to cross the upper rim of Cowcove and Cat Cove Beck. Beyond the ravine running below Cat Crags, our path breaks down to the left (straight on leads to the road above Wha House farm). Weave a way down the hillside to the track by the gate in the wall. Take the lower gate into the field and continue to Taw House farm.

A stile leads left to a corridor, formed by a stone wall and post and wire fence, leading to the footbridge over the River Esk. The path skirts Brotherilkeld farm to join the road at the foot of Hardknott Pass by the telephone kiosk.

◆ S C A 2 A ◆

SCAFELL PIKE VIA PEN, SCAFELL BY BROAD STAND

(A SUPPLEMENT TO WALK SCA 2)

Pen 2500ft/762m
Scafell Pike 3210ft/978m

Additional Length: 2.5miles/4km.
Additional Ascent: 375ft/115m.
Additional Approx Time: 1.25hrs.
Start: Great Moss (NY 219059).
Finish: Scafell Shoulder (NY 208067).
Difficulty: This addition to the Eskdale approach to Scafell is more than a walk. Reaching the independent summit of Pen involves scrambling of moderate difficulty. Ascending Broad Stand to reach the summit of Scafell is a difficult scramble/easy rock climb. It is extremely polished and exposed – a slip would result in serious consequences.

This outing is described as a supplement to Walk SCA 2, the Eskdale approach to Scafell, the reason being that it is the logical approach to reach the independent summit of Pen – a shapely and appealing top which could not be missed out. The problem for walkers is that reaching the summit does involve scrambling. Located amongst impressive mountain scenery, its position is remote and the going rough and difficult; this is not a place for the unwary. Having included Pen the logical link to Walk SCA 2A is to ascend Broad Stand from Mickledore. Although short, the difficulty is greater than that of Pen. The ground falls rapidly away below, resulting in considerable exposure; a slip on Broad Stand would be very serious indeed. To put an ascent of Broad Stand into context: for rock climbers it is very simple, they use it as an easy descent from the great crags on either side. For those walking the tops many do make an ascent and descent without a second thought. However, it is a climb involving both feet and hands and it is imperative to stay in contact with the rock and be able to continue or retreat in a steady and controlled manner. There have been many serious accidents here – take into account the weakest member of your party and if in any doubt stay away.

Cross the River Esk approaching the waterfall of How Beck (see Walk SCA 2), then bear right (a high line avoids most of the boggy ground) to cross beneath Esk Buttress, one of the finest rock climbing crags (incorrectly named Dow Crag and Central Pillar on the OS maps). Continue beneath a lesser crag with a prominent gash up its front: this is Thor's Buttress. Follow a vague path rising up into Little Narrowcove, but quickly move off left into a broad easy gully. Continue left to tackle the rocky pyramid summit of Pen by its left side.

After descending continue up the broad ridge beyond, taking the rocky wall on its left to make a rough bouldery ascent. When the angle eases the cairned rocky knoll to the left is the Eskdale Cairn. Cross the rocky plateau beyond to the summit of Scafell Pike. An easy path makes a stony descent to the wooden rescue box marking the start of the Mickledore edge connecting Scafell Pike to Scafell. Nearing the Scafell end of Mickledore, a path will be noted falling left to traverse beneath the rocks of the East Buttress. A short way down the rock face a narrow cleft in the rock, formed by a rock block to the left, provides the narrow squeeze access to Broad Stand.

The bottom section of Broad Stand in effect comprises of a series of stepped walls, each no more than 15ft in height. However, Mickledore falls rapidly away to the left and as the ascent involves traversing left there is immediately more exposure than the cumulative height of the individual steps.

Squeeze through the cleft and rise to a rock ledge beneath the first wall. Step left onto a very polished rock. Climb up and right to a ledge beneath the second wall (not very difficult but particularly exposed). Climb the second wall directly or by the corner (technically the most difficult section) – in either case only a few

The scene over Great Moss with Esk Buttress, topped by Pen, seen centrally.

feet need be made before a good handhold can be taken on the ledge above. Rock slabs lead out right to gently angled ground where it is again possible to assume a standing position.

The path continues up then left through a notch in the rocks to the easy top section of a gully (Mickledore Gully is a graded rock climb which offers no easy way below). Note that loose rocks and scree abound and it is imperative that nothing is dislodged, for rock climbers may be on the cliffs below. Continue up the gully until it is possible to bear left along the rocky top.

Shortly, to the right it is possible to observe twin rocky peaks located immediately north of the wide rim of Deep Gill. Famous and often photographed, the higher one is the top of Pisgah Buttress and the lower, Scafell Pinnacle. Continue to the path above Fox's Tarn and proceed along the broad shoulder plateau leading to the summit of Scafell.

The cliffs of Lingmell viewed from Scafell Pike.

• S C A 3 •

LINGMELL AND THE SCAFELLS FROM WASDALE

Lingmell 2649ft/807m
Scafell Pike 3210ft/978m
Scafell 3162ft/964m

Valley Base: Wasdale.
Maps: OS OD6, The English Lakes –
South West. L90 Penrith and Keswick.
Length: 6.25miles/10km.
Ascent: 3840ft/1170m.
Approx Time: 5hrs.
Start & Finish: The car park, alongside the camp site, at the head of Wast Water (NY 182074).
Difficulty: A strenuous outing, taking in some steep ground on Lord's Rake, though without undue technical difficulty. It is possible to miss out Scafell, descending directly from Mickledore before reaching Lord's Rake.

Climbing from Wasdale to Lingmell and on to Scafell Pike, offers one of the most direct ascents to England's highest peak.

Combining this with the short descent to Mickledore and traverse beneath Scafell Crag to climb Lord's Rake, so gaining the summit of Scafell, provides a logical continuation. For its directness in visiting the two main summits of the Scafells and for its spectacular rock scenery, this route from Wasdale is hard to beat.

After crossing the concrete bridge turn left to follow the stream bank, passing Brackenclose Fell and Rock Climbing Hut on the right. Cross a wooden footbridge and take the path rising with Lingmell Gill. Beyond a fence, a path bears off left to the shoulder of Lingmell. (Straight on leads up Brown Tongue to Hollow Stones and then via steep scree directly to Mickledore, the shortest route and a hard slog. This might be useful to the walker as a safe and quick descent from the deep gap of Mickledore.)

Although initially the going is steep, above the 1800ft/550m contour the angle recedes and pleasant walking leads to the left of Goat Crags and to the summit of Lingmell. An elegant cairn is bettered only by the sight of Great Gable, which looks most imposing from this outstanding viewpoint. Directly below to the north east lies the dark forbidding depths of Piers Gill.

Descend the grassy slope over a ruined

stone wall into the hollow of Lingmell Col (junction with the Corridor Route from Sty Head). The well-defined path rises to the right before sweeping back left over the rocky plateau to the summit cairn of Scafell Pike.

From the cairn a well-worn path makes a rocky descent to the ridge of Mickledore. Nearing the Scafell end of Mickledore a steep and rough scree slope (care must be exercised) leads down to a long ledge beneath the north facing precipice of Scafell Crag.

At the end of this Lord's Rake, running in the same line as the ledge, cuts upwards through the rocks. Before entering its bowels a cross cut on the rock face to the left may be observed. This commemorates a terrible accident in 1903 when four pioneer rock climbers making an ascent of the Scafell Pinnacle – which rises directly from this point – fell tragically to their deaths.

Lord's Rake has long been a popular way to climb to the summit of Scafell. Notice that much of the scree filling the rake has been emptied out leaving patches of hard slippery rock – it is now much more of a scramble than of old. Including this first immediately observed section the rake contains three rises and falls all continuing in a straight line to the open fell. A path leads up left onto the shoulder and in turn the summit of Scafell.

From the summit a vague path leads easily and quickly down the grass flanks of the mountain, over Green How to join the track above Fence Wood and Wasdale Head Hall farm. Popular in Victorian times this path is now relatively unfrequented, yet it is undoubtably the simplest way to descend from Scafell into Wasdale. Bear right through the sweet oaks of Brackenclose to Lingmell Gill.

•SCA4•

SCAFELL PIKE FROM SEATHWAITE IN BORROWDALE

Scafell Pike 3210ft/978m
Broad Crag 3054ft/931m
Ill Crag 3067ft/935m
Great End 2984ft/910m

Valley Base: Borrowdale.
Maps: OS OD4, The English Lakes – North West and OS OD6, The English Lakes – South West. L90 Penrith and Keswick.
Length: 8.5miles/14km.
Ascent: 3350ft/1020m.
Approx Time: 5hrs.
Start & Finish: The head of the Seathwaite Valley, by the side of the road beneath the farm. Do not block any field entrances or the road (NY 236123).
Difficulty: A long walk with a short section of moderate scrambling near the start of the Corridor Route and an exposed section traversing across the top of Piers Gill. The route can be considerably eased by rejoining the Corridor Route directly after ascending Scafell Pike.

Rising from Seathwaite on the Borrowdale side of the Scafells to traverse the Corridor Route from Sty Head to Scafell Pike, this represents yet another attractive route. Return can be made directly to the Corridor from the col between Scafell Pike and Broad Crag, or a continuation made along the northern spine of the group to include the summits of Broad Crag, Ill Crag and Great End. If the latter course is followed descend to Esk Hause,

then under the northern cliffs of Great End and down Grains Gill for a magnificent and truly memorable outing.

The track through the farm leads easily to Stockley Bridge over Grains Gill. From here it passes up through the gate in the fell wall and bears right to sweep up the shoulder above the larches of Taylorgill Force (you can hear the waterfall but cannot see it). The ascent eases and follows Styhead Gill, crossing it by a wooden footbridge before traversing the banks of Styhead Tarn. Peaceful Styhead Tarn is just as a high mountain tarn should be. If there is ice on its surface, then the Corridor Route should not be tackled without ice axe and crampons. Invariably, ice will have formed on the path and a slip would be fatal, particularly around the exposed head of Piers Gill.

Sty Head and the wooden rescue box, are just beyond the tarn. Wasdale lies below but our course rises up the shoulder of the col to the left. After a brief ascent, a slight descent is made to the right to the start of the Corridor Route beneath Spout Head. The path follows a natural course through rugged and exposed ground. The Corridor ends just above Lingmell Col from where the path leads directly up the stony slopes of Scafell Pike. It bears right then back left to cross the summit plateau

and reach the large cairn.

Heading north east across the plateau the path falls to the col beneath Scafell Pike and Broad Crag. It is now possible to escape directly back to the Corridor Route by descending the broad gully, the continuation of Piers Gill. Half way down the gully either bear right or continue directly down.

The hardy will climb the flanks of Broad Crag and bear left over rock and scree to its summit before returning to the central path along the northern spine of the group. A similar excursion to the right leads to Ill Crag. Regain the main path and proceed to the summit cairn of Great End. From here retrace your steps before following a course to the path descending to Esk Hause.

A cairn marks the junction of two routes, Esk Pike to the right, Esk Hause Shelter straight down. Our way bears left to the main Sty Head–Rossett Gill track, which should be followed under Great End. The stream on the right is crossed and a well- defined path taken down to the right of Ruddy Gill. A recently built footpath leads down to a bridge crossing Grains Gill. The path leads down the left bank of the gill to Stockley Bridge. The stony track beyond brings the welcome sight of Seathwaite Farm into view.

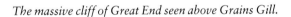

The massive cliff of Great End seen above Grains Gill.

The Screes tumbling into Wast Water.

THE SCREES

Tumbling from the high gullies and buttresses which crest its south eastern skyline, tons of rock sweep 2000ft down the hillside into the depths of Wast Water. The Screes, known locally as Wasdale Screes, provide one of the grandest and most rugged sights in the Lake District: an impressive gateway into the mountain valley of Wasdale.

Separated from the Scafells by the col carrying the ancient Wasdale Head to Boot Corpse Road, The Screes stretch as a high shoulder above Wast Water. Two main tops, Illgill Head and Whin Rigg, crest the shoulder before it falls to Irton Fell. This in turn slackens seaward to culminate in Irton Pike, beyond which lie the flat plains of the West Coast. While The Screes present a dramatic face, the actual crest of the ridge and the ground to the south east consist of gently rounded grassland curving down to Burnmoor Tarn and Miterdale. The craggy, granite outcrop of Great Bank forms an offshoot, standing above the wooded flanks of hidden Miterdale.

From Illgill Head to Whin Rigg, The Screes become progressively craggier. Beneath Whin Rigg, mighty rock buttresses appear to tower vertically. A series of gullies divide these buttresses: above the pumping station the awesome rifts of Great Gully and C Gully to its right are especially noticeable. These gullies of rot-

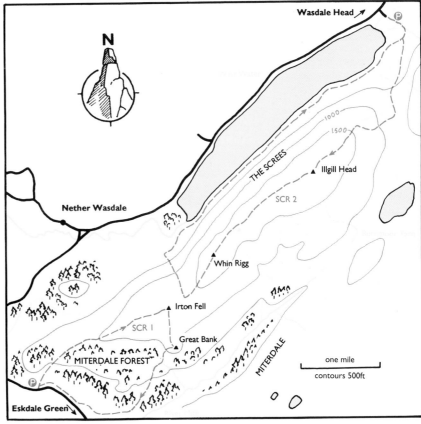

ten rock are formidably steep and present no walking opportunities. Indeed, walkers are advised not to be tempted to take any direct route up or down The Screes.

I have covered The Screes by two walks which take in the four tops over 1000ft. Proceeding from the western end, the first is a comparatively gentle stroll along Irton Fell and down over Great Bank above Miterdale. Lesser Irton Pike, a noted viewpoint, can also be visited. This is a sedate outing contrasting wooded Miterdale with the open fell above.

The second walk, a natural circuit, traverses the high shoulder via Illgill Head and Whin Rigg, returning across the foot of The Screes just above the level of Wast Water. Savouring at first hand the full drama and impact of this geological phenomenon, it is the keynote walk of the group.

The long shoulder declining from Whin Rigg holds the top of Irton Fell.

IRTON FELL

Irton Fell 1296ft/395m
Great Bank 1079ft/329m

Valley Base: Eskdale.
Maps: OS OD6, The English Lakes – South West. L89 West Cumbria.
Length: 4.25miles/7km.
Ascent: 1065ft/325m.
Approx Time: 2hrs.
Start & Finish: Old quarry car park by the side of the Eskdale Bridge to Santon Bridge Road (NY 121012) – marked Pit (dis) on the OS map.
Difficulty: A reasonably easy outing except for a short section of descent from Great Bank. This is pathless and a way must be struck through thick heather, bilberry, granite boulders and conifers.

Protruding above the ends of Wasdale and Miterdale, Irton Fell forms the south western shoulder of Whin Rigg and The Screes, its rainfall falling to the River Irt in the north and the River Mite to the south. In character, however, it still owes much of its allegiance to Eskdale. Thus the rocks, revealed in ancient piles of stones on the shoulder above Mecklin Park and the craggy face of Great Bank, are found to be made of Eskdale Granite.

By the side of the quarry in the direction of Santon Bridge, a signs reads 'Public Footpath Wasdale Head'. Rising above the quarry through the forestry, the path reaches a forest track. Follow this, bearing right at a junction. The track leads above a stone wall to exit the forest via a stile next to a gate. (Alternatively, ascend the forestry track bearing left to gain a shoulder leading to the top of Irton Pike, a popular viewpoint before the growth of the forest. From here a path leads through the forest to a stile and the open shoulder of Irton Fell.) Numerous piles of stones, optimistically marked 'Cairn Circle' on the OS map, lie mainly to the left.

The path continues easily along the grassy shoulder before an exposed section of paved road is crossed. The old track leads into a rift – an ancient mine indicated on the OS map. The red oven-baked rocks of Latterbarrow stand below, bared from their shroud of conifers at the time of writing. The path follows the stone wall, with afforested Miterdale lying to the right.

A stile leads over a wall until finally the shoulder levels. Bear right to the summit mound of Irton Fell, the most north easterly being the highest. An open aspect extends to Ravenglass and the coast. Either continue along the top to pick up the line of an old wall at the head of Greathall Gill, or descend directly towards Great Bank. In either case, the wall skirts forest to form a distinct corner from which access is made to Great Bank.

Stride the post and wire fence. At this point there is a clearing in the forest. Climb up through thick tussocks of grass and heather to the summit, then cross a ruined stone wall to the top.

Return to the neck and descend by the stone wall until the point at which it disappears into the forest. Bear left, past rough heather and boulders, until in a little way there is a break in the conifers below. Descend to this and continue in the same line through the trees to find a gap in a stone wall. On the other side of the wall an open gill, Merebeck Gill, tumbles below. A vague path leads down the bank above to enter a group of larches. On the left an stone gateway leads through the wall. Descend through the woods to reach a forestry track and bear right along this.

The track leads easily through the forest. Ignore the first branch to the right and, shortly afterwards, the bridleway crossing it. Continue straight along the track at the next junction, finally descending Crabtree Dale Wood to emerge briefly into open territory. Keyhow Coppice follows before the drive to Cubbens and shortly afterwards the road is reached. Strike right along this, noting the fine row of evergreen oaks on the right (they stay in leaf throughout the winter months) and the spreading cyprus tree on the left. The old granite quarry is reached in a short distance.

•SCR 2•

ACROSS THE SCREES

Illgill Head 1998ft/609m
Whin Rigg 1755ft/535m

Valley Base: Wasdale.
Maps: OS OD6, The English Lakes – South West. L89 West Cumbria.
Length: 8.25miles/13.5km.
Ascent: 2020ft/615m.
Approx Time: 4.5hrs.
Start & Finish: The car park alongside the camp site at the head of Wast Water (NY 182074).
Difficulty: Generally a straightforward outing with easy walking along the top. However, the magnitude of ascent, 2020ft, should not be forgotten. The final section of the walk, traversing The Screes just above the surface of Wast Water, is inescapable rough boulder hopping and can be especially tiring at the end of the day.

Contrasting fine mountain views with the dark serenity of Wasdale and the deep waters of Wast Water, this walk makes a logical circuit of one of Lakeland's most dramatic landscapes. From the head of the lake it rises quickly to traverse the tops of Illgill Head and Whin Rigg, below which The Screes plunge 2000ft. After descending from Whin Rigg by way of the flanks of the fell above the ravine of Greathall Gill, the walk cuts across the bottom of The Screes.

The track leads over a concrete bridge after which a left turn is made to follow the left bank of the stream bed. Skirt right through the oaks beneath Brackenclose, a 'Fell and Rock Climbing Club' Hut. Find a path emerging from the far corner of its grounds. This rises through Fence Wood to emerge onto the fell beneath the col. An old wall points up the shoulder of Illgill Head and the path leads directly to a group of stones and, according to the latest OS information, the rather nondescript summit. The trig point and cairn lie just beyond nearer the rim of the screes. Although lower in height, this is the spiritual summit.

The main path along the crest between Illgill Head and Whin Rigg traverses rolling grassland while below to the north, The Screes shoot precipitously into Wast Water. As you rise to the cairn of Whin Rigg, the scree slopes are replaced by precipitous rock buttresses of impressive size. Split by Great Gully and C Gully there is no safe way for the walker. Admire the view from the summit cairn, but do not venture any nearer.

Easy descent down the western shoulder leads towards the top of the ravine of Greathall Gill. A path bears right to pick a course over steep ground down the right flank of the gill – there is no need to enter the gill itself. Below the base of the ravine follow the line of a stone wall to the right which leads to a track above the lake shore. Continue along this passing the pump house, extracting water from the lake for the Sellafield Nuclear Plant. A path traverses the screes above the shore of Wast Water.

Steep scree and rock towers above, with deep water below. (Wast Water at some 258ft is Lakeland's deepest.) At first the path is well defined and quite straightforward, but it soon deteriorates to present a degree of strenuous boulder hopping. This is because The Screes are a living entity, constantly on the move, fed by rock from the disintegrating buttresses and slopes above. The path again takes shape and crosses brackened hillside to pick up the track leading past Wasdale Head Hall Farm. This continues over the concrete bridge to the car park.

The highest top of The Screes, Illgill Head (left), seen rising above Wast Water.

Great Gable seen over Styhead Tarn.

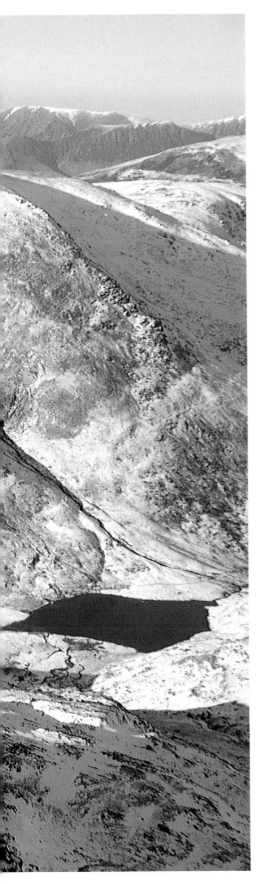

GREAT GABLE GROUP

•GRG•

Physically and spiritually the Great Gable Group lies at the heart of the Western Fells. Rising elegantly from the heads of Buttermere, Ennerdale, Wasdale and Seathwaite in Borrowdale, it is an upland area of high contrast. The smoothly aesthetic spur falling from Green Gable to Base Brown; the even-angled slopes of Kirk Fell suddenly truncating into a level top; that soaring edge of Fleetwith Pike above Gatesgarth in Buttermere; the tilted plateau of Grey Knotts and Brandreth; the rock, heather and

mountain tarn sanctuary of Haystacks – and rising dominant over them all, the rocky skull of Great Gable.

Four mountain passes link the deeply cut valleys and separate this group of mountains from others in the area. West of Kirkfell, Black Sail Pass runs between Mosedale and Ennerdale and splits this group from the Pillar Group. To the east Sty Head Pass links Wasdale Head with Seathwaite, distancing the latter from the Borrowdale Fells and the Scafells. Scarth Gap, the packhorse route between

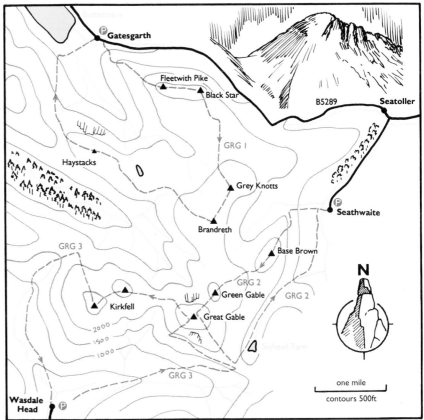

Buttermere and Ennerdale, falls between Haystacks and the long shoulder of the High Stile Group. Finally, Honister Pass between Borrowdale and Buttermere forms the northern boundary of these Western Fells.

The first walk selected, the Buttermere Horseshoe GRG 1, takes a greater traverse around Warnscale Bottom. Rising up the soaring Fleetwith Edge above Gatesgarth it takes in both Fleetwith Pike and Black Star before rounding Grey Knotts and Brandreth to descend over the hallowed ground of Haystacks. While undramatic in itself the highest top of this circuit, Brandreth, presents scenically sublime views along the lengths of Ennerdale and Buttermere.

Walk GRG 2 approaches Great Gable from Seathwaite. It begins by ascending alongside Sourmilk Gill to detour beneath Hanging Stone and so on to the top of Base Brown. Thereafter, the smooth spur dips through the col of Blackmoor Pols to rise to the summit of Green Gable. Across Windy Gap above Gable Crag to the north lies the ultimate prize, the stony summit of Great Gable. Descent to Sty

Head continues, passing Sty Head Tarn and Taylorgill Force waterfall.

Magnificent from any aspect, Great Gable casts its strongest influence over Wasdale. Here on its south facing flanks lie the finest crags – Kern Knotts, Tophet Wall, The Napes – all crowned by Westmorland Crags lying just below the summit. A great curtain of scree drops to sweep around the Napes via Great Hell Gate and Little Hell Gate before tumbling unchecked almost to the valley bottom.

These sun-kissed rocks were to inspire a new generation of adventurers. In 1866 Walter Parry Haskett-Smith climbed the Napes Needle – an act of considerable daring subsequently hailed as the birth of rock climbing. A growing band of pioneers followed his example and Wasdale Head became the mecca for British mountaineers. Its attraction and that of Great Gable remains undaunted to this day.

Walk GRG 3 rises from Wasdale Head, tackling Great Gable as it takes the Climber's Traverse across its Wasdale face. Descending to cross the two tops of Kirk Fell, it returns to Wasdale Head via Black Sail Pass and Mosedale. This is a

fine, rugged mountain course overlooking the wonderful rock architecture of Napes Needle and the Sphinx Rock.

◆ G R G 1 ◆

BUTTERMERE HORSESHOE

Fleetwith Pike 2126ft/648m
Black Star – Honister Crag 2077ft/633m
Grey Knotts 2287ft/697m
Brandreth 2344ft/715m
Haystacks 1959ft/597m

Valley Base: Buttermere.
Maps: OS OD4, The English Lakes – North West. L90 Penrith and Keswick.
Length: 6.25miles/10km.
Ascent: 2790ft/850m.
Approx Time: 4hrs.
Start & Finish: Car park by Gatesgarth Farm – small fee payable at the farm (NY 195150).
Difficulty: After a strenuous start the going eases and good paths predominate.

Fleetwith Pike rising from Buttermere.

Over Blackbeck Tarn and Haystacks with High Stile Group beyond.

OVER BASE BROWN AND GREEN GABLE TO GREAT GABLE

Base Brown 2120ft/646m
Green Gable 2628ft/801m
Great Gable 2949ft/899m

Valley Base: Borrowdale.
Maps: OS OD4, The English Lakes –
North West. L90 Penrith and Keswick.
Length: 5miles/8km.
Ascent: 2855ft/870m.
Approx Time: 4hrs.
Start & Finish: The head of the Seathwaite Valley, by the side of the road
beneath the farm – do not block any field
entrances or the road (NY 236123).
Difficulty: Some strenuous sections of
ascent and generally the going is rough and
stony. However, with the exception of a
short section of the path immediately
adjacent to Taylorgill Force, where it is a
little scrambly, there are no technical
difficulties.

Rising from Gatesgarth above Buttermere, a soaring edge shoots skyward to a
handsomely pointed peak. Fleetwith
Edge ascends to its sister pike cutting as
fine a trace as any in the Lake District. To
the north winds Honister Pass, defining
the boundary of this group and that of the
North Western Fells. This is a pass of
great drama, frowned upon by Fleetwith
Pike's most severe face, the extensively
quarried Honister Crag. To the south lies
the secluded valley of Warnscale Bottom,
its opposite flanks formed by the rock
buttresses of Haystacks. Above and
beyond stretches a sloping grass plateau
capped on its eastern edge by Grey Knotts
and Brandreth. The Buttermere Horseshoe takes in all these tops.

A good path blazes steeply up
Fleetwith Edge. Move right to gain the
White Cross, which can be seen from the
roadside. The inscription reads 'Erected
By Friends Of Fanny Mercer Accidentally
Killed 1887'. A straightforward ascent
follows to the top of Fleetwith Pike.

The path continues across the top,
soon reaching the mound of Black Star,
the actual top of Honister Crag. Descend
and follow the path through the slate
workings then over to the raised bank of
the dismantled tramway (which now
serves as the main path rising from the top
of Honister Pass). Keep on the path until

it stretches beneath the flanks of Grey
Knotts, whereupon bear left up the grassy
hillside with a broken crag to your left.
Here there is a trig point and just west,
with a better view, a cairned rock outcrop. Both are of equal altitude. Follow
the line of iron fence posts to Brandreth.

A straightforward descent leads to the
left of the craggy plug of Great Round
How and down to the waters of Blackbeck Tarn. Veer left at its head to traverse
a rock outcrop. Climb to a corridor
through the heather leading to a well-
defined path or proceed to its foot and
pick up the path immediately.

Either route gives access to the
Haystacks summit, a peaceful, gently
undulating area of heather, rock and
tarn. The path rises to crest a rocky ridge
running across it. Cairned at either end it
is the north point which is usually taken
as the summit. Beyond to the west lies
another shallow tarn, the Summit Tarn.
Pass this before a rocky descent leads to
Scarth Gap.

The rough track forming Scarth Gap
Pass, the old packhorse road between
Buttermere and Ennerdale, is followed
down the flanks of High Crag – Buttermere Fell. It provides an uneven but clear-
cut descent before crossing the bridge
over Warnscale Beck and returning over
the meadows to Gatesgarth Farm.

An undulating spur sweeps down from
Great Gable over Green Gable and Base
Brown to drop over Hanging Stone, ending abruptly above Seathwaite Farm.
After first breaching the defences of
Hanging Stone, reached by an ascent
alongside Sourmilk Gill, this circular outing ascends the spur. From the top of Base
Brown the shoulder falls to the hollow of
Blackmoor Pols before rising smoothly
up the flanks of Green Gable. Windy Gap
is crossed then a stony ascent made to the
summit of Great Gable. Descent down
the breast of the mountain leads directly
to Sty Head before returning along the
left bank of Styhead Gill to offer a grand-
stand view of Taylorgill Force.

In the farmyard turn right under the
arch. Take the footpath across the field to
the footbridge which crosses the beck
above its confluence with Sourmilk Gill.
Over to the right, spoil heaps mark the
site of the 'Plumbago Mines'. This was
once an important source of graphite and
the origin of the Keswick pencil industry.

The path follows the left side of Sourmilk Gill. Start by taking a stile over the

Sourmilk Gill above Seathwaite (left).

stone wall. Rising through the trees, the last association with sylvan Borrowdale, the path remains true to the gill until it zigzags to admire the topmost fall. Finally, bear left to a gap in the fell wall. Sourmilk Gill aptly lives up to its name.

The path emerges into the barren combe with Gillercombe Buttress ahead (this is the climber's name for the crag, on OS maps it is named Raven Crag). Rising to flank the slopes of Base Brown a large, balanced boulder is visible on the skyline to the left. Bear left off the path at this point to rise diagonally (no obvious path) to the craggy end known as Hanging Stone. Below the crag is a huge fallen block while balanced on top of the crag is another great block taking the distinctive shape of a gladiator's helmet. Pass left beneath the crag, with no difficulty despite initial appearances. Find a good path ascending the shoulder directly to the cairned summit of Base Brown.

Stroll down to the grassy col of Blackmoor Pols, where you join the main path rising from Gillercombe. Follow this directly to the stony summit of Green Gable. Drop to Windy Gap and climb steeply up rock and scree to cross the summit plateau and reach the topmost rocks of Great Gable.

There is something very special about

Great Gable, a hill of stature and grace from whatever angle or compass point it is viewed. Standing on its summit rocks it exudes a feeling of well-being – Great Gable even feels like a great mountain.

North of the summit rocks and looking in the direction of our approach, a bronze memorial plaque is dedicated by The Fell and Rock Climbing Club to its members lost during the First World War. Each November a Remembrance Service is held here. For the best view of Wasdale proceed beyond the summit rocks south to Westmorland Cairn standing above Westmorland Crags. The cairn was erected by the Westmorland brothers in 1876 to mark what they considered to be the finest mountain viewpoint in the area. Few would disagree with their choice.

Returning to the summit cairn a well-worn path heads off to Sty Head down the broad south eastern edge of the mountain. Bear left to take the path past Styhead Tarn and continue along the left side of Styhead Gill. Drop to skirt the Scots pine and larch surrounding Taylorgill Force. A little rocky scramble (straightforward) leads to a short wall and gate to the side of the waterfall. The path continues below, bearing left away from the river to make a gradual descent. Eventually the footbridge beneath Sourmilk Gill is re-crossed and retreat made through the arch into the farmyard.

GREAT GABLE AND KIRK FELL FROM WASDALE HEAD

**Great Gable 2949ft/899m
North Top – Kirk Fell 2582ft/787m
Kirk Fell 2630ft/802m**

Valley Base: Wasdale.
Maps: OS OD4, The English Lakes – North West. OS OD6, The English Lakes – South West. L90 Penrith and Keswick.
Length: 6.75miles/11km.
Ascent: 3640ft/1110m.
Approx Time: 4.5hrs.
Start & Finish: Car park at Wasdale Head Inn (NY 187088), or on the green below (where the track leads off the road to Burnthwaite).
Difficulty: There is a good deal of ascent on this route. If the Climber's Traverse is taken across the face of Great Gable beneath the Napes a little scrambling is also involved, although this can be avoided. Generally good paths prevail though the going is mostly rough and stony.

Whilst Kirk Fell rises directly from Wasdale Head it is lofty Great Gable which dominates the head of this narrow mountain valley. Known as Wasdale Fell the flanks of Kirk Fell rise uniformly to a truncated and flat summit, a place from which to pay homage to the nobler mountains which surround it. Perhaps this is the origin of its name, Kirk being Scottish for Church. The rocky skull of Great Gable stands higher. From its top plunges a scree, directed around the soaring rocks of the Napes via the corridors of Little Hell Gate and Great Hell Gate. From Wasdale in particular, Great Gable has a high profile.

The route described here first climbs to Sty Head before taking a rising diagonal rake across the face of Great Gable beneath the crags of Kern Knotts and the Napes. Known as the Climber's Traverse, this route does require a few short sections of scrambling (which can be avoided by using a lower path) yet is unparalleled in viewing the mountain's rocky architecture. Kern Knotts, Tophet Wall,

Great Gable towers above Wast Water and Wasdale Head.

Climbers on the Napes Needle, Great Gable.

the famous Napes Needle and Sphinx Rock, Great Hell Gate, Little Hell Gate and Westmorland Crags are all visited on this remarkable course.

Alternatively, easy ascent up the breast of the mountain above Sty Head leads directly to the summit where the rest of this route – on to Kirk Fell and then back to Wasdale Head by Black Sail Pass into Mosedale – can be followed.

From the car park outside the Wasdale Head Inn, cross the fields past the tiny Wasdale Church and join the track to Burnthwaite. In the surrounding grassland, in addition to the network of stone walls, the large piles of gathered stones emphasize the rocky nature of the terrain and the hardy constitution of the hill farmer here. Beyond the buildings of Burnthwaite, the final meadows are crossed before the mountains terminally squeeze the valley floor. Already the knife-edged ridges and deep-cut gullies of the Napes are plainly visible above. Picking out the 80ft high Napes Needle, a mere splinter beneath the extensive 300ft high haystack of crag, requires a patient and perceptive eye.

A footbridge leads over Gable Beck. To the left a steep path up Gavel Neese known as Moses' Trod provides the most direct line of ascent of Great Gable and a quick means of descent should the weather deteriorate. Soon the track begins to rise up the fell and scree to Sty Head. Not only the gateway between Wasdale and Borrowdale, Sty Head marks an important junction where many paths cross.

Our way follows the main path up the north east edge of Gable for only a little way before it branches off left to first traverse beneath the cleanly cut cliff of Kern Knotts. Rising slightly, the path moves across the hillside through an extensive area of scree, then levels as it crosses the head of a scree slope. It then intercepts the steep scree and boulder-filled runnel of Great Hell Gate. This chaotic stone slide fed from a huge basin above and overlooked by Tophet Wall presents an intimidating face. Fortunately, it is quickly crossed by our path.

The airy rock ridges of the Napes Crags rise above. Continuing beneath these rocks the path now splits. The lower path

The Sphinx Rock, Great Gable.

leads easily across to the next fan of scree, Little Hell Gate. The most interesting route is to take the higher path which rises up a gully on the left side of Napes Needle.

With its overhanging top block balanced precariously on a triangular base, The Needle is a gripping sight. First climbed solo by Walter Parry Haskett-Smith, its ascent in 1886 marked the birth of rock climbing as an activity in its own right. It is best viewed and photographed from a position to its left, from a comfortable ledge known as The Dress Circle. Our way passes over this ledge, making a rocky traverse left beneath the cliff to a narrow squeeze behind a great block. Climbing down from this corridor into the gully beyond constitutes the most technically difficult section. However, it is only a short distance and will be within the capabilities of those with a little scrambling ability. Beyond lies that remarkable rock sculpture, the superbly profiled Sphinx Rock.

Passing under Sphinx leads to Little Hell Gate just around the corner. A vague path leads up the right side of the scree corridor; it is steep going as far as Westmorland Crags and Westmorland Cairn above. Here the path bears left to rise up the final section of boulder scree to the summit of Great Gable.

Take the path leading down the north western shoulder of the mountain. Cross Moses' Trod and continue over the col of Beck Head to climb Rib End, following the path to the cairn marking the North Top of Kirk Fell. The higher summit of Kirk Fell lies beyond the two little tarns collectively known as Kirkfell Tarn. On arrival at the summit cairn of Kirk Fell, a small, ruined stone shelter will be revealed alongside particularly good views of the Scafells.

Follow the fence posts over the rocks and boulder debris of Kirkfell Crags. Care should be exercised and a controlled descent made to safely reach the head of Black Sail Pass. It is plain sailing down into Mosedale and along the valley. The path rises slightly again before finally dropping and bearing right to join the banks of Mosedale Beck. Pass Row Head and the old, stone-arched packhorse bridge to enter Wasdale Head Inn from the rear.

Pillar Mountain stands above the dark depths of Mosedale.

PILLAR GROUP

Forming the head of Mosedale to the south and looking down to the conifers of Ennerdale to the north, Pillar commands a range of high hills stretching westwards between Ennerdale Water and Wast Water. The mountain itself takes its name from the breathtaking 800ft high Pillar Rock, perhaps Cumbria's most spectacular cliff, perched below the summit on its northern flanks.

The craggy northern edge of the group presents a formidable skyline above Ennerdale. Among the mass of cliffs the bold rock architecture of the appropriately named Pillar Rock and Steeple stand out. For centuries they have been the focus of romantic attention – much favoured by the early walking and climbing pioneers. Wordsworth immortalised Pillar Rock in his poem *The Brothers* while local shepherds refer to it respectfully as a 'Grand Staen'.

Once gained, it is found that the tops along the Ennerdale rim are connected by a relatively gentle, undulating shoulder. A great stone wall known as 'The Ennerdale Fence' follows this shoulder from Scoat Fell over Haycock and Caw to Ennerdale Fell. This provides a useful aid to navigation should the mists descend. Even so, this remains one of the remotest areas in the region, large empty tracts of land rolling south and west. Anyone losing their way here would be in for a long

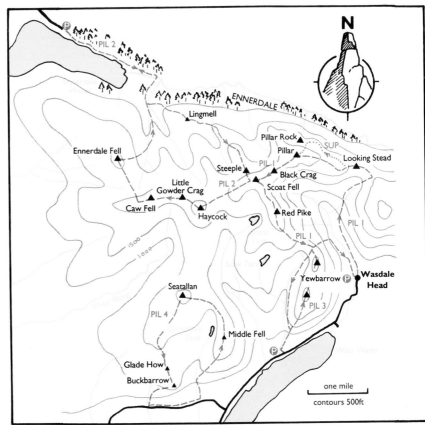

one mile

contours 500ft

and lonely hike back to home base.

Starting up Black Sail Pass and descending from Dore Head the rugged Mosedale Horseshoe, which takes in Looking Stead, Pillar, Black Crag, Scoat Fell and Red Pike, offers one of the most famous rounds in the Lake District. Beyond this to the south, Yewbarrow forms a cornerstone above Mosedale and Wasdale with Wasdale Head and Wast Water lying at her foot. From the western end of Wast Water, as Wasdale becomes Nether Wasdale, another horseshoe topped by Seatallan takes shape. This includes Middle Fell, Glade How and Buckbarrow.

The first selected walk, PIL 1, is the Mosedale Horseshoe. Also included is a supplement, PIL 1A, which is necessary to reach the independent top of Pillar Rock. Though the latter is classified as an easy *rock* climb, most of this route can be followed safely by *walkers* if they bypass the actual ascent of Pillar Rock.

When tackling the group from the Ennerdale side, because of vehicular access restrictions Ennerdale Youth Hostel at High Gillerthwaite is recommended as a base. Walk PIL 2 takes the superb north ridge of Steeple to reach the Ennerdale skyline. From Wasdale, Walk PIL 3 makes an anticlockwise circuit of distinguished Yewbarrow; while Walk PIL 4, a horseshoe around Nether Wasdale Common, provides a pleasant way to reach the summit of Seatallan.

◆ PIL 1 ◆

MOSEDALE HORSESHOE

Looking Stead 2057ft/627m
Pillar 2927ft/892m
Black Crag 2717ft/828m
Scoat Fell 2760ft/841m
Steeple 2687ft/819m
Red Pike 2709ft/826m

Valley Base: Wasdale.
Maps: OS OD4, The English Lakes – North West. OS OD6, The English Lakes – South West. L89 West Cumbria.
Length: 7miles/11.5km.
Ascent: 3430ft/1045m.
Approx Time: 4.75hrs.
Start & Finish: Car park at Wasdale Head Inn (NY 187088), or on the green beside the road before the Inn is reached.
Difficulty: Well-defined paths prevail. After the initial pull up Black Sail Pass the angle eases although the going is mostly rough and stony. Because the scree has now been eroded from Dore Head, a path on the open fellside to the left is taken, and this is both steep and exposed.

Certainly the most straightforward and popular way to tackle Pillar, the Mosedale Horseshoe provides a fulfiling round. Including the two other major fells of the group, Scoat Fell and Red Pike and

the tops of Looking Stead and Black Crag, it could easily be extended to take in Steeple. Although rugged throughout, once the crest of Black Sail Pass is reached the walk becomes less strenuous.

Perhaps taking Black Sail Pass, rising as it does from almost the head of Mosedale, does not at first appear to complete the Mosedale Horseshoe. Yet in my opinion it is the natural and logical way to approach the heights of Pillar. In its course it captures the very essence of this lonely mountain vale.

Gain the path along the bank of Mosedale Beck running behind the Wasdale Head Inn. Turn left through the gate marked 'Black Sail Pass' and climb up the fell to pass above Ritson's Force Waterfall before dropping down slightly to the floor of the remote vale of Mosedale.

The path bears right along the hillside – the famous Black Sail Pass. Gatherstone Beck is crossed and a steep shoulder climbed before the angle eases slightly. A low path crosses the hillside above the stream to make a final steep rise to the col marking the summit of the pass. It is possible to make a shortcut to the shoulder by following a steeper path bearing off to the left, though this demands more effort.

Once on the shoulder it is worth bearing right to the top of Looking Stead. A small cairn situated on a rock outcrop beyond the old iron fence posts offers a commanding vista. Although the main path continues to the south of the shoulder

From the summit cairn on Red Pike to Pillar Mountain.

of the hill through boulder and rock out-crops without difficulty to reach the col of Dore Head. Above stands Stirrup Crag which marks the northern end of Yew-barrow. Our way lies to the left down Dorehead Screes and Mosedale. Unfortunately, the top section of the screes has now been badly eroded by both humans and nature. The result is a steep and hard-surfaced gully offering little grip. Do not take it directly but first descend the flank of the open hillside to the north (left). This is not difficult though it is very steep and exposed. In frosty conditions or if the ground is wet and slippery, great care should be exercised.

After a little way it is possible to traverse back into the main line of the scree. Cross it and follow its southern side until the angle eases. The scree becomes a collection of small stones and can be followed to the floor of the vale. The path leads down Mosedale to join the beck and crosses over the packhorse bridge just before the Wasdale Head Inn.

The West Face of Pillar Rock.

·PIL 1A·

HIGH LEVEL ROUTE TO PILLAR ROCK

(A SUPPLEMENT TO WALK PIL 1)

Pillar Rock 2560ft/780m

Length: 1.25miles/2km (This is the actual length – no increase overall above that of 1A.)
Ascent: 985ft/300m (This is the actual ascent – little increase overall above that of 1A.)
Additional Approx Time: 1.5hrs.
Start: Looking Stead (NY 186118).
Finish: Summit of Pillar Mountain.
Difficulty: The High-Level Route leading to Robinson's Cairn, although traversing exposed ground, is technically straightforward. The climb beyond the cairn up the eastern edge of Pillar Rock is steep, exposed and often over unstable scree. The way up High Man, to the summit of Pillar Rock, is an easy rock climb, *not* a walk. The slope above Pillar Rock to the summit of Pillar mountain is steep with loose scree, but straightforward.

the northern edge can be followed and this is certainly more interesting. The summit and trig point of Pillar reveal the head of the mountain to be quite rounded and undramatic. A few paces to the north, however, and an exposed view can be taken down to the top of Pillar Rock (see supplement PIL 1A).

An easy descent is made to Wind Gap before rising to the boulder summit cairn of Black Crag, an independent top offering an open aspect to the summit of Pillar and along the rocky shoulder to Scoat Fell. Continue to the col above Mirk Cove then follow the northern edge of the wall to Scoat Fell. Divided into two tops, Little and Great Scoat Fell, on the OS map the

summit of Scoat Fell is, to say the least, indefinite. The highest section of the stone wall is the highest point of the mountain – find it if you can! Below to the right rising from the shoulder, lies the rocky tower of Steeple. If one wishes to extend the walk it can be reached in a few minutes. Gaining its summit is not difficult; unfortunately you have to re-ascend the shoulder of Scoat Fell to continue along the Mosedale Horseshoe.

The flanks of Scoat Fell fall to the shoulder of Red Pike, the path leading to a cairn midway along the shoulder. The cairn beyond and to the left, perched on the edge of the shoulder, marks the summit.

The path descends the northern edge

Pillar Rock, specifically the summit of High Man, must be considered a separate top. However, it is important to stress that it is a top that can only be reached by climbing; there is unfortunately no walking route to the summit.

The rock has a fascinating history. Wordsworth inspired a race for its summit with his poem *The Brothers*. He wrote about Pillar Rock:

You see yon precipice; it wears the shape
Of a vast building made of many crags;
And in the midst is one particular rock
That rises like a column from the Vale
Whence by our shepherds it is called
    the Pillar.

The first recorded ascent was made by a local shepherd, John Atkinson of Ennerdale on 9 July 1826. Pillar Rock remains an inspiration to mountaineers, its spire-like magnificence attracting many devotees.

Primarily this route is described for those wishing to ascend the top of Pillar Rock. However, if the actual climb to the rock is excluded – 'The Slab and Notch Climb' – walkers of average ability may enjoy it as a challenging and rewarding way to gain the summit of Pillar Mountain. The route consists of three sections: the High-Level Route to Robinson's Cairn; the ascent weaving up the eastern edge of Pillar Rock taking the sloping terrace of the Shamrock Traverse before continuing to the summit of Pillar Mountain; and the ascent of Pillar Rock from the path described in section two, by the easy rock climb known as 'The Slab and Notch'. Section three is only suitable for experienced climbers.

The High-Level Route begins from Looking Stead (see PIL 1A). Just beyond the summit a narrow path, (a small cairn marks the point) breaks off from the shoulder to cross the Ennerdale flank of Pillar Mountain. Make an exposed traverse across the hillside. There is no safe way off the path but the going is not technically difficult. Eventually, a broad boulder strewn rake leads to a shoulder and to Robinson's Cairn, the memorial to a great local cragsman and walker who explored these Lakeland Fells.

The route taking in Pillar Mountain via the Shamrock Traverse ascends the eastern flanks of Pillar Rock and continues up the hillside above to the summit of

Pillar Mountain, beginning from Robinson's Cairn. Descend slightly from the cairn to cross a rocky hollow and move up a minor rock ridge. A short section of scree gives access to a rake which rises diagonally right through the crag – the Shamrock Traverse. This is well-defined but very exposed. At the end of the rake there is a broad scree-filled basin down to the right . Do not attempt to descend into this. Fed by East Jordan Gully above, the basin empties directly over the steep cliffs below via two gullies, Shamrock Gully and Walker's Gully (named after the man who fell to his death there). These are both severe rock climbs.

Continue to make a rising traverse right until the path begins to climb more directly up the hillside. The head of Pillar Rock lies to the right. A steep but easy ascent leads directly to the summit of Pillar Mountain. Do not lose the path as cliffs lie directly below.

Pillar Rock by the Slab and Notch is section three of the route. East Jordan Gully falls from a rift in the crags above. This rift is Jordan Gap and separates Pisgah, the rocky buttress on the left adjoining the hillside, from the summit of Pillar Rock, standing independently to the right. At a suitable point on the second section of the route described above, descend into East Jordan Gully to find a series of rocky steps leading up the right wall. From here they continue up and right to cross a slab. Descend to a horizontal ledge further right until a short climb leads to the Notch, where the ridge levels off. A ledge is followed by a rising staircase after which a traverse right leads to a gully. This in turn continues easily up to the summit of Pillar Rock (this head of Pillar Rock being known as High Man).

This is a climb not a walk, and should be treated as such. The route is not straightforward and the consequences of a slip would be serious and most probably fatal. In the days when rock climbers wore nailed boots this route was well worn; today it is not so obvious. Remember, the route must also be taken in descent unless a rope is used, usually to abseil into the rift of Jordan Gap.

This route is recommended only for those with rock climbing experience . If in doubt, simply admire the distant summit of Pillar Rock from the easy top of Pisgah or from the hillside above.

◆ PIL 2 ◆

STEEPLE AND THE ENNERDALE FENCE FROM GILLERTHWAITE

Lingmell 1427ft/435m
Steeple 2687ft/819m
Scoat Fell 2760ft/841m
Haycock 2617ft/797m
Little Gowder Crag 2405ft/733m
Caw Fell 2288ft/697m
Ennerdale Fell 2113ft/644m

Valley Base: Ennerdale.
Maps: OS OD4, The English Lakes – North West. L89 West Cumbria.
Length: 8.75miles/14km.
Ascent: 3430ft/1045m.
Approx Time: 6hrs.
Start & Finish: Ennerdale Youth Hostel (NY 142141). Note vehicular access into the valley, apart from those with a pass authorised by the Forestry Commission, is prohibited. The distance from the car park beneath Bowness Knott to Char Dub Bridge is 2miles/3km.
Difficulty: A long walk with a considerable ascent to Scoat Fell. Its very remoteness must also be taken into account. Beyond Scoat Fell the route along the tops beside the stone wall known as the Ennerdale Fence is reasonably straightforward. Unfortunately, on the last section descending from Ennerdale Fell back to the valley floor the going through heather and boulder is rough.

Recent history has not treated Ennerdale kindly. The dark omnipresence of ranked conifers has descended plague-like to dampen her spirits, while the nearby nuclear industry sucks away her sweet waters. To add insult to injury the Forestry Commission have banned vehicular access to the valley without their permission. Perhaps this a mixed blessing, for it does mean the valley remains quieter than it would otherwise have been and free access on foot remains, as yet, unchallenged.

Thankfully too, the fells above remain inviolate and stand as proud and glorious as any in the region. Above rounded Lingmell it is the appealing north ridge of Steeple which draws the eye. Even among the rugged rock scenery which shapes Ennerdale's distinctive skyline it takes a high profile. Like Pillar Rock, the grand sounding and suggestive name of Steeple conjures up images of rocky defiance and mountain prowess. Indeed, this rocky tower provides a magnificent approach to these high tops.

After rising through the forest the open flanks of Lingmell lead across the base of Mirklin Cove to the north ridge of Steeple. Ascent gains the summit, followed in a short distance by that of Scoat Fell. Thereafter, the remarkable stone wall known as Ennerdale Fence is followed via the summits of Haycock, Caw Fell and the rocky top of Little Gowder Crag to Ennerdale Fell. A rough descent leads across Silvercove Beck and up to the pathed ridge which drops between Silver Cove and Great Cove. The route continues down through the forest to the valley floor and a completion of the circuit.

In view of the access problems it makes sense to start this walk from Ennerdale Youth Hostel. Proceeding from the car park beneath Bowness Knott would add a further four weary miles to an already substantial outing. After crossing the low concrete bridge above Char Dub, the track leads directly across the fields into the forest. Here it bears left. Follow it until another track cuts away to ascend diagonally right through the trees. From here it is easy progress onto the open shoulder of Lingmell.

The path crests the hill, with the summit – a cairn standing on a boulder – just above to the right. Descend slightly to cross Low Beck, then bear left and follow the north ridge falling from Steeple. Broad at first, it narrows and steepens as altitude is gained. Finally, impressive rock scenery leads you to the summit. Sharply triangular in section, Steeple is formed by a desert of stones falling to the west and steep crag to the east. This is an airy perch with fine views across the craggy heads of Windgap Cove to Pillar, and across Mirklin Cove to Haycock. A little drop followed by a short, steep ascent gains the head of Scoat Fell. Do not bother looking for a well-defined summit, for it does not exist. At some point to the east the stone wall attains the highest position.

The remarkable stone wall known as the Ennerdale Fence continues from this point all the way to Ennerdale Fell and down Crag Fell to meet Ennerdale Water. Follow it down the grassy shoulder to Haycock. Proceed to Little Gowder Crag and gain the summit cairn of Caw Fell just north of the wall. This is the highest point of Caw although its shoulder continues westwards for some distance with a number of cairned bumps. Follow the wall to the col beneath Ennerdale Fell.

Continue along the southern side of the wall, which from this point westwards has been restored to its former splendour. The easy rise up Ennerdale Fell leads to a gate through the wall with the summit cairn beyond. From the cairn it is possible to descend directly the Silver Cove flanks of the fell, but there is no path and care should be taken to avoid the cliffs of Iron Crag. The going comprises of thick heather and rocky boulders. Alternatively, return along the fell on the Ennerdale side of the wall to join the wall descending by Silvercove Beck. Where the wall bears off left, move right across the beck to a path descending the nose of the ridge between Silver Cove and Great Cove. The path falls easily into the forest and down to a footbridge. Up to the right lies the original track taken in ascent.

The rugged profile of Steeple towers above Ennerdale.

• PIL 3 •

YEWBARROW – SOUTH TO NORTH

South Top – Yewbarrow 2058ft/628m
North Top – Yewbarrow 2021ft/616m

Valley Base: Wasdale.
Maps: OS OD6, The English Lakes – South West. L89 West Cumbria.
Length: 3.75miles/6km.
Ascent: 1950ft/595m.
Approx Time: 2.5hrs.
Start & Finish: Overbeck Bridge car park (NY 168068).
Difficulty: Both the southern and northern ends of Yewbarrow are steep and craggy, demanding easy scrambling.

Yewbarrow may not be as tall as her neighbours in this mountain valley, yet in terms of immediate visual impact she lacks nothing. Resembling the upturned hull of a Viking longship, Yewbarrow has two steep, craggy ends connected by a long level top. From the Wasdale Road in particular she presents an elegant profile. Her sharp southern edge soaring to the impenetrable looking rocks of Bell Rib and Dropping Crag, marks the start of a long rocky crest. Standing as the cornerstone above the valleys of Wasdale and Mosedale, Yewbarrow offers a tremendous panorama of the mountains surrounding Wasdale Head. It is a view which extends to all of Lakeland's mountains over 3000ft.

Bell Rib and Dropping Crag form the southern prow; a route can be navigated between the two to Great Door and so on to the top. Stirrup Crag dropping to Dore Head marks the northern end. Fortunately, in descent its intimidating nature when seen from below is not as pronounced. The path is well defined and not too exposed; after a few sections of easy rocky scrambling it soon leads to the col. Thereafter an easy path traverses the flanks of the mountain above Over Beck to descend the lower half of the southern rib back to Overbeck Bridge car park.

A short stroll along the beck precedes a steep haul up the southern ridge. A stile leads left over the fence and wall and the path continues towards Dropping Crag. Take the higher path leading up to a gap in the rocks to the right of Dropping Crag. A vague path leads steeply up through loose scree and boulder; not very pleasant until the angle eases and further scree leads to a notch in the crest known as Great Door, from where a panoramic view unveils over the edge across Wast Water. Along the ridge to the south rises the head of Bell Rib. Note that there is no safe direct descent from here. Turn left to rise north up the ridge which leads to the almost flat shoulder of the mountain.

This upland plateau is easy in nature and pleasantly grassed. Sheep stroll at a leisurely pace, untroubled by the plunging rough slopes on either side. Continue to the large mound forming the summit of Yewbarrow, its Southern Top. Ten minutes on and the cairn of the Northern Top is reached before the path descends the little rocky walls of Stirrup Crag. From below, the crag looks continuous and unbroken. In reality, it comprises a series of short walls and grooves separated by comforting ledges. Its descent will trouble few although it is classified as an easy scramble. Alternatively, an even easier way can be found down a grassy slope to the west of the Northern Top.

Turning left at Dore Head, routine progress is made along the path moving across the flanks of the mountain above Over Beck. This rugged mountain dale provides a straightforward and reassuring conclusion to the exciting circuit of Yewbarrow.

The steep southern nose of Yewbarrow soars above Wast Water.

Seatallan and Middle Fell lit by the evening sun.

•PIL4•

CIRCUIT OF NETHER WASDALE COMMON VIA MIDDLE FELL AND SEATALLAN

Middle Fell 1908ft/582m
Seatallan 2270ft/692m
Glade How 1420ft/433m
Buckbarrow 1388ft/423m

Valley Base: Wasdale.
Maps: OS OD6, The English Lakes – South West. L89 West Cumbria.
Length: 5.5miles/9km.
Ascent: 2395ft/730m
Approx Time: 3.5hrs.
Start & Finish: Ample parking space by the side of the road at Greendale (NY 145056).
Difficulty: Generally the going is straightforward even though beyond the col above Greendale Tarn there is no definite footpath. There are two steepish ascents, to Middle Fell then to Seatallan, and a steepish descent from Buckbarrow.

A walk of surprising quality, this circuit contrasts the craggy ruggedness of Middle Fell and Buckbarrow with the gentler but higher grassy slopes of Seatallan. It approaches the latter in the most direct way possible. A short sharp ascent from the high col above Greendale Tarn is followed by an easy stroll down the long shoulder to the end known as Cat Bells. A final descent tops Glade How and Buckbarrow before reaching the road.

From the road a well-defined path leads across the grass and bracken to the steep shoulder descending from Middle Fell. Bear right to climb the shoulder, generally keeping to its right edge. Numerous crags are easily bypassed. The summit is notably more distant than first appearances would suggest – allow an hour to reach it.

Descent to the col is clear-cut and from here Haycock takes on its most imposing aspect. A steep ascent of the flanks above leads directly to the summit plateau of Seatallan. The extensive cairn (now partly shaped into a shelter) and the extensive dome of rubble on which it sits is reputed to be an ancient tumulus.

Dropping down through the tussocky grass of the gentle south western shoulder is a positive joy (in ascent it would be tedious). A cairn marks Cat Bells though in no respect could this be considered as a top in its own right.

Swing left to follow the shoulder leading towards Buckbarrow. After the initial section of descent the going levels. A prominent rocky hillock on the right is graced by a well-crafted cairn, the independent top of Glade How. In the distance, another rocky outcrop standing higher than the shoulder is considered to be the summit of Buckbarrow. Just beyond, a broad gully leads down to the right. Most will initially wish to continue to an independent rocky plateau, which marks the edge of the crags of Buckbarrow and provides an uninterrupted view across Wast Water.

The gully leads to the broader west flank of Buckbarrow. To avoid ground which is still steep and rough it is probably best to traverse across to Gill Beck before descending directly to the road. The journey back to Greendale provides splendid views of the craggy face of Buckbarrow, its rocks often lit a glowing red by the rays of the sinking sun.

Whoap and Lank Rigg seen at the head of the River Calder.

LANK RIGG GROUP

·LAK·

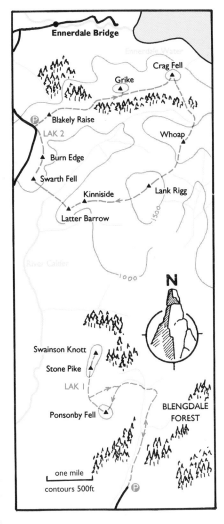

While these far western fells offer little of the grandeur of their higher cousins, they do command a certain solitude. With the exception of the herdwick sheep and the red fox, they remain relatively deserted. The fells included mark the western extremity of The Lake District National Park. To the east and rising to Caw, Seatallan and the glorious hills of the Pillar Group lies a considerable wilderness area – great tracts of barren land consisting of rough fell grass and the occasional rocky outcrop. To the west lies a short semi-industrialised plain before the Irish Sea stretches out to the Isle Of Man. Sadly, the massive, menacing nuclear power station at Sellafield dominates this view.

Although the landscape is now predominantly deserted there is much evidence of pre-history. Curious walls, cairns and boulders abound, the most visual being Kinniside Stone Circle just above the road over Blakeley Moss.

Ennerdale Water defines the northern limit. Seen from here, Grike and especially Crag Fell, with the rocky knoll of Angler's Crag standing above the lake, look most appealing. All the fells in this northern sector form a horseshoe around the watershed of the River Calder, the highest being the leader of the group, Lank Rigg. Walk LAK 2 is a long expedition, over nine tops in all. The going is straightforward on this route, with rolling grassland underfoot.

The little town of Gosforth with its famous Viking Cross located in the churchyard stands to the south. Above, the valley of Blengdale separates Ponsonby Fell and Swainson Knott from the flanks of Seatallan and Caw to the east. Despite the afforestation of its lower half before it turns eastward to rise towards Haycock, the valley provides a delightful route (see Walk LAK 1) to approach these two fells located above Scalderskew.

·LAKI·

PONSONBY FELL AND SWAINSON KNOTT FROM BLENGDALE

Ponsonby Fell 1020ft/311m
Stone Pike 1056ft/322m
Swainson Knott 1118ft/341m

Valley Base: Wasdale.
Town Base: Gosforth.
Maps: OS OD6, The English Lakes – South West. L89 West Cumbria.
Length: 6.25miles/10km.
Ascent: 1000ft/305m.
Approx Time: 2.5hrs.
Start & Finish: Blengdale Forestry Commission car park (NY 085053).
Difficulty: Good tracks prevail up Blengdale and although there are a few boggy sections and the grass is long above, there are no real problems.

Ponsonby Fell and Swainson Knott are two grassy hills marking the western limit of these Western Fells. Beyond to the east lies a vast swathe of high desolate grassland and deserted rough fell rising to Caw and Seatallan. This represents the best view for to the west, intervening before the Irish Sea, sits an ugly blight on the landscape – Sellafield/Windscale/Calder Hall Nuclear Power Plant. (Three names because public relations officials seem to rename it every time they wish to present a new image; currently Sellafield is in vogue.) Despite its afforestation, Blengdale is still a valley of considerable charm, and walking from here is certainly the most interesting way to tackle these fells. All bodes well until the actual top of Ponsonby Fell is reached. Thereafter until descent is made eastwards, Sellafield presents a disturbing backdrop.

From Wellington Bridge above Gosforth, a surfaced road runs parallel to the River Bleng to reach the spacious car park – ignore any sign indicating that vehicular access is forbidden. Proceed from the car park along the road to cross the bridge. Bear left following the excellent level track through the trees and along the east bank of the River Bleng. Where the track splits, take the higher route then bear left to the wooden footbridge. Exit left to reach a surfaced road snaking up the hillside. Follow this to a junction and veer left along the forestry track. After crossing Scalderskew Beck a wooden gate on the left (signposted) leads onto the open flanks of Ponsonby Fell. After an initial boggy section the open fell can be climbed without difficulty to the slightly domed, grassy summit marked by a tiny cairn.

Head north across the shoulder of the fell down to the col. Cross the overgrown track that once connected remote Scalderskew with Calder Bridge, go through the gate then move right over the stile to follow the post and wire fence through bog and rough grass. Climb up the fellside and bear left to the granite-walled enclosure of Stone Pike, entering through one of the numerous wall gaps. Continuing north, a slight descent leads to a post and wire fence and a foot stile. There is no path here, only long grass leading to the undistinguished top of Swainson Knott. This is cairnless and only a little hollow to the west indicates that peat was once extracted from the summit of this mound.

Return by the same route to the col then follow the path down past Scalderskew and on to the wooden gate beneath Ponsonby Fell. For those wanting to sample more of the wilderness area east of Ponsonby Fell there is a vague track rising over open moor to the long cairn of Sampson's Bratful (a prehistoric burial chamber). Otherwise, retrace earlier steps along the forest tracks to the car park.

Ponsonby Fell viewed from the walled enclosure of Stone Pike (below) and rowans by the River Bleng seen from the footbridge (right).

CALDER HORSESHOE

Blakeley Raise 1276ft/389m
Grike 1599ft/488m
Crag Fell 1716ft/523m
Whoap 1676ft/511m
Lank Rigg 1775ft/541m
Kinniside 1230ft/375m
Latter Barrow 1161ft/354m
Swarth Fell 1099ft/335m
Burn Edge 1050ft/320m

Valley Base: Wasdale or Ennerdale.
Town Base: Gosforth or Egremont.
Maps: OS OD4, The English Lakes –
North West. L89 West Cumbria.
Length: 7.5miles/12km.
Ascent: 2280ft/695m.
Approx Time: 4.25hrs.
Start & Finish: Beneath the flanks of
Blakeley Raise are a number of small
pull-offs beside the Coldfell Road
(NY 062130).
Difficulty: The walking, over pleasant
grassland, is easy throughout. Of course,
the length of the route and its remoteness
must be taken into consideration.

Taking in the numerous tops around the watershed of the River Calder this route provides a satisfying way to approach Grike, Crag Fell and the leader of this western group of hills, Lank Rigg. It cuts into the western leg of the shoe from the high Coldfell Road taking in Blakeley Raise before moving onto the Ennerdale edge of the group. From the 'Ennerdale Fence' – the southern terminus of the great stone wall leading along the Ennerdale skyline from distant Scoat Fell – it breaks around the head of the shoe topping Whoap before falling then steeply rising to Lank Rigg itself. Kinniside and Latterbarrow are included in the descent to the River Calder before the opposite leg of the shoe is completed with the inclusion of Swarth Fell and Burn Edge. Its chief merits are the ease of walking and the overwhelming air of solitude.

A scenic route providing the most direct link between Calder Bridge and Ennerdale Bridge, the high Coldfell Road provides a useful way to cut into the horseshoe. Make a direct ascent up the grassy slopes of Blakeley Raise. A walled compound by a small rocky outcrop may be spotted to the right (marked on the OS map as Bield).

Follow the fence line down the distinct shoulder to reach a sheep intake structure and a gate on the left. The gate may have to be climbed to reach a short track which crosses through a narrow neck of forestry to connect with the main forest road. Bear right here to pass a gateway in the fence beneath Grike, then swing immediately left to ascend above the track. Step over the remnants of a wire fence to continue steeply to the summit of Grike. There are three piles of stones acting as cairns/shelters; one predominates and gives the local name to the fell, Stone Man.

The path easily descends down the shoulder left of the fence line, passing a weather station on the right. A stile leads over the fence crossing the heathery shoulder. At a point where the fence rounds a corner to fall to the south, turn left. Climb to the furthest cairned outcrop of Crag Fell. A number of rocky hillocks rise along the summit crest of Crag Fell, yet the nature of the cragginess below as it falls defiantly to Angler's Crag and Ennerdale Water is undetectable. Traverse south along the crest until a path down the southern nose of Crag Fell leads to a stile over the forest fence.

Descent through a break in the forest leads to a track. Turn right then take a track left which leaves the conifers over a

Looking to the rocky knoll top of Crag Fell.

The little tarn on Lank Rigg rests in the hollow to the south west of the top.

stile beside an iron gate. Immediately in front lies the stone wall of the Ennerdale Fence. Follow the track running along the southern side of the wall (note a spring issues over to the right to a bend below a gate in the wall). Swing right here up onto the shoulder approaching Whoap from where a path leads to the grassy domed summit. A rock is reputed to mark the highest point, find it if you can. The northern slopes of Caw are shown to their best advantage from here – surprisingly they look quite precipitous and Caw actually looks like a mountain befitting its altitude.

Proceed down the shoulder of Whoap towards Lank Rigg. At the bottom our path crosses a dip. A path rising from Lank Rigg Moss traverses through it. The latter is an extension to the track that leaves the road at the corner above our starting point, where it is blocked off from vehicular access by a locked half-barrier. It forms a convenient escape route from the head of the horseshoe should bad weather move in.

After crossing the dip, rise steeply to the grassy summit marked by a stone trig point. Beyond lies a tarn and a cairned rocky mound providing a better view west. A little further south, follow what appears to be an ancient track striking an easy course down through the rocks to the grassy flanks below. To the left stands an impressive mound of boulders – an ancient tumulus. This tumulus and other evidence indicates Lank Rigg to be a site of prehistoric importance.

Crossing Poukes Moss in the hollow below is a rather peaty, boggy task but with care it should not provide too much difficulty. Reach the grassy bump of Kinniside before descending the shoulder to the final boulder strewn outcrop of Latterbarrow. A number of bouldery outcrops rise from the flanks here but no obvious tumuli. Three cairns mark the summit, and careful examination of the rocks reveals red sandstone among the Ennerdale Granophyre.

Descend tentatively towards the River Calder in the valley below. A little lower

to the right stands a small shepherd's cairn; this marks the easiest descent to the river, avoiding much of the bouldery scree. Cross the River Calder, usually no more than a narrow stream. On the far side a small section of bog leads to higher, drier ground and the edge of the fell bracken. It is now best to bear right until a path cuts through the narrowest portion of bracken, then cross directly up the open flanks of Scarth Fell. Pass a little bed of scree before continuing straight onwards to the rather elegant, circular summit cairn.

The whole horseshoe of the River Calder can be viewed from here. You are now qualified to reflect on its secrets.

Descend to Burn Edge. Keep walking, past the rise marked with a spot height of 311m on the OS map, to find scattered rocks of various geological origins. These mark the actual summit on the northern end overlooking Lankrigg Moss. Follow the grassy shoulder down towards the road, and join the track coming in from the river to meet the road.

High Crag (left) and Birkness Combe above Buttermere.

HIGH STILE GROUP

·HIG·

Defined by the valleys of Buttermere and Ennerdale, the high shoulder of High Stile consists of a long chain of peaks. Of these, Seat and High Crag rise from Scarth Gap while to the west Herdus tumbles steeply in a broad sweep to Floutern Pass and the end of Ennerdale Water. Together they form an imposing range of high fells divided centrally into two distinct sections, east and west. These have in common level high ground separating the tops.

The eastern half presents two quite different faces. Its least known side rises without excitement from the ranked conifers of the Ennerdale Forest; consisting of steep scree, bilberry, bracken and heather, it does little to tempt exploration. Above Buttermere, however, the eastern side presents a formidable face. Here stand the high peaks of High Crag, High Stile and Red Pike, between which the craggy combes of Birkness and Bleaberry hang dramatically.

Rising from Gatesgarth in Buttermere, Walk HIG 2 traverses this eastern section from Scarth Gap over the tops either side of High Stile to drop back down to Buttermere by the end of Bleaberry Tarn. This is a classic Lakeland outing with magnificent views.

The western section is generally more rounded, with the exception of the defiant, rocky knoll of Bowness Knott rising prominently above the northern shore of Ennerdale Water. The profile of this outcrop and that of Herdus, forming the end of this group, is a hallowed landmark to West Cumbrians, yet the higher tops of this section are not so well known. Great Borne and Starling Dodd are modest hills which hide their virtues behind unspectacular flanks. Walk HIG 1, climbing from the end of Ennerdale, gains the heights to make a complete traverse of this section before descending from Little Dodd via Gillflinter Beck to return along the shores of Ennerdale Water.

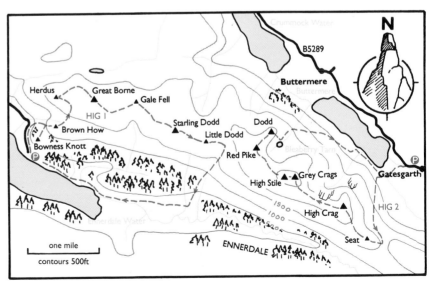

•HIG I•

GREAT BORNE AND STARLING DODD FROM ENNERDALE

Bowness Knott 1093ft/333m
Brown How 1056ft/322m
Herdus 1844ft/562m
Great Borne 2019ft/616m
Gale Fell 1699ft/518m
Starling Dodd 2077ft/633m
Little Dodd 1936ft/590m

Valley Base: Ennerdale.
Maps: OS OD4, The English Lakes –
North West. L89 West Cumbria.
Length: 7.75miles/12.5km.
Ascent: 2295ft/700m.
Approx Time: 4.75hrs.
Start & Finish: Car park beneath
Bowness Knott (NY 109153). Note this
car park marks the limit of permitted
vehicular access into Ennerdale.
Difficulty: After two sections of steep
ascent the route along the high level
shoulder is generally well pathed and
straightforward. Considering its length
and altitude the walk is remarkably gentle,
helped by the easy return alongside
Ennerdale Water.

This walk traverses the long upland plateau which forms the lower southern half of the great High Stile shoulder. Great Borne and Starling Dodd are the highest tops, though seen from West Cumbria above Ennerdale Water, it is the blunt nose of Herdus and the rocky knoll of Bowness Knott below which command the attention. After a strenuous start taking in Bowness Knott and Brown How en route to Herdus, the route traverses the upland plateau before descending from Little Dodd via Gillflinter Beck to Gillerthwaite. An easy return is made along the road by Ennerdale Water.

The Ennerdale face of Bowness Knott consists of steep scree and crag. To make an ascent it is necessary to walk back along the road from the car park until at the end of the woods a stile leads onto open brackened flanks. The path rises steeply up the hillside, bearing left slightly beneath the end of Ennerdale Forest

before rising with the wire fence to a wooden stile. Cross the stile and climb steeply up the back of Bowness Knott, following the vague path through bilberry and heather to the edge of the conifers. A dark passageway opens to the left. In a short distance it emerges into daylight again and the path bears right. Contour through further bilberry and heather to reach the summit of Bowness Knott. Despite the Pine Forest behind, good views remain across Ennerdale Water. For a short day, Bowness Knott is a worthwhile excursion in itself.

Descend the same route to the stile. Follow the wire fence until the going levels, then bear left to climb the rocky knoll of Brown How. On the descent, bear slightly right to find a path rising up the right side of the steep gill which descends from Herdus – Rake Beck. Follow this to find on the shoulder a perfectly preserved circular structure neatly built from red granite. Looking inside reveals that the back wall is built into overhanging rock, and the enclosing stone wall overhangs the floor. This is an ancient fox trap.

Above the shoulder the path continues to rise steeply until the gill falls back to cut into the plateau. At this point bear left, rising gently to the summit cairn of Herdus. From here, cross the plateau in a north easterly fashion to intercept the wire fence and main path that rises from

Floutern Pass. Bear right along the fence through the cleft which splits the rocky dome of Great Borne. South of the fence stands a trig point and ruinous summit shelter cairn – the highest top of Great Borne. The northern top on the far side of the cleft is slightly lower yet offers fine views over Loweswater Fells.

Return to the cleft and follow the well-defined trod beside the fence. When the fence turns sharply left, leave the path. Follow the fence to the grassy top of Gale Fell marked by a stout cornerpost. Bear right to regain the main trod, first crossing a dip – the surprisingly deep feeder of Clews Gill – before rising quickly to the stony top of Starling Dodd, a space-age combination cairn of metal fence post and stone.

Across the little tarn in the hollow beyond, it is only a short way to the rock strewn top of Little Dodd, which marks the end of this high-level excursion. Drop down its bouldery face to traverse left into the top of Gillflinter Beck as soon as possible. Descent by the side of the stream provides the easiest route. As the level eases and bracken takes hold, the path bears right away from the stream. Follow the break between the forest to reach the track/unsurfaced road. Bear right, passing High Gillerthwaite before joining the banks of Ennerdale Water. The road provides a level and pleasant return.

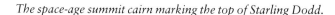

The space-age summit cairn marking the top of Starling Dodd.

Herdus rising distinctively above Ennerdale Water.

•HIG 2•

HIGH STILE AND THE BUTTERMERE EDGE

Seat 1840ft/561m
High Crag 2442ft/744m
Grey Crag – High Stile 2648ft/807m
High Stile 2644ft/806m
Red Pike 2478ft/755m
Dodd 2103ft/641m

Valley Base: Buttermere.
Maps: OS O4, The English Lakes – North West. L89 West Cumbria.
Length: 6.75miles/11km.
Ascent: 2725ft/830m.
Approx time: 4.5hrs.
Start & Finish: Car park opposite Gatesgarth Farm – small fee payable at the farm (NY 195150).
Difficulty: Some scree but generally well pathed. After a strenuous start the going round the edge is fairly level. A good path descends from Red Pike back to Buttermere.

The eastern half of the great High Stile shoulder is by far the most spectacular. Defined sharply by Ennerdale and Buttermere, its most profound influence lies over the Buttermere valley, from where it appears as a dark north wall, scalloped by the craggy hanging basins of Birkness Combe (incorrectly labelled Burtness on the OS maps) and Bleaberry Combe. Guarding the entrances to these combes are the formidable sentinels of High Crag, High Stile and Red Pike.

Rising from Gatesgarth to traverse High Crag, High Stile and Red Pike, the Buttermere Edge is a Lakeland gem. From Scarth Gap it includes the top of Seat before ascending Gamlin End to gain High Crag and the start of the shoulder. Despite appearances from below, walking along the top is easy going. Descent from Red Pike takes in Dodd before reaching Bleaberry Tarn. Dropping eastwards, the path leads away from Sourmilk Gill and returns to Gatesgarth, traversing above Buttermere.

Cross the fields from the farm until a

gate leads to open fellside. After the initial section of steep ascent Scarth Gap Pass, an important packhorse route in times gone by, rises more gradually off to the left. Follow it, making a rough and stony diagonal ascent to the col. A convenient corridor in the rocky ridge, the Scarth Gap, connects Buttermere with Ennerdale.

Climb towards the right up steep scree to find the summit cairn of Seat, where a tiny tarn exists in the hollow beyond. Steep ascent follows up Gamlin Edge. This is partially by bucket footholds worn into the grass but chiefly by scree. Look out for the large rock with the in situ iron fence post, found on the initial third of the ascent – it is called the Marble Stone. The edge leads to the summit cairn of High Stile. From here there is an excellent viewpoint, particularly over the head of Ennerdale.

Looking along the undulating ridge of grassy col and stony hillock towards the next objective, High Stile, observe the black head of Eagle Crag at the top of Birkness Combe. Beyond lie the sunlit

Looking north to High Stile.

cliffs of Grey Crags, whose top stands above that of High Stile by a few feet.

Begin the traverse to ascend High Stile, moving right before the distinguished cairn to gain the rocky top of Grey Crags. Observe again the black and monstrous buttress of Eagle Crag across Birkness Combe before facing Red Pike and Dodd over Bleaberry Tarn. Head to the summit cairn of High Stile, taking in the stupendous view in all directions: seaward to the Isle of Man and the Galloway Hills, and inland to the giant skull of Great Gable and over Buttermere and Crummock to the North Western Fells of Robinson and Grasmoor.

First descending and then ascending to the red granite rocks of Red Pike the path, although rocky, is quite straightforward. Excellent views prevail over the western half of this group from Starling Dodd to Great Borne. Across Floutern Pass lie all the hills of the Loweswater Fells. Take the path of stone and scree into the saddle between Dodd and Red Pike. Do not miss out on Dodd, for it is a worthy and quite independent top requiring little extra effort. Ascend from the main path to find the best uninterrupted view over Crummock Water. From here it is best to return to the saddle, for descent down the nose of Dodd is mostly pathless and involves negotiation of much rough, bouldery scree. Continue down the main trod to Bleaberry Tarn.

Initially, the way follows a broken stone wall before swinging to the right away from Sourmilk Gill. The gill is a hazardous place, best left alone. Descending in a series of zigzagging steps, the path begins to level above the forest fence.

The main path continues descending to the shore of Buttermere. However, it is possible to join the forest fence at this point. Follow it to the right above the trees. Cross the stream to find a small but adequate shepherd's track rising slightly to traverse the hillside. It rounds a craggy outcrop before terminating above a wooden stile placed beyond the end of the conifers. Climb the stile over the stone wall and descend the open slope of Horse Close to gain the main path leading to the gate at the foot of Scarth Gap Pass. From here, the flat fields lead back to Gatesgarth.

Mellbreak above Crummock Water.

LOWESWATER FELLS

·LOW·

An air of secrecy and intrigue prevails over the tightly grouped circle of the Loweswater Fells. Chiefly grassy and rounded, the western half of the circle has a concentrated number of tops. Of these, from the lowly coastal plains beyond only Knock Murton stands out prominently. The eastern half comprises the independent fells of Hen Comb and Mellbreak. With her eastern flanks falling directly into Crummock Water, Mellbreak dominates the entire eastern perspective, of which Loweswater defines the northern limit and Floutern Pass the south.

Burnbank Fell, the Loweswater End of Carling Knott, Hen Comb and the gable end of Mellbreak are all visible over Loweswater. Floutern Cop and Banna Fell across Floutern Pass are best observed from the High Stile group to the south. Within these perimeters, at the heart of the group even Blake Fell, the highest, takes a low profile as it merges in a long grassy shoulder with Gavel Fell to its south. To the east, two valleys rising from Loweswater cut deep into the group. One contains Whiteoak Beck, and the other is known as Mosedale (with the Mosedale holly tree standing beneath Mellbreak specifically marked on the OS map). These valleys separate Hen Comb from the western fells of the group and Mellbreak from Hen Comb. This is a quiet yet fascinating group whose tops can all be visited by the four circular walks I have described here.

Remote from Loweswater and beyond her charms lies the south western corner of the group. Here, rising from lowly

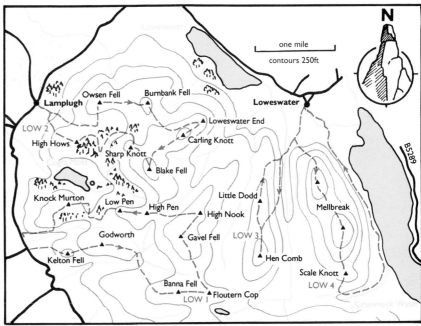

Kelton Fell over to Banna Fell and Floutern Cop to Gavel Fell, Walk LOW 1 makes a western circuit, descending over High and Low Pen before rising once more to the distinctively domed top of Knock Murton. These extensive grassy fells are in no way spectacular, yet exude a certain charm.

Beginning from Lamplugh and sweeping in an arc over Owsen Fell, Burnbank Fell and Carling Knott above Loweswater, Walk LOW 2 ascends Blake Fell, the highest of the group. The views across Loweswater are particularly fine. Sharp Knott and High Hows above Cogra Moss are included in the return.

Hen Comb is an entity in herself. Walking to her head is a pleasant exercise, rewarded by a classic view through Floutern Pass into Buttermere. Walk LOW 3 includes the knoll of Little Dodd in descent. Twin-topped Mellbreak is a magnificent hill, locally very much a favourite.

Walk LOW 4 traverses Mellbreak from north to south, descending over Scale Knott before making a return along the shores of Crummock Water. In all, there is much of interest to be discovered within the Loweswater Fells.

Numerate signpost at the start of the walk.

◆ · LOW 1 · ◆

WESTERN CIRCUIT OF GAVEL FELL

Kelton Fell 1020ft/311m
Godworth 1197ft/365m
Banna Fell 1496ft/456m
Floutern Cop 1480ft/451m
Gavel Fell 1726ft/526m
High Nook – Gavel Fell 1601ft/488m
High Pen 1558ft/475m
Low Pen 1427ft/435m
Knock Murton 1467ft/447m

Valley Base: Loweswater.
Maps: OS OD4, The English Lakes – North West. L89 West Cumbria.
Length: 6.5miles/10.5km.
Ascent: 2035ft/620m.
Approx. Time: 4 hrs.
Start & Finish: A wide verge with ample parking spaces by the Croasdale to Lamplugh road just above junction and sign that reads 'Kirkland 1 Rowrah 2' – a numeric curiosity (NY 087183).
Difficulty: Generally straightforward over rough fell grass, although frequently pathless and boggy in places. The steepest ascent, that of Knock Murton, is reserved for last.

A grassy cluster of tops forms the south west corner of the Loweswater Fells. To the north the reservoir of Cogra Moss and the afforested flanks of Lamplugh Fell are topped by Blake Fell, while the trough of Floutern Pass defines the southern periphery; to the west lie open plains, and to the east rise the bold craggy hills of the North Western Fells.

Blake Fell forms the head and highest point of this meandering circuit, which takes in nine individual tops. Mainly an area of rough fell grass and occasional heather, the most distinguished mounds (being the most independent and best formed, if not the highest) are Floutern Cop and Knock Murton, both made of Skiddaw slate. The rest provide easy if unexciting walking.

Behind the signpost 'Kirkland 1 Rowrah 2' a gate leads onto the track. Follow this past a number of great circular pits on the right. With their raised rims standing above the field and their now grassy basins some 15ft below, it is not difficult to associate them with the iron mining industry which once flourished here. After the next gate, cross the stile on the right and climb the field to the top of Kelton Fell.

Beyond the summit, stride over the fence using the extra height of the ruinous wall and up to the grassy top and small cairn of Godworth. Continue up the shoulder. Bear right to make a descent, passing sheepfolds, into the upper ravine of Croasdale Beck which is fed from above by Combe Gill and Ill Gill. Cross the stream, avoiding the waterfall and contour to cross Grain Gill before ascending to the left of High Bridge Gill. This gains the shoulder of Banna Fell immediately above a subsidiary lower top, which is conveniently outside the wire fence delineating a disputed access area. Only slightly higher than the grassy shoulder leading to it and the falling plain beyond, the summit of Banna is undistinguished, apart from its vantage point overlooking the Irish Sea out to the Isle of Man.

Pass the old boundary fence and descend to the left of the modern wire fence. Make a steep climb up the western end of Floutern Cop, a thinly grassed whaleback of Skiddaw slate. A longish top is apparent on arrival, with a worthwhile view eastwards along the corridor of Floutern Pass. Descend the same way,

Knock Murton (above) and a boundary marker on Gavel Fell (below).

then bear right through the cotton grass and over rough and boggy ground to follow the fence line rising over White Oak to the summit cairn of Gavel Fell. Frequent headstone-like blocks of sandstone stand in the fence line, the old boundary markers presumably carried by pony from the distant west coast.

To the north west stands a prominent and isolated rocky knoll unnamed on the OS map. High Nook, a subsidiary top of Gavel Fell is reached by following a direct but pathless course over the rough heather. Descend passing a small boulder field of marble white quartz, and set another course across to Fothergill Head. A stile leads over the fence. Follow a grassed track, before bearing right to the shoulder. Descend this and step over the fence line to gain the summit of High Pen. From here, move down to Low Pen. Ahead lies the conical shape of Knock Murton, while beyond it over the plains in the distance lies the Isle of Man to the west and the Solway leading to the Galloway Hills to the north.

From Low Pen continue down the shoulder following the fence line to gain the forestry track. Take this, bearing right and descending towards the waters of Cogra Moss. Further on, a path bears off left through the trees. Follow it to ascend through the thinning tree cover, heading left at the top. A stile leads over the wire fence, which marks the extent of the afforestation, and onto the open bilberry covered fellside of Knock Murton. Make a steep ascent and then cross to a distinguished summit cairn of slate, stained mauve by iron deposits and seamed with white quartz. This is the last, and in many ways the best summit of the round.

Easy descent down the shoulder leads to the top levels of the old iron mines, which in 1888 alone produced 46,100 tons of ore. Now aim directly down the flanks of the hill, passing the numerous tips and levels to gain the track beneath. Follow this and over a stile bear left along the line of the old railway track. Finally, descend over a stile to the road just below the junction and original starting point.

•LOW 2•

BLAKE FELL AND LOWESWATER FELLS EAST OF LAMPLUGH

Owsen Fell 1342ft/409m
Burnbank Fell 1558ft/475m
Loweswater End – Carling Knott
1703ft/519m
Carling Knott 1785ft/544m
Blake Fell 1878ft/573m
Sharp Knott 1581ft/482m
High Hows 1027ft/313m

Valley Base: Loweswater.
Maps: OS OD4, The English Lakes –
North West. L89 West Cumbria.
Length: 6miles/9.5km.
Ascent: 1705ft/520m.
Approx time: 3.5hrs.
Start & Finish: Lamplugh, parking oppo-
site the church – The Green (NY 089209).
Difficulty: Despite the fact that much of
this circuit is without paths the going,
mostly over fell grass and heather, is quite
straightforward.

Rising to the highest top of the group, Blake Fell, and taking in six other tops, this circuit provides an enjoyable outing. Starting and returning to the village of Lamplugh it makes rapid progress to the heights above Loweswater, Owsen Fell, Burnbank Fell and the two tops of Carling Knott before scaling Blake Fell. A particular feature of this walk are the clear views down to and over beautiful Loweswater. From Carling Knott and the high open summit of Blake Fell, the plains to the west contrast vividly with the rugged hills to the east and south.

From The Green in Lamplugh, take the stile and track (signposted footpath) leading through the fields. After a double gate a sign indicates that the footpath swings to the right. Ignore this and take the track bearing left, rising up the hill to the edge of the forestry. A stile left of the gate gives access. Follow the track, bearing left at a junction. This leads to the far side of the plantation from where you can exit through a stile and bear left along its edge. Pass a gate then climb left over a fence to rise up the open fellside along the side of the forestry. With smooth, easy walking over grass and bilberry, follow the remnants of an old fence line, which

leads directly to the rounded summit of Owsen Fell.

Continue down into the dip beyond, then make the simple rise over the top of Burnbank Fell. The fence turns a corner at the highest point, where a distinctive rusty straining post adorned with the remnants of an iron fence post makes an artistic statement. From here, Grasmoor comes into view. Follow the fence line in a slight descent then rise until another wire fence crosses in front to join it. Take the stile over this, stride over the fence to the left and contour around the head of Holme Beck, aiming for the Loweswater End of Carling Knott. This is the most arduous section of the walk, boggy around the head of the beck with rough heather beyond. It can be avoided by tak-ing a higher line.

A cairn marks the commanding top of the Loweswater End of Carling Knott. From here, a narrow path climbs the easy shoulder to the top of Carling Knott. Despite the fact that it is set lower than distant Blake Fell, it is a distinguished summit. An extensive stony plateau area holds a number of cairns and is topped by a circular cairn/shelter. There are com-manding views over Highnook Tarn

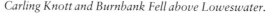

Carling Knott and Burnbank Fell above Loweswater.

To Burnbank Fell above Loweswater (above) and the rusty straining post atop of Burnbank Fell (right).

(unnamed on the OS map) and Black Crag to Hen Combe, Mellbreak, Grasmoor and southwards to Red Pike and Fleetwith Pike.

Descend the craggy south eastern edge of the shoulder. From the hollow of a steep rise, cross a wire fence near the top, leading to the summit of Blake Fell. A low, circular shelter constructed from Skiddaw slate acts as a windbreak for those seeking protection within its walls. This is a broad, mainly grassy summit offering a commanding view.

Proceed down the shoulder, taking care to locate the narrow path which very quickly bears off left towards Sharp Knott. From the col behind the grassy knoll, make a short, steep ascent to the top. Once there, it makes an interesting point from which to view the forestry, Cogra Moss and Knock Murton opposite. Just beyond the summit, extensive slate workings ring the top of this outcrop alongside curious sunken, circular hut structures. The best descent is to return to the col and take the very steep, grassy path descending to the head of Wisenholme Beck as it enters the forestry. Immediately to the left, find the head of a broad forestry track. Take this to a junction then bear right. The track itself bends left, and a little further left again. At this point, bear right before, in a short distance, a stile leads into the open. Stride the low fence line on the left and follow the edge of the open field by the stone wall. At the highest point, bear right to the grassy mound of High Hows.

The church tower can be seen from here. Descend the field in its general direction, bearing left to a gate in the first wire fence (always use the gates when crossing the fences). Soon a gate leads to a track descending to another, at which point turn right. After crossing a stream and climbing a stile, the original track is regained. Return to your starting point across the fields.

·LOW 3·

HEN COMB

Hen Comb 1670ft/509m
Little Dodd 1188ft/362m

Valley Base: Loweswater.
Maps: OS OD4, The English Lakes – North West. L89 West Cumbria.
Length: 4miles/6.5km.
Ascent: 1310ft/400m.
Approx. Time: 2 hrs.
Start & Finish: A large car park at the Kirkstile Inn, opposite the church in Loweswater Village (NY 142209). If the inn facilities are used the landlord permits parking and walking but ask permission first.
Difficulty: Straightforward walking, the most demanding section being the dry crossing of Mosedale Beck.

Looking over Black Crag to Hen Comb.

Rising from Loweswater Village the long and tapering grassy wedge of Hen Comb, which ends in a great dome at its southern end and sports the knoll of Little Dodd at the other, is seldom visited. It is easy to see why. Effectively, it is cut off from the other Loweswater Fells by the bogs of Floutern Pass to the south, by the equally boggy Whiteoak Moss and Whiteoak Beck to the west, and by Mosedale to the east. There is only one practical line of approach to Hen Comb; that is to climb from the Loweswater end of the wedge and return the same way.

Hen Comb is a one-off. Overshadowed by her more glamourous neighbour, Mellbreak, therein also lies her strength. She is independent. Her summit stands equal in altitude to that of the northern top of Mellbreak's and the view from here into Buttermere is nothing short of classic. Hen Combe can be climbed in a short day or evening, and the walker who appreciates quiet beauty can extract as much pleasure here as on the most celebrated Lakeland tops.

From Loweswater Village a lane leads over Church Bridge past Kirkgate Farm. Pass earthworks to emerge into open Mosedale. Cross the beck (in flood this would be difficult, if not impossible) and follow the path along the left bank beneath the flanks of Hen Comb. Before reaching the old mine workings (grassed over and difficult to recognize) ascend diagonally up the hillside to the shoulder beneath the steepening of the summit dome. An old zigzagging path exists here, though it requires some effort to locate. Once found, climb up the path to gain the summit of Hen Comb.

From here descend the shoulder, taking in the picturesque scene across Loweswater, before rising slightly to the knoll of Little Dodd. Below, the path leads to the intake wall then bears right down to Mosedale Beck. Re-cross this and return to the Kirkstile Inn.

•LOW 4•

MELLBREAK

Mellbreak – North Top 1670ft/509m
Mellbreak – South Top 1678ft/512m
Scale Knott 1109ft/338m

Valley Base: Loweswater.
Maps: OS OD4, The English Lakes – North West. L89 West Cumbria.
Length: 5miles/9km.
Ascent: 1950ft/595m.
Approx. Time: 3.25hrs.
Start & Finish: A large car park at the Kirkstile Inn, opposite the church in Loweswater Village (NY 142209). If the inn facilities are used the landlord permits parking and walking but ask permission first.
Difficulty: A steepish ascent, daunting to look at though not technically difficult, is followed by gentler going. The area beneath Scale Knott and on the footpath beside Crummock is boggy in places.

Twin-topped and saddle-backed Mell-break is a moody and slightly mysterious hill. Her public face, the northern gable seen above Loweswater Village, stands craggy and sharply angular, and her dark, eastern flanks fall directly into Crummock Water. Seen in silhouette, her scree and crags cast in shadow, she appears as a high crown. Beyond, to the west the complete massif of the remaining Loweswater Group shield Mellbreak. To the south she faces Scale Force, Lakelands highest single fall of water.

Climbing the steep gable above Loweswater leads to the crossing of the summit plateau. Descend over Scale Knott and return along the shores of Crummock Water. The best views are observed in this direction; in particular, the return beside Crummock Water under the high crags and steep scree is a magical experience.

Leave the Kirkstile Inn to follow the lane over Church Bridge. Beyond the earthworks a path leads up to the open shoulder marking the northern flanks. Initially rising diagonally to the left, it soon begins zigzagging through the scree and heather. At the head of the scree a short gully leads to more open fellside. Above, the path runs more gently through grass, heather and outcrops of Skiddaw slate. A glance over the edge to the left reveals Crummock Water stretched out below in all her glory. Further on, the path rises to the North Top of Mellbreak where a tremendous feeling of open exposure is experienced, as you stand there transfixed with deep valleys slicing away the flanks of the top on both sides.

The path leads on over bilberry and heather to the higher Southern Top of Mellbreak – the summit. Although the path in descent is rather vague, the going is over grass and very easy. The slight rise onto Scale Knott may be taken before further descent to the south meets a wire fence. Stride over this and continue the descent, picking the easiest line for there is now no definite path. Reach a well-defined path crossing above the stream of Black Beck. This is Floutern Pass, once an important packhorse route though now mainly lost in bog. A small, circular ruin lies below while above stands the great rift of Scale Force.

Take the path down to a gate through a wire fence to pass a number of ruined stone walls and circular enclosures (marked as a settlement on the OS map). Continue to the main footpath following the shores of Crummock Water. Follow this, passing the curious, curving peninsula leading to Low Ling Crag. Further on, another boulder emerging from the clear waters is known as the Iron Stone. Adjacent to this, the path begins to rise and pull away from the lakeshore. Follow it above the stone wall to a stile. A gate leads past Highpark after which the road continues to Park Bridge and left to Loweswater Village.

Over the Buttermere Valley to Mellbreak.

A view north to the Fellbarrow Group.

FELLBARROW GROUP

·FEL·

Rising above Loweswater to the south and separated from the North Western Fells by Lorton Vale, a sprawling and predominantly grassy upland area lies dormant. Fellbarrow is the most northern group in the Western Fells, with open agricultural land encircling the northern and western boundaries, and beyond these plains the ebb and flow of the Solway Firth.

Although the flanks of Darling Fell, Loweswater Fell and Low Fell represent the steepest and craggiest aspect, the group is known as Fellbarrow after the grassy domed top of Mosser Fell, the most prominent feature when viewed from the north. While scant evidence now remains, the boggy hollow between Darling Fell and Low Fell – which feeds Crabtree Beck – was once damned. In 1828 the dam burst with tragic conse-quences; the resulting deluge of water washed away a portion of Crabtree below and two of its inhabitants were killed.

Ironically, the top of Low Fell consti-tutes the highest point and, uniquely, all seven tops include 'fell' in their name. The underlying rock is Skiddaw slate, which explains the generally rounded appear-ance of the group. Unlike most other Lakeland areas, it is all neatly fenced and individually parcelled into different sheep pastures. On the walk selected all fences are crossed by stiles and access does not present a problem.

Rising from Loweswater, Walk FEL 1 takes in all the tops in an anticlockwise direction, before making a pleasant return along the Mosser Road (which is unfit for cars but highly suited to fell walkers). Taken as a whole, this is a splendid outing.

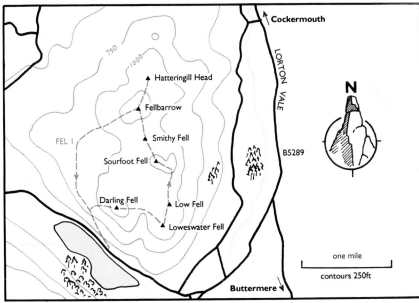

•FEL I•

FELLBARROW ROUND FROM LOWESWATER

Darling Fell 1283ft/391m
Loweswater Fell 1352ft/412m
Low Fell 1388ft/423m
Sourfoot Fell 1348ft/411m
Smithy Fell 1286ft/392m
Fellbarrow – Mosser Fell 1363ft/416m
Hatteringill Head – Whin Fell 1263ft/385m

Valley Base: Loweswater of
Lorton Vale.
Town Base: Cockermouth.
Maps: OS OD4, The English Lakes –
North West. L89 West Cumbria.
Length: 6 miles/9.5km.
Ascent: 1805ft/550m.
Approx Time: 4hrs.
Start & Finish: Pull-offs for a small
number of cars exist by the side of the
road above Loweswater near the
track/road signposted 'Mosser unfit for
cars' rising from the main road (NY
128218). If these are full, a larger car park
exists above the end of the lake, a little
way along the road in a westerly direction.
Difficulty: A pleasant low fell outing.
Initially, ascent is steep and again from the
dip below Loweswater Fell, yet there is a
good path for most of the way. Once on
the tops, the walking is straightforward
over gently undulating grassland.

From the Scots pines above the waters of
Loweswater this is a notable circuit of
low Lakeland Fells; a journey through a
quieter part of Lakeland whose airy
disposition and ease of walking make for
a delightful excursion.

On the route detailed there are no
access problems, with all the boundary
fences crossed by stiles. However,
Hatteringill Head on Whin Fell lies out on
a limb beyond and slightly below Fellbarrow. To avoid crossing the fields bounded by stone walls, it is recommended that
Fellbarrow is re-climbed. You can then
descend down her flanks through a gate
onto the Mosser Road.

Leave the sweet smelling pines and
walk up the road to Mosser to a sign on
the right which says 'Public Footpath
Foulsyke'. Climb the ladder stile and bear
left along the zigzagging path up the steep
flanks of Darling Fell. A post and wire
fence lies to the left of the path for most of
the way, before veering off left near the
top. Cross the stile in front to the first
summit. Beyond is a longer spur which
appears to be of equal altitude and offers
the best view.

Separating Darling from Loweswater
Fell, a deep hollow holds Crabtree Beck.
Initially, its descent and subsequent
ascent appears a daunting prospect, but
thankfully appearances are deceptive in

*Walkers on Low Fell (below) and the
view over Loweswater to the Fellbarrow
Group (right).*

this case. Follow the line of the fence,
cross Crabtree Beck at the bottom (where
it is no more than a narrow stream) and
rise again. After a short distance, leave the
ascent and bear right to the rocky knoll of
Loweswater Fell.

A good path rises up the nose, crossing
a stile to the cairned top of Low Fell.
Beyond a dip leading to another stile, an
unexpected view materializes down into

Lorton Vale. Note the old building on the right and a grassed track that has risen from Thackthwaite. Follow this and cross a stile, then bear left to the top of Sourfoot Fell. Descend to the short length of stone wall, before rising again to the top of Smithy Fell where the fence changes direction. There is no definite path, but this is easy walking over short grassland.

A few wistful larches stand on the eastern flanks of Fellbarrow. Step over the stile on the left and follow the fence up the flanks. The broad summit is marked by a stone trig point. A few surplus trig construction rocks of various geological origin can be seen scattered nearby. Follow the fence down into the dip and mount the stile over the stone wall. Climb over and skirt the scree of Skiddaw slate to ascend the last northern outpost of the Western Fells – Hatteringill Head of Whin Fell.

For access purposes, retrace your steps back to the top of Fellbarrow. Take the summit dome westwards for a straight-forward descent down Mosser Fell. Crossing the moss below, aim for a short track beyond Mosser Beck which leads through an iron gate onto the road. Turn left to return back to your starting point.

2

North Western Fells

Dale Head Group DAL (11 tops) • Grasmoor Group GRA (18 tops)
Grisedale Pike Group GRI (15 tops) • Lord's Seat Group LOS (12 tops)

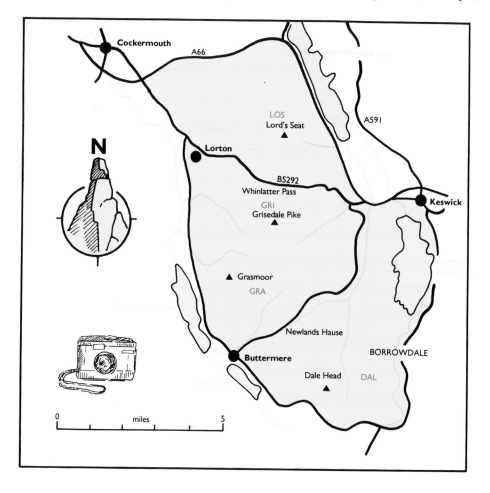

Cockermouth

A66

Basenthwaite Lake

LOS
Lord's Seat ▲

A591

N

Lorton ●

B5292
Whinlatter Pass

GRI
Grisedale Pike ▲

Keswick ●

▲ Grasmoor
GRA

Newlands Hause

BORROWDALE

● Buttermere

Dale Head
▲

DAL

0   miles   5

Between Bassenthwaite Lake and Derwent Water, Buttermere and Crummock Water, this intriguing area of fells offers a number of fine, powerful peaks. The region's smallest area covering a mere 80 square miles, it is noted for its graceful, often spectacular ridges. Bulky Grasmoor is the highest top, rising sheer above Crummock Water. Yet, it is the Sphinx Head of Causey Pike, and that Lakeland Matterhorn, the pyramidal Grisedale Pike, which best represent the aesthetic appeal of the area.

Dale Head above Honister Pass marks the southern boundary with the Western Fells, while Sale Fell above the Vale of Cockermouth guards the northern extremity. In all, the area falls into four distinct groups covering some 56 tops. The Lord's Seat Group lies north of Whinlatter Pass, while the Grisedale Pike Group (which includes Whiteside and Hopegill Head) lies to the south. The valleys of Gasgale Gill and Coledale join at Coledale Hause, separating the latter from the mighty Grasmoor Group. Finally, the Dale Head Group lies to the south of Newlands Pass.

It is the regular symmetrical shapes of the ancient and weathered Skiddaw slate which are dominant throughout. The great domed tops and craggy features of Grasmoor and Crag Hill; the pyramidal points of Grisedale Pike, Hopegill Head and Whiteless Pike; the sharply defined ridges and conical turrets of Cat Bells and Causey Pike – these are the stuff of fine art, lifted from the canvas and elevated to perfection.

The Borrowdale Volcanics join the older slates above Honister Pass, briefly running together through Dale Head and High Spy. Eel Crags and Dalehead Crags are formed of volcanics, yet set within the scene of rugged grandeur around the head of Newlands few would be able to discern any outward physical difference. Predominantly, the scene south of Whinlatter Pass is of nature wild and unbridled. Yet within the heart of this magnificence and nowadays for the most part hardly detectable, man has wrought an extensive industry. Mineral mining was long an important component of the local economy. Lead and copper were the mainstay, yet gold was once extracted from Goldscope below Scope End in Newlands, and cobalt from the Coledale side of Scar Crags. Whinlatter Pass marks a distinct change in the nature of the hills. More gentle and rolling here, their cladding of heather and flanks of pine add a distinct Scottish flavour to their character. Overall, this is an exceptionally lovely area offering generally amenable walking across a wide spectrum of interest.

AREA FACT SHEET

THE VALLEY BASES

Bassenthwaite
Camping: Traffords in Bassenthwaite Village, Gaskells near Lane Foot Farm at Thornthwaite.
Youth Hostels: None.
Inns: The Sun in Bassenthwaite Village, The Swan Hotel and The Pheasant Inn.
Bus services: Keswick to Cockermouth, and Keswick to Carlisle.

Borrowdale
Camping: Seathwaite Farm, Thornythwaite Farm, Borrowdale Village, Stonethwaite, Ashness Farm, Dalt Wood Grange.
Youth Hostels: Longthwaite, Barrow House.
Inns: The Scafell Hotel.
Bus services: Keswick to Seatoller.

Buttermere
Camping: Gatesgarth Farm.
Youth Hostels: Buttermere, Honister Hause.
Inns: The Fish.
Bus services: None.

Lorton Vale
Camping: Whinfell Hall Farm.
Youth Hostels: None.
Inns: Kirkstile Inn, Scale Hill Hotel.
Bus services: None.

Newlands
Camping: Braithwaite Village.
Youth Hostel: None.
Inns: Swinside Inn.
Bus services: None.

THE TOWN BASES

Cockermouth
Camping: Graysonside Farm and Violet Bank.
Youth Hostel: Double Mills.

Keswick
Camping: The Headlands, Derwent Water, Castlerigg Hall and Castlerigg Farm.
Youth Hostels: Keswick.
All facilities except railway station.

Dale Head seen over Honister Pass.

DALE HEAD GROUP

·DAL·

Above Derwent Water the dark curve of Catbells outlined against a crimson sky represents the epitome of picturesque Lakeland. In effect, three mountain ridges rise from the north to the high summits of Dale Head, Hindscarth and Robinson. In turn, these heights are linked by Littledale Edge and Hindscarth Edge. Two mountain horseshoes have been described to tackle the main tops while a third walk visits the noted viewpoint of High Snockrigg.

This prized triangle of high hills is separated from Grasmoor by Newlands Pass and from the Western Fells by Buttermere, Honister Pass, Borrowdale and Derwent Water. Those rising from Catbells to High Spy are often referred to as the Derwent Fells, while the steep flanks rising to Robinson and Dale Head are called the Buttermere Fells. Within the range lie the quiet valleys of Newlands and Little Dale. Walk DAL 1 samples the delights of Catbells, Maiden Moor and High Spy before ascending Dale Head.

Walk DAL 2 climbs Scope End from Newlands to round Little Dale en route to the summit of Robinson. A steep descent leads to High Snab Bank. Then down Hindscarth via Scope End leads to the Newlands Valley.

Finally, Walk DAL 3 climbs High Snockrigg from Newlands Hause via the waterfall of Moss Force.

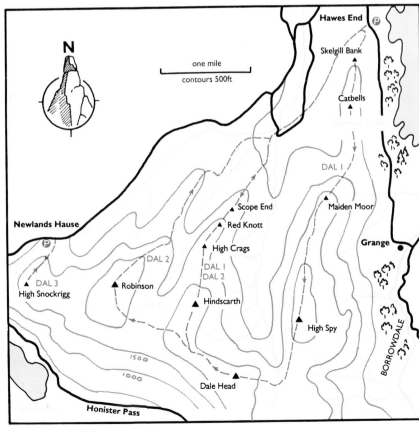

•DAL 1•

DALE HEAD HORSESHOE

Skelgill Bank 1109ft/338m
Catbells 1481ft/451m
Maiden Moor 1890ft/576m
High Spy – Scawdel Fell 2143ft/653m
Dale Head 2472ft/753m
Hindscarth 2385ft/727m
High Crags 1736ft/529m
Red Knott 1483ft/452m
Scope End 1352ft/412m

Valley Base: Borrowdale, Newlands.
Town Base: Keswick.
Maps: OS OD4, The English Lakes –
North West. L90 Penrith & Keswick.
Length: 10miles/16km.
Ascent: 2855ft/870m.
Approx Time: 5.5hrs.
Start & Finish: Car Park at Hawes End
(NY 248212).
Difficulty: Considering its length and
mountain setting, apart from the short
strenuous pull up Dale Head this is a
remarkably straightforward walk. Good
paths prevail and the going is easy.
However, its length should not be
underestimated and escape, save down
the length of Newlands Valley from Dalehead Tarn, is not straightforward. Steep
cliffs and deep mine shafts abound on the
slopes below.

Summit cairn of High Spy.

Seen from Keswick or along lower
Borrowdale, the ascending heights to
Catbells float above Derwent Water as
inviting as any in the land. The route rises
to Dale Head, then follows the heights
around the secluded Newlands Valley.
This is one of the loveliest mountain
walks in Lakeland, overlooking Derwent
Water in Borrowdale to the east and the
heart of the Western Fells to the south.

A well-worn path climbs from the
road to the blunt nose of Skelgill Bank. An
easy shoulder of sheep-cropped grass
leads to the steeper climb up the bell-
shaped dome of Catbells. Marked Cat
Bells on the OS maps the name is probably a corruption of Cat Bields ('shelter of
the wild cat'). The summit is a slate dome
worn clear of vegetation by millions of
walkers' boots. Nevertheless, the beauty
of the scene defies description.

Easy walking leads to the rise up
Maiden Moor before the path splits. Keep
to the right along the flat edge of the moor
above Newlands Valley. A small cairn on
a rise denotes the top of Maiden Moor.
Bull Crag lies below and excellent open
views across the valley reveal the glory of

the ridges beyond. Above Newlands and
Goldscope, Scope End falls from Hindscarth and High Snab Bank from Robinson. Easy walking continues with the
path climbing gently to the northern end
of the High Spy shoulder of Scawdel Fell.
After the initial climb bear left to the
prominent cairn on the rocky bump
above Blea Crag for a last look along
Derwent Water. Return to the main path
and proceed along the flat shoulder
which hides the rocky steeps of Eel Crags.

A substantial cairn marks High Spy,
the top of Scawdel Fell sometimes known
as Lobstone Band. The rock here is
Borrowdale Volcanic.

Descend easily to cross the stream
above the head of Newlands. The path
then flanks Dalehead Tarn, with a rock
knoll and ruined stone shelter to the right,
before rising steeply to climb Dale Head.
Although shorter than appearances
would suggest, this is the most strenuous
section of the outing. Keep to the right,
above the precipitous rocks of Gable
Crag, for the most spectacular outlook
across the depths of Newlands. From the
summit cairn take time off to admire the

Down Hindscarth Edge from Dale Head (above) and Scope End rising from Newlands (below).

outstanding views in all directions.

The route continues down Hindscarth Edge and is not difficult. Two rocky knolls lead to a third lower but distinctly separate pinnacle (unnamed) marked by a substantial and ancient cairn. Descent continues until an easy ascent leads up the Buttermere end of Hindscarth. The rocks are now Skiddaw slate. The junction with Borrowdale Volcanics takes place somewhere along Hindscarth Edge. A short cut bears right but it is better, if slightly longer, to climb directly to the crest of the shoulder which leads to the summit cairn.

Follow the broad back of Hindscarth to a large, ancient circular shelter, after which the edge steepens dramatically. Take care until the little top of High Crags brings an easing in the angle of ascent. The main path passes beneath the top of Red Knott and leads to Scope End.

From Scope End the path steepens to a wire fence. Bear right above Low Snab Farm and below the extensive workings of Goldscope Mine. This rift running up the hillside continues through the mountain and out the other side. Gold was mined here and the workings were of such importance that Queen Elizabeth claimed them from Thomas Percie, Earl of Northumberland. The trial went in favour of Elizabeth, Percie being infuriated to the point of starting an armed rebellion. He lost and was beheaded.

Cross the footbridge over Newlands Beck and proceed along the track to Little Town. A lane on the right signposted 'Skelgill' leads to a house and then continues across open fields. It leads to the surfaced road beyond Skelgill Farm.

·DAL 2·

ROBINSON HORSESHOE

Scope End 1352ft/412m
Red Knott 1483ft/452m
High Crags 1736ft/529m
Hindscarth 2385ft/727m
Robinson 2417ft/737m

Valley Base: Newlands.
Town Base: Keswick.
Maps: OS OD4, The English Lakes – North West. L90 Penrith & Keswick.
Length: 6.5miles/10.5km.
Ascent: 2495ft/760m.
Approx Time: 4hrs.
Start & Finish: Small car park above Chapel Bridge, Little Town, Newlands Valley (NY 232194).
Difficulty: A high mountain walk ascending and descending two steep ridges. Paths are good throughout and although exposed in places there is no great technical difficulty.

Two steep, impressive ridges rise from Newlands to Hindscarth and Robinson. Between them lies Little Dale. Ascending one and descending the other, thereby linking Hindscarth and Robinson by the Littledale Edge, provides a perfectly defined mountain outing. The three separate tops of Scope End, Red Knott and High Crags are best appreciated in ascent of the ridge. As this was descended in Walk DAL 1 it is this ridge which will be taken in ascent.

Proceed down the road to cross Newlands Beck via Chapel Bridge then bear left to Newlands Church. (Chapel and Church are one and the same here.) Turn left down the track leading to Low Snab Farm and pass through the farmyard to a gate. The path bears right to the snout of the ridge then steeply climbs Scope End above Goldscope Mine. Next comes Red Knott and High Crags before a steep ascent leads to the shelter cairn on the edge of Hindscarth. From here, the path continues easily to the summit.

Move along the shoulder to a path junction, and bear right to traverse the Littledale Edge. To the west stands shapely Fleetwith Pike with Gatesgarth Beck running along the valley bottom below. To the east lies the high deserted basin of Little Dale. A gentle ascent leads above Robinson Crags and past Hackney Holes (100 yards to the right of the path). These curious excavated holes were possibly one-time mineral explorations. As the angle eases you reach the summit plateau. Take stock of the fine view to the west before bearing right to the summit cairn of Robinson located on the most westerly of two parallel rock outcrops.

Proceeding from the summit, a cairn marks a distinct steepening in the ridge. From here on the going is extremely exposed and caution should be taken not to stray left onto the precipitous face of Robinson Crags. As Blea Crags are reached the route changes direction slightly, bearing left and descending over three rocky steps. The path is well defined and the technical difficulties slight, though the position is dramatic. Easier going follows the sharp edge of High Snab Bank. The path bears right, making a straightforward grassy descent to a track and gate. Follow the track past Low High Snab after which the road leads past Newlands Church.

•DAL 3•

HIGH SNOCKRIGG ABOVE NEWLANDS HAUSE

High Snockrigg 1726ft/526m

Valley Base: Buttermere, Newlands.
Town Base: Keswick.
Maps: OS OD4, The English Lakes – North West. L90 Penrith & Keswick.
Length: 1.25miles/2km.
Ascent: 655ft/200m.
Approx Time: 1hr.
Start & Finish: Car park at the summit of Newlands Pass – Newlands Hause (NY 193176).
Difficulty: A little easy scrambling is involved in ascent and the descent is steep in places.

This walk can be extended by following the old sled route directly from Buttermere or by combining with Walk GRA 2. A well-worn path leads directly to a waterfall. A large hanging block impressively splits the flow on the upper section. Continue steeply up to the right of the fall, following a natural weakness. For a short distance the going is steep and exposed and involves a little easy scrambling.

The climb quickly crests the gentle edge of Buttermere Moss to follow the raised grassy rim of the plateau. Note the corridor which cuts down from the moss as a well-defined trod while zigzagging its way to Buttermere. This was the old sled route which was used to transport peat cut from Buttermere Moss to the waiting fires of Buttermere.

You reach the summit cairn of High Snockrigg without incident. Buttermere, Crummock Water, the high craggy Birkness Combe and the rugged cirque of Haystacks are all revealed in their best light from here.

Return along the edge of the moss. The path bears left before reaching the point taken in ascent from the waterfall. With one or two steeper steps it winds its way down to Newlands Hause.

High Snockrigg falling from Robinson as viewed over Buttermere.

Grasmoor above Crummock Water.

GRASMOOR GROUP

·GRA·

Seen from the west, Grasmoor rises from the Buttermere Valley as a steep and striking mountain. From all the higher mountains of the Lake District, save the Eastern Fells, it forms a distinct addition to the high-level landscape. It is not only the leader of this group but also the highest mountain of these North Western Fells. However, from the east over Derwent Water it is Crag Fell at the head of Coledale and her satellite, Causey Pike, that steal the scene.

As a whole the group is bound by the deep rifts of Gasgale and Coledale, meeting at Coledale Hause to the north; by Newlands Pass to the south, by Crummock Water to the west and Derwent Water to the east.

Within these boundaries lie the two main mountains along with high deserted valleys, hanging combes, spectacular ridges and fine peaks. This is a hill walking area of the highest quality with three walks selected to cover eighteen tops.

Beginning above the bridge of Stoneycroft, Walk GRA 1 climbs Causey Pike directly via Rowling End. Taking the high-level edge over Scar Crags, it continues over Sail and then follows the exposed ridge to Crag Fell. A return is made to Sail Pass before descent under the old Cobalt Mines enables a sweeping tour of Outerside, Stile End and Barrow.

The ascent of Knott Rigg from Newlands Hause and the walk along the shoulder to Ard Crags provides a pleasant upland excursion with the minimum of effort. This is described in Walk GRA2.

Walk GRA3 tackles the leader of the group, Grasmoor. It makes a high circuit including Wandhope and Whiteless Pike. Finally, it traverses along Low Bank to the viewpoint of Rannerdale Knotts, which is placed strategically to look along both Buttermere and Crummock Water, and across to Mellbreak.

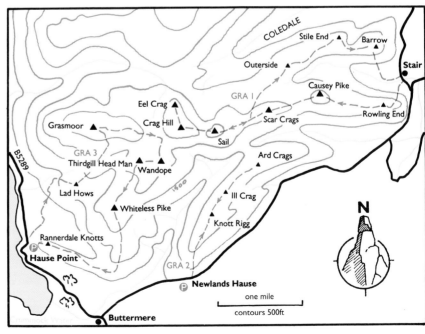

·GRA I·

CAUSEY PIKE, CRAG HILL AND THE FELLS ABOVE COLEDALE

Rowling End 1421ft/433m
Causey Pike 2090ft/637m
Scar Crags 2205ft/672m
Sail 2536ft/773m
Crag Hill 2751ft/839m
Eel Crag 2649ft/807m
Outerside 1863ft/568m
Stile End 1467ft/447m
Barrow 1494ft/455m

Valley Base: Newlands, Borrowdale.
Town Base: Keswick.
Maps: OS OD4, The English Lakes –
North West. L90 Penrith & Keswick.
Length: 6.75miles/11km.
Ascent: 3280ft/1000m.
Approx Time: 4.5hrs.
Start & Finish: Stoneycroft. There is
parking along the verge either side the
arched bridge (NY 232212).
Difficulty: Mountainous terrain prevails
although the paths are generally good.
Steep ascent of the summit cone of
Causey Pike constitutes an easy scramble,
as does the exposed edge, The Scar,
ascending from Sail to Crag Hill. This is
not a route on which to go astray.

*High exposure on the ridge between
Sail and Crag Fell.*

This mountain route links Causey Pike
with Crag Hill, the central pivot of these
North Western Fells, via a long high
shoulder. The going is always open, the
views breathtaking and in places there is
considerable exposure. Return over the
fells that stand on the southern edge of
Coledale offers a logical circuit and
completes a particularly fine outing over
high hills.

From the stone arched bridge which
crosses Stoneycroft Gill, climb steeply up
the grass hillside. Numerous old tracks
and water leats are crossed – a testimony
to the extensive mining operations that
were once carried on here – before the
path bears left to the heathery shoulder of
Rowling End. Easy progress along the
shoulder leads to a crossing of Sleat
Hause towards the nose of Causey Pike.
The edge rears impressively and the climb
is steep. Near the top, hands as well as feet
may be needed.

Beyond the rocky summit dome the
hill forms a cocks-comb crest, with alter-
nate peaks and troughs, before dropping
to the shoulder. Rise to the top of Scar
Crags. The shoulder is sharply defined to
the left by steep craggy ground which falls
to Rigg Beck. Beyond the summit cairns
the going increases in difficulty again as
you descend to the col and crossroads of
Sail Pass.

A long diagonal ascent leads up the
flanks of Sail with a little detour right to
reach the summit cairn. Returning to the
path you might imagine yourself crossing
an Alpine ridge, as the cliffs plunge away
on both sides. A little pinnacle leads to

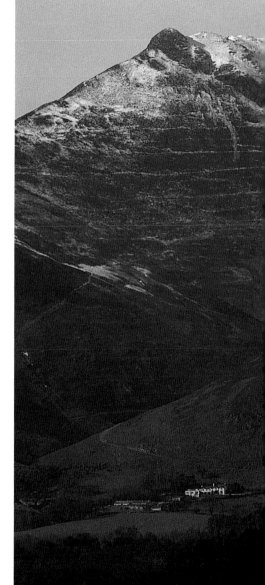

steeper ground as the edge climbs
towards the summit of Crag Hill. On its
final section a few rocky outcrops may
require the hands-on approach and warrant its classification as an easy scramble.

A cairn marks an easing in the angle
from where the final approach to the trig
point lies over a stony, gently domed
plateau. Although Crag Hill is sometimes
referred to as Eel Crag, this is in fact a
separate top, marked by an ancient cairn.
It can be reached by descending slightly to
the north.

Causey Pike, Sail, Crag Fell, Eel Crag and Barrow above Stoneycroft.

Follow the same route in return to Sail Pass; compared with the ascent it is considerably easier. Turn left at Sail Pass, following a path which at first drops steeply but then eases. Above on Long Crag are the old levels of the ancient Cobalt Mine. Before reaching High Moss the path meets the track which once served the mine. Our route leaves it a short distance later and bears left across High Moss to climb the nose of Outerside to its summit cairn. A straightforward descent and ascent lead to the top of Stile End. Set slightly out from Outerside and the next objective, Barrow, it provides a first-class view to Skiddaw. Bear right and descend to the grassy hollow of Barrow Door. An ascent leads to the heather-covered summit of Barrow.

Direct descent down the southern flank of Barrow involves a short, steep section of thick heather before the easier open shoulder of fell grass is reached. There is no distinct path yet this is the quickest way back to Stoneycroft. From the shoulder make a simple descent to the mine track above Stoneycroft Gill. Follow the mine track until a path bears off down to the right. This picks up an ancient (now dry) man-made water course hewn through solid rock. Its purpose was to divert the stream to enable mining below the bed of Stoneycroft Gill where a rich lead vein was discovered. To achieve this the stream was dammed. Tragically for the ancient miners the dam broke, the workings flooded and lives were lost. The water course leads back to the gill just above the bridge.

Ascending Ill Crag with Ard Crags beyond. Causey Pike can be seen on the ridge behind.

•GRA 2•

KNOTT RIGG TO ARD CRAGS

Knott Rigg 1824ft/556m
Ill Crag 1791ft/546m
Ard Crags 1906ft/581m

Valley Base: Buttermere, Newlands.
Town Base: Keswick.
Maps: OS OD4, The English Lakes –
North West. L90 Penrith & Keswick.
Length: 3.5miles/5.5km.
Ascent: 1230ft/375m.
Approx Time: 2hrs.
Start & Finish: Car park at the summit
of Newlands Pass – Newlands Hause
(NY 193176).
Difficulty: A straightforward ridge walk.

Clean cut and roof-like, the high shoulder
between Knott Rigg and Ard Crags
makes a delightful and straightforward
excursion. Starting from Newlands
Hause at an altitude of 1093ft/333m
provides a distinct advantage. Its only
failing, if it could be called that, is that
there is no circuit or logical link which

provides an enjoyable alternative return
to Newlands Hause.

A minor preliminary climb leads to the
nose from where the path becomes
straightforward. Grassy slopes climb past
a number of rocky outcrops of Skiddaw
slate before the climb eases to the highest
grassy knoll. To the left, Knott Rigg
plunges shudderingly to Sail Beck before
rising even more dramatically to Whiteless Edge and Wandhope. To the right
Keskadale Edge sinks down to Keskadale
Farm. Beyond this stretch the fine ridges
of High Snab Bank, Scope End and
Maiden Moor.

The middle hump of the shoulder, Ill
Crag, arrives quickly. Hanging above Sail
Beck is the imposing Addacomb Hole.
Beyond the dip in the ridge and its tiny
tarn, the shoulder gathers momentum. It
rises distinctly to its highest top, the
heather-clad dome of Ard Crags. Steep,
craggy ground falls away beneath this to
the right. A natural forest of indigenous
sessile oaks, Lakelands' traditional
woodland, clings to the hillside scree
above Ill Gill.

A descent and a little energetic ascent
to the top reveals a small cairn, atop of
which the spire of Causey Pike stands
proudly. It only remains to turn around
and walk back to Newlands Hause.

•GRA 3•

GRASMOOR TO WHITELESS PIKE CIRCUIT

Lad Hows 1398ft/426m
Grasmoor 2795ft/852m
Wandope 2533ft/772m
Thirdgill Head Man 2402ft/732m
Whiteless Pike 2165ft/660m
Rannerdale Knotts 1165ft/355m

Valley Base: Buttermere.
Town Base: Cockermouth.
Maps: OS OD4, The English Lakes –
North West. L90 Penrith & Keswick.
Length: 6.25miles/10km.
Ascent: 2950ft/900m.
Approx Time: 4hrs.
Start & Finish: Parking area by the
roadside where the track leaves for
High Rannerdale, beneath Rannerdale
Knotts (NY 163184).
Difficulty: Despite making a relatively
direct attack on the heights of Grasmoor
and descending the exposed Whiteless
Edge, good paths prevail and the going is
generally straightforward.

Cast your eyes up from the road by Crummock Water, between Rannerdale Knotts and Rannerdale Bridge. A formidable mountain array is revealed. To the left, perched on the soaring flanks of Grasmoor lies Lad Hows. To the right stands Whiteless Pike. Lad Hows proves to be a ridge, rather than a crag, snaking easily to the summit plateau of Grasmoor, while Whiteless Pike is a point on the opposite edge of the steep-sided combe at whose base lies Rannerdale Beck. In all, this high circuit links Grasmoor and Whiteless Pike via Wandope and continues across Low Bank to Rannerdale Knotts.

The track beneath Rannerdale Knotts leads through a gate and bears right to a footbridge over Squat Beck. Bear left along the track and take the gate/stile past the stone wall. Just beyond to the right, a path begins to lead directly up the hillside. After an initial section of ascent it bears left to strike a diagonal line through the bracken, emerging onto a grassy shoulder above Cinderdale Beck. After a further short section of ascent it bears right to the summit and cairn of Lad Hows.

The ridge beyond, although rising through heather and Skiddaw slate above, is quite straightforward and leads to a cairn marking the edge of Grasmoor's summit plateau. Proceed to the large shelter cairn which indicates the highest point.

For an uninterrupted view south and west find a little shelter cairn on the edge overlooking Crummock Water. There are numerous ancient cairns along the summit plateau, marking the points where the main paths arrive and descend. Although the summit area is grassed, in addition it has more shale areas where the Skiddaw slates lie bare. The 'Gras' part of the name Grasmoor derives from grise, meaning wild boar.

Strike a well-defined course to the easternmost cairn perched on an elevated top. The path falls directly to the col between Grasmoor and Crag Hill. At this high-level crossroads our route lies straight on up the steep flanks of Crag Hill. Bear right to intercept the steep edge above Addacomb Hole, where there is a sudden transition from mundane slope to

screaming exposure. Follow the edge to the cairn of Wandhope.

A simple descent leads to the cairn ('man') of Thirdgill Head Man. Standing commandingly above the combe of Rannerdale Beck it marks the start of Whiteless Edge, a beautiful mountain ridge which plunges elegantly down to the col of Saddle Gate. This route is considerably exposed, yet without technical difficulty. From the col a short steep ascent leads to the rocky summit of Whiteless Pike.

The path descends steeply towards Whiteless Breast and bears right, slightly slackening in gradient, before finally steepening again to drop to the col above High Rannerdale. Climb slightly, then follow the crest of Low Bank. Pass over a cairned rocky top to a second higher top. This is the summit of Rannerdale Knotts. The path continues north a little distance (care should be taken, for steep crags lay beyond) before bearing left to descend the nose of Rannerdale Knotts, from where it heads directly for Hause Point. On reaching a saddle, a short steep path down to the right leads to the start.

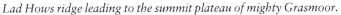

Lad Hows ridge leading to the summit plateau of mighty Grasmoor.

A northerly aspect of Grisedale Pike.

GRISEDALE PIKE GROUP

•GRI•

Viewed from the east, a long ridge rises to a perfect pyramidal peak. This is Grisedale Pike – 'The Matterhorn of Lakeland'. Whinlatter Pass defines the northern edge of the group, while below to the south lies Coledale. Beyond and hidden when viewed from the east stands Hopegill Head. The western flank of the group is dominated by Whiteside standing at the end of Crummock Water above Lorton Vale. Nine of the twelve tops stand above 2000ft.

The valleys of Coledale and Gasgale Gill meet at Coledale Hause to form the southern boundary of the group, Gasgale Gill separating Whiteside from Grasmoor. The southern face of Whiteside takes a precipitous plunge to form a face reminiscent of the Wasdale Screes. Above

it runs an exposed edge ending in the peak of Hopegill Head. Placed centrally within the massif, Sand Hill falls sedately to the high-level crossroads of Coledale Hause. The north face of Hopegill Head stands as the highest point of both Hope Gill and Hobcarton Crag (its local name being Hobcarton Pike).

Rising by the north ridge and descending by the east ridge of Grisedale Pike, Walk GRI 1 provides a relatively short circuit around the valley of Grisedale. Walk GRI 2 takes the east ridge and continues over Hobcarton Head, before descending the west ridge and veering down to Coledale Hause. Pass Force Crag to follow the track down Coledale. The Hope Gill Horseshoe, Walk GRI 3, visits Hopegill Head, taking in eight other tops.

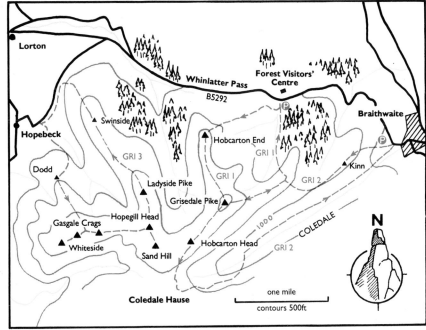

•GR11•

GRISEDALE PIKE BY THE NORTH RIDGE

Hobcarton End 2080ft/634m
Grisedale Pike 2593ft/791m

Valley Base: Bassenthwaite, Lorton Vale.
Town Base: Keswick.
Maps: OS OD4, The English Lakes –
North West. L90 Penrith & Keswick.
Length: 3.75miles/6km.
Ascent: 1705ft/520m.
Approx Time: 2.5hrs.
Start & Finish: Car park in Hospital
Plantation Forest (opposite side of the
B5292 to the Visitors' Centre) above
Grisedale Gill, Whinlatter Pass
(NY 209242).
Difficulty: A straightforward outing, gen-
erally on good paths. Grisedale Pike and
her ridges are rocky and exposed offering
little possibility of shelter.

With the advantage of starting at the 300m contour this is an uncomplicated and direct way to reach the summit of Grisedale Pike.

Take the track beneath the car park, crossing the stream and rising to a junction. Bear right for a short way until an overgrown track rises to the left. This continues onto open fell, leaving the forest to climb the heathery slopes above Black Crag.

Along the north ridge of Grisedale Pike the path reaches the first of three cairns on Hobcarton End. The other two cairns lay beyond a post and wire fence which is crossed via a stile. The middle cairn, although the least substantial, stands at the highest point.

To the right, up the Vale of Hobcarton stands Hopegill Head. The black and rather awesome looking cliffs of Hobcarton Crag lie below.

From the col the ascent gradually steepens. You then join the line of the ruined wall which ascends the north east ridge to the summit of Grisedale Pike, an airy exposed top with its cairn standing astride a saddle of rock, which offers only limited shelter from the frequent winds which buffet this peak.

Head east from the summit down the east ridge. The route is not obvious from above and a compass bearing may be necessary in bad weather. However, the path soon becomes well defined. Steep throughout, there are a few steps where special care is needed.

The ridge eases to a rounded shoulder over Sleet How. The route bears left until brought to a halt by the forestry fence of the Hospital Plantation. The name comes from when Lakeland View beside Whinlatter Pass used to be an isolation hospital for contagious diseases.

Drop down to the left beside the fence where a vague path descends through thick heather. On reaching the base of Grisedale Valley bear left. Cross the gill to find a gate leading through the fence and onto a forest track. Once on this track bear right, cross a little bridge and follow the track directly back to the car park.

On Grisedale Pike North Ridge with Hobcarton End in the background.

Down Grisedale Pike's East Ridge.

•GR12•

GRISEDALE PIKE BY THE EAST RIDGE

Kinn 1227ft/374m
Grisedale Pike 2593ft/791m
Hobcarton Head 2425ft/739m

Valley Base: Bassenthwaite.
Town Base: Keswick.
Maps: OS OD4, The English Lakes –
North West. L90 Penrith & Keswick.
Length: 6.5miles/10.5km.
Ascent: 2085ft/635m.
Approx Time: 3.5hrs.
Start & Finish: Car park available in the
old sand pit by the side of the B5292
Whinlatter Pass Road just above
Braithwaite Village. (NY 227237)
Difficulty: Generally straightforward and
on good paths throughout. However,
Grisedale Pike is an exposed mountain
offering little shelter and the final section
of the east ridge is steep with a number of
little rocky steps.

The long aesthetic line of its east ridge
takes a high profile and is understandably
the most popular way to tackle the might
of Grisedale Pike. Linking this with the
descent, first to Coledale Hause, then
down to Force Crag Mine and back along
the Coledale Valley, provides an excellent
circular outing.

A path climbs the flanks of the hill to
the right of the parking area. It offers a
gentler approach than the more direct
route which climbs from the elbow in the
bend of the road below. Once the shoulder is gained, it gives a straightforward
ascent over the gentle top of Kinn. Pass
the natural spring of Lanty Well to the
left. Steeper ground leads to the shoulder
of Sleet How. The final section of the east
ridge steepens to the pyramidal head of
Grisedale Pike.

Pass the summit cairn and descend the
south west shoulder. Rise over the elevation which I have called Hobcarton Head
(it is unnamed on the OS). This distinct
top, with Hobcarton Crag below to the
right, is commonly mistaken for Sand

Hill. Sand Hill lies beyond but could also
be included in this round.

Before the levelling off, follow a good
path down to the left which leads diagonally down the hillside to Coledale
Hause. (From here the Coledale Horseshoe climbs the west face of Eel Crag to
top Crag Hill, Sail and Causey Pike.
Allow a minimum of 5hrs for this round.)

Below lies the upper basin of Coledale
with High Force Waterfall plunging into
its depths. Do not be tempted to enter.
Between it and Coledale lies the great
precipice of Force Crag. From the crossroads of Coledale Hause follow the distinct path along the southern edge of the
basin. This picks up a mine track and
leads safely past Force Crag to cross
Coledale Beck below the mine buildings.
(Force Crag Mine, Lakeland's last mineral mine, has been kept open by a group of
enthusiasts.) A great waterfall, Low
Force, plunges down Force Crag. The
barrier of rotten rock is a place best left to
the swooping dive of the peregrine falcon.
Return down Coledale via the mine track.

The tops of Hope Gill Horseshoe, Ladyside Pike, Hopegill Head and Whiteside as seen above Lorton Vale.

·GR13·

HOPE GILL HORSESHOE

Dodd 1489ft/454m
Whiteside – East Top 2359ft/719m
Whiteside – West Top 2319ft/707m
Gasgale Crags 2306ft/703m
Hopegill Head 2525ft/770m
Sand Hill 2480ft/756m
Ladyside Pike 2306ft/703m
Swinside 1670ft/509m

Valley Base: Lorton Vale, Buttermere.
Town Base: Cockermouth.
Maps: OS OD4, The English Lakes –
North West. L90 Penrith & Keswick.
Length: 6miles/9.5km.
Ascent: 2655ft/810m.
Approx Time: 3.5hrs.
Start & Finish: On the open fell side of
the little road above Hopebeck and below
High Swinside Farm. Just above the gate,
an old cutting in the hillside offers parking
space (NY 169242).
Difficulty: The going is a little rough in
places and exposed along the tops. Care
should be taken in descending the rocky
face of Hopegill Head. A walk of no great
technical difficulty.

Hope Gill is a quiet, almost forgotten
place. The steep-sided valley is roughly
clothed in thick heather which rises to the
fine peak of Hopegill Head. Numerous
stone structures, tracks and evidence of
past mining activity suggest that the valley has not always been deserted.

From the road the path skirts the stone
wall before dropping to cross Hope Beck
by the stone sheepfold. Climb to intercept
an ancient grassed track and follow it as it
rises to the left. The path steepens after
passing a ruined building. Shortly after
this bear right, up steep heathery slopes to
the summit cairn of Dodd.

A ridge extends to the col behind,
which is cut off by a craggy end of
exposed Skiddaw slate. Proceed round
this to the right; the col provides a distinct
pass. Descend it to the left to find a vague
path cutting through rough heather and
rising up the ridge above. The going is
never steep and finally leads to the East
Top of Whiteside. This is the highest
point, though the top to the west takes a
higher profile from the valley. Once
regarded as the highest top of Whiteside,
the West Top is worth a visit for the views
extending across the Solway to the
Scottish Hills.

Return to the main top and proceed
along the knife-edged ridge from where
spectacular views are available down
Gasgale Crags to Gasgale Gill. Cross the
flat table top of Gasgale Crags. Descend
into a hollow and then climb to Hopegill
Head. In local circles the distinct peak
below is known as Hobcarton Pike. The
stroll to Sand Hill is simple and offers a
good prospect of Grisedale Pike.

Whiteside and Gasgale Crags viewed from Grasmoor (top) and along the ridge of Whiteside and Gasgale Crags to Hopegill Head (bottom).

A steep descent leads north down the Hopegill Head. This route is initially extremely exposed, with the precipice of Hobcarton Crag off to the right. Things become less hazardous as the path moves away from the edge to descend a stepped rocky slab. When the angle eases, traverse a rocky knoll on the left to gain the line of

an old wall. This leads to Ladyside Pike. Move down the shoulder to the field boundary junction, walk along the left side of the wall and continue to proceed down the shoulder.

The wall soon becomes a fence and the highest point of Swinside lies just to the right. The ancient cairn that once repre-

sented the top of Swinside lies lower and further to the right. To reach this it is necessary to stride the fence. Most walkers will be content to follow the fence directly down to the road lying just above High Swinside Farm.

From here a vague grassy track just above the road leads back to the cutting.

Over Whinlatter Pass and Thornthwaite Forest to the snowy dome of Lord's Seat.

LORD'S SEAT GROUP

• LOS •

Lying between Bassenthwaite Lake and Lorton Vale, and stretching north from Whinlatter Pass to the Vale of Cockermouth, these are the most northerly group of hills within the North Western Fells. Above Bassenthwaite Lake the heights are dominated by a steep impenetrable barrier of conifers. Only the craggy triangular face of Barf stands proud. Above Whinlatter Pass and the Vale of Cockermouth lie steep and uninviting slopes.

The key to their exploration, with the exception of Barf, is by two hidden valleys. Aiken Valley rises above Spout Force

and Whinlatter Pass to penetrate the heart of the main cluster of hills while enchanting Wythop, with its mixture of fellside whin, bracken, green pasture and trees, rises towards Skiddaw.

Three contrasting walks cover all the tops within this group. Walk LOS 1 passes beneath the Bishop of Barf to climb to its summit before continuing to the leader of the group, Lord's Seat. Further on, Ullister Hill leads to the superb viewpoint of Seat How with a return along the tracks of Thornthwaite Forest.

Walk LOS 2 makes a high circuit of the Aiken Valley. Beginning with a traverse

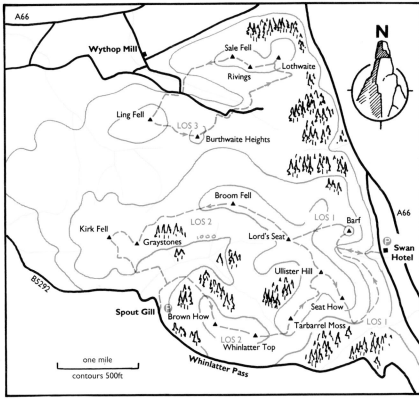

high above Whinlatter Pass to Lord's Seat, you return over Broom Fell and Widow Hause to Graystones and Kirk Fell. With its heady mixture of deserted heathery slopes, pines and far reaching open views this walk has more than a flavour of the distant Scottish hills.

Ling and Sale Fell stand either side of the cross-cut Wythop Valley. Walk LOS 3 begins above the valley base and makes an anticlockwise circuit, dipping back into the valley at midpoint. It is a lovely walk, exploring both dale and fell.

◆LOS 1◆

BISHOP OF BARF TO LORD'S SEAT

Barf 1536ft/468m
Lord's Seat 1811ft/552m
Ullister Hill 1722ft/525m
Seat How 1627ft/496m

Valley Base: Bassenthwaite.
Town Base: Keswick.
Maps: OS OD4, The English Lakes – North West. L90 Penrith & Keswick.
Length: 4miles/6.5km.
Ascent: 1870m/570m.
Approx Time: 2.25hrs.
Start & Finish: Directly beneath Barf, within the community known as Powter How, there is extensive pull-in space by the side of the old A66 opposite the Swan Hotel (NY 220264).
Difficulty: The initial ascent to Barf is energetic, with one craggy section. The going above is boggy in places although there are well-defined paths throughout.

Craggy Barf presents a bold face, free from the conifers which have crept insidiously over the flanks of the fells. This is an attractive walk, offering fine viewpoints and much of interest.

Just behind the pull-in, a surfaced road leads towards Beckstones. Follow the road for a few yards. A kissing gate on the right takes you through a haven of silver birch to the foot of the scree which tumbles from the face of Barf. Above stands the unmistakable figure of the Bishop of Barf (regularly whitewashed, he is locally known as the White Bishop).

The path bears left and crosses the tumbling waters of Beckstones Gill. Climb a stile over a wire fence. The path begins to rise steeply to the right allowing you ample opportunity to visually inspect the White Bishop through the canopy of larch. The Bishop, a natural outcrop of Skiddaw slate and remarkably life-like, stands on a grand plinth at the point he supposedly fell from his horse. Above, the twisted contortions of slate look incredibly unstable. (Indeed, they frequently come crashing down onto the scree below.) As the larch turns to conifer a

craggy outcrop will be encountered. This looks at first rather alarming and care should be exercised. The path follows a natural fault, leading at first right then back left to make a technically easy ascent through the barrier. It emerges onto a forestry track (Junction No. 21).

Bear right to find, in a short distance, a path which leads to a stile over the boundary fence of the forest. After crossing the head of Beckstones Gill the path winds around the face of Barf. It then emerges onto the little rocky perch which constitutes the top, from where there is a

Over the head of Bassenthwaite Lake to Barf.

grand view along Bassenthwaite Lake and over to Skiddaw.

The well-defined path descends into the hollow beyond the summit. It then climbs up to the shoulder which falls from Lord's Seat. As the angle steepens and the final pull to the grassy dome of Lord's Seat begins, the most boggy section of the walk is encountered. The top reveals an extensive vista stretching across the Solway to Criffell.

A swift descent of Lord's Seat's south flank leads to a stile over the boundary fence of Thornthwaite Forest. The Forestry Commission have constructed a splendid path over the bogs and through the heather. Where the path splits (Junction No. 5) take the left fork. After a few yards, a vague path strikes off right climbing through heather to the summit of Ullister Hill.

Descending southwards and now skirting the edge of the conifers, a course through the trees opens to the left. Take the path through this green corridor, which is well maintained by the Forestry Commission. The trees part to reveal the rocky-edged top of Seat How with a panorama over Keswick to Skiddaw, Grisedale Pike, Barf and beyond.

From here, take the path as it descends quickly down the nose of Seat How to meet a broad forestry track. Follow this through the pines to a junction (No. 9) and bear left. The track levels and at a further junction (No. 8) bear right. Descend beneath rock cuttings, with Barf ahead and Skiddaw to the right. This track is the one intercepted by the original footpath which rises beside Beckstones Gill. At Junction No. 21 bear right and descend steeply.

•LOS 2•

LORD'S SEAT CIRCUIT

Brown How – Whinlatter 1696ft/517m
Whinlatter Top 1722ft/525m
Tarbarrel Moss 1617ft/493m
Ullister Hill 1722ft/525m
Lord's Seat 1811ft/552m
Broom Fell 1676ft/511m
Graystones 1496ft/456m
Kirk Fell – Lorton 1437ft/438m

Valley Base: Lorton Vale, Bassenthwaite.
Town Base: Cockermouth, Keswick.
Maps: OS OD4, The English Lakes – North West. L90 Penrith & Keswick.
Length: 6.75miles/11km.
Ascent: 2065ft/630m.
Approx Time: 4hrs.
Start & Finish: Spout Gill Car Park (NY 181256).
Difficulty: Although the path is vague in places, the going is generally straightforward and reasonably level once the initial ascent of Brown How has been made.

Looking westwards from Lord's Seat to Broom Fell and Graystones.

Starting above Spout Force Waterfall this logical circuit around the high, grassy rim of the hidden Aiken Valley makes for a long but worthy outing. Where the forest encroaches upon the high rim of the circuit between Tarbarrel Moss and Lord's Seat, the Forestry Commission have made an excellent system of paths. This is also the case on the ascent to Brown How and descent to Spout Force through Darling How Plantation.

The track leads to the lane of Darling How. Bear right and follow the lane past the farm. Pass through two gates, before a third gate through a stone wall leads to a break in the conifer plantation. Although thickly covered with Corsican pine, the trees stand in parallel lines which allow relatively easy access.

Climb through the pine trees to reach a fence. Bear left along it to find a stile which leads onto a forestry track. Immediately above an avenue sweeps through the trees to emerge through a gap in the fence onto open hillside. The gap is closed by a section of timber-framed fence that can be opened for entry. Ascend the open hillside directly to the top of Brown How.

The summit is marked by a semi-circular stone shelter with an open view to Hobcarton Crags and Grisedale Pike.

A grassy path leads along to the small cairned summit of Whinlatter Top. Descend down the shoulder to the boundary fence of Thornthwaite Forest. The scene of heather, pine and solitude is remarkably reminiscent of the Scottish Highlands. Climb to the cairned top of Tarbarrel Moss and a corner in the fence. A stile leads to a little path falling to the main forestry track. Cross this and bear right along a track. When this splits, bear left until another path breaks off to the right. This skirts the forest to gain a little hollow then rises to the summit of Ullister Hill. A path falls quickly down the heathery shoulder and meets an excellent path. After an extensive boggy area, which is crossed dry by the path, climb to the open grassy shoulder of Lord's Seat. A stile leads to the summit. This, the highest summit north of Whinlatter Pass, lies at the head of the Aiken Valley. Views extend over Keswick and the Solway to Criffell.

A straightforward ridge gives access to Broom Fell. Its summit cairn stands immediately west of the ruinous stone wall which traverses the summit from north to south. The highest point lies slightly south east of the cairn, though few will accept it so. Walk down the shoulder to cross through a gap in the stone wall. Follow the edge of Darling How Plantation over Widow Hause. At the end of the plantation a gate gives access to a grassy track which leads

diagonally up the hillside to the left. Follow this track, first left then right, to an open shoulder. Walk to the left to a cairned grassy bump. This is the north top of Graystones. It provides a good view of the whole circuit walked so far. The true summit lies on a little rocky knoll further to the south.

From the latter continue past an obvious circular pit and rise with the stone wall to a rocky head and junction of stone walls. A stony descent leads to the little col to the west before a gentle ascent to the summit of Kirk Fell, which is marked by a cairn of small stones and a wooden post. From here there is a fine view to Mellbreak. Those wishing to catch a quick glimpse of the Vale of Lorton may proceed west to a cairn.

Move down steep grassy slopes to enter Sware Gill by an old stone wall. Cross the gill and follow a ruined stone wall across the fellside to the edge of Darling How Plantation. Descend directly along its edge until a stile gives access to a forest track. Follow this until a cleared break drops steeply right to the banks of Aiken Beck just above Spout Force. Follow a path on the right until the beck can be crossed. A little section of ascent leads to a fenced-off viewing point for Spout Force. This is rather misplaced. The waterfall, a fine sight, cannot be seen from it. For a better view of the fall (still obstructed by foliage in summer) it is necessary to risk life and limb by descending through the pine to the south. Climb the break above the viewing point to regain the track which leads back to the car park.

•LOS 3•

LING AND SALE FELL ABOVE WYTHOP

Ling Fell 1224ft/373m
Burthwaite Heights 1043ft/318m
Lothwaite 1132ft/345m
Rivings 1099ft/335m
Sale Fell 1178ft/359m

Valley Base: Lorton Vale, Bassenthwaite.
Town Base: Cockermouth.
Maps: OS OD4, The English Lakes – North West. L90 Penrith & Keswick.
Length: 4.25miles/7km.
Ascent: 1560ft/475m.
Approx Time: 2.25hrs.
Start & Finish: An old quarry provides parking space beside the road (leading to Kelswick Farm) above Brumston Bridge in the Wythop Valley (NY 185293).
Difficulty: Although the paths are vague in the early stages, the going is generally good underfoot and there are no technical difficulties.

Standing either side of the timeless little valley of Wythop, these hills represent the northernmost outpost of the North Western Fells.

Follow the road across Brumston Bridge and climb the steep hill which bears right, opposite the buildings of Eskin. The road levels and is joined by two tracks. Take the gate on the right. Join the Old Copse Road across the open hillside, passing a track which merges from the left. A short distance beyond this a vague path leads up through bracken. It follows the edge of a tiny stream which is fed by a small spring that issues from a pile of stones. Above the spring, the path continues up a hollow past a pile of stones to a terrace. Ascend this, passing further piles of stones until it is better to bear left and climb more directly. Pass another terrace which bears a track rising from the right, then walk over a series of natural terraces to the top of Ling Fell. There is a stone trig point and a cairn a little further to the east. This is a good vantage point to view Wordsworth's birthplace – the market town of Cockermouth.

Head straight down the heathery flanks in the direction of Burthwaite Heights to a field with a curved and stepped edge. Beyond, lies a brown, dreary wasteland of 'seers' and bog. A vague path steers south across the moss to the bank of a drainage ditch. Follow this to an iron gate. Beyond the gate proceed along the right bank of another ditch, then continue up the flank of Burthwaite Heights. The gently sloping, grassy table top is highest at its northern edge.

Descend to the east. Join the line of a stone wall and follow it to an iron gate just above the plantation. Move down to a grass track and bear right along it. Pass two huge, ancient sycamore trees. The path ends with two massive hollies and a gate leading on to the surfaced road which runs up the Wythop Valley.

Pass Old Scales Farm and continue up the road to a sign 'Public Bridleway' on the left (the second, there is also one opposite the farm). Follow this (signposted) across the fields to Chapel Wood. The ruins of the old chapel stand to the west. Bear right along the leafy and muddy track. When you leave the wood pass a gate, bearing left then left again when the track splits. Shortly afterwards a smaller track rising diagonally left cuts a well-defined course through the whin bushes. Before reaching a grassy shoulder bear right. Then make a more direct ascent of the hillside, passing through a small

outcrop of Skiddaw slate to reach a long shoulder. Bear right along this to a rocky outcrop which marks the summit of Lothwaite. There is a supreme view to massive Skiddaw, which can be seen climbing majestically from the shores of Bassenthwaite Lake.

To descend, head west back along the shoulder to the ascending track. At a pile of stones (an old quarry) move left up the grassy hillside to the unmarked top of Rivings. The fell is so called, perhaps, because of the scratches in the earth surface hereabouts which mark old quarrying activity.

Head on to the flanks of Sale Fell along a grassy track. Take the opening through two ruined stone walls. This leads to a ridge and small cairn, which marks the summit of Sale Fell. Beyond, a rocky knoll can be seen to have been quarried for Skiddaw slate. Pass over this. Before descending, walk 20 yards to the north to the edge which overlooks the Vale of Cockermouth. Here, the rock pinnacles are not made of Skiddaw slate but an attractive red microgranite.

The path descends centrally down the shoulder, with the flat plain of the west coast lying ahead in the distance. A natural corridor leads between rocky piles of quartz, before you reach a stone wall. Bear left and make a steep descent back to the road and gate above the old quarry.

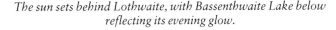

The sun sets behind Lothwaite, with Bassenthwaite Lake below reflecting its evening glow.

3

NORTHERN FELLS

Blencathra Group BLE (13 tops) • Skiddaw Massif SKI (20 tops)
North O'Skiddaw Group NOS (25 tops)

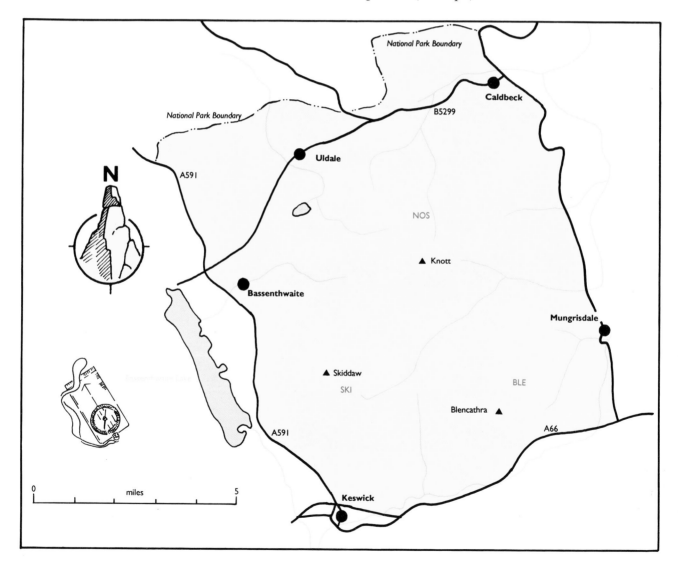

North of Keswick and high above Threlkeld stand two of the most aesthetic and grandest mountains in the Lake District – Blencathra and Skiddaw. Skiddaw is Lakeland's fourth highest mountain, with the main top of High Man standing at 3053ft/931m. Blencathra meanwhile offers Sharp Edge, Lakelands most spectacular and demanding knife-edged ridge. Both are enormously popular, yet behind this impressive face lies a wild expanse of fells which is little known and seldom trod. Notably the Uldale and Caldbeck Fells, which make up the Back O'Skiddaw Group, and are the most northerly fells in the Lake District.

These Northern Fells are bounded by the A66 to the south and the A591 to the west; Mungrisdale and the plains of Eden line the east while Caldbeck and the plains of the Solway extend to the north. The roughly circular concentration of hills lies at the northern end of the Lake District National Park. From their heights you can look south along Derwent Water and north across the Solway into Scotland. In all, this group constitutes some 85 square miles of fells and offers 58 tops.

Three groups of fells are clearly defined. The deep fault corridor of Glenderaterra Beck separates Blencathra from Skiddaw and allows a rare glimpse from the south of Great Calva and the North O'Skiddaw Group. Beyond Skiddaw and Blencathra, Dash Beck runs west and the River Caldew east forming a wide valley that divides the North O'Skiddaw Group.

To the casual tourist Skiddaw appears as a stately and gentle mountain, a legacy of the weathering of her old slates. There is, however, far more to Skiddaw than meets the inexperienced eye, it being a complex massif of 20 individual tops. Likewise, beyond the imposing south face of Blencathra there is unexpected depth extending to Souther and Bowscale Fell, to Bannerdale Crags, and even to Little Eycott Hill.

Of the hills, Knott in the North O'Skiddaw Group forms the highest point, offering a central advantage over the fells. Visually, it is hard to penetrate this wilderness area of rolling grass and dark heather north of Dash and Caldew. Further exploration, however, reveals Carrock Fell which is topped by a large hill fort; and, with their igneous intrusion into the slate, a richness and variety of minerals that was once said by Wordsworth to be 'worth all England else'. Not forgetting Binsey beyond the main group, with the one-time home of John Peel lying below.

AREA FACT SHEET

THE VALLEY BASES
Bassenthwaite
Camping: Traffords in Bassenthwaite village, Gaskells near Lane Foot Farm at Thornthwaite.
Youth Hostel: None.
Inns: The Sun in Bassenthwaite Village, The Swan Hotel and The Pheasant Inn.
Bus Services: Keswick to Cockermouth, Keswick to Carlisle.
Borrowdale
Camping: Seathwaite Farm, Thorneythwaite Farm, Rosthwaite, Stonethwaite, Ashness Farm, Dalt Wood – Grange.
Youth Hostels: Longthwaite, Honister Hause, Barrow House.

Inns: The Scafell Hotel.
Bus Services: Keswick to Seatoller.
Mungrisdale
Camping: None. Camping barn in Mungrisdale.
Youth Hostel: Carrock Fell at Hesket Newmarket.
Inns: Old Crown Inn, Hesket Newmarket.
Bus Services: Carlisle to Caldbeck (School Bus Service).
Threlkeld
Camping: Burns Farm, Setmabanning.
Youth Hostel: Skiddaw House.
Inns: Horse & Farrier, White Horse Inn by A66.
Bus Services: Keswick to Penrith.

THE TOWN BASES
Cockermouth
Camping: Graysonside Farm and Violet Bank.
Youth Hostel: Double Mills.
All facilities except railway station.
Keswick
Camping: The Headlands, Derwent Water, Castlerigg Hall and Castlerigg Farm.
Youth Hostel: Keswick.
All facilities except railway station.

Blencathra over St John's in the Vale.

BLENCATHRA GROUP

·BLE·

The magic of Blencathra, with her frontal ridges soaring from Threlkeld to intercept a finely arched skyline, is plain for all to see. It is often unappreciated, however, that beyond the dipping high shoulder of Saddleback (Blencathra's alternative name) she is connected to a rarely visited horseshoe of hills.

Between the hamlets of Mungrisdale and Bowscale, a narrow entrance guards the secretive valley of Bannerdale. This secluded area is split by The Tongue and encircled by Bowscale Fell, Bannerdale Crags and Souther Fell. The River Glenderamackin snakes through all four points of the compass. First it runs beneath Atkinson Pike, then turns into

Bannerdale. It then turns again in Mungrisdale, before finally heading west beneath the end of Souther Fell and along the Threlkeld Valley.

Eycott Hill stands on the eastern edge of the National Park Boundary overlooking Bannerdale. Walk BLE 1 examines its attractive green rocks, known as the 'Eycott Hill Lavas'. These prove to be quite different to those of the Skiddaw slates which make up the remainder of the group. Bowscale Fell is covered by two walks. Walk BLE 2 rises from Bowscale hamlet to cut across the fell via Bowscale Tarn before descending The Tongue into Bannerdale. Rising and ending at Mungrisdale, Walk BLE 3 provides a great horseshoe around wild, deserted

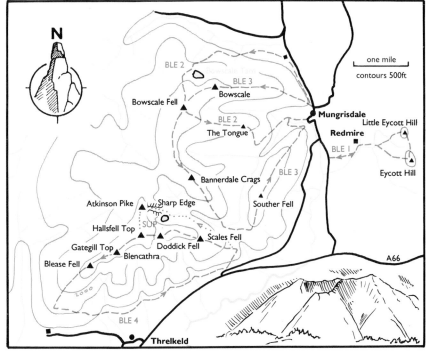

Bannnerdale. Taking in both tops of Bowscale Fell and Bannerdale Crags, it makes a full traverse along the top of Souther Fell, which according to local legend if visited on midsummer's day may also be occupied by the ghosts of a long deceased army.

Buttressed by Blease Fell to the west and Scales Fell to the east, the south face

of Blencathra is a grand sight. Three truncated fells, Gategill Fell, Hallsfell and Doddick Fell, taper from their broad bases to rise as slim ridges. To the north east and climbing centrally between the steep rocks of Tarn Crags and Foule Crags lies Sharp Edge, Lakelands' most difficult ridge. Walk BLE 4 encircles the entire south face of Blencathra, topping all the aforementioned fells in the process before returning beneath the foot of the mountain. The supplement Walk BLE 4A climbs Sharp Edge to reach the top of Atkinson Pike (also known as Foule Crag). It then continues along the saddle to Hallsfell Top which marks the summit of Blencathra. In contrast, north of Blencathra is a rolling expanse of grassland and bog known as Mungrisdale Common. This falls unexcitingly to the River Caldew.

• BLE I •

EYCOTT HILL

Eycott Hill 1132ft/345m
Little Eycott Hill 1099ft/335m

Valley Base: Threlkeld, Mungrisdale.
Town Base: Keswick.
Maps: OS Pathfinder 576 & OS OD5, The English Lakes – North East. L90 Penrith & Keswick.
Length: 3miles/5km.
Ascent: 490ft/150m.
Approx Time: 1.75hrs.
Start & Finish: By the side of the Mungrisdale Road the verge allows limited parking opposite a stile and signpost 'Public Footpath' (NY 368295). The track to Redmire Farm lies just beyond in the direction of Mungrisdale.
Difficulty: Straightforward, although Naddles Beck must be crossed and it is a little boggy on the open fell.

Lying east and very much in the shadow of the Blencathra Group, Eycott Hill could not be called grand. However, despite a bland appearance from below, hidden charms await. A fine view to Souther and Bowscale Fells and the saddle of Saddleback is one. A wilderness which belies the ease of access is another. To geologists she is quite famous, particularly

The unusual stone slab bridge over Barrow Beck, taken en route to Eycott Hill.

for her wonderfully green coloured crystalline volcanic rocks, known as the Eycott Hill Lavas.

Climb the stile over the fence and cross the field, following the fence line to a further stile/gate. Continue by the wall to Barrow Beck and a marvellous stone bridge. The bridge is made from a single slab of rock that has a slight natural arch. Some 12ft in length, 3ft wide and 4in thick, this stone slab is the longest such single span bridge this author knows of in the Lake District.

Cross the bridge and bear left along the river bank, to a gate in a stone wall. Continue along the bank to the track just below the barn of Westing (now in a ruined condition). Cross this track by the end of a bridge. Continue to a small gate which gives access to a field. Walk through the field by the bank of Barrow Beck, crossing a narrow side stream by a ruined stone slab bridge. At the top of the field the wall is broken away and there is open access to the fellside. Cross Naddles Beck and strike a line up the hillside. There is no path and initially the going is

a little boggy through long grass and rushes. Rise to the spine of a long rock ridge. Cross the boggy canyon behind and continue up to a level plateau beneath some craggy outcrops. Walk directly up the steeper ground above to the summit of Eycott Hill. Evidence of past quarrying activity is now obscure, but many of the exposed rocks have been chipped by the geologist's hammer.

Strike a line due north, passing a little walled bield (in ruins) before descending into the dip and crossing the stream. Above stand three little tops. The middle one, fringed with small crags, is Little Eycott Hill. Beneath the furthest one there is a tiny ruined building made from beautiful green rock. On banging a stone against the old lintel (do not damage it) note the musical chime. Long ago in Victorian times the brittle 'singing' rocks of Eycott Hill were used to construct a type of xylophone.

Descend the hillside, avoiding the rocky bluffs until it can be traversed to pick up the line of ascent and crossing of Naddles Beck.

BOWSCALE FELL BY BOWSCALE TARN

Bowscale Fell 2305ft/702m
The Tongue 1814ft/553m

Valley Base: Threlkeld, Mungrisdale.
Town Base: Keswick.
Maps: OS Pathfinder 576 & OS OD5, The English Lakes – North East. L90 Penrith & Keswick.
Length: 5.5miles/9km.
Ascent: 1525ft/465m.
Approx Time: 3hrs.
Start & Finish: Bowscale, limited parking by the roadside (NY 358317).
Difficulty: Generally the going is straightforward and on well-defined paths. A short section of road walking is involved.

In days gone by Bowscale Tarn was a considerable tourist attraction. It is set high on the mountain's side and trapped by

Looking from Bowscale Fell's East Ridge to The Tongue.

Looking over Mungrisdale into Bannerdale; Bannerdale Crags stand above, Blencathra's saddleback beyond.

moraine in its ice-carved basin. This walk ascends Bowscale Fell from Bowscale via Bowscale Tarn and descends The Tongue into Bannerdale.

Where the road enters the village and narrows to make a tight turn through the buildings, a path turns off to the left. Beyond the gate it rises easily to the tarn. Above to the right, a grassy rake cuts through the steep rocky basin to exit onto the shoulder above Tarn Crags. An easy ascent leads first to a cairn then to a ruined stone shelter, which marks the top of Bowscale Fell.

The steep northern end of Blencathra, Atkinson Pike, looks most impressive from here. The view to the right of it extends to the distant Western Fells, and includes Pillar and Red Pike.

A gentle slope descends before rising again to the highest point of The Tongue. A path leads down to the right, along the edge of its craggy eastern face. You join a track by an old stone bield. Bear left along the track and cross Bullfell Beck where it joins the River Glenderamackin. Pass some houses and join the road by a telephone kiosk in Mungrisdale. Follow this past the Church and back to Bowscale.

•BLE 3•

BANNERDALE HORSESHOE

East Top – Bowscale Fell 2185ft/666m
Bowscale Fell 2305ft/702m
Bannerdale Crags 2240ft/683m
Souther Fell 1713ft/522m

Valley Base: Threlkeld, Mungrisdale.
Town Base: Keswick.
Maps: OS Pathfinder 576 & OS OD5, The English Lakes – North East. L90 Penrith & Keswick.
Length: 6.75miles/11km.
Ascent: 2395ft/730m.
Approx Time: 3.75hrs.
Start & Finish: Mungrisdale, verge parking near the road junction (NY 364306).
Difficulty: A reasonably straightforward walk mainly on grassy paths, though a little boggy in places. A sign in the field at the foot of Souther Fell reads 'Keep Out'. So detour over the River Glenderamackin, which can be dangerous in spate conditions.

This round of Bowscale Fell and Bannerdale highlights the contrast between the craggier face of these Northern Fells and their gentler more rolling regions.

Above the road junction in the direction of Bowscale, take the gated track to the left of the quarry – now housing a Water Authority building. Just past the quarry, a small path rises to the right directly up the hillside. Initially the path is vague, though the route through the gorse and bracken is quite clear. Above, hill grass predominates and the ascent proves quite sublime.

A small rise (unnamed but cairned) leads to the higher cairned East Top of Bowscale Fell. Descend to the dip before rising again, passing first a cairn then a ruined stone shelter which marks the summit of Bowscale Fell. The Skiddaw slate has been changed here to resemble pumice stone.

Aim south and descend the broad grassy shoulder until it begins to level. At this point bear left to pick up a well-defined sheep trod which traverses the rim of Bannerdale Crags. This provides a splendid view down the craggy slopes, which in their less precipitous climes are

Above Threlkeld lies Blencathra's South Face with the snow clad tops of Blease Fell, Gategill Fell, Hallsfell and Doddick Fell set against a blue sky.

populated with silver birch and heather. A broad slab of rock sweeps up from a steep, dark gully before the path ascends to a gravestone-shaped cairn. Note the dramatic profile of Bannerdale Crag's east ridge just beyond. The cairn, despite appearances, is of some antiquity. Graffiti alone dates it to 1850, but the reference to 'Curricks' on the 6in OS map indicates it to be much older; for a 'Currick' is an early Bronze Age burial chamber from around 2000 BC. The summit actually lies a little way to the west and is marked by a pile of large flat slates. These rocks are flecked with thin needle-like crystals and are known as Chiastolite Slate. From here the view of Sharp Edge is quite stunning. Set centrally between the steep crags of two glaciated combes, it resembles not a ridge offering a popular walk but an alpine pillar of formidable difficulty.

Drop down the grassy shoulder over the steeper lower slopes, known as White Horse Bent. Cross a grassed track leading to the wooden footbridge over the River Glenderamackin. Rise up the track to Mousthwaite Col then bear left. A vague path up the grassed fellside forms the southern shoulder of Souter Fell. This leads to a substantial circular cairn topped by a rock of white quartz. Strike a line over the level top of the fell to a single rock on a tiny outcrop. This is the highest point of Souter Fell.

Continue, losing height gradually, to the northern edge of the summit plateau, then fall more steeply down the nose. Beyond a stone wall and little field, a gate opens onto the road opposite The Mill Inn in Mungrisdale. Unfortunately, a sign on the wall (once taken by a stile) says 'Keep Out'. So make a detour along the wall to the left until it turns in the direction of the winding River Glenderamackin. Cross the river, hopping the most convenient boulders (only possible in dry conditions) to gain the track which leads into Mungrisdale by the telephone kiosk.

•BLE 4•

BLENCATHRA

Scales Fell 2238ft/682m
Doddick Fell Top 2434ft/742m
Hallsfell Top – Blencathra 2847ft/868m
Gategill Fell Top 2792ft/851m
Blease Fell 2638ft/804m

Valley Base: Threlkeld.
Town Base: Keswick.
Maps: OS OD5, The English Lakes – North East. L90 Penrith and Keswick.
Length: 6miles/9.5km.
Ascent: 2295ft/700m.
Approx Time: 3.5hrs.
Start & Finish: Lay-by along the A66 above Threlkeld (NY 339267).
Difficulty: Good paths prevail, although invariably the ascent requires sustained effort.

This route makes a grand tour of Blencathra's south face, and includes all of her tops save that of Atkinson Pike (which could be included with little further effort).

Pass the roadside cottage and bear left rising to open fellside. A path cut deep through the grass and bracken rises diagonally across the hillside to the right. Climbing the craggy edge above Mousthwaite Comb, the path splits. Go left up the grassy shoulder of Scales Fell. The second and higher hump constitutes the summit of this, Blencathra's most easterly fell. Skirt the rim of the upper bowl feeding Scales Beck and ascend to the rocky head of Doddick Fell. Continue up the shoulder to Hallsfell Top, the summit of Blencathra. The view is extensive and very fine indeed.

The south westerly traverse along the edge of the south face includes the distinct rise of Gategill Fell Top. The most westerly top reached is Blease Fell. The going, over small shingly Skiddaw slates or close cropped turf, proves flat and easy. A straightforward descent down the grassy shoulder leads to a distinct track which cuts a course diagonally east down the hillside. The path is followed to a stone wall before descending directly down to the fell wall. Bear left along the marked path, which traverses the hillside above the fell wall. In turn, cross Gate Gill, Doddick Gill and Scales Beck before finding the opening back to the A66.

•BLE 4A•

BLENCATHRA BY SHARP EDGE

(A SUPPLEMENT TO WALK BLE 4)

Atkinson Pike 2772ft/845m

Additional Length: 0.5miles/1km.
Additional Ascent: 165ft/50m.
Additional Approx Time: 0.5hr.
Start: Where the path splits above Mousthwaite Comb (NY 343276).
Finish: Hallsfell Top, the summit of Blencathra (NY 323277).
Difficulty: This route climbs Sharp Edge, which is a popular route but by far the most demanding ridge in the Lake District. If taken along its crest it can be classified as a mild scramble. This is technically not too difficult yet extremely exposed and polished. A path just below the crest to the north is easier.

Sharp Edge is possibly the most popular way to ascend Blencathra. It is certainly the most exciting. In anything other than perfect conditions an ascent of Sharp Edge should be considered as a mountaineering expedition. The rocks are slippery and extremely exposed; a slip would have disastrous consequences.

Bear right above Mousthwaite Comb and traverse the hillside to join Scales Beck. The path here is well defined. Climb to Scales Tarn then bear right. (Alternatively, if at this point Sharp Edge proves too daunting bear left to take a path rising above the tarn to Hallsfell Top.) A stony climb leads to the ridge of Sharp Edge. Traversing the crest needs a cool head. There is a section that involves crossing a polished slab (lethal in the wet or if verglassed) where a sense of balance is essential because there are no handholds. Below to the north lies an easier path, but this too is exposed. Towards the end of the ridge the ground steepens and it is best to follow a chimney groove just right of the edge. When blocked by snow or ice even this weakness can prove tough going.

Finally, the angle falls back and Atkinson Pike is reached. Easy going into the trough and up to Hallsfell Top leads to the actual saddle of 'Saddleback' – the alternative name for Blencathra.

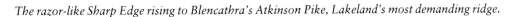

The razor-like Sharp Edge rising to Blencathra's Atkinson Pike, Lakeland's most demanding ridge.

Alpenglow illuminates the Skiddaw Massif to perfection.

SKIDDAW MASSIF

·SKI·

Skiddaw smiles inscrutably like a goddess above Derwent Water. She is a sacred mountain of evocative curvature and balanced symmetry. Her head rises centrally, the summit ridge of High Man appearing as a volcanic cone. Beneath stretch long shoulders, each constructed from a series of graceful arcs. Carl Side, Long Side and Ullock Pike stand to the west; Low Man, Jenkin Hill and Lonscale Fell to the east. At her feet lie the loving cubs of Dodd and Latrigg.

Skiddaw's summit ridge is substantial and runs from the South Top over Middle Top to High Man, ending with North Top. It declines as a broad shoulder over Broad End before dividing into Bakestall and Cockup. Between this ridge and that of her western shoulder lies the hidden basin of Southerndale. On her north eastern flanks two further ridges rise from the remote climes of the Caldew Valley. These include the tops of Hare Crag and Sale How.

One penalty for Skiddaw's instant panorama over Keswick and for being the fourth highest mountain in the Lake District is popularity. The main tourist route, which rises from the high car park behind Latrigg over Jenkin Hill and behind Low Man to the summit ridge, is a veritable motorway. That is not to say that this walk is not worthy but there are other ways to explore Skiddaw.

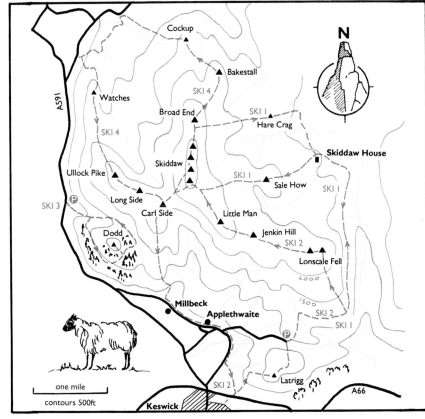

Walk SKI 1 starts from the car park, then traverses right using the deep fault rift of the Glenderaterra Valley to reach Skiddaw House and Back O'Skiddaw. From here the ridge of Sale How is climbed and that of Hare Crag descended to traverse the length of the summit ridge.

Of course, little Latrigg is a hill in her own right. The Greater Traverse of Skiddaw, Walk SKI 2, makes the traditional start from Keswick to first ascend Latrigg before climbing directly to the prominent upturn of Lonscale Pike. The eastern shoulder, topped by Low Man, leads to the summit ridge. Descent is made to Carl Side and down the White Stones ridge.

Dodd, with its unruly collection of conifers, is treated as a separate entity. Walk SKI 3 makes a circuitous route through its forest. This route offers a considerable contrast with the open grass, heather and slate scree which clads the rest of Skiddaw.

Walk SKI 4 makes a high horseshoe around hidden Southerndale. Shapely Ullock Pike and Longside Edge form a sharply defined ridge. This is taken in ascent before Carlside is crossed and a steep climb made to Skiddaw's summit plateau. Finally, Bakestall and Cockup are taken in descent.

Looking along the track to lonely Skiddaw House, now a Youth Hostel.

◆SKI 1◆

SKIDDAW BY SKIDDAW HOUSE

Sale How 2185ft/666m
South Top – Skiddaw 3034ft/925m
Middle Top – Skiddaw 3044ft/928m
High Man – Skiddaw 3053ft/931m
North Top – Skiddaw 3024ft/922m
Hare Crag 1765ft/538m

Valley Base: Borrowdale, Bassenthwaite, Threlkeld.
Town Base: Keswick.
Maps: OS Pathfinder 576. OS OD4, The English Lakes – North West. L90 Penrith & Keswick.
Length: 11miles/18km (3.5miles/5.5km to Skiddaw House).
Ascent: 2130ft/650m (605ft/185m to Skiddaw House).
Approx Time: 4.5hrs (1.25hrs to Skiddaw House).
Start & Finish: Latrigg car park (NY 281254). Alternatively, Skiddaw House (NY 287291), now a Youth Hostel, can be used as the base (reached by walking from Latrigg car park as described).
Difficulty: Straightforward as described, though the remote nature of Back O'Skiddaw should be noted.

This walk follows the old packhorse route to Skiddaw House and climbs 'Back O'Skiddaw', exploring a very different mountain to that most commonly viewed. To take in the full atmosphere and break up the expedition, a stay at Skiddaw House is recommended.

Turn left from the head of the small car park, following the main tourist route up Skiddaw. Turn left again onto the shoulder. Almost immediately, a grassed track bears off to the right. However, a little higher up the tourist route stands the 'Shepherd's Memorial'. This attractive stone is inscribed with a simple yet moving verse:

Great shepherd of thy heavenly flock,
These men have left our hill.
Their feet were on the living rock,
Oh guide and bless them still.

Pass the memorial to find a grass track which zigzags steeply down and joins the

Skiddaw's Lonscale Pike stands above the great corridor of Glenderaterra.

Proceed north, passing the little cairn which marks the North Top, and drop to the north col. (Or missing out Hare Hill, you can return by taking the tourist route directly to Latrigg car park – allow 1.25hrs.) Bear right, making an easy descent down the shoulder of Blake Hill to Hare Hill. A swathe through the thick heather extends across Dead Beck directly to the road leading to Skiddaw House.

•SK12•

SKIDDAW – THE GREATER TRAVERSE

Latrigg 1207ft/368m
Lonscale Pike 2306ft/703m
Lonscale Fell 2344ft/715m
Jenkin Hill 2411ft/735m
Lesser Man – Skiddaw 2674ft/815m
Little Man – Skiddaw 2837ft/865m
South Top – Skiddaw 3034ft/925m
Middle Top – Skiddaw 3044ft/928m
High Man – Skiddaw 3053ft/931m
Carl Side 2447ft/746m

Valley Base: Threlkeld, Borrowdale, Bassenthwaite.
Town Base: Keswick.
Maps: OS OD4, The English Lakes – North West. L90 Penrith & Keswick.
Length: 10miles/16km.
Ascent: 3675ft/1120m.
Approx Time: 5.5hrs.
Start & Finish: At the end of Spooney Green Lane, behind Briar Rigg housing estate, Keswick (NY 268241). A wide verge allows restricted parking; no vehicular access up the lane.
Difficulty: A long, high mountain walk. The terrain varies from rough and stony to smooth and grassy, although the going is generally straightforward. There are a number of steep ascents and one long steep descent.

track just before it crosses the Beck. Continue along the track over a gate/stile to round the corner and enter the great fault corridor of Glenderaterra Beck.

This deep ravine, with crags above the path and steep ground below, is a place of considerable atmosphere. Often a cold north wind whistles through here, making for a stark contrast to the sunny and gentle climes of Skiddaw's southerly aspect. As the route progresses, bleached white spoil and other evidence of ancient mining activity will be detected. As the track makes a stony descent an old quarry can be observed above, before a large combe opens to the left. Cross the stream which issues from it by a small wooden footbridge. In front stands the shoulder of Burnt Horse and a little further on numerous ruined buildings.

After a gate/stile the corridor opens into the Caldew Valley and the area known as Skiddaw Forest. Heather abounds here, but only a few trees are evident. Meanwhile, Great Calva stands across the way. The feeling of openness and space generated by this meeting of valleys amid the mountains feels like that of a great Scottish Glen. Ahead of the path a larch plantation can be seen with a few ruined buildings beneath. After crossing a wooden footbridge over Salehow Beck, Skiddaw House becomes visible on the edge of the larches.

To the right of the plantation a grassy path leads up to Sale How. Beyond the highest point is a little bump with a cairn. From the col beyond continue up the flanks of Skiddaw to intercept the main tourist path. Bear right to cross a wire fence. The path leads to the stony summit ridge of Skiddaw, then traverses South Top and Middle Top before reaching the large shelter and trig point of High Man – the summit of Skiddaw. The scene is breathtaking.

This walk follows the traditional route to Latrigg and Skiddaw, shunning the high car park behind Latrigg. Proceed up Spooney Green Lane – signposted 'Public Bridleway Skiddaw'. This takes the

Skiddaw looms over peaceful Derwent Water.

bridge over the A66, passing a gate by a house. Continue up the hill through a further gate until a lane branches off to the right. At this point, marked by two stone gateposts, a path climbs directly up the hillside skirting the edge of the larch wood. This straightforward if strenuous ascent offers an excellent view of Skiddaw. The highest little rocky knoll that you reach marks the summit of Latrigg.

Continue along the dyke, traversing the rim of the hill. On reaching a stone wall bear left. At the end of the wall a stile leads down to a track on the right which is followed to the head of the car park. Turn right and follow the avenue between the wall on the left and the wire fence on the right to meet a kissing gate and the open shoulder. Bear right on the track, crossing Whit Beck, to the stile/gate running down the edge of Lonscale Fell. Climb left along the fence to follow the edge of Lonscale Crags directly to the little upturned point of Lonscale Pike. Walk across the shoulder to the summit cairn of Lonscale Fell.

Continue to a ruined wall and fence. Take the gate on the right and proceed along the shoulder, following the fence. Rise again until the going slackens. A cairn marking the flat top of Jenkin Hill stands over the fence to the right. It is necessary to stride the fence to reach it, but just beyond there is an old iron gate taken by the main tourist track. After crossing the line of the fence bear left. Climb steeply, first to Lesser Man then up to the final rocky top of Low Man. The prospect over Derwent Water from here is one of the finest in Lakeland. Indeed, this is generally regarded as one of the best viewpoints over the Lake District.

Suitably invigorated, descend to the col with the fence line to your right. Ascend directly to join the main tourist route at the end of the main ridge of Skiddaw. South Top and Middle Top lead in turn to High Man, its shelter and trig point marking the summit of Skiddaw. To the west of the trig point stands a circular 'Silver Jubilee' plaque which serves to identify some of the tops to be seen

from here. The view from this point is extensive in all directions.

Return to the cairn of Middle Man, then bear right to pick up a well-defined path which makes a diagonal descent over the screes of the western flank. At the col by Carlside Tarn, bear left. Ascend to the broad summit and cairn of Carl Side. The rough stony path leads down the shoulder to the remarkable White Stones. This massive outcrop of pure white quartz, gently coloured by grey and green lichens, offers a good view to Little Man to the east and Dodd to the west. Cross an old wall and the craggy Doups before a stile leaves the brackened hillside. Field grass leads to a little lane beside a house.

Bear left along the surfaced road through Applethwaite, rising to turn right at the junction by the hotel. Now descend the road past Birkett Wood Farm until on the left a sign 'Public Footpath' points through a kissing gate. Follow the path through the fields to round the house beside Spooney Green Lane. Re-join the original track back to the start.

•SKI3•

DODD

Dodd 1647ft/502m

Valley Base: Bassenthwaite.
Town Base: Keswick.
Maps: OS OD4, The English Lakes –
North West. L90 Penrith & Keswick.
Length: 3miles/5km.
Ascent: 1610ft/490m.
Approx Time: 2hrs.
Start & Finish: Dodd Wood car park, by
The Old Sawmill tea room (NY 235281),
above the A591 Keswick to
Bassenthwaite road.
Difficulty: A straightforward outing.

The ascent of Dodd is largely afforested.
A mix of coniferous trees and a smatter-
ing of deciduous make this particular
walk enjoyable, ideally a pleasant family
or short day outing. Above the building of
The Old Sawmill and to the right of Skill
Beck a series of steps lead up through the
forest. Climb these and the path beyond,
to gain a forest track. Continue up this to
a junction and bear right.

About 25yds on a path cuts off
through the forest on the left beside a
green marker post. This climbs steeply at
first through dark conifers until levelling
of and swinging right to traverse the face
of the hillside. Here the forest becomes
more varied and open with oak, beech
and Scots pine. Rising again the path
intercepts another forestry road. Continue in the same direction across the junction, to join a forestry track which
ascends to the right. This steepens and
begins to zigzag until at a col on the
southern shoulder of Dodd a sign reads
'Dodd Summit 300m'.

Follow the steepening path to the left.
Enter the summit group of trees by a steep
rocky knoll. After first levelling the path
rises again to the summit cairn of Dodd. A
little outcrop of Skiddaw slate and a
memorial stone are surrounded mainly
by conifers. Move forward to a little
clearing above the western face for the
best view over Bassenthwaite Lake.

Take the same path back to the col and
turn left along the track. This passes
beneath the craggy shoulder of Long
Doors. At the time of writing, due to tree
felling, this offers an excellent view over
Keswick and Derwent Water. The path
falls to a larger forest road. Descend this,
bearing right at the junction. Continue
down the track, bearing left at a further
junction to keep Skill Beck on the left. A
little further a marker post indicates a
path which breaks off to the left. This contours back to a wooden footbridge over
the beck. From here the path, continues to
a forestry track. Descend this to find the
original junction about 200 yards on, and
Find the steps back to The Old Sawmill.

Skiddaw above the shore of Bassenthwaite Lake; Dodd is the lowest tree clad protuberance.

The final slopes leading to the summit of Dodd.

• S K 1 4 •

ULLOCK PIKE AND LONGSIDE EDGE TO SKIDDAW

Watches 1093ft/333m
Ullock Pike 2270ft/692m
Long Side 2408ft/734m
Carl Side 2447ft/746m
Middle Top – Skiddaw 3044ft/928m
High Man – Skiddaw 3053ft/931m
North Top – Skiddaw 3024ft/922m
Broad End 2726ft/831m
Bakestall 2208ft/673m
Cockup 1657ft/505m

Valley Base: Bassenthwaite.
Town Base: Cockermouth, Keswick.
Maps: OS Pathfinder 576 & OS OD4, The English Lakes – North West. L90 Penrith & Keswick.
Length: 6.75miles/11km.
Ascent: 3330ft/1015m.
Approx Time: 4hrs.
Start & Finish: Lay-by (NY 237311) at the side of the Orthwaite Road a little beyond the junction of the A591 above Bassenthwaite Village.
Difficulty: A generally straightforward high-mountain route on well-defined paths.

The curved spur of Ullock Pike and Longside Edge rising to Carl Side maintains a high profile over Bassenthwaite Lake. Just above the lay-by a sign reads 'Public Bridleway'. Take the stile and follow the path/track leftwards over the stream until a zigzag can be made to the right. The grassed track, initially lined by ancient thorns on the uphill side, leads across the field and rises to a stile/gate.

On passing through the gate bear right off the track. Ascend the field by the wall to a narrow gate through the fell wall. This leads onto the toe of the edge. Ascend this directly to the distinctive summit of Watches.

Beyond the summit look for a strange area of block-like pinnacles. This outcrop of igneous rock among the Skiddaw slates gives the appearance of once being quarried. Pass this and the dark slate again takes over. Numerous rises are ascended before the going steepens to the shapely cone of Ullock Pike, which has dominated the scene from below. However, this is not the true summit of the pike. A twin top proves to be the significantly higher Ullock Pike.

Longside Edge ascends to the rocky top of the ridge known as Long Side. Steep broken crags sweep down to the head of Southerndale on one side while a fine open prospect across Bassenthwaite Valley lies on the other. After a short

descent, the path rises up the grassy flanks of Carl Side. At the high point, strike rightwards across the summit plateau to find the cairned top of Carl Side.

Follow a well-defined path down to the col and tarn. A diagonal path then rises to the left across the great scree flanks. This emerges on the summit shoulder of Skiddaw by the cairn/shelter of Middle Man. Continue north along the summit ridge to High Man – the highest top of Skiddaw. Descend north to find the little cairn of the North Top then a col,

before rising to the plateau of Broad End. Despite numerous little cairns the actual top is illusive. Bear right and follow the line of the wire fence down the shoulder to the top of Bakestall. Dead ahead and below are Dead Crags. To the right, Birkett Edge falls to the Dash Falls (named Whitewater Dash on OS Map).

Our route, despite the magnetism of Birkett Edge, lies to the left. Descend the flanks and cross Dead Beck above the trees and the old mine entrance. Then head out onto the summit of Cockup.

Near the edge of Cockup Gill find an ancient track which leads to a gate through the fell wall. The path leads on down through the field following the line of the wall.

Cross through a gate and follow a track. Just before the road, bear left to take another track. This passes Mill Beck and rises to a field with an old pit to the right. A gate on the left gives access to a vague path which contours the field. This eventually joins a track which descends to a wooden bridge over Barkbeth Gill

below Hole House. Climb towards the buildings but then bear left following the sign 'Public Bridleway'.

In a short distance a sign 'Permissive Path' will be found and should be followed (ignore the sign 'Public Bridleway'). It leads past Barkbeth Farm and then directly onto the footpath which runs along the wall above. This emerges through a gate into a field passing a well-worn rubbing stone. It then contours left to a little gate which leads back onto the original track.

Looking up to Longside Edge from Ullock Pike.

Looking over Skiddaw Forest and along the Caldew Valley, the great divide of the Northern Fells, to Carrock Fell (seen far left).

NORTH O'SKIDDAW GROUP

·NOS·

The Northern Fells provide a real wilderness area in which there are no lakes, only two tarns, and but a few trees. This is an upland mass of rough grass, heather, peat, boulder, fell and deeply scoured gills. It is an area of great solitude, where the merlin swoops unruffled over the purple heathers of Skiddaw Forest.

This has not always been the case. In days past, mining operations were so extensive and productive it was said 'Caldbeck and Caldbeck Fells are worth all England else'. Geologically this is a fascinating area, rich in minerals and rare metals. Ancient Britons made their homes here; hence the great hill fort on Carrock, the excavations on Meal Fell, the earthworks on little Aughertree Fell and the tumulus which marks the top of Binsey.

The wide valley formed by Dash Beck and the River Caldew isolates this group of hills, the desolate area surrounding the heads of both being known as Skiddaw Forest. The Uldale Fells lie to the west and the Caldbeck Fells to the east; Great Calva stands guard to the south and Knott, the highest of the group, acts as the centre pin from which all the other heights radially decline. The outlying fells of the main group are Binsey and Aughertree Fell.

Walk NOS 1 leads over Carrock Fell to High Pike and on to Knott. It then returns by the River Caldew. This is the key to unlocking the complexity of these fells. Great and Little Calva, on the other hand, are best walked independently. Walk NOS 2 does this by approaching them along Dash Valley past the white cascades of Dash Fall.

Walk NOS 3 climbs Orthwaite Bank to visit Little Cockup before ascending Great Cockup. The natural corridor of Trusmadoor is crossed and Meal Fell climbed before the Sca Fells, Great and Little, lead to Knott. The return over Frozen Fell and Burn Tod offers fine views over the Dash Valley.

The final walk, Walk NOS 4, takes a

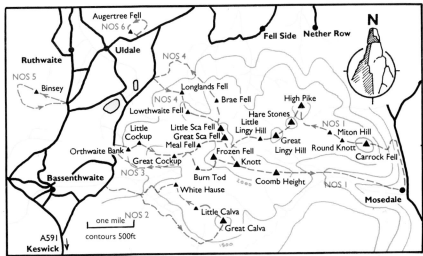

horseshoe around Charleton Gill, ascending the grassy ridge of Longlands Fell and Lowthwaite Fell to reach Little Sca Fell before descending Brae Fell. Beyond, come the oddities of Binsey and Aughertree Fell. Binsey's volcanic dome stands above John Peel's Ruthwaite home offering open views across the Solway. This and the limestone shoulder of Aughertree Fell are covered by Walks NOS 5 and 6.

• N O S I •

OVER CARROCK FELL, HIGH PIKE AND KNOTT

Carrock Fell 2174ft/663m
Round Knott 1978ft/603m
Miton Hill 1991ft/607m
High Pike 2157ft/658m
Hare Stones 2057ft/627m
Great Lingy Hill 2021ft/616m
Little Lingy Hill 1998ft/609m
Knott 2329ft/710m
Coomb Height 2057ft/627m

Valley Base: Mungrisdale, Threlkeld.
Town Base: Keswick.
Maps: OS Pathfinder 576. L90 Penrith & Keswick.
Length: 10.5miles/17km.
Ascent: 2510ft/765m.
Approx Time: 5.5hrs.
Start & Finish: Above the Mosedale to Caldbeck road, past Stone Ends Farm. A short track leaves the road and leads to numerous parking places – the site of a long abandoned mine (NY 353338).
Difficulty: The going is occasionally boggy, otherwise this is a straightforward expedition of some length.

The starting point for this walk beneath Carrock's main crag has apparently been the site of both quarrying and mining activities. Known as 'Apronful of Stones', the grassy fellside here abounds with boulders. Many are made of gabbro, the same rock that forms the Black Cuillin Ridge of Skye. Rising diagonally towards the left on the hillside beneath the crag is an ancient trackway known locally as Rake Trod. Follow this into a gill past two lonesome Scots pines, then rise directly up

the heather-clad shoulder above. Pass a cairn and an ancient stone enclosure of curious construction to ascend a steep knoll of heather and boulders. This is Pike, and on its rocky top stands a cairn offering an unobstructed view.

The path leads across the stone wall of the summit hill fort, some 10ft wide in its ruined state. The fort was roughly circular in construction, draped around the highest point of the fell. Pass a mound of stones, possibly a tumulus, and rise to the summit cairn of Carrock Fell, which is situated on a high rock plinth above the western edge of the wall. This is a commanding position with the deep valleys of Carrock and Caldew, north and south respectively, and the Plain of Eden stretched out to the east.

Cross the wall and descend the shoulder, bearing left to go around the bog. Climb up to a circular bandstand of rock with a flat grassy top. This is Round Knott. Proceed past a cairn and scattered rock outcrops to the flat table top of Miton Hill. Descend into the dip beyond, Red Gate, to find an intersection of tracks. Ascend the shoulder by way of a track until a path branches off right, skirting the top of Dry Gill. It then rises up the shoulder of High Pike. The top of High Pike is marked by a large pile of rocks, a stone bench and a trig point. Just below on the shoulder to the north stands the remains of an old building. This is a better shelter should the wind blow keenly from the north or west.

A path leads down the shoulder past an old collapsed mine entrance which is now hardly recognizable. You then briefly join the substantial miners' track that has risen across the eastern flanks of High Pike. At its highest point bear right to find the few stones on Hare Hill. Descend over heather into the dip to a wooden plank conveniently crossing a water-filled peat hag. Climb to Great Lingy Hill, which is marked by a small cairn. Beyond lies the dome with a cairn which must be Little Lingy Hill (the OS accredit an insignificant hump across Miller Moss with this name).

A short way beyond, a little stream cutting drops into the ravine of Roughton Gill. Directly opposite, above an old mine entrance which looks unstable, a groove or channel cut into the hillside leads up Balliway Rigg where it ends at a curious

circular pit. Both features presumably relate to mining activities in Roughton Gill, once the most productive site in all these mineral rich Caldbeck Fells.

Climb through rough, boggy ground to reach the grassy shoulder which rises to Knott. The central and highest point of

these fells, Knott puts the whole of this sprawling North O'Skiddaw Group into proper perspective.

Head east down the shoulder to cross the boggy plateau of Rigg and on to the cairn and defined top of Coomb Height. From here the path descends along the crest of the shoulder. As it begins to steepen, Brandy Gill and the old Wolfram Mine workings over Grainsgill Beck appear to the left and a long ditch is crossed. There is danger here – do not under any circumstances follow it. This is the top of an ancient mineral stope, where the ore has been extracted to a considerable depth underground. In places it opens and falls vertically. Continue down the shoulder to a track. Cross the bridge and follow the road by the River Caldew. Pass the 'Friends Meeting House 1702' and bear left into the hamlet of Mosedale.

The track by the River Caldew with Carrock Fell rising beyond.

• N O S 2 •

GREAT CALVA

Great Calva 2265ft/690m
Little Calva 2106ft/642m
White Hause 1525ft/465m

Valley Base: Bassenthwaite.
Town Base: Cockermouth, Keswick.
Maps: OS Pathfinder 576. L90 Penrith & Keswick.
Length: 6.75miles/11km.
Ascent: 1705ft/520m.
Approx Time: 3.25hrs.
Start & Finish: Lay-by beside the Orthwaite Road (NY 249324). Virtually opposite Peter House Farm there is a gate and signpost 'Public Bridleway' pointing up a surfaced road beyond a gate.
Difficulty: Short sections of thick heather and boggy ground make the going difficult in places, though a good track occupies most of the route.
Note: Skiddaw House YHA also makes a good base for this walk (see Walk SKI 1).

Although standing above the isolated tract of Skiddaw Forest and north beyond the higher mountains of Blencathra and Skiddaw, the pyramidal southern face of Great Calva can be seen from afar. This is because it stands at the northern end of a great fault corridor, which offers an unobstructed view and cleaves south through the Lakeland hills.

Beyond the first gate the surfaced road continues through the fields via three further gates. At a point where the road falls to Dash Beck the bridleway, signposted Skiddaw House, bears off up to the right. Follow it through a gate/kissing gate and under Dead Crags. The track rises above the cascading waters of Dash Falls and crosses a gate/stile below Birkett Edge. It then crosses a small bridge and rises again. As it levels Candleseaves Bog lies to the right. A considerable wilderness stretches out before you.

Continue along the track until it begins to fall, after which it crosses Dead Beck and turns towards Skiddaw House. At this point bear left and climb the flanks of Great Calva. As height is gained the vague path swings right to ascend the heathery nose of the pyramid. A boulder field adorns what appears to be the summit with a small shelter before the cairn. On arriving at the cairn, which is prominent from below, it becomes obvious that this southern tip of Great Calva is not actually the highest point. The ridge continues to rise to rocks and a fine cairn marking the summit. From here the view extends along the geological fault corridor through the Glenderaterra Valley, along St John's in the Vale and Thirlmere, and over Dunmail Pass to Grasmere, Ambleside and beyond to the low hills above Windermere.

It is best to follow the line of the ruined fence to avoid the bog on the route to Little Calva. The cairn and highest point lie just south of the fence line. Move down the shoulder through peat bog, heather and long fell grass to pick up a track which leads to White Hause. Leave the track and climb right to a boulder of volcanic origin which defines the top. Walk down the steep flanks to cross the track and continue to Dash Farm. A track leads through the farm and becomes the surfaced road which began from the lay-by.

Looking to Dash Falls from the white quartz of Brockle Crag; Little Calva is the highest top seen to the left, with Bakestall and Birkett Edge to the right.

·NOS3·

GREAT COCKUP TO KNOTT

Orthwaite Bank 1142ft/348m
Little Cockup 1296ft/395m
Great Cockup 1726ft/526m
Meal Fell 1804ft/550m
Little Sca Fell 2083ft/635m
Great Sca Fell 2135ft/651m
Knott 2329ft/710m
Frozen Fell 2050ft/625m
Burn Tod 1952ft/595m

Valley Base: Bassenthwaite.
Town Base: Cockermouth, Keswick.
Maps: OS Pathfinder 576. L90 Penrith
& Keswick.
Length: 7.5miles/12km.
Ascent: 2115ft/645m.
Approx Time: 3.75hrs.
Start & Finish: A public bridleway leaves
the road just south of Orthwaite, where a
wide verge allows limited parking – do not
block any field entrances or the road
(NY 253337).
Difficulty: A straightforward outing
mainly over rolling, grassy fellside though
there is a fair amount of ascent and the
going is rough and boggy in places.

The gap of Trusmadoor from the flanks of Burn Tod.

Follow the bridleway through the gate, then ascend left by the wall. Carry on in the same line, climbing the open fellside by way of a groove with a spring at its top. Continue past an interestingly shaped boulder to the summit of Orthwaite Bank. Pudding stone boulders worn smooth by sheep rubbing themselves litter the hillside.

Little Cockup is the prominent hill to the left. To find its summit traverse left to the boulder which marks its top. Then work back right to the nose of Great Cockup to find a level plateau and cairn below the final tower.

Ascend leftwards, crossing a diagonal line of shooting butts. Of curious construction, most of these relics are sunk into the ground with only about 2ft of wall exposed. Walk to the cairned western tip of Great Cockup. This is the best viewpoint and looks as though it should be the top. However, according to OS information this is not the case. The highest point is a slight grassy rise in the middle of the plateau to the east. A small cairn marks this, the top of Great Cockup.

Cross the summit plateau over another rise. Follow the path/track down by an edge of Skiddaw slate into Trusmadoor. Cross the gap and take the track which rises across the southern flank of Meal Fell. After a little way, bear left.

Ascend directly to the summit outcrop of rock, which is marked by a large circular shelter (like a hollow cairn). Around its summit rock outcrop it appears that the ground has been quarried away. Above this hollow, a raised rim of rock seems to guard the northern edge. From above on Frozen Fell, the quarrying or hollowing seems to extend in a full circle around the summit knoll. Could this be the remains of another hill fort along the lines of Carrock Fell?

Descend east to the col, with a view into Frozenfell Gill revealing a hidden waterfall in a scene of surprising drama. Find a prominent grassy rake which leads up diagonally left to the gap between Great Sca Fell and Little Sca Fell. A little pile of stones on the col marks the top of this path. Go left to the cairn and shelter on Little Sca Fell.

A straightforward path leads to the broad top of Great Sca Fell and on to the summit plateau of Knott. Make a rough descent to the grassy shoulder of Frozen Fell. Contour south over feeder streams, peat hags and long grass onto the declining shoulder of Burn Tod. The shoulder rises slightly to a single white rock of quartz marking the top. Beyond lies a short stone wall. Immediately down to the right lies a distinct path/track. This zigzags down the hillside to Trusmadoor.

Cross the stream and bear left along the path above Burntrod Gill. When the path diverges take the lower, more distinct path to the stone bield. Follow the path across the basin of field grass and rise up again below the rough heather which clads the flanks of Great Cockup. This is a bridleway and leads easily across the hillside, with views over the lovely Dash Valley.

The distinct head of Brockle Crag lies just below the track. It is worth a visit to examine the rocks of brilliant white quartz. From here, the track falls gently to join another level track. Bear right to the take the road back to your starting point.

•NOS4•

LONGLANDS FELL TO LITTLE SCA FELL AND BRAE FELL

Longlands Fell 1585ft/483m
Lowthwaite Fell 1670ft/509m
Little Sca Fell 2083ft/635m
Brae Fell 1923ft/586m

Valley Base: Bassenthwaite, Mungrisdale.
Town Base: Cockermouth, Keswick.
Maps: OS Pathfinder 576. L90 Penrith & Keswick.
Length: 4.5miles/7.5km.
Ascent: 1675ft/510m.
Approx Time: 2hrs.
Start & Finish: Longlands, parking space by the water pumping station below the hamlet (NY 266358).
Difficulty: A gentle outing over rolling grassy fells. Keeping the feet dry over Charleton Wath Ford is tricky.

Setting aside the outlying hills of Binsey and Aughertree Fell, Longlands Fell is the most northerly in Lakeland. However, it is Brae Fell that assumes a purely Scottish name as it looks with yearning across the Solway and the plains of Carlisle to its distant cousins. These outlying shoulders of Sca Fell, with Little Sca Fell at the head, form a horseshoe around Charleton Gill.

Take the gate just above the pumping station and immediately bear right. Break

To Lowthwaite Fell and Longlands Fell.

off left and ascend the shoulder. Keep to the edge on the right of some hollows to reach Thwaite, then continue directly above to the cairned top of Longlands Fell. A grassy track runs over the top, having risen from the north, and descends into the dip in the shoulder beyond. Follow it and rise to the top of Lowthwaite Fell. From here descend to Broad Moss and cross it to re-discover the grassy track. On taking this, bear left beneath the summit of Little Sca Fell and make an ascent to the cairned top and pit shelter of Little Sca Fell.

Cross the plateau to find a track which descends the shoulder towards Brae Fell. The going is easy and rapid progress is made before ascent leads to the boulder-strewn cap of Brae Fell. Proceed down the grassy shoulder, bearing slightly left to find another vague grassy track. This leads down to the ford at Charleton Wath. Bear left to follow the track to Longlands.

◆ N O S 5 ◆

BINSEY

Binsey 1466ft/447m

Valley Base: Bassenthwaite, Mungrisdale.
Town Base: Cockermouth, Keswick.
Maps: OS Pathfinder 576. L90 Penrith & Keswick.
Length: 2.5miles/4km.
Ascent: 575ft/175m
Approx Time: 1.25hrs.
Start & Finish: At the junction of the little Bewaldeth Road and Ruthwaite Road there is a derelict building – this is Binsey Lodge. Just beyond this, towards Bewaldeth there is an iron gate and a wide verge parking area (NY 235352).
Difficulty: None.

The circular dome of Binsey should not be underestimated. That famous Lakeland huntsman, John Peel, was content to live in Binsey's shadow and called his pony after the fell. Certainly the ascent is simple, and true there are few features likely to set the pulse racing. Yet its position is quite magnificent. Unlike its near neighbours its mass is volcanic, with some green Eycott Hill lavas. Its summit is capped by a great tumulus with much evidence of ancient occupation.

A gate enters a sheep pen. Exit this by another gate on the left. Bear left beneath the grassed hollow of a long deserted quarry and find a vague grassy trod that leads directly to the summit. On the top of Binsey you find that what appears to be a pyramid on approach is in reality a long ridge of dark rock. The large pile of boulders represents an ancient tumulus and there are numerous shelters. A cairn stands at the highest point and the trig

The snow clad Binsey from the flanks of Cockup.

Aughertree Fell as seen above Longlands, and out over the Solway the distinctive shape of Criffel.

point lies just beyond it. Beyond this there is a stone shelter.

Continue in the same direction to discover another long whaleback ridge of rock, cairned and offering an open vista. Descend with the craggy shoulder of West Crag rising to the left. Beneath this bear left. There are a number of paths at different levels that contour the hillside. Continue traversing above the stone wall until the path drops through the clusters of ancient hawthorn.

It should be noted that nearby Latrigg (not to be confused with the one above Keswick) which stands above Over Water has not been included. While over 1000ft/305m, it is a fenced hill of cultivated pasture rather than a fell. In any case, it is private and the owners want it to remain so.

•NOS 6•

AUGHERTREE FELL

Green How – Aughertree Fell 1053ft/321m

Valley Base: Bassenthwaite, Mungrisdale.
Town Base: Cockermouth, Keswick.
Maps: OS Pathfinder 576. L90 Penrith & Keswick.
Length: 1.5miles/2.5km.
Ascent: 165ft/50m.
Approx Time: 0.5hr.
Start & Finish: Large car park over the brow of the hill above Uldale (NY 262374).
Difficulty: None.

Although lying outside the main group of the Northern Fells and beaten in height by Sandale Hill's transmitting mast to the north, Aughertree is still considered to be the most northerly fell within the Lake District National Park. Its top, Green How, lies a few feet above a grassy track and only a little further from the road. Nevertheless, it has a certain independence of character.

It is best tackled in an anticlockwise direction. Proceed to the old limestone quarry, which is usually flooded, then bear right over the rough fell grass to the little cone of Dale Hows. On the northerly flanks below lie ancient earthworks, circular ditches and mounds. Pass these and walk over to a stone wall, along which Elfa Well lies. From here make the short climb to Green How.

·4·

CENTRAL FELLS

Great Mell Group MEL (7 tops) • Dodds Group DOD (25 tops)
Helvellyn Massif HEL (10 tops) • Fairfield Group FAR (24 tops)

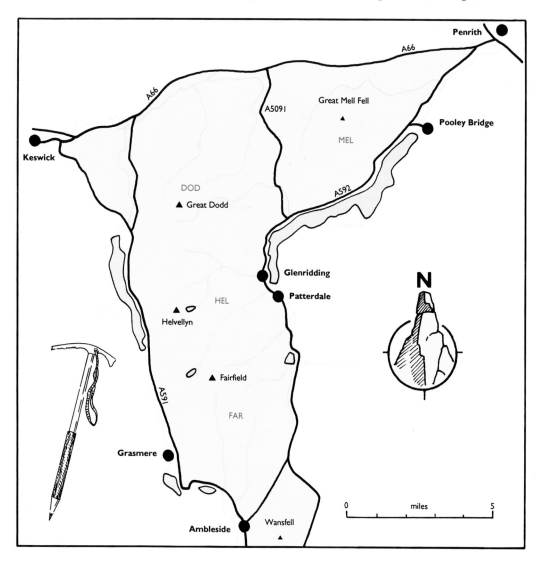

The monolithic massif of the Central Fells is a high integral plateau which stretches for 16 miles north to south. From its shoulder rise a series of distinguished tops, the most notable being those of the Helvellyn Massif – second only to the Scafells in altitude – followed by the Fairfield Group. Here can be found some of Lakeland's classic mountain walks: from the exposed Striding Edge as it soars to Helvellyn, to the genteel circuit around Wordsworth's Rydal in the Fairfield Horseshoe.

Situated at the very heart of Lakeland, this area comprises four groups: the Great Mell Group appears appendaged, wing-like, to the east of the Dodds while the Dodds, in turn, are situated at the northern head of the main shoulder of the Helvellyn and Fairfield Groups.

Wansfell stands above Ambleside, providing the finely tapered southernmost tip of the range. To the west lie the valleys of Grasmere and Thirlmere through which runs the A591 between Ambleside and Keswick. To the north, the Threlkeld Valley stretches eastwards along the A66 from Keswick to Penrith, while the Ullswater Valley and the A592 from Penrith to Ambleside border the eastern boundary. Taken as a whole, this area of some 87 square miles offers 66 individual tops.

The Great Mell Group extends from the northern shore of Ullswater to the A66. Naddle Fell lies on the opposite side of the secluded St John's in the Vale to the Dodds. These two are outliers to the main range, as is little Wansfell, the southern tail. All the tops within the central spine stretching from Clough Head to Red Screes are remote and guarded from the valleys either by distance, steep craggy ground or both. The eastern faces of Helvellyn and Fairfield are particularly impressive.

From the remote and grassy expanses of the Dodds, the pyramidal Catstycam, the gully-seamed St Sunday Crag, and the overhanging buttresses of Dove Crag and Castle Rock, to the beauty of Grasmere and Rydal Water and the glittering majesty of Ullswater – Lakeland's central bastion is clearly a region of powerful contrasts.

AREA FACT SHEET

THE VALLEY BASES

Matterdale
Camping: Rookin House Farm.
Youth Hostel: None.
Inn: Royal Hotel in Dockray.
Bus Services: None.

Thirlmere
Camping: Dale Bottom, Bridge End Farm.
Youth Hostel: Thirlmere.
Inns: Thirlspot/King's Head.
Bus Services: Ambleside to Keswick.

Threlkeld
Camping: Burns Farm, Setmabanning.
Youth Hostels: None.
Inns: Horse & Farrier, White Horse by A66.
Bus Services: Keswick to Penrith.

Troutbeck
Camping: Limefitt Park.

Youth Hostel: Windermere.
Inns: Mortal Man, Queen's Head.
Bus Services: None.

Ullswater
Camping: Sykeside by Brotherswater, Side Farm in Patterdale. Various sites above Watermillock. East of the lake are Park Foot, Hill Crest, Waterside House.
Camping Barn: Swirral Barn above Glenridding.
Youth Hostels: Patterdale, Helvellyn.
Inns: Kirkstone, Brotherswater, Travellers' Rest in Glenridding.
Bus Services: Penrith to Patterdale.

THE TOWN BASES

Ambleside
Camping: None.
Youth Hostel: Ambleside (Waterhead).
All facilities except railway station.

Grasmere
Limited facilities, no camping.
Youth Hostels: Butterlip How and Thorney How.

Keswick
Camping: The Headlands, Derwent Water, Castlerigg Hall and Castlerigg Farm.
Youth Hostel: Keswick.
All facilities except railway station.

Penrith
Camping: None.
Youth Hostel: None.
All other facilities.

Over Gowbarrow Fell looking to Great Mell (left) and Little Mell (right).

GREAT MELL GROUP

◆ MEL ◆

Appendaged like a wing to the main body of the Central Fells, this small area of low fells projects eastwards. Sandwiched between the Northern Fells and Ullswater it occupies an interesting position, with an open corridor extending beyond Penrith to the Vale of Eden.

Like father and son, Great and Little Mell appear as grassy domes rising from the surrounding flatlands. Located in relative isolation, nevertheless they do have merit and even a certain stature, with their profile akin to that of the keel of an upturned boat.

A further dimension is added to this group by the shoulder which stretches east from Aira Force, running above the shores of Ullswater and Matterdale over Gowbarrow Fell to Little Mell Fell at the Hause. While Aira Force waterfall and the initial slopes of Gowbarrow Park have long been popular, few bother to visit these tops. For those who make the effort, however, there are superlative views over Ullswater and a rich diversity of wildlife to be experienced.

Great Mell Fell is best tackled as an entity in itself. Walk MEL 1 explores the rich mixed woods and offers two finishes. Walk MEL 2 follows the shoulder from Gowbarrow Fell to Little Mell Fell and returns along the flanks above Ullswater.

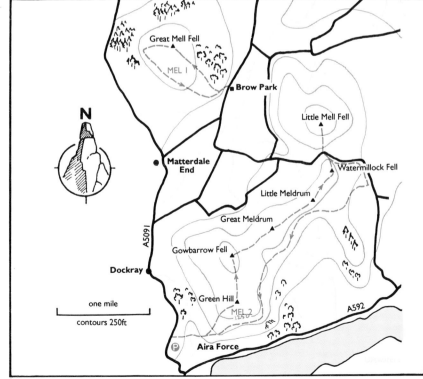

Great Mell Fell flanked by deciduous woods and Scots Pine, as seen above Matterdale.

GREAT MELL FELL

Great Mell Fell 1760ft/537m

Valley Base: Threlkeld, Ullswater.
Town Base: Keswick, Penrith.
Maps: OS OD5, The English Lakes –
North East. L90 Penrith & Keswick.
Length: 2.75miles/4.5km.
Ascent: 920ft/280m
Approx Time: 1.5hrs.
Start & Finish: An unsurfaced lane
leaves the Matterdale End to Motherby
road beneath the south eastern toe of the
fell. There is limited parking in the verge
but do not obstruct the lane (NY 406247).
Difficulty: Straightforward. Now that
firing has ceased in the rifle range to the
north, there is also little danger.

Although a great many people look out
on the pronounced dome of Great Mell
Fell as they pass by on the A66, few set
foot upon it. They do miss out, though,
for this peaceful walk requires little effort
while offering ample reward. Its mixed
woods of oak, rowan, silver birch, holly
and Scots pine shelter a splendid variety
of wildlife; a protective screen behind
which badger setts adorn the slopes, shy
roe deer roam free and the green wood-
pecker drums wantonly. In contrast, the
summit offers a fine open aspect with
striking views to Blencathra.

Access can be gained as in the following description or alternatively from the
bend in the A5091 just outside the hamlet
of Troutbeck, where a path leads alongside the old rifle range. Once the open fell
is gained the hill can be ascended or
descended at virtually any point.

Follow the rough unsurfaced lane past
a gate and stile on the right to a second
gate and stile. Step right over this and follow the path, bearing left above the fell
wall/fence. After leaving the mixed deciduous woods, a vague grassy path rises to
the right. This makes a circuitous climb to
the shoulder of the fell. Continue up the
shoulder, passing through the western
extremities of an apparently ancient
planting of Scots Pine. The shoulder levels and thick, tussocky grass leads to the
top. The view extends along the length of
these Central Fells through the upper corridor of Ullswater to Red Screes.

Continue in the same direction,
towards Troutbeck. Make a steep descent
to an old fence above the disused rifle
range. The path extends in two directions
around Great Mell Fell. Either bear right
to make a clockwise traverse through
woods back to the first gate mentioned,
or go left and take an open anticlockwise
route back around the foot of the fell to
the initial point of ascent.

·MEL 2·

GOWBARROW FELL TO LITTLE MELL FELL

(OVER AIRA FORCE WATERFALL)

Green Hill – Gowbarrow Park
1450ft/442m
Gowbarrow Fell 1579ft/481m
Great Meldrum 1434ft/437m
Little Meldrum 1325ft/404m
Watermillock Fell 1391ft/424m
Little Mell Fell 1657ft/505m

Valley Base: Matterdale, Threlkeld, Ullswater.
Town Base: Keswick, Penrith.
Maps: OS OD5, The English Lakes – North East. L90 Penrith & Keswick.
Length: 8miles/13km.
Ascent: 2200ft/670m.
Approx Time: 4.25hrs.
Start & Finish: Park Brow National Trust car park (free) above A5091 and below Aira Force waterfall (NY 398206).
Difficulty: Generally straightforward, although its length should not be underestimated. (No public right of access over the Great Meldrum to Little Mell Fell section.)

Crossing over the fine waterfall of Aira Force, a beguiling circular walk heads east along the tops and climbs above the north eastern shores of Ullswater before returning along thee southern flanks.

Drop through the wood below the car park on the constructed path which leads to a gate and an open field beyond. Enter the wood surrounding Aira Force by another gate and take the high path left across the stone arched bridge perched above the brink of the main fall. Bear left then right to find a stile leading to open fellside. Ascend directly along a path to crest the rocky knolls of Hind Crag and Bernard Pike. From here, climb further to reach the fine cairn marking the top of Green Hill.

The best path along the top keeps initially to the left. It picks a course through the humps of heather, bilberry and cotton grass before topping a higher grassy mound and then finally falling beneath a rocky knoll. Round the knoll –

whose ascent offers a fine view of Ullswater – to reach a higher craggy knoll. This is the summit of Gowbarrow Fell.

From the trig point (bearing a National Trust plaque) the way ahead is clearly displayed. The rocks below to the south are known as Airy Crag. Take the path eastwards down the steep snout of the crag and follow it until a vague path bears left. Climb a stile where the stone wall makes a corner and contour right to meet the edge of the wire fence bounding the Swinburn Park forestry plantation. Rise with it, then continue directly up the hill to the highest point of Great Meldrum.

Continue east across a saddle formed from red crumbling rock. Walk easily down the grassy shoulder to a distinct corner in the fence line. Climb the fence and bear right to skirt the edge of the conifers. Pass the head of a track which breaks through the trees then fall and rise through thick grass past bushes of gorse to the furthest and highest rock outcrop. This is the summit of Little Meldrum. (Alternatively follow the track then bear left to reach the same point.)

A pond lies ahead. Descend to the left of this to pick up a track. Follow this through the tress to a gate in the wall, continue along the track then bear right to ascend the slopes of Watermillock Fell. The top of the fell is cleaved by a canyon which runs south to north.

Descend to the track and follow it to the gate onto the road. Bear right past the fenced reservoir compound to take the

second gate on the left. This is signposted, rather confusingly, 'Public Footpath' and 'No Public Right Of Way To Top Of Fell', with a 'Bull In Field' sign thrown in for good measure! Climb through the field to a stile/gate which leads to the open flanks of Little Mell Fell. A curious, grassy runnel leads directly up the steep fellside to a banked path (possibly an old water leat) traversing the hillside. Cross this to reach the trig point that marks the top of Little Mell Fell. The view extends to the Lakeland Fells and east across the Vale of Eden to the Pennines, with the little seen Martindale on the far side of Ullswater.

Return to the road. Descend to find a sign which marks the return to Aira Force through a gate on the right. Cross beneath the craggy flanks of Watermillock Fell and rise to the shoulder above Hagg Wood. From here, traverse above Swinburn Park to exit via a stile over the fence. Cross the stream and take a second stile over a wall, then bear left past the ruins of an old Shooting Lodge. Cross a gill and wooden bridge to round a rocky knoll. Continue to where the path splits, whereupon you take the lower branch which leads around the spur of Green Hill onto its face above Ullswater. A stone 'memorial seat' marks an excellent viewpoint. Below, notice the cairn over the fence. Yew Crag lies beyond. Our walk continues along the path descending behind Lyulph's Tower. Take the track rising to the right which leads back to the stone arched bridge above Aira Force.

The summit trig point of Gowbarrow Fell, looking to Little Mell Fell.

Over the Thirlmere Valley and above Castle Rock lie (from left to right) Great Dodd, Watson's Dodd and Stybarrow Dodd.

DODDS GROUP

· DOD ·

The Dodds form the northern head of these Central Fells. A substantial high plateau is topped first by Clough Head, then by Great Dodd and Stybarrow Dodd before Sticks Pass divides the group from that of Raise and Helvellyn beyond. Calfhow Pike and Watson's Dodd, both visible from Thirlmere, sit between the higher tops.

The valleys of Thirlmere, Threlkeld and Matterdale physically define the perimeter of this group. The western flanks above Thirlmere, St John's in the Vale and the north face of Clough Head are impressively steep. In contrast, the eastern side of the group comprises mainly extensive rolling grasslands: Mosedale, rising to Calfhow Pike and intersecting Clough Head and Great Dodd, and Deepdale rising to Watson's Dodd between Great Dodd and Stybarrow Dodd. Above these deserted eastern valleys lie grassy shoulders of great interest.

Naddle Fell is a low but rugged shoulder that is isolated from the main group by St John's in the Vale. Walk DOD 1 begins at Legburthwaite and tackles the length of this shoulder. It then drops down to St John's Church before returning along the vale.

Castle Rock dominates the southern entrance to St John's in the Vale. A sharp ascent, it makes a worthy outing in its own right. This is the chosen route for Walk DOD 2.

Clough Head marks the northern end of the Dodds and the Central Fells. Walk DOD 3 tackles it head on over Threlkeld Knotts before looping around Mosedale over Calfhow Pike to Great Dodd. Randerside above Matterdale Common is taken in descent, while the edge of Wolf Crags gives access to the Old Coach Road and the return to Wanthwaite.

The keynote outing of the whole group is Walk DOD 4. This makes a high

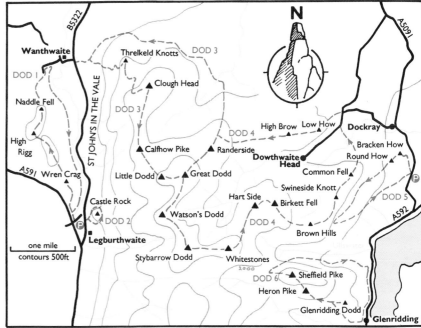

circuit around Deepdale (the source of Aira Beck feeding Aira Force) and includes Great Dodd, Watson's Dodd and Stybarrow Dodd. Ascent over Matterdale Common includes Low How and High Brow with Randerside leading to Great Dodd. Then Watson's Dodd, with an open vista over Thirlmere, is followed by Stybarrow Dodd. From here, a descent is made down the long eastern arm of Green Side, Hart Side and Birkett Fell before the tops of Watermillock Common offer superb views over Ullswater.

Walk DOD 5 visits the minor tops of Round How and Bracken How before making a delightful excursion through Glencoyne Park and the ancient larch, Scots pine, beech and alder.

Rugged Sheffield Pike with Heron Pike and Glenridding Dodd are tackled on Walk DOD 6. Steep ascent, firstly up bracken-covered slopes then along the rocky south east ridge reveals more great views over Ullswater.

•DOD 1•

NADDLE FELL ABOVE ST JOHN'S IN THE VALE

Wren Crag 1020ft/311m
High Rigg 1125ft/343m
Naddle Fell 1171ft/357m

Valley Base: Thirlmere, Threlkeld.
Town Base: Keswick.
Maps: OS OD5, The English Lakes – North East. L90 Penrith & Keswick.
Length: 5miles/8km.
Ascent: 1115ft/340m.
Approx Time: 2.75hrs.
Start & Finish: Car park at Legburthwaite, head of St John's in the Vale (NY 318195).
Difficulty: A straightforward low fell walk on good paths.

Pass through the head of the car park to find a small gate leading onto the old road. Turn left to the kissing gate which opens onto the verge of the A591. Turn right along this over Smaithwaite Bridge. Climb over the stile and take the path which rises to the left. This leads through magnificent Scots pines with a fine view to Castle Rock and Wren Crag.

Descend steeply into the dip and take the gap in the wall. Climb again to follow along the rocky outcrops of Long Edge. A grassy incline leads to a stile over the wire fence to the left. Cross this then go right, first rising then falling to pass a little tarn in a hollow. The path descends to the left, dipping to reach a stile over a stone wall. Beyond the stile, the path runs along the wall. It then climbs to pass through a corridor formed by the rocky knoll of Moss Crag. Immediately beyond the crag, turn left beneath it where there is a small tarn to the right. Make a steep ascent to the top of High Rigg.

Looking north along Long Edge to Naddle Fell with mighty Skiddaw profiled in the distance.

A Scots Pine on Wren Crag.

•DOD 2•

CASTLE ROCK

Castle Rock 1112ft/339m

Valley Base: Thirlmere.
Town Base: Keswick.
Maps: OS OD5, The English Lakes –
North East. L90 Penrith & Keswick.
Length: 0.5mile/0.8km.
Ascent: 605ft/185m.
Approx Time: 1hr.
Start & Finish: Car park at Legburth-
waite, head of St John's in the Vale
(NY 318195).
Difficulty: Steep ascent and descent,
exposed in places. In descent there is a
short section of difficult scrambling,
though this can be avoided quite easily.
The path is vague in places and all mem-
bers of the party should be competent.

Guarding the narrow entrance to St
John's in the Vale stands the rocky bastion of Castle Rock. The 'castle' comprises three rock precipices – the formidable
North Crag, some 300ft of sheer rock; to
its right, separated by an area of trees and
vegetation, the sunnier and friendlier
South Crag; and above them all to the left
of the North Crag and separated by a
deep gully stands the summit tower. In
literary terms Walter Scott immortalized
it in his poem *The Bridal Of Triermain*:

> But midmost of the vale, a mound
> Arose, with airy turrets crown'd,
> Buttress, and rampires circling bound,
> And mighty keep and tower;

Today it has become a famous rock
climbing cliff. Its precipitous North Crag
was first ascended by my father, Jim Birkett on All Fools' Day 1939. The route he
took is called 'Overhanging Bastion' and
it pioneered a new order of difficulty in
rock climbing.

The route described here is much sim-
pler. Leave the car park by an overgrown
narrow path opposite the toilets and cross
the road. Climb the steps through the
kissing gate and bear right to a gate in a
stone wall. Do not take the gate but bear
left by the wall to cross a track. Rise above
the track where the path bears first left
then back right to the top corner of the

A high grassy ridge leads above the
tarns of Paper Moss to a hollow and
pond. Ascend to the summit of Naddle
Fell (unnamed on OS map). The cairned
rocky knoll has an unbroken view to
Skiddaw and Blencathra. The stone circle
at Castlerigg is also just visible. A wide
path falls down the hillside, steepening
near its end, to the buildings by the road
above St John's Church (this gives the
vale its name and is well worth a visit).
Turn right down the road past the church
to a gate and stile leading to a grassy
track. Skirt the foot of the fell along this
track. Pass a ruined farm surrounded by
large sycamore trees and a giant yew
which overhangs the track. Deviate to the
right on a path taking the high side of Low
Bridge End Farm. The track meets the
bank of St John's Beck beneath Wren
Crag and then stops. It appears that the
river was once forded at this point. A narrow and exposed path continues above
the river, rising through the trees to the
grassy shoulder above the wooden stile
leading onto the A591.

Castle Rock guarding the entrance to St John's in the Vale (above and right).

wood. Here an aqueduct traverses the hillside and enters a tunnel. Ignore the wooden footbridge and instead take the stone slab stile over the wall to the right. Notice the little rock face immediately above. The path follows above the tunnel and rises to a high point among the Scots pines. Cross the fence on the left using some stones. The path bears up through the bracken past a rocky knoll on the left towards the South Crag. Ascent can be made by the side of the South Crag, however the steep scree is badly eroded so it is best to make a zigzag ascent up the knoll to the right. Near the top a gap will be found in a stone wall from where another ruined stone wall is followed. Cross a further ruined wall to gain the highest grassy break leading across Castle Rock. There are four grassy breaks which lead almost

horizontally across. Each is blocked by a stone wall in order to keep sheep away from the cliffs.

Before reaching the wall on the top break, move right up a rough shoulder to the top of a rocky knoll. Beyond and connected by an easy grassy saddle lies a higher flat, stepped table of rock. Move around its right side for an straightforward ascent to the highest point of Castle Rock. Although there is no difficulty, the exposure here is great. Extreme care should be exercised at all times.

Descend to the saddle then bear left down to a ruined wall which runs behind Castle Rock. Veer left along it until it meets the crag, where a gap is found. Take this and descend to a level shoulder. A path cuts back beneath the crag. Follow this to the gully that falls between the wall

of the summit tower and the North Crag. Here a choice can be made to traverse into the gully directly or to move down a broad grassy break beneath. The former is exposed and for a short section constitutes quite a difficult scramble. The latter leads easily but less pleasantly down to a point beneath the foot of the gully. In either case, a clear-cut path leads from the base of the gully to a gap in a stone wall directly beneath the centre of this cliff. If climbers are operating above, a careful watch should be kept to guard against falling stones. Walk through the gap then bear right, descending by the stone wall through the trees to find a wooden footbridge over the aqueduct. A path leads down through the bracken and left onto a track. Descend this to the point crossed in ascent, then bear right to the road.

OVER CLOUGH HEAD TO GREAT DODD

Threlkeld Knotts 1686ft/514m
Clough Head 2381ft/726m
Calfhow Pike 2175ft/663m
Little Dodd 2575ft/785m
Great Dodd 2811ft/857m
Randerside 2391ft/729m

Valley Base: Thirlmere, Threlkeld.
Town Base: Keswick.
Maps: OS OD5, The English Lakes –
North East. L90 Penrith & Keswick.
Length: 8miles/13km.
Ascent: 3000ft/915m.
Approx Time: 4.5hrs.
Start & Finish: The wide junction
signposted 'Matterdale Unsuitable For
Motors' above the St John's in the Vale
Road at Wanthwaite provides limited
parking (NY 316231).
Difficulty: Despite its formidable appear-
ance, the north face of Clough Head is not
technically difficult. A well-defined path
broaches the steep ground. Elsewhere the
going is straightforward, and good grassy
paths prevail.

This high mountain outing scales Clough
Head by Red Screes and then continues to
Great Dodd, the highest of the Dodds.

Walk along the lane which is the start
of the 'Old Coach Road'. Pass the house
on the right and go through the gate to
bear left at the junction. At the end of the
stone wall a stile climbs the wire fence to
the right. A path then continues up
through the old quarry tips, bearing right
to a track. From here, a signposted path
climbs directly up the grassy bank above
the track by the side of a wire fence. Cross
this to follow the path, which rises to
cross another stile over the fell wall.

Climbing the grassy slopes of Wanthwaite Bank, first follow what appears to
be a ditch or runnel in the hillside. This
develops into a well-defined grassy track
zigzagging up the fell. Cross through a
rock cutting, passing a sheep fold below
to the right. Here the track levels slightly
and bends to the right. At this point, bear
left following a grassy path to a col. To
the left there is a cairn and viewpoint, to

the right the grassy summit cone of Threlkeld Knotts.

Descend over the spoil of past mining activity and cross the hollow, before rising over a grassy hummock to pick up the main path. This rises first to the left then climbs diagonally rightwards out to the shoulder. A cairn marks the head of this path, from where an easy ascent leads to the top of Clough Head.

Locate a broad, well-defined path leading down the grassy flanks of Great Dodd and up to the distinct, rocky knoll of Calfhow Pike. Beneath stand the ruins of a rectangular bield. The pike resembles a Dartmoor tor. Your path continues up the grassy flanks of Little Dodd to the summit cairn. Great Dodd is also reached easily and marked with a cairn. A little to the south a stone shelter offers a better viewpoint than the summit.

A straightforward path leads down the shoulder from the top to the cloven-hoofed, stony outcrop of Randerside. To the right a cairn marks the highest point. Follow the main path in descent to where ponds of water lie in the peat moss. Bear left here to the western end of Wolf Crag. Note that there is no distinct path and the going is a little boggy underfoot.

When Mosedale Beck appears directly below, you are correctly located on a grassy shoulder which descends by the western end of the crag. Circumnavigate the small rocky bluffs and descend to the Old Coach Road, then bear left to follow its now rough and stony course back to Wanthwaite and the start.

◆ DOD 4 ◆

THE DODDS: GREAT, WATSON'S AND STYBARROW

Low How 1631ft/497m
High Brow 1886ft/575m
Randerside 2391ft/729m
Great Dodd 2811ft/857m
Watson's Dodd 2588ft/789m
Stybarrow Dodd 2766ft/843m
White Stones – Green Side 2608ft/795m
Hart Side 2481ft/756m
Birkett Fell 2378ft/725m
Brown Hills 1808ft/551m
Swineside Knott 1814ft/553m
Common Fell 1811ft/552m

Valley Base: Ullswater.
Town Base: Ambleside, Keswick, Penrith.
Maps: OS OD5, The English Lakes – North East. L90 Penrith & Keswick.
Length: 9miles/14.5km.
Ascent: 2525ft/770m.
Approx Time: 5hrs.
Start & Finish: Parking area by the New Road/Dockray/Dowthwaitehead road junction at the Matterdale End of the Old Coach Road (NY 380218).
Difficulty: A grassy walk throughout, despite a little bogginess in places. Though technically without difficulty its length and altitude should not be underestimated.

Along the shoulder to Calfhow Pike.

This represents a considerable horseshoe around Deepdale and Dowthwaite, taking in the essence of the Dodds. A little gate for walkers and a larger gate for track users provides entry to the grassy wastes of Matterdale Common at the eastern end of the Old Coach Road. Immediately bear left off the track to rise up the grassy shoulder to Low How. Descend into the dip and rise by the stone wall, passing an ancient collapsed mine level. Continue from here to the broad grassy summit of High Brow.

Move down slightly and cross the moss beyond. Begin to rise by a small stream and continue to the main path leading up to the summit cairn of Randerside. The path steepens to the cairn and summit of Great Dodd. To the south, the shelter cairn provides a better location to stop on this, the highest of the Dodds.

The path leads on to Watson's Dodd, which offers a splendid view along Thirlmere. A simple climb reaches the northern cairn, the mid and the highest point of Stybarrow Dodd, while to the south the summit plateau spurs to another cairn. The southern end is slightly lower in altitude but offers a commanding view in all directions. Return to the top then make an easy descent west to a grassy col. The shoulder rises to a bouldery top and cairn marking the White Stones top of Green Side. The extensive lead mine above Glenridding, once the largest in England, takes the name Greenside from this fell. The next cairn, a little further on, offers a better view. Bear left and rise to the top of Hart Side. Some 20yds beyond the summit a fine cairn on a rock outcrop offers a panoramic view down over Dowthwaite.

Proceed along the grassy heights. Bear right then left to the cairn and name plaque, which marks the top of Birkett Fell. This fell was recently named in honour of Lord Birkett. He did much to preserve the natural shape and environment of Ullswater from the demands of the Water Authority.

Descend and follow the line of a ruined stone wall until a gap leads out onto the grassy shoulder of Brown Hills. Pass a couple of rocky knolls to gain the top of Brown Hills. From here, move on to the rocky knoll and cairn of Swineside Knott, then cross the boggy expanse of Watermillock Common to ascend the

Birkett Fell and Hart Side standing above the hamlet of Dowthwaitehead.

final top of the round, Common Fell. (Note that on the current OS 1:25 000 scale map (OD5), a contour is missed and this fell is accredited with the same height as Watermillock Common.)

You could extend the walk to include the tops of Round How and Bracken How, but this would involve a considerable walk back to the car. There is a very neat solution. Beyond the summit cairn of Common Fell stands a balanced rock of green stone. Pass it, then descend by the left bank of Blake Sike. Cross the latter halfway and descend to the fir plantation. Just to the right through the wall is a little gate. Pass through it and follow the fence above the river until an opening allows a descent to the footbridge. Cross Aira Beck then bear right across the field to a boggy and overgrown lane. Follow this to its top, bear right through a gate, then turn left onto the road past Crookwath. Climb this and pass the building of 'Penrith RDC Waterworks 1932'.

·DOD5·

ROUND HOW AND BRACKEN HOW ABOVE GLENCOYNE PARK

Bracken How 1224ft/373m
Round How 1270ft/387m

Valley Base: Ullswater.
Town Base: Ambleside, Keswick, Penrith.
Maps: OS OD5, The English Lakes – North East. L90 Penrith & Keswick.
Length: 3.75miles/6km.
Ascent: 1330ft/405m.
Approx Time: 2hrs.
Start & Finish: Old quarry car park beside the A5091 on Park Brow (NY 397211).
Difficulty: A straightforward outing.

Whilst Bracken How and Round How in themselves are tops of a very minor nature this walk, returning through Glencoyne Park, is quite delightful. Leave the old quarry car park by an overgrown path on its right side. Pass an old ruined building and climb a stile. Ascend steeply along the line of the wall until a further stile climbs the wall to the right. Follow the wall until the going levels. Bear right, picking the best route through the bracken over small rocky ridges and two little green valleys. The second of these carries a path from the pasture below, by which stands a stone of five regular sides (possibly a marker stone). In the middle of a rocky-edged basin of grass stands a knoll and slight cairn; however just above to the west a grassy mound marks the highest point of aptly named Bracken How. The view up Matterdale throws Great Mell Fell into the position of guardian of the dale.

Descend the shoulder into the bracken

Looking down to the grassy dome of Round How.

village and past the Travellers' Rest Inn. Continue past the cottages on the right to a cattle grid. Beyond is another row of cottages but to the right a grassy track zigzags up the hillside. Follow this to the cottages by an electric post and small scree, whereupon a small path rises up to the right. Follow this steep, narrow but well-defined path through bracken to a levelling behind a rocky knoll. This is the top of Blaes Crag. Bear left, following a path known as the Rake and ascend a grassy col.

In front there is a stone wall and an opening that was once gated. Bear right along it and follow it around the corner. A path ascends the easy shoulder to the

before ascending the more open flanks of Round How. For those intent on top accumulation only, return can now be made to the car – an outing accomplished with ease in half an hour. However, the walk from here on is quite splendid and well worth doing for its own sake.

Descend to the stone wall and bear right into a dip of unsuspected depth. Ascend steeply by the wall until it levels and turns a corner. Follow along the wall, in part now replaced by a fence, and pass beneath Swineside Knott. A little further and the view over the length of Ullswater becomes supreme. The mountain perspective over the head of the lake, including Hartsop, Threshwaite Mouth and Ill Bell, is magnificent. Further on the path traverses the green scree tumbling down the face of Brown Hills. A narrow opening through the wall marks the top of the path which makes a diagonal descent through Glencoyne Park.

Follow the path through thick woods of mature beech to a stile over the wall. The diverse woods are delightful and numerous little gills are crossed: Near, Middle and Far Swan Becks. Continue over Groovegill Beck. The path is now quite narrow and boggy to the extent that alder becomes the common tree. At its end a stile leads onto the A5091 opposite the high National Trust car park for Aira Force.

Alternatively, it is possible to bear left about 50 yards on to join an old track leading back up Park Brow towards the quarry. Follow this as it spirals left to become overgrown, before levelling and leading directly to the perimeter fence which surrounds the quarry. Down to the right a gate leads onto the road just by the car park.

•DOD 6•

SHEFFIELD PIKE

Glenridding Dodd 1450ft/442m
Heron Pike 2008ft/612m
Sheffield Pike 2215ft/675m

Valley Base: Ullswater.
Town Base: Ambleside, Penrith.
Maps: OS OD5, The English Lakes – North East. L90 Penrith & Keswick.
Length: 5miles/8km.
Ascent: 1920ft/585m.
Approx Time: 3.25hrs.
Start & Finish: Glenridding car park (NY 386169).
Difficulty: Steepish and rough in places but pathed throughout.

This route rises from Glenridding and provides lively walking and splendid scenic views. From the car park find the road through the centre of Glenridding

right. Round the initial hump to find a stone boundary marker post. There is a letter 'M' (the Marshall estate of Patterdale) inscribed on its Glenridding face and 'H' (the Howard estate of Greystoke) on its Glencoyne face. Beyond lies a large cairn marking the top of Glenridding Dodd. Framed by larch rising from its northern slopes, this is a prized viewpoint with an excellent view of Ullswater.

Return to the col and rise with the line of the wall. Make a scrambly ascent up the initial rocky knoll of the south east ridge of Sheffield Pike. There is a good view of Heron Pike on one side and the great concave face of Birkhouse Moor on the other.

Where the path levels bear right to the grassy top and little cairn of Heron Pike. Its craggy east face falls steeply and frames a superb view down Ullswater. Notice the old iron stake on the rocky end inscribed 'M 1912' and 'H 1912'.

Regain the path and follow this to the summit cairn of Sheffield Pike. The Helvellyn Massif and, particularly, Catstycam looms large to the south west. Below lies the now quiet site of Greenside Lead Mine, in the past one of the most productive in England.

Descend the easy shoulder to the deep groove of Nick Head and turn right along the path which rises through it. Follow the well-defined path, making a diagonal ascent above Glencoyne. Pass a broken dam, straddling Glencoyne Beck to skirt along a stone wall. Take a stile and enter the woods above Seldom Seen. Pass the cottages and continue along the track to the road.

On the far side of the road a path traverses above the shores of the lake. Beneath the impressive form of the overhanging Stybarrow Crag, the road itself must be followed. On passing the crag, a constructed path leads off to the left just above the lake. Pass a little crag in the woods then take steps leading up to the right. You gain a viewpoint before continuing along the path to where it joins the road by the signpost for Glenridding.

The view north east down the middle leg of Ullswater from Heron Pike.

Looking along Striding Edge to the high summit plateau of Helvellyn.

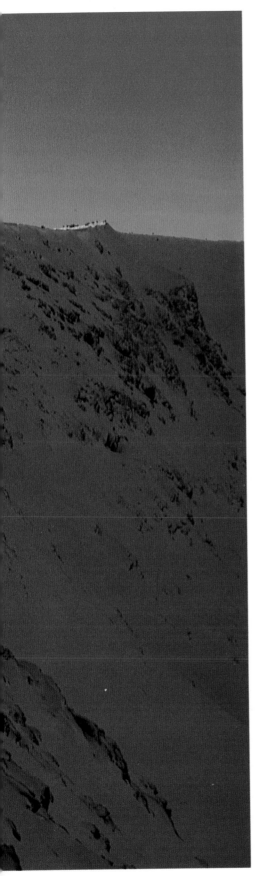

HELVELLYN MASSIF

•HEL•

While second only to the Scafells in height, the Helvellyn Massif first appears as a benign giant. Massive yet unthreatening, its great back, long and broad, sweeps upwards firmly but unspectacularly from the tree-lined shores of Thirlmere. Its east flank, distanced by the valleys of Grisedale and Glenridding, remains largely out of sight. Its edge is defined by the high crest which runs over Dollywaggon Pike, High Crag, Nethermost Pike and Helvellyn, forming a formidable and relatively unbroken face from Grisedale Tarn to Lower Man. Here lies the danger. Distances are considerable, particularly in winter, and many traps await the unwary.

Sticks Pass lies to the north of the massif and Grisedale Pass to the south. Raise rises from the high col of Sticks Pass. An undulating grassy shoulder extends over White Side to a col beneath the steep edge which falls from Lower Man. Finally, the high plateau of Helvellyn stretches from Lower Man to Dollywaggon Pike before finally plunging to Grisedale Tarn.

Striding Edge finds a way through Helvellyn's eastern defences as does the steeper Swirral Edge, which falls to Catstycam. Otherwise most of Helvellyn's safe walking routes lie to the west.

Walk HEL 1 makes a gentle approach up Sticks Pass from Stanah before taking the rollercoaster shoulder over Raise to

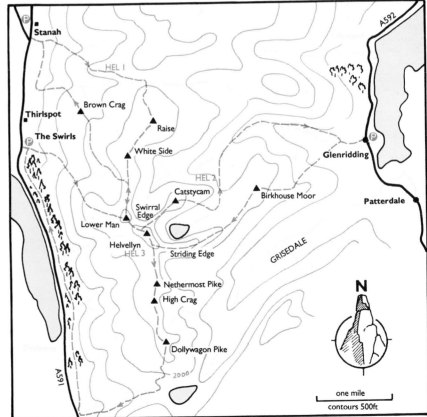

Helvellyn. This offers the easiest way to climb Helvellyn, the walk descending via Brown Crag to the foot of Sticks Pass.

Walk HEL 2 climbs Helvellyn via Striding Edge and descends via Swirral Edge over Catstycam. This is one of Lakeland's classic mountain walks.

Walk HEL 3 ascends easily from near Thirlspot to traverse the entire length of Helvellyn's High Massif. From Lower Man it rises over Helvellyn, Nethermost Pike, High Crag and Dollywaggon Pike before dropping to Dunmail Pass. An easy return leads through the woods above Thirlmere.

◆ HEL 1 ◆

STICKS PASS TO RAISE, WHITE SIDE AND HELVELLYN

Raise 2897ft/883m
White Side 2832ft/863m
Lower Man – Helvellyn 3033ft/925m
Helvellyn 3118ft/950m
Brown Crag 2001ft/610m

Valley Base: Thirlmere.
Town Base: Ambleside, Keswick.
Maps: OS OD5, The English Lakes – North East. L90 Penrith & Keswick.
Length: 7.5miles/12km.
Ascent: 3200ft/975m.
Approx Time: 4.5hrs.
Start & Finish: Limited parking by telephone kiosk in the centre of Stanah (NY 318189), just beyond the St John's in the Vale B5322 junction with the A591.
Difficulty: A high mountain outing. Good paths prevail and Sticks Pass provides an amenable route of ascent to Helvellyn, Raise and White Side.

Rising from Stanah by way of Sticks Pass provides a relatively easy access route to the spine of the plateau. The pass was once an important packhorse route, marked by sticks because of its mountain environment. Often snow clad in Winter it reaches an altitude of some 2500ft.

From the square ascend the surfaced

The path leading to Helvellyn Lower Man.

road following the sign 'Bridleway Glenridding Via Sticks Pass'. Beside a barn on the left, a stile leads over a stone wall. Take the next stile and cross the aqueduct as it enters a section of tunnel. In a short distance a little gate gives access to a bridge across Stanah Gill. Climb steeply with the rushing waters of the gill to the left. Soon the path enters a well-worn groove and the angle slackens. Where the remains of an old stone structure stand to the right, the path/track bears left and moves into a high grassy basin. A substantial sheepfold provides a worthy viewpoint.

Climb from the basin onto the shoulder on the right and ascend this before cutting diagonally right towards Sticks

Gill. Rise from the head of the gill to a broad, grassy col and the summit of Sticks Pass. The main path now traverses along the spine of these Central Fells. The rocky turreted top of Raise, evident against the skyline, lies to the right while Stybarrow Dodd lies to the left. Follow the deeply grooved path up a little bouldery scree to Raise. A cairn stands on the highest rocky turret of this mountain sanctuary. Its rocks resemble pumice stones and provide one of the most aesthetic tops in the area, from which enticing mountain views stretching south to Helvellyn lead you quickly on to the broad grassy rump of White Side and its summit cairn.

Descend to the col and make a steep,

rough ascent to the top of Lower Man. A little stony descent and ascent up the edge of the shoulder leads to the edge of the summit plateau above Swirral Edge. Follow the curving edge past the trig point with a spectacular view down to Red Tarn. Continue to the summit cairn of Helvellyn beyond. Beneath this find the crossed walls of the summit shelter. (Take care to avoid the bandit sheep.) The view in all directions, particularly to the west, is quite superlative.

Just south of the shelter lies a commemorative cairn and plaque which reads: 'The first aeroplane to land on a mountain in Great Britain did so on this spot on Dec 22nd 1926. John Leeming

and Bert Hinkler in an Avro 585 Gosport landed here and after a short stay flew back to Woodford'.

Retrace your steps to Lower Man and down to the col beneath the north ridge. Bear left immediately on a vague path, to find a well-defined path beyond. This skirts the western flanks of White Side to allow the minor ascent of the rocky outcrop of Brown Crag to be made.

Finally, the path steepens and leads down through the bracken to a path which traverses above the stone wall. Bear right, following the path above the wall to cross Fisherplace Gill on a wooden footbridge. Continue on to cross the Stanah Gill at the foot of Sticks Pass.

·HEL 2·

HELVELLYN BY STRIDING EDGE, DESCENDING SWIRRAL EDGE TO CATSTYCAM

Birkhouse Moor 2356ft/718m
Helvellyn 3118ft/950m
Catstycam 2919ft/890m

Valley Base: Ullswater.
Town Base: Ambleside.
Maps: OS OD5, The English Lakes – North East. L90 Penrith & Keswick.
Length: 7.5miles/12km.
Ascent: 3000ft/915m.
Approx Time: 4.5hrs.
Start & Finish: Glenridding car park (NY 386169).
Difficulty: A high mountain route. The going is easy along Striding Edge although exposure is considerable. A head for heights is desirable if not essential. Descent of Swirral Edge is very exposed, steep and eroded, though it is not technically difficult. Use of hands is helpful in places.

This is a great mountain day, one of Lakeland's finest outings and perhaps the most popular. Nevertheless, its length and difficulty should not be underestimated. Walk through Glenridding following the road to the junction at the bend. Bear left to cross Glenridding Beck by Rattlebeck

Bridge. Pass the caravan site and continue to make progress on the track through the fell wall. Follow the path, bearing left to cross Mires Beck, and make an ascent up Little Cove to a stone wall running along the shoulder above.

The path follows the wall to the boggy ridge of Birkhouse Moor. The undistinguished highest point lies by the stone wall to the left. Cross it and proceed to the rocky end cone of Striding Edge, rightly called High Spying How. En route admire the view above Grisedale across the precipitous east face of Helvellyn from Nethermost Pike to Dollywagon Pike. It is now time to take stock. Steep ground plunges away to both sides, Nethermost Cove to the south and Red Tarn to the north. Following the very crest of Striding Edge is a tricky task, though with a little care an easier way can be found and the exposure minimized. At its end the going steepens. Fortunately the shoulder falling from Helvellyn has widened so that, although the ascent is a little scrambly, there is little difficulty. Pass the Gough Memorial erected in memory of Charles Gough of Winchester who perished at the foot of Helvellyn in 1805, and follow the path to the summit shelter and the cairned highest point of Helvellyn.

Proceed along the curving rim of the summit plateau, past the trig point on to the top of Swirral Edge. The path seems to plunge into an abyss and looks impossibly steep. Take heart, for although exposed, it is not anywhere near as bad as it looks. The going eases rapidly after the first section of descent. Continue along the ridge to the col then ascend to the top of Catstycam. This is an aesthetically shaped peak that is positioned impressively. If it were composed of bare rock rather than grass and scree it would be one of Lakeland's most prized summits. As it is, descend down the east ridge, where the path is vague in places but soon joins the main highway in the vicinity of Red Tarn Beck.

Follow the path down into the head of Glenridding. Cross Red Tarn Beck by a little footbridge. Continue above Glenridding Beck and cross it by another footbridge. Proceed down the track, passing the old mine buildings (now a youth hostel) to the Greenside Road. Beyond a cattle grid the road becomes surfaced and passes the Travellers' Rest to the car park.

Striding Edge, Lakeland's classic ridge.

•HEL 3•

HELVELLYN HIGH MASSIF

Lower Man – Helvellyn 3033ft/925m
Helvellyn 3118ft/950m
Nethermost Pike 2922ft/891m
High Crag 2903ft/885m
Dollywaggon Pike 2815ft/858m

Valley Base: Thirlmere.
Town Base: Ambleside, Keswick.
Maps: OS OD5, The English Lakes –
North East. L90 Penrith & Keswick.
Length: 9miles/14.5km.
Ascent: 2675ft/815m.
Approx Time: 4.75hrs.
Start & Finish: North West Water
Authority car park (NY 317169) by the
side of the A595, above Thirlspot,
Thirlmere.
Difficulty: A long, high mountain outing.
Good paths prevail and there is no
technical difficulty on this walk.

This route traverses all the main tops of Helvellyn, skirting the high crest of the massif in its entirety. Follow the path from the back of the large car park to rise up the flanks of Helvellyn by the side of Helvellyn Gill. The going steepens as you climb over the end of Browncove Crags. From here, the path becomes easier above the crags until it is possible to bear left and gain the top of Lower Man. Descending to the col beneath and following the main trod leads to the summit of Helvellyn.

Continue following the main trod south past the shelter. Bear right across the broad shoulder of Helvellyn to reach a low point and junction with the eastern edge of the plateau overlooking Nethermost Cove. Just beyond, the trod divides. First take the left fork, then leave the main path to follow the eastern edge along to the summit cairn of Nethermost Pike. The view across Nerthermost Cove to Striding Edge is quite dramatic.

Proceed across the summit, striking a line south to regain the eastern edge of the massif before climbing up to the large summit cairn of High Crag. This is an independent top which offers impressive rock scenery overlooking Ruthwaite Cove and Hard Tarn (immediately beneath the flanks of Nethermost Pike).

Move south along the eastern edge, first falling then rising again to a cairned bump on the flank of Dollywaggon Pike. The summit lies a little further on. A cairned dome, narrowing to the east, marks the highest point of Dollywaggon Pike, though the rise to its west bears the major cairn. Remnants of the old iron fence may be found, indicating the old county boundary dividing Westmorland (east) from Cumberland (west). Join the main trod that lies below to the south and descend the zigzagging route to Grisedale Tarn. The head of Grisedale Pass leads to Grasmere with the Fairfield Group above. Look for a glint of gold in its dark waters. King Dunmail is said to have fled this way and tossed his crown into the tarn while escaping from a battle on the Pass below.

Follow the path above the shores of the tarn, cross the line of the old boundary and proceed down the southern side of Raise Beck. Just above the pass of Dunmail Raise a gate leads through the wall on the right. To the left the present-day carriageway splits around the ancient cairn which marks the site of King Dunmail's battle. The path leads to a footbridge over Birkside Gill beneath the waterfalls. Continue along the level track/path and make an easy return through the wood of conifers above Thirlmere. Walk over Whelpside Gill above Wythburn Church and cross a footbridge over an unnamed gill. Continue until a slight descent leads back to the car park.

Looking along the snow corniced eastern rim of Helvellyn with the tops of Nethermost Pike, High Crag and Dollywaggon Pike beyond.

St Sunday Crag beyond Grisedale Tarn.

FAIRFIELD GROUP

·FAR·

A high mountain plateau of venerable shape and form, the Fairfield Group stands head and shoulders with the gods. Yet her many long arms stretch out to Grasmere, Rydal, Ambleside, Patterdale and Hartsop. In her shadow lived Wordsworth, the most influential of the romantic poets. On her slopes, as witnessed by the remarkable network of stone walls, hill shepherds have long kept watch.

To the east and west lie the passes of Kirkstone and Dunmail Raise. At her foot, Lake Windermere extends south whilst Grisedale Tarn nestles secretly in her northern confines. Above these boundaries the high spine of the Fairfield Group stretches over Hart and Dove Crags, dipping over Scandale Pass and rising again to Red Screes. Beyond Red Screes, sweet Wansfell belongs to Ambleside. And declining gracefully from these heights are a series of fine ridges. It is their presence which provides numerous choices of ascent and descent and makes the Fairfield Group so appealing to the average hillwalker.

Walk FAR 1, the Deepdale Horseshoe, is a tremendous circuit rising from Patterdale to encompass all the tops around Deepdale. St Sunday Crag, Cofa Pike and Fairfield herself are the star prizes yet the whole trip, which takes in nine tops, is quite superb. But note: take care with navigation. The summit plateau can be very misleading in poor visibility.

Red Screes is tackled from Hartsop in Walk FAR 2 by way of Middle Dodd. The route continues over the head of Scandale Pass to Little Hart Crag and High Hartsop Dodd. Walk FAR 3 is the great classic, the Fairfield Horseshoe. It rises from Ambleside to round the valley of Rydal, ascending and descending two sublime ridges which offer easy walking and fine open views. In all, it offers seven tops, including the summit of Fairfield. Although it is described in anticlockwise

mode, it can just as easily be tackled in the opposite direction.

Seat Sandal curves to the west while dropping precipitously to the east. Although slightly outside of the main massif, it links naturally into an ascent of Fairfield. Walk FAR 4 follows this route and leads over Great Rigg, from where it continues over the rocky castle of Stone Arthur back to Grasmere. Wansfell, although beyond the main massif, forms the tail of the Central Fells and of the Fairfield Group. It is reached by Walk FAR 5.

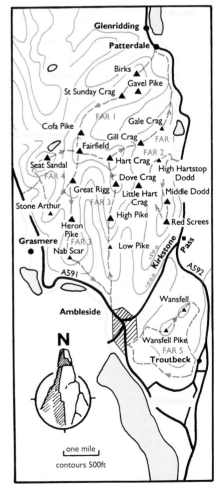

•FAR I•

DEEPDALE HORSESHOE

Arnison Crag 1422ft/433m
Birks 2040ft/622m
Gavel Pike 2572ft/784m
St Sunday Crag 2758ft/841m
Cofa Pike 2700ft/823m
Fairfield 2863ft/873m
Hart Crag 2698ft/822m
Gill Crag – Hartsop above How
1909ft/582m
Gale Crag 1680ft/512m

Valley Base: Ullswater.
Town Base: Ambleside.
Maps: OS OD5, The English Lakes –
North East. L90 Penrith & Keswick.
Length: 9.5miles/15km.
Ascent: 3495ft/1065m.
Approx Time: 5.25hrs.
Start & Finish: Car park (fee charged)
on the opposite side of the A592 to the
Patterdale Hotel (NY 396159).
Difficulty: Long and fairly arduous with
some steep sections of ascent and
descent. The ascent of Cofa Pike and
descent from Hart Crag are both exposed
and care is required, although technical
difficulties are minimal.

This is a long circuit through impressive
mountain scenery, with views of Fairfield's rugged north face. Pass the right
end of the Patterdale Hotel to find a footpath which leads to a kissing gate through
a wire fence. A broad path rises through
bracken and over a rise to descend to a
gate through a stone wall. Do not pass
through the gate but bear left following
the side of the stone wall as it ascends the
hillside, passing Oxford Crag to the left.
As the wall levels and turns a corner a
path continues the ascent to the left. Follow this to a level shoulder, then ascend
steeply left to a corridor. This runs to the
north of Arnison Crag. A little rocky step-
up provides access to the summit.

Regain the shoulder and continue
along the path. Initially, the path bears
left but then swings back right towards a
mound. Either energetically ascend and
descend this or go round it to the right.
Take a central course through the hollows and hummocks to find the grass

corridor of Trough Head. Cross it at its
head and ascend the shoulder which rises
beyond. Gradually curve to the right.

In a hollow beneath a craggy outcrop,
pass a little stone structure before gaining
the line of a ruined ancient stone wall.
Ascend this and continue in the same
direction when it peters out to gain the
path cresting the shoulder above. This
leads to the grassy and flat summit of
Birks, an unspectacular top yet one that
offers fine views.

Continue along the grassy shoulder
past slate outcrops. Gain the main trod
which rises from Grisedale to St Sunday
Crag directly in front. After a short section of ascent a well-defined path bears
off left for a comfortable diagonal climb
to Gavel Pike. The summit offers a commanding view around the impressively
craggy head of Deepdale.

The path back along the shoulder continues in a short way to the summit cairn
which marks the rocky top of St Sunday

Crag. The view of Helvellyn's steep eastern aspect, including Striding Edge, is
particularly fine.

A long shoulder falls to the col of
Deepdale Hause. To the right rise the
steep crags of Dollywaggon Pike that
guard Grisedale Pass. The ascent appears
to be formidable yet proves reasonably
straightforward. Nearing the top, boulder balances upon boulder and the going
is a little scrambly before it relents to
reveal a grassy, broken rock edge topped
by a cairn. This is the summit of Cofa
Pike. The path continues to traverse a
rocky point beyond, before beginning the
ascent of the final flanks of Fairfield. Here
the path splits, the left fork giving the
steepest but most direct ascent to the summit shelters of Fairfield. The first of these
perches directly above the precipitous
north face and is a good place to rest.

The summit plateau of Fairfield is
rather flat and featureless. A proliferation
of cairns and the meeting here of four

The Grisedale face of St Sunday Crag.

Red Screes and Middle Dodd above Kirkstone Pass.

◆ • FAR 2 • ◆

RED SCREES BY HARTSOP ROUND

Middle Dodd 2146ft/654m
Red Screes 2545ft/776m
Little Hart Crag – West Top 2091ft/637m
High Hartsop Dodd 1702ft/519m

Valley Base: Ullswater.
Town Base: Ambleside.
Maps: OS OD5, The English Lakes –
North East and OS OD7, The English
Lakes – South East. L90 Penrith
& Keswick.
Length: 5.25miles/8.5km.
Ascent: 2933ft/894m.
Approx Time: 3.5hrs.
Start & Finish: On the Hartsop side of
Kirkstone Pass there is a lay-by
(NY 402113) within the double bends of
the A592, a little south of Cauldale Bridge
and the Brotherswater Inn.
Difficulty: The path is a little vague (and
boggy) to start. There are steep sections
of grassy ascent and descent, though no
technical difficulties, and generally the
going is straightforward throughout.

major routes, also make it notoriously treacherous to navigate correctly and safely in poor visibility.

Pass the most northerly shelter to find, about 20yds to the south, another large stone shelter. At this point bear left to follow the northern rim of the plateau across the head of a gully known as Flinty Grave. Once located the path becomes well defined and leads along the spine of the mountain. Descend slightly past the head of Scrubby Crag before making a steep rocky descent to Link Hause. Beyond the dip ascend directly up Hart Crag, bearing right at the top of the rise to find the long, rocky summit crest marked by a cairn.

Cross the main path and bear slightly left to find a path leading down to the long ridge of Hartsop above How. After a short way the path skirts the edge of Link Cove to the left. It then bears right to follow a central line down the nose. Move left, with a short rocky scramble down a rock slab, to a steep descent leading to the

flatter ground below. The path leads over Blake Brow and through peat hags and bogs. Finally a short ascent leads to the top of Gill Crag on Hartsop above How (the latter name is attributed to the ridge as a whole). Continue down the shoulder through a corridor to follow a stone wall before rising again to the definite summit of Gale Crag, with its little rocky tops. Follow the wall and then squeeze through a narrow corridor to descend the ridge. Cross the wall which rises from the left by a stile, then follow the path to the left. The path leads down the broadening shoulder into the woods of Deepdale Park.

Enter the woods until after a little way the path splits. Bear left to a stile over a wall and an old barn beyond. Follow the path to a track, which leads onto the main road by the telephone kiosk at Deepdale Bridge near Bridgend. Beyond the bridge pavements, which seem to swap from one side of the road to the other, lead intermittently back to Patterdale.

After a short distance along the road a stile (signposted 'Public Footpath') leads into the field. Strike a diagonal line across the field until, above a barn to the right, a further sign points to a wooden bridge over Kirkstone Beck. Beyond this, a stile crosses the wall (note the footbridge over Caiston Beck to the right; this will be used on the return). A vague path leads up to the ruined fell wall. Ascending steeply, follow the line of the wall up and across the flanks of Middle Dodd. Keep with the wall as it levels. Where it drops over a little crag, it is best to ascend directly up the nose of the fell. The path becomes better defined as the ascent progresses. Nearing the top it bears right before rising to the summit cairn of Middle Dodd. This is a stirring viewpoint with an excellent prospect over Ullswater to St Sunday Crag and to Fairfield.

Walk past a hollow to a saddle. Cross the old wall to climb Smallthwaite Band, which contours around the rim of the rocky combe below (note the gargoyle formation on its left). The going eases and

On Dove Crag looking to Hart Crag and Fairfield's summit beyond.

This much celebrated round well deserves its popularity. It offers wonderful views over scenes of great beauty and the walking quality is first class throughout.

Bear right and cross the road to ascend the Kirkstone Road for a short distance only, before Nook Lane rises off to the left (the Golden Rule Pub lies to the right). Follow Nook Lane to Nook Farm. The track continues across Low Sweden Bridge before rising through the fields. Detailed description is unnecessary, the path is unmistakable as it rises up the eastern leg of this great horseshoe. Above the fields the main path bears right. An alternative to this follows the crest by the wall, rejoining the main trod a little further on

the trig point and summit cairn of Red Screes are gained. The view reveals the High Street Group to the east, and gives a real depth to the Lake District.

Circumnavigate the summit tarn and continue until a well-defined path splits down to the right from the rocky plateau. Cross a large rock slab near the bottom and follow the line of the wall which falls to the head of Scandale Pass. Cross the pass and ascend again, following the wall as it turns left and until joined by a fence. In front now lie the mysterious depths of Scandale Tarn. Our way lies to the right. Ascend by the line of the fence until the path bears off right, from where it ascends to the shoulder west of Little Hart Crag. Climb to the first and highest top, which is the West Top of Little Hart Crag. Cross to the second top, which is more shapely though lower, before finding an easy descent down to the left.

A grassy shoulder leads easily down to the final cairned grassy rise which is taken to be the summit of High Hartsop Dodd. Plunge steeply down the nose of the fell, following the well defined path with an excellent view across Brothers Water. As the angle slackens, scattered boulders begin to litter the hillside. A barn stands below while in the field beyond lie the curving earthworks of an ancient settlement. Before the barn bear right and follow the path through a gate in the wall. Walk along the flanks of the fell above the wall, until the path rises from the wall. After a little way, before a kissing gate a

path bears down to the left to the footbridge over Caiston Beck.

◆ FAR 3 ◆

FAIRFIELD HORSESHOE

Low Pike 1667ft/508m
High Pike – Scandale Fell 2152ft/656m
Dove Crag 2598ft/792m
Hart Crag 2698ft/822m
Fairfield 2863ft/873m
Great Rigg 2513ft/766m
Rydal Fell 2037ft/621m
Heron Pike 2008ft/612m
Nab Scar 1450ft/442m

Town Base: Ambleside, Grasmere.
Maps: OS OD5, The English Lakes – North East, and OS OD7, The English Lakes – South East. L90 Penrith & Keswick.
Length: 10.25miles/16.5km.
Ascent: 3430ft/1045m.
Approx Time: 6hrs.
Start & Finish: The central car park beside the Rydal Road (A591) out of Ambleside (NY 376046).
Difficulty: Extremely popular, on well-defined paths throughout and with no technical difficulty. This classic walk should not be underestimated. In less than perfect visibility, the summit plateau of Fairfield can be very misleading.

by the craggy little scar of High Brock Crag. Thereafter, the path follows the stone wall faithfully.

Surmounting the craggy face of Low Pike directly involves a short rocky scramble which can be easily bypassed to the right. Low Pike has a cairned top and offers a worthwhile view. Next comes the gentler height of High Pike and this is followed by the summit of Dove Crag. A descent and a slight ascent lead to the stony ridged top of Hart Crag. A steep dip into Link Hause is followed by a very stony ascent, before the angle eases and the path leads rapidly up to the summit plateau of Fairfield. The central shelter cairn is the best resting place on this walk.

Before moving off take great care to ensure the correct route is selected. Head initially east, then go south to find the plunge down the western leg of the horseshoe. Dip over Calf Cove and ascend to the cairned top of Great Rigg (sometimes called Greatrigg Man). It is easy to be excited by this viewpoint and impossible not to be moved. In front of you lies a scene of matchless beauty.

Plunge over the undulations of Rydal Fell towards its summit, then carry on to Heron Pike. Grasmere, Windermere and Coniston shine silver below. If it is late in the day the lights of Ambleside will be twinkling ever so brightly against the evening sky.

Nab Scar, a prominent cairn, soon follows. Steep craggy ground and Rydal Water lie directly below. Bear left, following the path until it intercepts the track which rises from the hamlet of Rydal. Descend the surfaced road past Rydal Mount, the final home of William Wordsworth. A track bears off to the left. This passes above Rydal Hall and across Rydal Beck by a stone arched bridge. A lovely return through Rydal Park leads to the A591 just outside of Ambleside.

Seat Sandal, Stone Arthur and Great Rigg above Grasmere.

OVER SEAT SANDAL TO FAIRFIELD

Seat Sandal 2415ft/736m
Fairfield 2863ft/873m
Great Rigg 2513ft/766m
Stone Arthur 1652ft/504m

Town Base: Ambleside, Grasmere.
Maps: OS OD5, The English Lakes – North East. L90 Penrith & Keswick.
Length: 6.25miles/10km.
Ascent: 2805ft/855m.
Approx Time: 3.5hrs.
Start & Finish: Limited verge parking by the side of the A591 (at the junction with a minor road to Low Mill Bridge) above Mill Bridge, Grasmere (NY 335091).
Difficulty: Steep sections of ascent and descent but no technical difficulties.

A strong mountain atmosphere pervades the tops of this delightful round high above Grasmere, with fine open views to the south and west.

Opposite the junction a lane, signposted 'Public Bridleway Patterdale' leads up past the houses. This was once the packhorse route between Grasmere and Patterdale rising over Grisedale Pass. It is now best known as 'Wainwright's Coast to Coast' route. A stone set in the last building on the right (a modern barn conversion) reads 'St Bees 40, Robin Hood's Bay 150'. The lane opens to Tongue Gill on the right and continues past a gate and barn on the left. Traditionally, the route went through this gate and made its way up through the fields on a track/path gated through the walls. This led onto the

Seat Sandal, Fairfield (in cloud) and Great Rigg above Dunmail Pass.

open fell for a direct and logical route up the nose of Seat Sandal. Now, however, the gate bears a sign 'Private' and the following alternative serves as a rather more indirect route to reach the same point on the open fell.

Continue up the lane to the confluence of Little Tongue Gill and Tongue Gill. Cross the first footbridge and follow the track which rises up to the left, with the spur of Great Tongue above to the right. The track crosses the stream and on to a gate. Bear right, following the line of the wall. Stay with the wall as it swings left. Take the path that leads horizontally left through the bracken, across the flank of the fell onto the long southerly nose of Seat Sandal.

Ascend steeply and continue to a grassy rise which offers a bird's eye view of Dunmail Raise. The route continues to make a stiff ascent until the angle eases

and the path becomes less well defined. Keep in the same line past cairns and continue over the summit plateau to the substantial cairn. Look north to Criffel across the Solway and south to Heysham across Morecambe Bay.

Cross the wall and follow it east to Grisedale Hause. Cut past the Grisedale Pass packhorse route and climb along the line of the ruined stone wall up the scree flanks of Fairfield. The path here is well defined, zigzagging before it gains the stony summit plateau of Fairfield.

First move east then leave the summit due south. Descend, then ascend the shoulder to Great Rigg and follow the main trod over the initial rocky top of Great Rigg until a grassy path swings off to the right. This leads down the spur, winding its way between rocky knolls. Pass the remains of a curious small square building on the way to the rocky castle of

Stone Arthur (also known as Arthur's Seat). A path takes a slight corridor through this rock outcrop. The highest point is a cairned rock to its left, and the best viewpoint is from the rocky edge to the right. This western wall is perhaps 30ft above the fellside below, so take extra care.

Bear right, above the cliffs. Descend past the ruins of a stone building to Brackenwife Knotts, then continue down the fellside to the line of the stone wall. Follow this to the old packhorse track just above Tongue Gill. Note the red colour of the rocks and observe the long abandoned workings of man. This was once the site of an old haematite mine.

Pass the fenced reservoir and proceed across Tongue Gill by the footbridge. Make another crossing, this time Little Tongue Gill, to follow the packhorse route back to the main road.

•FAR 5•

WANSFELL

Wansfell Pike 1588ft/484m
Wansfell 1597ft/487m

Valley Base: Troutbeck.
Town Base: Ambleside, Grasmere.
Maps: OS OD7, The English Lakes –
South East. L90 Penrith & Keswick.
Length: 6.75miles/11km.
Ascent: 1875ft/570m.
Approx Time: 3.5hrs.
Start & Finish: Fisherbeck car park by
the side of the Windermere Road (A591)
out of Ambleside (NY 377038).
Difficulty: A straightforward outing over
a popular low fell.

A much loved hill, Wansfell is to Ambleside what St Paul's is to London. Leave the back of the car park and turn left along the road. At the first junction walk uphill to the right. Follow this road and bear left to a junction with the Blue Hill Road. Continue up this to a walled lane leading up and left across the flanks of the fell.

Continue along the track until, at its walled end, it meets the main path which rises directly up the slopes of Wansfell. Follow the well-defined path, which steepens at the top and winds leftwards up to the rocky summit knoll of Wansfell Pike. (Below the summit knoll a stile on the right provides an easier alternative.) The dramatic aspect of Windermere, stretched out below, is one of the finest glories that any Lakeland fell can offer.

Take the stile just beyond the summit and continue along the undulating spine of the fell. A stile over the second wall gives access to the summit of Wansfell. This is marked by a few stones but the view is more restricted than from Wansfell Pike, which should be regarded as the spiritual summit. The path follows the line of the wall towards Troutbeck to intercept Nanny Lane. This leads directly into Troutbeck Village.

The Mortal Man Inn lies up to the left. Its sign reads: 'Oh Mortal Man Who Lives By Bread, What Is It That Makes Thy Nose So Red, Thou Silly Fool That Looks So Pale, Tis By Drinking Sally Birkett's Ale.'

This walk proceeds to the right towards the Post Office, which offers home-made teas. Immediately beyond the Post Office take the track, Robin Lane, which rises to the right. Follow this until it continues rising to the right, where it is named as Hundred's Road. A signed path bears off horizontally to the left. Follow this to High Skelghyll and continue along the track through Skelghyll Wood. Jenkin Crag to the left offers a celebrated viewpoint over Windermere. Continue along the track to the road within a short distance of the car park.

Wansfell Pike above the silver birch of Ambleside's Stock Ghyll.

5

EASTERN FELLS

Loadpot Hill Group LOA (12 tops) • Branstree Group BRA (11 tops)
Shap Group SHA (25 tops) • Kentdale Group KEN (6 tops)
High Street Group HST (25 tops) • Martindale Group MAR (16 tops)

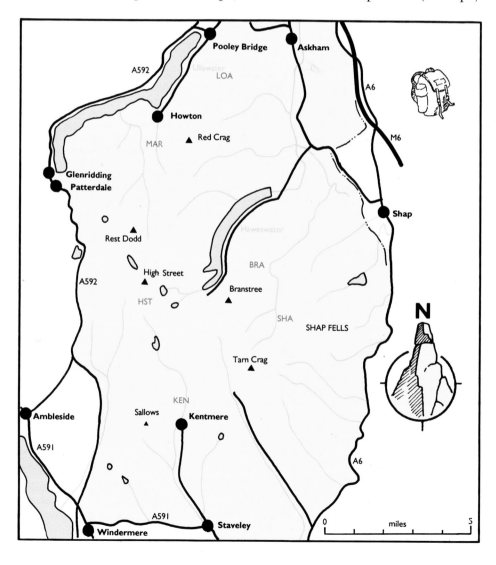

Between Ullswater and the rolling expanse of moorland above Shap, there are perhaps greater extremes of character than in any other area of Lakeland. Stretching between Penrith and Kendal with their west side unequivocally Lakeland and their east more Pennine in nature, these fells form the eastern fringe of the Lake District. They are a complex group of fells dominated by a broad high spine stretching south to north, the route utilized by the High Street Roman Road.

The key to understanding the area is to realize that High Street (the great broad shouldered fell of that name, not the Roman road) acts as the central pivot. Falling from this high ground are the shoulders and valleys that radiate from this central hub.

The area is a large one, consisting of some 139 square miles and 95 tops which may be divided into six identifiable groups. The Loadpot Hill Group forms the northern tip of the High Street Roman Road. Its western face, lying above Martindale and Ullswater, is steep and abrupt. To the east distances are long and rolling. This group is fringed at its extremity by a white cap of limestone which manifests itself as Heughscar Hill and Knipe Scar.

The Branstree (a corruption of the name Brant Street) Group forms the eastern flank of Haweswater Reservoir. It is a long declining shoulder that divides around Little Naddle Valley.

Forming the eastern extremity of Lakeland, the Shap Fells line the A6 and the famous pass of that name, which was once the arterial link between England and Scotland. Save for the oases of Longsleddale and the Sleddale Fells, they present a uniformly desolate scene.

The fells either side of lower Kentmere above Staveley and the plains stretching south to Kendal, I have called the Kentdale Group. They are low level and offer interesting walking suitable for short days.

The High Street Group is, of course, the highest and most important, with no less than seven tops over the 2500ft mark. The classic Kentmere Horseshoe and the Mardale Skyline are outings par excellence. Finally, within in the crook of Ullswater and beneath the long arm of High Street, bask a cluster of glorious fells known as the Martindale Group.

AREA FACT SHEET

THE VALLEY BASES

Kentdale
Camping: Rather Heath and Ashes Lane.
Youth Hostels: None.
Inns: Several in Staveley.
Bus Services: Kendal to Keswick.

Lowther
Camping: Bampton and Shap.
Youth Hostels: None.
Inns: Several in Askham, Helton, Shap and Bampton.
Bus Services: None.

Troutbeck
Camping: Limefitt Park.
Youth Hostel: Windermere.
Inns: Mortal Man, Queen's Head.
Bus Services: None.

Ullswater
Camping: Sykeside by Brotherswater, Side Farm in Patterdale. Various sites above Watermillock. East of the lake are Park Foot, Hill Crest, Waterside House.
Camping Barn: Swirral Barn above Glenridding.
Youth Hostels: Patterdale and Helvellyn.
Inns: Kirkstone, Brotherswater, Travellers' Rest in Glenridding.
Bus Services: Penrith to Patterdale.

THE TOWN BASES

Ambleside
Camping: None.
Youth Hostel: Ambleside (Waterhead).
All facilities except railway station.

Kendal
Camping: None.
Youth Hostel: Kendal.
All facilities.

Penrith
Camping: None.
Youth Hostel: None.
All facilities.

Windermere
Camping: Park Cliffe, Tower Wood.
Youth Hostel: Windermere.
All facilities.

The High Street Roman Road stretching over Red Crag and Wether Hill to distant Loadpot Hill.

LOADPOT HILL GROUP

·LOA·

The western flank of the Loadpot Hill Group is abrupt with steep, grassy ground falling from Red Crag, Wether Hill and Loadpot Hill to overlook the quiet Martindale Fells. A grand craggy rim topped by the cairns on Arthur's Pike and Bonscale Pike continues to run above Ullswater's sparkling waters. To the east a vast sprawling upland of hill grass, peat hag and heather falls slowly to the Lowther Valley. The deep and largely unfrequented valleys of Fordingdale, Cawdale and Heltondale penetrate the sprawling expanse. Across Moor Divock and the Lowther Valley spreads a limestone cap, adding yet a further dimension of interest to this often fascinating region.

This an area worthy of exploration beyond the High Street Roman Road. Rise from Ullswater along the craggy heights of Arthur's Pike to view one of Lakeland's most majestic Lakes. Follow the long nose of The Hause ascending

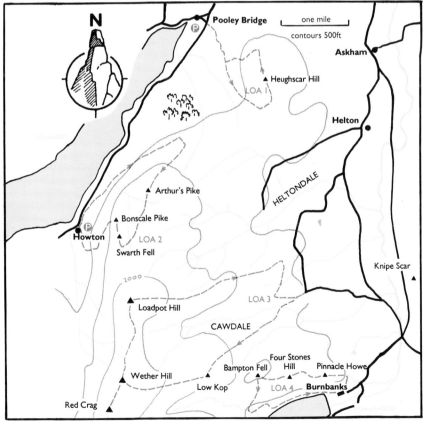

through a wilderness untamed. Stroll to Heughscar Hill and traverse the white limestone of Knipe Scar. And inspect the length of Haweswater from Bampton Fell. In all, five walks have been selected to cover this little known area between Haweswater and Ullswater.

Making a gentle ascent and offering rewarding views, Walk LOA 1 leads from Pooley Bridge over Heughscar Hill and provides a pleasant half-day outing; while a gentle rising traverse from Howtown with a return along the rocky rim of Arthur's Pike and Bonscale Pike is the route taken by Walk LOA 2. Experience a wonderful ambience and scenery of constant splendour over Ullswater.

Taking a horseshoe around Cawdale, Walk LOA 3 visits the highest tops of this group – Red Crag, Wether Hill and Loadpot Hill – and rises up the slender nose of The Hause to reach the High Street shoulder from the east.

Above the dam at Haweswater and the small community of Burnbanks stands a series of hills, including Pinnacle Howe and Four Stones Hill, topped by Bampton Fell. Walk LOA 4 explores these with a fine view along Haweswater to the rugged Mardale Head skyline.

•LOA1•

HEUGHSCAR HILL

Heughscar Hill 1231ft/375m

Valley Base: Lowther, Ullswater.
Town Base: Penrith.
Maps: OS OD5, The English Lakes – North East. L90 Penrith & Keswick.
Length: 4.25miles/7km.
Ascent: 740ft/225m.
Approx Time: 1.75hrs.
Start & Finish: Pooley Bridge (NY 471244), public car parks on either side of the bridge.
Difficulty: A straightforward walk suitable for a family afternoon's outing.
Note: Pooley Bridge is well endowed with many facilities.

Gentle and accessible, this is a pleasant outing over green turf and white limestone pavement. It offers rewarding views and interesting relics of antiquity.

Through the village centre take the Howtown Road past the church. Cross the main road at the junction. Continue in

the same direction and rise with the road until it becomes a track. Follow the track which rises up the flanks of the hill with ever widening views. A cairn marks the position where the High Street Roman Road descends from Loadpot Hill to cross our track and the flanks of Heughscar Hill. For those wishing to spend some time exploring the relics of pre-history bear right along the Roman road to the remains of a stone circle. Here a track bears back left onto the main route described. For those content with the main ascent, continue straight on past a boundary stone and path bearing off left. Rise with the path. Keep the plantation to the right and climb to the summit plateau of Heughscar Hill. Pass the distinct Boundary Stone and continue to the cairn that marks the top of Heughscar Hill. The view along Ullswater backed by Helvellyn is famous. To the east over the Vale of Eden looms Cross Fell.

Take the path descending to the north and cross above the limestone outcrop of Heugh Scar before gaining a track. Bear left, cross the Roman road, and descend to the corner of a wall. Deviate right by the wall to regain the original track taken in ascent.

Looking east from the heights of White Knott to Heughscar Hill.

Over Howtown to Bonscale Pike and Arthur's Pike beyond.

•LOA2•

ARTHUR'S PIKE AND BONSCALE PIKE ABOVE ULLSWATER

Arthur's Pike 1747ft/532m
Swarth Fell 1788ft/545m
Bonscale Pike 1718ft/524m

Valley Base: Ullswater.
Town Base: Penrith.
Maps: OS OD5, The English Lakes –
North East. L90 Penrith & Keswick.
Length: 5.5miles/9km.
Ascent: 1445ft/440m.
Approx Time: 3hrs.
Start & Finish: Howtown. Limited
parking at the public launching site
(NY 444199). The best way to start this
walk is by taking the steamer from either
Glenridding or Pooley Bridge (summer
service only).
Difficulty: Gentle in ascent, steep in
descent. A little boggy along the top
though generally straightforward.

The beautiful views that prevail over Ullswater are a feature throughout this walk. Cross the road to a metal gate and signpost 'Public Footpath, Pooley Bridge, Askham'. Rise through the field to exit via a garden gate on the left. Leave the garden by steps and a gate to the right, to gain the track running above the fell wall. Pass beneath the crags of Bonscale Pike with the cairns of Bonscale Pike, Bonscale Tower and Arthur's Pike (the cairn, not the summit) all visible. Continue along by the wall above the bridge that crosses over Swarthbeck Gill.

Proceed along the track beyond a barn, when the track splits. Bear right and rise diagonally up the hillside, following the sign 'Moor Divock, Helton'. Cross boggy ground either side of a covered reservoir and rise above the edge of the wood of Barton Park. Here a path bears off right from the track and climbs a sward of grass directly up the hillside. Follow this to the shoulder, then follow the grassy trod on the right to the top of White Knott.

Continue along the slight path, which runs along this Ullswater edge of Barton

Fell, past another cairned knoll on the right. Rise to a cairn then bear right out to the cairn on Loup Knott. Follow the path, traversing right to a stone cairn which stands below Arthur's Pike. This is possibly the most commanding viewpoint of the whole walk.

Climb the hill behind to a cairned knoll marking the summit of Arthur's Pike. Beyond can be seen the High Street Roman Road. Follow the vague path towards it, then bear right to intercept a grassy track falling from it towards the hollow of Swarth Gill. Cross the beck (immediately above the sheepfold) then ascend to the left over boggy ground to reach the flat and grassy summit of Swarth Fell.

Bear right and descend the shoulder to a col. As you ascend again, a grooved grassy track will be observed on the left edge. This is a man-made track that appears to serve a number of quarried levels on the steep flanks below. Follow the track to a cairn located on the summit of Bonscale Pike.

A path runs to the right, above the old track, across steep hillside to the lower

The cairn on the Ullswater edge of Arthur's Pike.

rectangular masonry pillar known as Bonscale Tower. Above stands another 'tower' of rather inferior construction, and a further smaller cairn. Rise to the higher tower. Find to its north an ancient path descending steeply to meet the elbow of the track that ran past Bonscale Pike.

This track runs diagonally down the hillside, below the crags of Bonscale Pike. Follow it until a path bears off left, traversing to the easier ground of the shoulder which stands above the bay of Howtown Wyke. Keep bearing left across it to find a grooved track, falling from above, which continues to make a diagonal ascent across the slopes of the hillside. Midway down the slope a track cuts off to the right and descends to the fell wall. Bear right to find the gate into the garden.

Valley Base: Lowther.
Town Base: Penrith.
Maps: OS OD5, The English Lakes – North East. L90 Penrith & Keswick.
Length: 8.75miles/14km.
Ascent: 1540ft/470m.
Approx Time: 3.75hrs.
Start & Finish: The road below Moorahill Farm provides limited parking in the verge (NY 495182).
Difficulty: Generally good paths prevail and the grassy walking is quite straightforward.

◆ LOA 3 ◆

AROUND THE CAWDALE HORSESHOE TO LOADPOT HILL

Low Kop 1877ft/572m
Red Crag 2333ft/711m
Wether Hill 2205ft/672m
Loadpot Hill 2201ft/671m

The narrow band of The Hause rising steeply above Cawdale Beck provides the most aesthetic and appealing route to the sprawling heights of this group. A grassy path follows the wall south of the road to continue across open ground before falling to an ancient stone slab bridge across Cawdale Beck. Rise steeply onto the plateau past the circle of Towtop Kirk. Known locally as the Druid's Circle, it comprises a slight raised, circular earth mound enclosing the remains of various stone structures. An excavation was carried out in 1902.

The path continues across the grassy plateau to join a well-defined track which rises up Hause End. The track levels, passing numerous knolls before moving

Loadpot Hill above the head of Cawdale.

between two plantations either side of the nose. Pass a cairn to the left and continue with the track to Low Kop. Below, there is a small sandstone boundary stone and a view to Haweswater.

Continue along the centre of the shoulder and rise again to the levelling of High Kop. There is no definite top here. Below to the south notice another small Boundary Stone. Beyond there are hollows and ridges, from where peat was once extracted. Make a level traverse out onto the shoulder and continue to the main track and path of the High Street Roman Road.

The independent top of Red Crag lies up to the left. Descend left to the col, then rise with the track through the gap in the wall up onto Red Crag. A fence stands to the right. To get the best views this should be climbed and a route taken up the western edge of the hill. A large cairn and post stand centrally just to the west of the fence which is holed at this point. The highest point is an uncairned grassy mound just to the south. An old quarry cutting lies immediately below.

Join the High Street Roman Road and follow it back down to the col. Climb the first grassy top of Wether Hill and continue to the next, the most northerly, which is taken to be the summit. The summit cairn of Wether Hill lies just above the track/path. Continue along High Street, descending to the col then ascending the grassy hillside beyond. Pass ruined Lowther House, which at one time served as a shooting lodge. On the summit plateau fell ponies can usually be found grazing. The path leads past a boundary stone to the stone trig point and top of Loadpot Hill. This extensive yet flat summit is relatively featureless. It is easy to lose direction in poor visibility.

Find the grassy path heading due east and follow it, making an easy and rapid descent down Hart Hill. A length of ancient stone wall on the left, marked as Bield on the OS map, is joined and a track enters from the right. Follow the track in descent as it leads leftwards across the boggy expanse of The Pen. As the track winds down Pen End above a coppice of trees behind the fell wall, bear right along the path above the wall. Pass a barn and move down to Carhullan Farm. A gated lane leads through the farm to the surfaced road below Moorahill Farm.

•LOA 4•

BAMPTON FELL ABOVE HAWESWATER

Pinnacle Howe 1257ft/383m
Four Stones Hill 1362ft/415m
Bampton Fell 1604ft/489m

Valley Base: Lowther.
Town Base: Penrith, Kendal.
Maps: OS OD5, The English Lakes – North East. L90 Penrith & Keswick.
Length: 4.25miles/7km.
Ascent: 1180ft/360m.
Approx Time: 2.25hrs.
Start & Finish: In the hamlet of Burnbanks, beneath Haweswater Dam. Either park at the end of the road opposite the houses (do not obstruct local parking) in the centre or by the locked gate on the track that continues along the northern shore. A track is signed 'MCWW Public Footpath' leading off right from the road (NY 506161).
Difficulty: Straightforward, though undulating and occasionally pathless.

Below Bampton Fell stands Four Stones Hill and its historical relics.

Erratic boulders rest on the white limestone pavement of Knipe Scar.

Follow the track through the bungalows and wood, rising to a locked gate and stile. Beyond the stile bear right along a grassy trod which cuts through the bracken. The track crosses another and traverses the hillside before making an ascent. To the right of the Aika Sike stream, stands the gorse covered Aika Hill and a well-defined track. Bear right to this track and follow it behind Drybarrows Farm. Bear left to climb the angular grassy mound of Pinnacle Howe.

Descend to the west across the low boggy area via a prominent mound. Continue straight up the flanks of Birkhouse Hill. Head south, picking a route over the numerous grassy hummocks to a view over Haweswater on the edge of the plateau. Beyond, on the flanks of Four Stones Hill stands a prominent cairn. Descend and cross to the cairn which provides a remarkable viewpoint along Ullswater to the rugged head of Mardale. Make a steep scrambly ascent direct to the top of Four Stones Hill. In the col beyond lies a path and the remains of a circular stone structure marked as Cairn on the map. Climb directly up the hillside beyond to cross a track rising from Drybarrows. Proceed up to the cairned top of Bampton Fell (unnamed on the OS map).

Descend the shoulder, aiming for a cairn on a rocky knoll. The track crossed previously runs beneath the cairn. Cross it again to work directly down the flanks of the hill to the track that passed behind Four Stones Hill. It leads to a wooden footbridge over Measand Beck. Do not cross the bridge but bear left along a path which falls to the main track above the eastern shore of Haweswater.

◆ L O A 5 ◆

KNIPE SCAR

Knipe Scar 1122ft/342m

Valley Base: Lowther.
Town Base: Kendal, Penrith.
Maps: OS OD5, The English Lakes – North East. L90 Penrith & Keswick.
Length: 3miles/5km.
Ascent: 500ft/150m.
Approx Time: 1.25hrs.
Start & Finish: Beyond the cattle grid leading onto the open ground of Knipe Moor there is limited parking on the verge (NY 521187).
Difficulty: A mild outing suitable for an afternoon stroll.

A path signposted 'Public Footpath' leads off to the right and crosses the moor. It rises to turn right and runs parallel to the fell wall. A track rises to old lime kilns and quarries but the path takes the stile in front over the wall. The signposted path continues to traverse the hillside before bearing left to rise past Low Scarside onto Knipescar Common.

Turn left and walk along the rim of the scar. The white bones of the limestone pavements reveal the darker erratic boulders deposited on top. At the most distinctive point of the scar the rim slopes inwards. A sunken circular trig point marks the top of Knipe Scar.

The extensive view across the breadth of the Eastern Fells is quite magnificent. To the east lies a platform of limestone pavement which is interspersed with golf-green grass. A stone enclosure (which is a listed ancient monument) is difficult to locate when the bracken is high. Beyond there are views to Cross Fell and the distant Pennines.

Proceeding north the scar diminishes and a way can be found down onto the shoulder below. A green swathe of grass cuts through the bracken down the hillside. Follow this path as it crosses a hollow and rises before finally falling back to the road.

Passing the cairn on Artlecrag Pike.

BRANSTREE GROUP

·BRA·

Overlooking Haweswater Reservoir, the great dome of Branstree stands at the head of four valleys. Drowned Mardale, damned and flooded in 1940 to supply water to Manchester, runs to the west; Longsleddale falls south; Mosedale (the higher continuation of Swindale) and Swindale run to the east. The Old Corpse Road between Mardale and Swindale separates the higher grassy domes of Branstree, High Howes and Selside Pike from the lesser knolls to produce a horseshoe around the vale of Naddle. The main attractions of the group are its position above Haweswater, its views to the rugged Mardale skyline and its quiet, relatively deserted landscape.

The Naddle Horseshoe, Walk BRA 1, starts at the base of Swindale. It gains the southern leg of the horseshoe via Scalebarrow Knott and then proceeds to encircle the valley. Visiting the highest top, Hare Shaw, the route strikes a way back above Haweswater. Finally dipping to Naddle Farm, the walk crosses the valley before rising to the southernmost shoulder of the horseshoe.

Walk BRA 2 takes the north ridge to Branstree. It continues over High Howes and Selside Pike before falling down the sharp shoulder of Selside End to the Old Corpse Road. The top of Brown Howe is reached before the Corpse Road provides a dignified end to the outing.

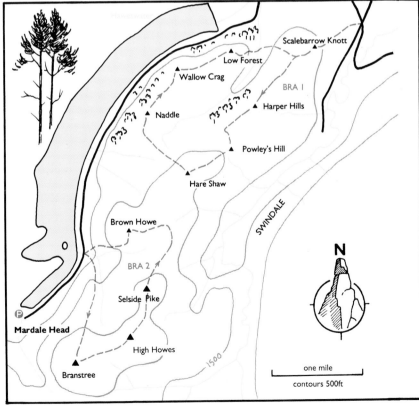

•BRA I•

NADDLE HORSESHOE

Scalebarrow Knott 1109ft/338m
Harper Hills 1375ft/419m
Powley's Hill 1526ft/465m
Hare Shaw 1650ft/503m
Naddle High Forest 1427ft/435m
Wallow Crag 1421ft/433m
Naddle Low Forest 1398ft/426m

Valley Base: Lowther.
Town Base: Kendal, Penrith.
Maps: OS OD5, The English Lakes –
North East. L90 Penrith & Keswick.
Length: 6.75miles/11km.
Ascent: 1706ft/520m.
Approx Time: 3.5hrs.
Start & Finish: A track rises from the
concrete road (NWWA – North West
Water Authority) just above the junction
with the Rosgill to Swindale road
(NY 528157).
Difficulty: Rough and undulating for
perhaps half its length.

This exploration of quiet hills encircles and then crosses the open end of the Naddle Valley. From the start the track leads quickly to the heights of Scalebarrow Knott. Bear right at the division and then right again from the track; the second cairned, grassy dome is the highest. Regain the track and follow it up Harper Hills. To the right nearing the top is the NWWA reservoir/pumping station and above to the left a cairned knoll. This is taken as the representative top for Harper Hills. Beyond, pick a route between the numerous grassy knolls before bearing right back to the track. Take the gate through the fence line and continue beneath the flanks of Powley's Hill. Ascend directly up the hillside, clipping the left edge of the bracken, to find the highest point. It appears to be a bouldery outcrop on the north east edge of the summit area, though the OS map indicates a point to the south.

Undulating terrain leads to a rise with two standing stones. The next objective is the cairned shoulder, indicated on the OS map, which extends eastwards from the heights of Hare Shaw. Intervening below there is a flat boggy hollow which is best circumnavigated by its left edge. Pass a small chambered mound before rising to the cairn on the knoll. The cairned summit of Hare Shaw is now in view. Make directly for it over rough and sometimes boggy ground. Although the cairned knoll appears to be the top of Hare Shaw and was apparently once an OS trig point, the OS now indicate that a rise to the south is actually the highest point.

Descend from here, picking the best route through the brackened knolls and flat bogs before ascending a shoulder and falling to the stone wall. Follow it to the left. Cross the col and make a short descent to a hurdle gate. Walk through this and right over another hurdle gate to find a track which traverses left across Naddle High Forest. At a gate in a fence bear left and ascend directly to the bilberry and heather top of Naddle High Forest. It is probably best to continue along the undulating rim, through sections of thick bracken and heather, directly towards the next prominent top of Wallow Crag. This cairned top stands beyond a wire fence, which must be climbed.

From Wallow Cràg to the heathery heights of Naddle Low Forest (Hugh's Laithes Pike stands to the left).

Beyond lies the raised edge of Naddle Low Forest. To its left and lower is the upturned knoll of Hugh's Laithes Pike. It supports a large ancient cairn and is a commanding viewpoint over the lower part of Haweswater and its dam. Unfortunately, barring your way is a wire deer fence. There is no stile so a visit depends on your personal philosophy (and agility). To the north east stands another, lower, cairned knoll. Although unfenced, this also is relatively inaccessible due to head-height heather and extensive bog. Bear right and south, descending to a wooden fence. Stride this and walk down rough pasture to the head of a track. This falls in turn to a further track, which can be followed through extensive woods of alder to a junction above Naddle Farm.

Bear right through a gate and stile to cross Naddle Beck by the ford. Below, the beck is crossed by the Swindale Aqueduct feeding Haweswater. A gate and stile above to the right lead to a track. Follow this through the woods to a gate. Beyond, the track becomes open. Rise to a gate in the fell wall, bear left along the shoulder and crest Scalebarrow Knott once again.

• B R A 2 •

BRANSTREE

Branstree 2339ft/713m
High Howes 2208ft/673m
Selside Pike 2149ft/655m
Brown Howe 1736ft/529m

Valley Base: Lowther.
Town Base: Kendal, Penrith.
Maps: OS OD5, The English Lakes –
North East. L90 Penrith & Keswick.
Length: 4.75miles/7.5km.
Ascent: 1755ft/535m
Approx Time: 2.5hrs.
Start & Finish: Lay-by/verge by the
Haweswater road (NY 480118).
Difficulty: After the initial steep section
of ascent easy grassy going prevails.

A mild-mannered round providing an excellent vantage point from which to view the wild grandeur around the head of Mardale. A little gate over the bridge gives access to Branstree's north ridge. A

From Branstree's Artlecrag Pike along the flanks of High Howes to Selside Pike and the lower fells beyond.

path leads up to the right out of the gill, zigzagging steeply. Pass beneath the large boulder with a cavernous base, named Hollow Stone. Continue past two ruined stone buildings to gain the easier angled grassy shoulder above. Head directly up the shoulder to the broad and flat summit plateau, from which the best views are achieved by touring its western edge. A circular basin trig point and little cairn mark the summit.

A grassy path leads out to an airier and much better perch – the rocky shoulder of Artlecrag Pike. Descend, bearing right to the fence line and stride over it to pass an old masonry survey tower (once used by the Water Authority to plot the course of the Haweswater Aqueduct). Pass the little tarn on a grassy neck between what is usually black peat water to the right and mud to the left. Continue up the tuffeted

grass to the top of High Howes (unnamed on the OS map). Descend directly down the shoulder to meet the fence line where it bends. Stride over this and continue to the cairn and shelter marking the top of Selside Pike.

The pronounced shoulder of Selside End falls to the Old Corpse Road. Make a grassy descent. At its base swing left to the Corpse Road by an old wooden post. This ancient track was last used to take the dead from Mardale to Shap for burial in 1736.

Follow the track towards Haweswater, bearing right to ascend the cairned top of Brown Howe. Return to the track beneath Rowantreethwaite Well and descend through the zigzags. Pass two ruined buildings, and walk through a rock cutting past the split ravine, with its cascading waterfalls and fine trees.

Sadgill Bridge,
Longsleddale.

SHAP FELLS

·SHA·

Massed along the eastern edge of the National Park, running parallel with England's main lines of communication with Scotland, scarred by quarrying and wounded by water extraction, the grassy tops of the Shap Fells are of stubborn character. They look towards the east with ease, yet refuse to acknowledge the presence of Lakeland to the west.

The Shap Fells are largely Pennine in nature, devoid of tarns or lakes with the exception of Wet Sleddale Reservoir and tiny Haskew Tarn. There is little of typical Lakeland in these hills.

The valleys of Longsleddale, Mosedale and Swindale divide these fells from the rest of the region, with the National Park Boundary and A6 defining the eastern limit. Of the many tops in these fells, only the three above Longsleddale rise above the 2000ft mark.

Within the complex, the valleys of Wet Sleddale, Wasdale, Crookdale, Borrowdale and Bannisdale all radiate eastwards, fan-like, from the high point of Harrop Pike. The grassy, heathery and sometimes boggy shoulders and plateaus between these forgotten valleys provide the high ground described. Only Longsleddale truly feels like a Lakeland dale; there is beauty in solitude here.

Of course, these fells do have their devotees, especially those who have a

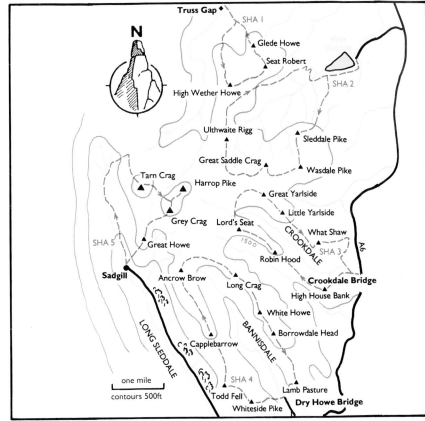

preference for isolation, length and arduous walking. Walk SHA 1 makes a circuit around Haskew Tarn on the high plateau of Ralfland Forest between Swindale and Wet Sleddale, while Walk SHA 2 takes in the tops above Wet Sleddale.

The Crookdale Horseshoe, Walk SHA 3, is an unexpectedly long outing which starts beneath the summit of Shap Pass. Whilst the names Robin Hood, Lord's Seat and Great Yarlside (tops visited en route) may sound grand its chief merit lies in its desolation.

Bannisdale, with its working farms and wooded slopes, is an attractive valley quite hidden from the public. Our chosen Walk SHA 4 makes a circuit around its heights, allowing a full inspection of this secluded valley.

Finally Walk SHA 5, Sleddale Fell, makes a circuit above Longsleddale, taking in all three of the tops above 2000ft.

•SHA 1•

OVER TRUSS GAP TO SEAT ROBERT

High Wether Howe 1742ft/531m
Seat Robert 1688ft/515m
Glede Howe 1562ft/476m

Valley Base: Lowther.
Town Base: Kendal, Penrith.
Maps: OS OD5, The English Lakes –
North East. L90 Penrith & Keswick.
Length: 4.25miles/7km.
Ascent: 1165ft/355m.
Approx Time: 2hrs.
Start & Finish: Swindale. Between the
North Western Water Authority intake
dam and the footbridge below Truss Gap
Farm there is limited parking (NY 516132).
The road up Swindale is extremely narrow
and parking is encouraged where the open
expanse of Rosgill Moor becomes a walled
lane into Swindale (NY 521142). This
lengthens the walk by 1.5miles/2.5km.
Difficulty: Although undulating and a little
boggy in places this is otherwise a straightforward outing over rough low fell.

This walk makes a high horseshoe around Haskew Tarn, taking in the highest and best defined tops of an otherwise

Truss Gap above Swindale Beck with Gouther Crag to the right.

desolate expanse of myriad rocky knolls, rough fell grass and peat bog. Truss Gap, above the farm of the same name, rises as an ancient track from the ford, stepping stones, and footbridge over Swindale Beck. It was reputedly once the continuation of the Old Corpse Road between Mardale and Shap.

Cross the bridge. Bear right to the track which rises through the bracken. The track zigzags and bears left away from the gill, before again bearing right to gain the plateau. An ancient cairn marks the top of Truss Gap (NY 519129). Its location should be noted.

Bear right. Cross Haskew Beck above the little waterfall and continue along the fell wall. Cross a knoll and traverse beneath the west face of Beastman's Crag. Cross a boggy area and head right onto the lower shoulder which falls from Fewling Stones. Climb the shoulder to the summit area, which resembles an elephant's graveyard. Continue easily along the undulating broad edge, where a track will be found to the right, to gain the rocky knoll of High Wether Howe. This is the highest top of this wilderness region between Swindale and Wet Sleddale.

A fence lies below. Bear left taking a line parallel to it but picking a higher, drier route through the boggy depressions. Tiny Haskew Tarn lies in the rough grassy basin to the left and, as often as not, a herd of red deer can be found grazing here. Seat Robert appears as a saddle in front. Climb its south hump to reach its higher northern dome. It bears a fine cairn and a considerable stone shelter to its right. A 'ring' trig point is sunk below the cairn to the south.

A high grassy shoulder falls north and this is followed to Glede Howe. There are two rocky knoll tops of apparently equal altitude. The first is larger, yet the second feels the most independent and has a cairn standing upon a flat rock. Below to the right is a ruined bield. Observe ahead the cairn which marks the head of Truss Gap Pass. Head for it, passing a knoll with a rowan growing from its face. Avoid boggy ground and pick up the right side of Haskew Beck as it turns around the corner of the fell wall. Pass the head of Gouthercrag Gill and return to Truss Gap.

•SHA 2•

SLEDDALE PIKE AND WASDALE PIKE ABOVE WET SLEDDALE

Sleddale Pike 1659ft/506m
Wasdale Pike 1852ft/565m
Great Saddle Crag 1850ft/564m
Ulthwaite Rigg 1648ft/502m

Valley Base: Lowther.
Town Base: Kendal, Penrith.
Maps: OS OD5, The English Lakes –
North East and OS OD7, The English
Lakes – South East. L90 Penrith
& Keswick.
Length: 8.5miles/14km.
Ascent: 985ft/300m.
Approx Time: 3.5hrs.
Start & Finish: Car park by Wet Sled-
dale Dam (NY 555114).
Difficulty: Paths are vague on the higher
regions of this walk and the going is rough,
alternating between thick heather and bog.

This is a walk for the enthusiast intent on treading all Lakeland tops, for man has lent heavily on this environment. Follow the track above Wet Sleddale Reservoir (where the dam appears massively out of proportion to the trapped water) to the first building at New Ings. A vague path rises to the left to a gate through the fell wall. Follow Poorhag Gill to a track which terminates in a curious wooden structure known as the Lunch House. Continue the ascent by Howe Gill before traversing right to a large boulder of beautiful pink Shap granite known as the Gray Bull. Long Fell to the east is the source of this granite and is the home of Shap Pink Quarry. Continue the right-wards traverse to the cairned summit of Sleddale Pike.

Proceed to the cairned heights of Great Saddle Crag then take a circuitous route down to Ulthwaite Rigg. The bridleway falling from Mosedale is the next objective; cross the wet hollow to reach it. Bear right along the track until another track leaves it, zigzagging as it falls to Sleddale Hall. Pass the Hall and descend along the track to a footbridge across the beck. The way back is via a further footbridge to New Ings.

The River Lowther (top) and Wet Sleddale reservoir (bottom).

•SHA3•

CROOKDALE HORSESHOE

High House Bank 1625ft/495m
Robin Hood 1617ft/493m
Lord's Seat 1719ft/524m
Great Yarlside 1952ft/595m
Little Yarlside 1691ft/516m
What Shaw 1593ft/485m

Valley Base: Kentdale, Lowther.
Town Base: Kendal.
Maps: OS OD7, The English Lakes –
South East. L90 Penrith & Keswick.
Length: 6.75miles/11km.
Ascent: 1705ft/520m.
Approx Time: 3.5hrs.
Start & Finish: Parking in the open
grassy verge below Crookdale Bridge
(NY 552055).
Difficulty: Although technically easy,
thick uncropped grass makes the initial
section of this walk particularly arduous
in summer.

Crookdale Beck twists out of sight of the
famous Shap Pass between the grassy
mounds of High House Bank and What
Shaw. A circuit of this hidden valley,
flanked on either side by grassy shoulders, provides a walk which may well be
of interest to the etymologist, ornitholo-
gist or botanist. Indeed, escape down the
bog strewn valley bottom is not by any
means an attractive proposition.

From a point just beyond the old stone
barn, climb the hillside directly to the fell
wall topped by a fence. Through-stones
provide a convenient stile. Bear left over
thick grass to the prominent cairn on the
shoulder. Just above the cairn find the
grass and bilberry mound top of High
House Bank.

Descend the shoulder through the gate
in the fence to gain the col. Slightly boggy
ground rises to a stone wall and gate.
Beyond, bearing slightly left, make a steep
ascent to the grassy summit of Robin
Hood. There is a fine ancient cairn below
to the west overlooking Borrowdale. The
going now improves considerably as does
the general ambience of the walk. Follow
a vague but satisfactory track all the way
along the shoulder to the grassy platform

The multicoloured wall on Great Yarlside.

of Lord's Seat. It is slightly ridged to the
south and this must be regarded as the
top. There is no cairn here.

Harrop Pike lies a considerable distance and height away at the head of

upper Crookdale. The terrain of rocky
knolls and peat hag do not allow it to be
easily reached from here. It is better to
swing right across the head of Crookdale
through the peat hags, over three little

With High House Bank (left) and What Shaw (right), Crookdale rises beyond Crookdale Bridge.

streams and above the stone walls of Crookdale Fold. A vague grassy path rises steeply up the hillside to the right of the ravine formed by the third stream.

Cross a small rocky outcrop and gain the easier terrain of Lawyer's Brow before striking rightwards to join an attractively coloured stone wall. Its main rocks are a crystalline rhyolite, hued from white to pink, and these are capped by those of dark Bannisdale slate.

Follow the wall across the indistinct summit of Great Yarlside to a grass mound on the right. Descend along the shoulder until a gap in the wall leads to the highest point of Little Yarlside. This turns out in actual fact to be the rim of a quarried hollow.

Descend on the right side of the wall, through Scotch thistles to the col. Rise again, taking the stile over the fence before bearing right over rough ground which rises to a fine cairn on a ruined wall. Follow the old wall line to stride a fence and gain the highest grassy top of What Shaw. Proceed along the fence to the left and rise to the second lesser top of What Shaw. Descend to another fence. Bear right to a track and follow it through the gate, beyond which it is joined by another track from the right through the gates to Crookdale Bridge Farm.

·SHA 4·

BANNISDALE HORSESHOE

Whiteside Pike 1302ft/397m
Todd Fell 1314ft/401m
Capplebarrow 1681ft/512m
Ancrow Brow 1816ft/553m
Long Crag – Bannisdale Fell 1617ft/493m
White Howe 1737ft/530m
Borrowdale Head 1734ft/528m
Lamb Pasture 1205ft/367m

Valley Base: Kentdale.
Town Base: Kendal.
Maps: OS OD7, The English Lakes – South East. L90 Penrith & Keswick.
Length: 8miles/13km.
Ascent: 2180ft/665m
Approx Time: 4hrs.
Start & Finish: Limited parking by the junction above Dryhowe Bridge, Bannisdale (NY 531017).
Difficulty: A long outing. Once altitude has been gained it becomes gently undulating and is thereafter mainly straightforward grassy plodding. However, there are substantial sections of bog and long, troublesome tussocky grass.

Walk SHA 4 is a substantial outing not to be underestimated. The tops are never exciting, though Bannisdale itself is a delightful and lonely valley, well hidden from general view. Above the road take the gate through the fence and head straight up the hillside of rough pasture. Stride the fence and continue the ascent to a cairned knoll. Bear right along the wall until ahead of a boggy hollow a stone stile crosses the wall to the left. Bear left of the little tarn and climb to the rock and heather cairned knoll of Whiteside Pike. The blue-grey rock outcrops are of Bannisdale slate. The view extends to the Howgills, across Morecambe Bay to Blackpool Tower and then west over Longsleddale to the Scafells.

Follow the path through heather, bearing left to the hog-hole in the stone wall. Take the stone slab stile and ascend the grassy flanks beyond to Todd Fell. Along the shoulder the next stone wall is surmounted using the through-stones as a stile. Progress along the shoulder until barred by a wire fence. Stride the lesser fence to the right and pass a rocky knoll which is joined by a further fence rising from Dub Ings Wood in Bannisdale. Stride this and climb to the top of Capplebarrow. The summit point is itself traversed by the fence. Fall down the grassy shoulder beyond, taking the gate through a fence before rising again to pass a boggy tarn. The ground here is very soft and it is probably wisest and safest to make a wide detour to the right. Continue the ascent to a corner in the fence. A cairn stands beyond it on the Longsleddale side – the highest top of Ancrow Brow and the highest point of this round.

Follow the old wall around the grassy shoulder, passing the pits from which the stones of its construction – Bannisdale slate – were once dug. The tiny fragments which now form the remains of the wall were originally much larger. From the highest grassy point at the head of Bannisdale descend down the shoulder. Cross boggy ground to a little rock outcrop. The bog behind this is best circumnavigated to the right before an ascent leads to a stile over the fence and gap in the ruined wall. Beyond, find the knoll of Long Crag – Bannisdale Fell.

Pick the best line over uneven grassy terrain to cross the line of a ruined stone wall. Begin ascending the heathery and peaty flanks of White Howe. Bear right away from the wall to a grass plateau capped by a concrete trig point. This is the top of White Howe. Dip down to a col and cross the fence by a stile and the ruinous wall by a gap to rise again to the top and little cairn of Borrowdale Head.

From here, descend the shoulder to a wet hollow. Follow down the left side of a drainage ditch or stream, which is the source of Priest Gill, and then bear left through the rushes to a gate in the stone wall. Take the gate and climb directly to the top of Lamb Pasture. Long, tussocky grass makes this short section of ascent an arduous challenge.

Make your way right to the edge of the craggy ground. To the right a grassy cleft leads steeply but safely down. A crag stands to the south. Below, pick the best way through the bracken to pass an ancient settlement, which is invisible when the bracken is high. Find a path falling to the road just before a wooden gate opens onto the lane which crosses Bannisdale Beck by Dryhowe Bridge.

·SHA5·

SLEDDALE FELL

Tarn Crag – Sleddale Fell 2178ft/664m
Harrop Pike 2090ft/637m
Grey Crag 2093ft/638m
Great Howe 1621ft/494m

Valley Base: Longsleddale.
Town Base: Kendal.
Maps: OS OD7, The English Lakes – South East. L90 Penrith & Keswick.
Length: 6.25miles/10km.
Ascent: 1770ft/540m.
Approx Time: 3.5hrs.
Start & Finish: Sadgill Bridge, Longsleddale (NY 483057).
Difficulty: Energetic sections of ascent and descent, on ground that varies from track to track, and negotiation of steep and craggy brackened fellside. No technical difficulties, though a degree of route finding ability is essential.

Whiteside Pike (right) overlooking the entrance to Longsleddale.

Longsleddale is both desolate and appealing. It is a narrow-bottomed valley running deep into the craggy steeps of the high fells. Beginning by Sadgill Bridge at the end of the surfaced road, this walk has a true Lakeland flavour, exploring the full length of the dale before making a high return over the tops of Sleddale Fell.

Follow the walled lane along the valley base to pass Buckbarrow Crag up to the right. As the track rises it becomes pitched with slate and begins to zigzag to break the grade. Down this route many a ton of fine Lakeland slate has been carried from the extensive quarries above. Pass a gate to continue to the walls of a sheepfold.

Bear right, signposted 'Public Bridleway Swindale Head', beneath the stone walls. Follow an indefinite path that crosses and re-crosses the stream along Brownhowe Bottom. Rise to a gate on the col above the head of Mosedale, then bear right by the fence line to rise with the fence up the grassy north shoulder of Sleddale Fell. Stride the old fence and continue to a rise. Where the original line of fence turns a corner, bear right to the rocky top of Tarn Crag standing above a masonry survey tower. The latter is a relic of the Longsleddale aqueduct originating from Haweswater.

Relocate the fence and follow it into the hollow with the boggy ground of Greycrag Tarn (usually no tarn exists) on the right. Rise with the fence to its high corner. Bear left to follow it along the boggy shoulder towards Harrop Pike. Stride the fence, and follow its left side to the rocky knoll of Harrop Pike. A splendid circular cairn marks the top.

Return along the fence, bearing left (south) at its corner to follow a vague path to the summit cairn of Grey Crag, located on a little knoll higher than the rest. Head west to pick a way through the rocky outcrops and grass troughs, before descending to a built-in gap in the fence at its corner point. Pass through it and proceed along the spur of Great Howe. Another survey tower will be seen to the left before the highest knoll of Great Howe is located. Below stands an independent little top and it is this which gives the best view along the length of Longsleddale. Again the path becomes indistinct and care must be exercised.

Bear right, picking the best route down to a line of fence which, to the right, becomes the fell wall. Cross the fence where it joins the wall then bear right to find a natural corridor leading down through the craggy ground. Thick bracken lies below but a path beats a way through it to a stile over the wall. Bear diagonally left across the field to a gate immediately above Sadgill Bridge.

The Survey Pillar on the summit of Tarn Crag (below), and the walled track leading up Longsleddale (right).

Looking east across Kentmere (from Kentmere Park) to Green Quarter and Brunt Knott.

KENTDALE GROUP

◆ KEN ◆

The Kentdale Group forms the southern extent of these Eastern Fells while Kentdale is the name given to the plains around the river Kent. Effectively, the group comprises the two shoulders of grassy fell either side of the lower half of the Kentmere Valley.

The Troutbeck Valley lies to the west with Longsleddale to the east. Two mountain passes separate these fells from their higher neighbours. Similar in nature, they provide low-level and easily accessible walking above the little town of Staveley. Although of meagre altitude, views are surprisingly extensive. Beyond Staveley the River Kent flows on through the 'old grey town' of Kendal.

Walk KEN 1 ascends Brunt Knott, the highest top of the group lying east of Kentmere. (Note: Due to access problems the three tops of Potter Fell, which provide a logical route, have been omitted.)

Walk KEN 2, a round of Skeggles Water, does just that. It starts from Kentmere Church to visit the highest tops of Kentmere's Green Quarter. The revealing view to the head of Kentmere, from Hollow Moor, is quite the best available and deserves much acclaim.

To the west of Kentmere, only the fells of Kentmere Park above the Garburn Pass are of sufficient altitude to be included. The three tops taken by Walk KEN 3, Capple How, Sour Howes and Sallows, form a little horseshoe around Kentmere Park. This is a splendid lofty outing.

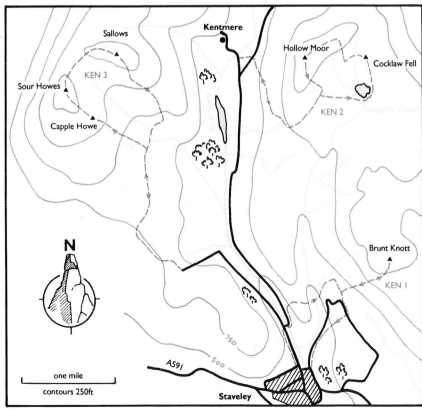

•KEN 1•

BRUNT KNOTT ABOVE STAVELEY

(EXCLUDING POTTER FELL)

Brunt Knott 1400ft/427m

Valley Base: Kentdale.
Town Base: Kendal.
Maps: OS OD7, The English Lakes –
South East. L90 Penrith & Keswick, L97
Kendal & Morecambe.
Length: 5miles/8km.
Ascent: 1085ft/330m
Approx Time: 2.5hrs.
Start & Finish: Staveley. Above Barley
Bridge and the Weir on the Kentmere
Road a lay-by provides parking space
(SD 470988).
Difficulty: A straightforward outing on
road, tracks and paths.

(Note: Unfortunately Potter Fell and its three tops, including that of Ulgraves, have had to be excluded from this walk because of access problems.)

Beginning from Staveley, beside the Kent where wild salmon jump the weir in autumn, this walk rises steadily through picturesque wooded countryside to the major top of the area. Proceed up the road by the river to cross Scroggs Bridge. Continue to a small road, just before the hamlet of Fellside Cottages, which climbs to the right towards Elf Howe. Bear right on a lane between the houses of Middle Elfhowe and Lower Elfhowe and ascend to the surfaced road of Hall Lane. A little way along this a sign on the right points out a path which climbs the field towards the farm of Ghyll Bank.

Intercept a track beneath the farm and bear right to a junction. Go left and ascend the road to Brunt Knott Farm. Pass through the farm, through a gate and over a stile, to follow the track which bears right up the fellside. When the track divides, bear left to a grassy plateau. There is evidence here of an ancient settlement although this is not indicated on the OS map. Continue to bear left up the grassy flanks of Brunt Knott. The top of Brunt Howe is marked by a distinctive stone trig point.

Return through Brunt Knott Farm, bearing left at the junction and left again where the surfaced road is joined. In a short distance a signposted path bears down through the fields to the right, to join Hall Lane. Descend the lane, bearing right at the bottom of the hill to cross Barley Bridge.

To the heights of Brunt Knott.

•KEN 2•

ROUND OF SKEGGLES WATER

Cocklaw Fell 1197ft/365m
Hollow Moor – Green Quarter Fell
1398ft/426m

Valley Base: Kentdale.
Town Base: Kendal.
Maps: OS OD7, The English Lakes –
South East. L90 Penrith & Keswick.
Length: 6miles/9.5km.
Ascent: 1295ft/395m.
Approximate time: 3hrs.
Start & Finish: Kentmere. Limited parking by the Church (NY 456041). Please park with all consideration to others, locals in particular. Do not restrict the road or block access points.
Difficulty: A little boggy in parts, there is no established path over the heights above Skeggles Water.

Skeggles Water is a lonely and desolate mountain tarn. It was once under threat of being excavated for diatomite (the present elongated shape of Kentmere Tarn is due to such activity), but now its tranquil future appears secure.

Looking over Skeggles Water to Cocklaw Fell.

From the church descend the road to cross Low Bridge and turn left at the junction. In a short way a signed path rises through the field to the right. Above the buildings and the surfaced Lowfield Lane, a track leads up to the right, signposted 'Public Bridleway To Longsleddale via Cocklaw Fell'. Follow this, taking the left fork at the junction. This grassy track ascends the shoulder of Green Quarter Fell, with Skeggles Water now in sight. Descend to just beyond the large ruined barn, joining a further track. Leave this and take the path right across the low ground to traverse the southern edge of Skeggles Water.

Take the wooden footbridge across the exit stream to bear left across boggy ground. A drainage ditch feeding the tarn is double-fenced for a way and must be crossed to the right. Proceed to the next inlet arm of the tarn and stride the single fence where it meets the water. Take the rise beyond and cross above the little crag and lonesome ash. Climb the grassy flank of Cocklaw Fell. Bear left across a ruined wall and ascend to the summit of Cocklaw Fell. Just to the north runs a wire fence line (unmarked on OS maps). Cross it by climbing the sturdy post at its corner point. Above lies the boggy and overgrown grassy bridleway to Longsleddale. Bear left along it to a stile and gate in the wall. Beyond this, bear right through a wall gap to climb the grassy shoulder above. Traverse left across a swampy hollow, then follow the edge of the shoulder with an open view to the right. Stride a fence line and ascend the top of Hollow Moor on Green Quarter Fell. The view into Upper Kentmere is magnificent.

Descend the flanks of the hill through rough pasture in the general direction of Skeggles Water to regain the grassy bridleway (not obvious). Take the gate through the new fence and the wall gap beyond, to return to the original junction of tracks by the old barn – a fascinating structure worthy of inspection. Bear right, making a slight ascent before the long descent home.

·KEN 3·

SALLOWS AND SOUR HOWES ABOVE KENTMERE PARK

Capple Howe 1460ft/445m
Sour Howes 1585ft/483m
Sallows 1691ft/516m

Valley Base: Kentdale.
Town Base: Kendal.
Maps: OS OD7, The English Lakes –
South East, L90 Penrith & Keswick.
Length: 6.5miles/10.5km.
Ascent: 1265ft/385m.
Approx Time: 3hrs.
Start & Finish: The end of Browfoot
Lane above Kentmere provides limited
parking (NY 448004). Do not obstruct the
road/tracks or the gate.
Difficulty: Generally straightforward,
although long tussocky grass prevails on
the ascent of Capple Howe.

The start from the end of Browfoot Lane
provides a gentle approach to this pleas-
ing and airy round. It is the same distance
as the approach from Kentmere, with the
advantages that it avoids the melee for
parking by Kentmere Church, and is
significantly easier.

Take the walled track heading north.
Keep right at the first junction and continue to a gate. The track splits again. To
the left can be found Hugill Village, an
ancient settlement. Take the gate on the
right and follow the track, with open
ground to the right and pasture over the
wall to the left. Continue past a walled
enclosure and wood over to the right.
Pass over a boggy section and follow the
track through a gate in the corner of the
wall to the right. Notice further on a circle of large rowans standing on the hill
above the track. A path bears left before
these fine trees and crosses a stream to
round the corner of the fell wall. Keep
right of the wall, avoiding the bracken as
best as possible, to find a gate at the wall
corner. This leads onto the open flanks of
Capple Howe.

Bear right and make a strenuous
ascent past the remains of stone grouse
butts en route to the top of Capple Howe.
Beyond, a wall crosses the shoulder and
behind it there is a triangular parcel of
fenced land. To its left, above the ruined
wall a stile climbs the fence. From here

ascend directly to the summit of Sour
Howes, from where there are tremendous
views to the west and up to Threshwaite
Mouth at the head of Troutbeck.

A distinct path falls through the grassy

*Along the lane to Kentmere Park with Sallows ahead and Capple Howe to the left
(below), and Sallows seen beyond the wall running from Sour Howes (right).*

hillocks along the line of the wall to the right. Rise to a wooden stile over a gated gap in the wall, take it and move directly to the top of Sallows. There is a raised ridge, with a little cairn placed centrally, known as Kentmere Park. Proceed eastwards down the shoulder to a stone shooting butt. Bear right, falling directly down the flank of the hill to join the old quarry track, then follow this down to enter a gated field. Walk down to the bridleway and bear right, leaving by a gate in the wall. Park Beck flows directly in front. Bear left before crossing to find the track rising to the hill alongside the rowans.

The great high spine of the High Street Group, seen over the head of Ullswater, profiled against a wintry sky.

HIGH STREET GROUP

·HST·

From High Street and its Roman road, the imposing jagged edge of the Mardale skyline stretches over the three pyramidal domes of Froswick, Ill Bell and Yoke to high Hartsop Dodd and Stony Cove Pike. Classic horseshoes, craggy steeps, stark edges, secretive tarns and soaring ridges abound. High Street, undoubtedly the most prized group of these Eastern Fells, holds the highest tops and is the central point from which all the other groups radiate.

The Romans recognized its principal asset when they drove their high-level road from Troutbeck over Thornthwaite Beacon, High Street, High Raise and on to Penrith. Despite their often ferocious appearance from below, once gained the tops are in the main gently inclining and grassy. Crest the heights and great distances can be traversed in superb scenery, with comparatively minimal effort. On these heights you can enjoy the company of red deer and Lakeland fell ponies in addition to red foxes and golden eagles.

Walk HST 1 tackles the classic

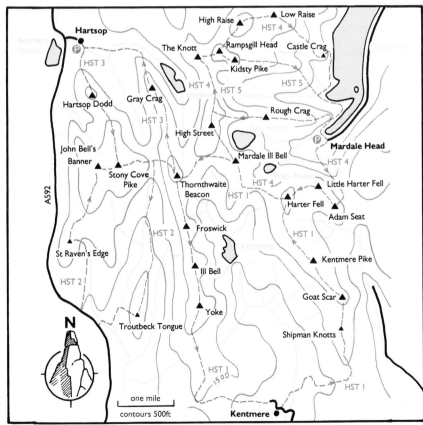

Kentmere Horseshoe in anticlockwise mode, leaving the best for last: Caudale Moor, with its tops of John Bell's Banner and Stony Cove Pike, rising to the east of Kirkstone Pass. Walk HST 2 takes in this fine round, starting up Woundale to crest St Raven's Edge before traversing the heights and descending to Threshwaite Mouth. Troutdale Tongue is included by way of a finale.

Plunging with intimidating steepness towards the hamlet of Hartsop, the two sharply honed ridges of Hartsop Dodd and Gray Crag feature in Walk HST 3. The Hartsop Horseshoe rounds Threshwaite Cove by connecting Stony Cove Pike with Thornthwaite Beacon via Threshwaite Mouth.

The Mardale skyline is one of Lakeland's most dramatic. Walk HST 4 makes this great traverse over Harter Fell, Mardale Ill Bell, High Street, and Rampsgill Head to High Raise. This is a long and thoroughly rewarding expedition.

Within this greater traverse the horseshoe of Riggindale has not been forgotten. Walk HST 5 rises up the classic ridge of Rough Crag to round the high tops and pass the Straits of Riggindale before returning over Kidsty Pike.

•HST I•

KENTMERE HORSESHOE

Shipman Knotts 1926ft/587m
Goat Scar 2054ft/626m
Kentmere Pike 2396ft/730m
Harter Fell 2552ft/778m
Mardale Ill Bell 2496ft/761m
Thornthwaite Beacon 2572ft/784m
Froswick 2360ft/720m
Ill Bell 2483ft/757m
Yoke 2316ft/706m

Valley Base: Kentdale.
Town Base: Kendal.
Maps: OS OD7, The English Lakes – South East. L90 Penrith & Keswick.
Length: 12miles/19.5km.
Ascent: 3440ft/1040m.
Approx Time: 6.5hrs.
Start & Finish: Kentmere. Limited parking by the Church (NY 456041). Please park with all consideration to others, locals in particular. Do not restrict the road or block access points.
Difficulty: A high mountain outing of some length.

This walk represents one of the classic horseshoes of the Lake District. Take the walled lower lane below the church past Rook Howe Farm. Keep on the lane, dipping around a bend to find before a gate a narrow squeeze stile gap in the wall on the right (not very well signposted – do not continue through the gate).

A wooden footbridge crosses the young river Kent and a path rises to cross the walled track of Low Lane by two stiles. Climb the grassy path directly to a stile leading onto the surfaced road of High Lane. Bear left through a gate to find a signposted 'Public Bridleway to Sadgill & Longsleddale' unsurfaced track rising to the right. Follow this past the barns of Stile End to the left, until it begins to level and a grassy hillock and old quarry working stand to the left. Before the gate in the wall lying at the highest point of this path, bear left to join the line of the wall and follow it steeply up the hillside. The angle eases, the wall turns a corner and the grassy knoll of Wray Crag stands to the left. Keep with the path by the wall over a hollow of cotton grass before again making a steep ascent. The first knoll is cairned either side of the wall. It is the second knoll which constitutes the top of

Over the head of Kentmere to Froswick (nearest), Ill Bell and Yoke with a Lakeland fell pony in the foreground.

Troutbeck Tongue.

Shipman Knotts. Follow the path to a stile. Above the stile follow the wire fence to the right to the top of Goat Scar, found within the corner of the fence. Beyond the fence, a cairned knoll gives an excellent view over Longsleddale.

Follow the fence up the grassy shoulder of Kentmere Pike to its summit. The trig point stands just on the other side of the wall. Descend to Brown Howe, then follow the fence directly up the shoulder to the large cairn on Harter Fell.

The path to be followed bears west off the edge of the plateau. Taking on a new order of drama while descending to the head of Nan Bield Pass, the path now traverses the exposed skyline between the head of Kentmere and Mardale. Small Water lies at your feet to the right while Kentmere Reservoir nestles below the bulk of Ill Bell to the left. Though the going is straightforward, exposure is considerable. At the head of the pass, a small ruined building forms an effective windbreak. There is also an opportunity to escape from the horseshoe by following the old packhorse route back down the length of Kentmere.

Our path rises, first to the left then swings back right. It levels along the shoulder before dividing into two. Bear right and make a steep ascent to the cairned top of Mardale Ill Bell. Move left across the summit, leaving the path leading to High Street to join with a lower path to the south: This path traverses the grassy hillside, with an impressive aspect across the head of Kentmere to Froswick, Ill Bell and Yoke.

Intercept the broader route of the High Street Roman Road. Bear right around the head of the hanging valley which holds Hayeswater, then climb up to the unmistakable column of Thornthwaite Beacon. This is the highest top on this horseshoe.

Below, on the western leg of this round are situated the most dramatic and widely acclaimed tops of the outing: Froswick, Ill Bell and Yoke. Descend the sweeping grassy shoulder and climb up to the first, the cairned top of Froswick. A descent and steep ascent gains the queen of the horseshoe, the slaty top of Ill Bell. Three cairns adorn the summit rocks of this fine mountain top.

Proceed down the shoulder, negotiating a few peaty hollows, to the broader summit of Yoke. The path leads on down the shoulder to a stile over a stone wall. Cross the stile and follow the west side of the wall down to the head of the Garburn Pass. Take the gate on the left and follow the Garburn Pass to Kentmere.

•HST 2•

CAUDALE MOOR ABOVE TROUTBECK

St Raven's Edge 1946ft/593m
John Bell's Banner – Caudale Moor
2477ft/755m
Stony Cove Pike 2503ft/763m
Troutbeck Tongue 1194ft/364m

Valley Base: Troutbeck.
Town Base: Ambleside, Windermere.
Maps: OS OD7, The English Lakes – South East. L90 Penrith & Keswick.
Length: 7.5miles/12km.
Ascent: 2345ft/715m.
Approx Time: 4hrs.
Start & Finish: Small lay-by by the west side of the Kirkstone Pass A592 road (NY 412063).
Difficulty: Although rough and stony in places with steepish sections of ascent and descent generally good paths prevail, except Troutbeck Tongue which is little visited.

Thornthwaite Beacon.

A sheepfold stands to the west of the wall. Proceed up the road to a gate and stile on the right. Follow the track into the beguiling wilds of Woundale through a gate, and cross an ancient stone slab bridge. The path follows the wall to the right of the beck to move steeply up the hillside. Rise to a large sheepfold. Bear left across the beck to climb grassy and boggy flanks to the track which leads to an old slate quarry. The slate here was known locally as 'pheasant eye' because of its rather ball- bearing like composition.

Ascend the hillside above the quarry to the crest of St Raven's Edge. A large cairn stands to the left and looks down to the Kirkstone Pass Inn.

Cross the rocky knoll to the north, which is indicated by the OS to be the highest point. The path continues by the wall into the dip before climbing up the long grassy flanks of John Bell's Banner. Follow the ruined wall line over a rocky outcrop until the path bears out left to a wooden cross in a cairn. This is known as Atkinson's Monument.

Ascend beyond the cairn then bear left to the prominent cairn of John Bell's Banner which marks the top of Caudale Moor, a superlative viewpoint. Cross the moor past the tarn and return to the ruined wall. A little way along the wall, notice the cairns that mark the highest top of Stony Cove Pike.

Bear east along a path which traverses the rim of Park Fell Head, before joining the main trod by the stone wall. A steep descent leads to the col of Threshwaite Mouth. Bear right along a little path over a wide spread of stones and continue down the hillside. The path leads out onto a grassy tongue between two streams. Pleasant woods line the ravines. Bear right to cross the small stream above the trees and continue along the path to a sheepfold. Cross Troutdale Beck at this point to walk above its east bank. Take a high contour to reach the gate in the stone wall, which encloses Troutdale Tongue (properly known as The Tongue of Troutdale Park).

Beyond the gate you reach a sheepfold.

Exit this by a further gate to the left. Follow the track for only a little way before bearing right to gain the grassy shoulder. Continue along the crest, passing curious stone structures to stride a wire fence. Bypass rocky knolls to the right to stand on the end knoll of Troutdale Tongue.

Double back for a short way until a route can be plotted to avoid the worst of the bracken down to the wire fence just above a large ash tree. Continue down the hillside, skirting the northern edge of an alder wood, to an ancient stone slab bridge. This is one of the most impressive of its type in the Lake District.

Cross the bridge and bear left along the west bank of Trout Beck. Above the confluence with Woundale Beck rise up the hillside to the right and follow a stone wall. Thick bracken prevails. At the field head cross the wall, then cross Woundale Beck to the left to ascend a leaning stone wall. Climb the field above to a gate situated to the right of a sheepfold. This exit takes you directly onto Kirkstone Pass and your return journey.

•HST3•

HARTSOP HORSESHOE

Hartsop Dodd 2028ft/618m
Stony Cove Pike 2503ft/763m
Gray Crag 2293ft/699m

Valley: Ullswater.
Town Base: Ambleside.
Maps: OS OD5, The English Lakes –
North East. L90 Penrith & Keswick.
Length: 5.5miles/9km.
Ascent: 2755ft/840m.
Approx Time: 3.5hrs.
Start & Finish: Parking area beyond the
hamlet of Hartsop (NY410130).
Difficulty: Steep sections of ascent and
descent, and surprising length, make this
walk more of an outing than first
impressions may suggest.

Take the kissing gate from the car park and immediately bear right, crossing the bridge over Pasture Beck. Ascend the stony lane and walk through the gate or stile to bear right up the steep grassy pasture by the stone wall. A narrow gate to the left leads through the fell wall. Continue to bear right to ascend by the stone wall climbing the hillside. Old mine workings can be observed to the left. At the high corner of the wall the grassy path leads directly up the nose. It gains a ruined wall before cresting Hartsop Dodd.

The path climbs the shoulder to the right of a stone wall. The going is easy and allows time to observe the extensive workings of Caudale Slate Quarry, once reputed to have been served by the steepest track in Lakeland. As the going levels, the cairn topping Stony Cove Pike is found to the left of the wall. Another wall falls to Threshwaite Mouth and the main path follows this down steps of rough

rhyolite. The path rising to Threshwaite Beacon now lies above. It is very steep here and the loose scree makes the going both awkward and strenuous in places. However, the ascent is comparatively short and the going soon levels. The path then bears right to the circular stone column of Thornthwaite Beacon, a remarkable structure approaching 12ft in height.

Head north to the grassy path which descends to Gray Crag. Proceed over a knoll to the cairned end of the ridge. Although lower, this is hailed as the top of Gray Crag and offers the better view.

The path falls steeply down the crest of the nose. About halfway down it steepens and becomes a little craggy. It then zigzags to avoid the worst and eventually joins the track descending from Hayeswater.

Bear left and take the gate into the walled 'avenue'. Continue along the track past a barn on the left to get across Haweswater Gill. The track, passing old mine workings and the site of a waterwheel, leads back to the car park above Hartsop and your starting point.

The Mardale skyline seen above Small Water on descent from Harter Fell.

•HST4•

MARDALE SKYLINE

Adam Seat 2185ft/666m
Little Harter Fell 2234ft/681m
Harter Fell 2552ft/778m
Mardale III Bell 2496ft/761m
High Street 2718ft/828m
The Knott 2423ft/739m
Rampsgill Head 2598ft/792m
High Raise 2633ft/802m
Low Raise 2474ft/754m
Castle Crag 1296ft/395m

Valley Base: Lowther.
Town Base: Kendal, Penrith.
Maps: OS OD5, The English Lakes –
North East. L90 Penrith & Keswick.
Length: 10miles/16km.
Ascent: 3315ft/1010m.
Approx Time: 5.5hrs.
Start & Finish: Car park at Mardale
Head at the head of Haweswater
Reservoir (NY 469107).
Difficulty: A long, reasonably arduous
mountain outing. Escape down Nan Bield
Pass cuts the distance considerably.

The Mardale skyline as viewed from the Old Corpse Road to Swindale, over the head of Haweswater.

Although the Dun Bull along with the rest of Mardale now lies drowned beneath Haweswater, the skyline around Mardale Head remains inviolate.

Leave the car park, cross the bridge and rise to the left. Follow the bridleway up Gatescarth Pass. At the col, bear right and follow the fence. The main path rises diagonally to the right of the fence and bears away from it – do not take this.

At the corner stride the fence to the top of Adam Seat. Return over the fence and follow it north along the shoulder to intercept the main path. Above the path to the right lies the rocky top of Little Harter Fell. Beyond this, you can climb the grassy shoulder of Harter Fell. Round the corner of the fence to a large cairn and viewpoint. Continue easily across the broad back to the summit cairn of Harter Fell. Take the path which bears west down the exposed edge between Mardale and Kentmere to the head of Nan Bield Pass. This is a useful escape route.

Follow the path up to the shoulder, which falls from Mardale Ill Bell. To reach the summit take the path bearing right. A well-defined route cuts directly up the grassy shoulder of High Street to intercept a stone wall. Follow the wall to

the concrete trig point and the cairn to its right, which marks the top of High Street. The highest of these Eastern Fells, this expansive, gently domed plateau is also given the name Racecourse Hill.

Descend along the wall to pass the little rise of Short Stile. The High Street Roman Road enters from the left at the point known as the Straits of Riggindale. Beyond the col keep to the path which bears left. Continue along above the stone wall until the grassy cone of The Knott stands to the left. Follow the wall rising to its cairned top. Return to the path and cross it to climb up the grassy flanks of Rampsgill Head. Intercept the main path and bear left to a cairn. To the north near the cliffs stands a further cairn. Between lies the highest point of Rampsgill Head.

Take the path along the cliffs and descend to a grassy col. A straightforward ascent leads to the rock strewn top of High Raise.

Break from the main trod of the High Street Roman Road and take a lonely, narrow path east to Low Raise. Its top is marked by a substantial cairn along with a circular stone shelter.

Follow the south east edge of Low Raise. Steep craggy ground lies to the left

above Whelter Bottom. Eventually, the edge steepens and a way must be picked through little craggy outcrops, below which stand two roofless buildings. Continue down the edge, picking the easiest line through the craglets to Lady's Seat. To the left stands the independent top of Castle Crag, which is separated from the hillside by two channels through the rock. Its top appears to be a high and flat-topped, curving bank of excavated slate. Whether it is a quarry site or an ancient fortification is open to interpretation. Nevertheless, it occupies a commanding position above Haweswater.

The face of Castle Crag is a steep cliff. Descent is probably best made to the north where an ancient track becomes submerged in bracken. Alternatively, to the south a very steep slope leads to scree and on down to the main path. This is only for the sure-footed.

It is probably best to descend to the small enclosed wood before bearing right to the main path which follows the contours above Haweswater. Take the path south, climbing at first to a col beneath Castle Crag. Here, the path is well defined and crosses the foot of Riggindale to return to the car park at Mardale Head.

•HST 5•

RIGGINDALE HORSESHOE

Rough Crag 2060ft/628m
High Street 2718ft/828m
Rampsgill Head 2598ft/792m
Kidsty Pike 2560ft/780m

Valley Base: Lowther.
Town Base: Kendal, Penrith.
Maps: OS OD5, The English Lakes –
North East. L90 Penrith & Keswick.
Length: 6.75miles/11km.
Ascent: 2395ft/730m.
Approx Time: 3.5hrs.
Start & Finish: Car park at Mardale
Head at the head of Haweswater
Reservoir (NY 469107).
Difficulty: A shorter version of the
Mardale skyline traversing above steep
craggy ground to the highest summit of
the group.
Note: This walk may be deemed out of
bounds by the RSPB if the golden eagles
are nesting between April and July inclusive.

Remote Riggindale takes its name from the finger-like peninsula protruding out into Haweswater (once Mardale). Circumnavigated by this excellent walk, a deserted valley surrounded by high hills provides a considerable wilderness experience. Sad relics, ruined buildings and field boundaries of the once thriving community of Mardale grace the valley floor and are passed on the return.

Take the kissing gate, cross the bridge and then bear right. The path bears right again to cross the bridge over Mardale Beck, rounding the head of Haweswater. Continue to rise above the sweet smelling conifer woods which now occupy The Rigg. Bear left up the path, skirting the bracken along the toe of the ridge. Follow the steepening path up the increasingly rocky ridge on the left side of the wall to crest the cairned top of Rough Crag. Enjoy a tremendous view and a real mountain feel, for both sides of this sharply defined ridge fall over crags to the valleys below; Blea Water lies to the south with Riggindale to the north.

Descend to the col and tarn of Caspel Gate. At this point a path rises from remote Blea Water, below to the left.

Make a steep ascent up Long Stile to emerge suddenly by the cairn on the edge of the flat and grassy plateau of High Street. The summit trig point lies a little way over to the left.

Descend by the wall, passing a short stile standing above the head of Riggindale to the right, to reach the col and Straits Of Riggindale. Take the path which rises to the right over Twopenny Crag with an open view into empty Riggindale below. Bear left to the cairns of Rampsgill Head before returning right to the obvious upturned nose of Kidsty Crag. Enjoy this commanding and airy summit marking the top of a crag poised above steeply sweeping fellside.

A path bears easily down the shoulder to find a natural corridor leading safely through the crags of Kidsty Howes. Descend to join the main valley path just beyond the stone arched bridge over Randale Beck. Bear right along the path and cross the footbridge over Riggindale Beck to enter an aisle of standing stones. Climb the rocky steps to pass through the corner of a larch wood. The path now bears out rightwards from the ancient aisle to climb the fields and round The Rigg.

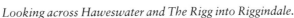

Looking across Haweswater and The Rigg into Riggindale.

Hallin Fell, guarding the entrance to Martindale, across Ullswater's Howtown Wyke.

MARTINDALE GROUP

· MAR ·

This blissful cluster of fells shelters itself within the crook of Ullswater, beneath the long arm of High Street. Place Fell is the most prominent, rising serenely above the head of Ullswater. Above the lakeshore to her north east, stands the rounded dome of Hallin Fell. Hidden beyond, outside the main tourist flow, there is the solitude of Boredale, Bannerdale and Martindale.

Martindale lies beyond Howtown, which in itself is only reached by a drive up the narrow cul de sac road on the east shore of Ullswater. There are two churches, St Peter's and the Old Church of St Martin, while the ruins of another rest on the heights of Boredale Hause. Patterdale and Hartsop offer some opportunity to penetrate the group, yet Martindale is undoubtably the best location from which to explore the area.

On examination, Place Fell will be found to form a high horseshoe around Scalehow Beck. Walk MAR 1 rises from Sandwick, with the towering profile of The Knight beckoning from an early

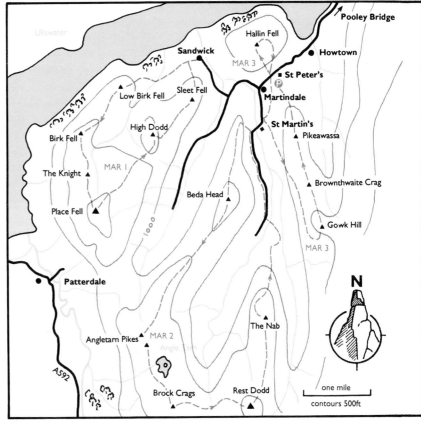

Place Fell above Ullswater.

stage, to ascend Birk Fell. It rises to the summit of Place Fell before falling over High Dodd and Sleet Fell for the trip back to Sandwick.

Walk MAR 2 rises from Martindale over the rocky pyramids of Winter Crag to the long ridge of Beda Fell. This considerable horseshoe, which lies at the heart of the group, extends around the lonely head of Bannerdale. Angletarn Pikes and Brock Crag lead to the high point of Rest Dodd before descent is made down the shoulder of The Nab.

The Martindale Edge, Walk MAR 3, is rather an oddity sprouting from the flanks of Wether Hill. From the bulbous Gowk Hill it narrows and proceeds over Brownthwaite Crag and Pikeawassa on Steel Knotts, falling to the pass between Howtown and Martindale. Beyond, between Ullswater's Sandwick Bay and Howtown Wyke stands the stately dome of Hallin Fell. Walk MAR 3 begins from the pass by St Peter's Church. The walk proceeds by way of Martindale before rising to Gowk Hill. Thereafter, the edge is followed north as it crosses the pass and rises to a worthy culmination and fine view on Hallin Fell.

• MAR 1 •

PLACE FELL ROUND

Low Birk Fell 1224ft/373m
Bleaberry Knott – Birk Fell 1680ft/512m
The Knight 1778ft/542m
Place Fell 2154ft/657m
High Dodd 1644ft/501m
Sleet Fell 1240ft/378m

Valley Base: Ullswater.
Town Base: Penrith.
Maps: OS OD5, The English Lakes – North East. L90 Penrith & Keswick.
Length: 5miles/8km.
Ascent: 2425ft/740m.
Approx Time: 3.5hrs.
Start & Finish: The hamlet of Sandwick (NY 423196), limited parking by the end of the surfaced road.
Difficulty: Steepish sections of ascent and descent; the going is rough in places.

For exquisite views and a fine position this walk is second to none. Leave Sandwick by the track signposted 'Patterdale';

a route described by Wainwright as 'the most beautiful and rewarding walk in Lakeland'. Move above the stone wall to an old stone barn on the right. Shortly after this the route bears right to a footbridge across Scalehow Beck. Rise with the track until at its highest point, above the corner in the wall, a path rises directly up the open fellside to the right. Note how Scalehow Force is visible to the left through the trees.

The path bears left slightly until the angle eases on a slight shoulder. It then zigzags to the right above little rocky craglets, rowan and holly to the nose of the fell. Ascend this directly to the top of Low Birk Fell marked by a large cairn.

Descend along the path through the brackeny hollows with rocky mounds to the right and past ancient ruins of stone buildings. Proceed across the hollow to the rim, with a view above Ullswater. Bear left over the bracken of Kilbert How to find a rising diagonal path across the steep flanks above. Follow the path for some 20yds, then climb directly up the steep hillside to a cairned, bilberry-clad top above Smeathwaite. This offers a view north to Carrock Fell and out across the Solway. Proceed across the heather and bilberry shoulder to the dome of Bleaberry Knott, which is the summit of Birk Fell. Pause to take in the view over Ullswater to the Central Fells – for it is nothing short of magnificent.

Ahead lies the towering shape of The Knight with Place Fell visible beyond. Skirt the low boggy ground to the right to cross an area of whaleback rocky knolls and grassy, boggy hollows. Suddenly appearing beyond the undulations, a well-defined path rises from Ullswater and climbs the grassy flanks above. At a col, bear left along the narrow rocky ridge to find the summit of The Knight. Note the slate embankment and distinct cairn below to the right.

Return to the path at the col and continue the ascent over a subsidiary ridge to the summit of Place Fell. A cairn stands to the west, offering the best vistas over Ullswater. The trig point lies on the rocky spur just to the east. The view in all directions captures the quintessential beauty of the Lake District.

A good path leaves the summit rocks to pass a little tarn in a hollow and heads north east along the shoulder of Hart Crag. This leads on down to the col of Low Moss, past a clear water spring to the left and a stone-walled sheepfold. Beyond this the path divides. Take the right fork, rising to a shoulder on the flank of High Dodd. At this point, as the path levels before descending, bear left to climb directly to the summit of High Dodd.

The best descent is found to the right down the grassy eastern flank. A route directly down the nose is steep and dangerously craggy so should be avoided. Descend through the bracken to gain the main path. Follow this until it bears right to make a steep zigzagging descent towards Boredale. At this point bear left along the shoulder. The path leads to the top of Sleet Fell. A cairn stands on a grassy mound just to the left of the path. Continue to the final grassy rise. Beyond, there lies an old ruined wall and over this a large cairn.

The most straightforward descent is to follow the line of the wall down the western flank of the fell. Near the bottom the wall disappears into thick bracken. However, a path prevails. It bears slightly left before falling to a track (which has descended from the col of Low Moss). Continue on this track directly back to the hamlet of Sandwich.

Trig point on the top of Place Fell.

•MAR 2•

MARTINDALE'S BANNERDALE HORSESHOE

Beda Head – Beda Fell 1670ft/509m
Angletarn Pike – North 1860ft/567m
Angletarn Pike – South 1854ft/565m
Brock Crags 1842ft/561m
Rest Dodd 2283ft/696m
The Nab 1890ft/576m

Valley Base: Ullswater.
Town Base: Penrith.
Maps: OS OD5, The English Lakes – North East. L90 Penrith & Keswick.
Length: 8.75miles/14km.
Ascent: 2740ft/835m.
Approx Time: 5hrs.
Start & Finish: Parking below the Old Church of St Martin, Martindale (NY 434183).
Difficulty: A long walk, undulating with steep sections of ascent. The going is rough and boggy in places, though for the most part paths prevail.

Rising from quiet Martindale to round the deserted head of Bannerdale, this walk makes an interesting voyage of discovery. Cross Christy Bridge and pass the farm buildings which stand to the right. Take the path rising to the right. Cross a track and ascend the hillside by the wall. When the track crests the brow, bear left along it over the rocky turrets of Winter Crag. Beyond, a grassy ascent up the nose of Beda Fell passes an ancient cairn on a rocky knoll to the right, before gaining the top of Beda Head. A small cairn stands on a knoll of rock.

A well-defined path continues along the ridge, first falling then rising again to the cairned shoulder of Bedafell Knott. Beyond this the ridge is crossed by an ancient packhorse route rising from Boredale Hause and falling to Dale Head. This remarkably exposed trod is still much in use by pony trekkers.

Continue along the ridge past a cairn on a knoll, until the path levels to cross an area of grassy hummocks above Heckbeck Head. Bear right off the path to the highest grass dome. Make a bee-line for

Angle Tarn from Angletarn Pike.

the rocky tower of Angletarn Pike North. This the highest of the Angletarn Pikes and offers a grassy bower fringed by stone. Leave it and cross the divide to scramble easily to the top of the second pike, Angletarn Pike South.

Pick the the easiest line of descent and weave a way through the craggy ground below. Cross two paths and descend to the hollow by the tarn. Stride the little stream from the tarn, and pass through a gap in the stone wall to ascend Cat Crags. The most central offers an excellent view over Angle Tarn.

The vague path continues. Cross a further gap in the wall before bearing right, by an old structure of flat slab stones, to the summit cairn of Brock Crags.

Leave the summit, taking the path over boggy ground to the left of a little tarn. Follow the line of an old stone wall to a junction with the path rising from Angle Tarn. Take the gate on the right and continue along the well-trod path. Satura Crag lies unseen below to the left. Bear right when the path appears to diverge and continue along the line of a fence. The path bears right at a point where the line of an old wall sweeps directly up the grassy flanks of Rest

Dodd. At the end of the line of wall, bear left to the substantial summit cairn of Rest Dodd. It offers a view over the wild valley of Ramps Gill.

Descend the steep northern nose of Rest Dodd to find a stone wall that crosses its flanks. This is the one-time barrier of the deer park. Today, however, the red deer can be seen wandering at will over these wild fells. To the right, as the wall begins its steep plunge towards Ramp Gill, find a gap. Cross through this and follow the path down and across the shoulder, through peat hags and bog, to rise up the broad and grassy head of The Nab itself.

Do not descend the nose directly (due north), as this is steep and precipitous. Nab End is a substantial cliff, hidden from above.

Initially, head south west to find an old stalkers' track. This turns to traverse the steep western flank of The Nab, passing beneath Nab End, before descending the lower section of the nose. A gate leads through the wall and the path/track continues directly down the easier shoulder below. Bear right at the next stone wall to find a gate. Take this and cross to the unsurfaced track beyond. Bear left to gain

the road and follow this down Long Grain to Martindale.

•MAR 3•

MARTINDALE EDGE

Gowk Hill 1545ft/471m
Brownthwaite Crag 1457ft/444m
Pikeawassa – Steel Knotts 1417ft/432m
Hallin Fell 1273ft/388m

Valley Base: Ullswater.
Town Base: Penrith.
Maps: OS OD5, The English Lakes – North East. L90 Penrith & Keswick.
Length: 5miles/8km.
Ascent: 1725ft/525m.
Approx Time: 2.75hrs.
Start & Finish: Lay-by opposite St Peter's Church, Martindale (NY 436192).
Difficulty: Good paths prevail and although undulating, the going is grassy and easy underfoot. Care should be exercised to safely circumnavigate the two-tiered crag of Birkie Knott above St Peter's Church.

This walk begins with a descent. Pass the church gate to gain the open fellside by Lanty Tarn. Bear right, away from the main track, on a small path. This makes a high traverse beneath the craggy lower face of Birkie Knott, to follow above the stone wall. Although thick bracken prevails, the path is continuous. When open ground falls away to the right to the Old Church of St Martin, descend to intercept a path which rises from the surfaced road. Follow the path above the fell wall to take the gap (the highest one) in the wall which forms the boundary of Martindale Forest. The forest is now a thin natural wood of hardy deciduous trees. The path rises to cross a bank of slate and passes the opening marked on the OS map as 'Cave'. Continuing to traverse the hillside, the path is now little more than a sheep trod. Pass above the next wooded area and cross a small gill. At a point where the curious red roofed building of The Bungalow is in sight below, and before reaching Mell Beck, the path disappears. Ascend the grassy flanks to the dome of Gowk Hill. A few stones stand on its western edge. The top will be found across a hollow of marshy ground to the east.

Now begins the traverse of the edge, with Martindale below to the west and Fusedale to the east. Bear right down the grassy flanks to meet a well-defined path (a barn stands over the stone wall to the right). Follow the path until it splits. Take the right fork which climbs to the summit of Brownthwaite Crag. Following the line of the wall, make a descent down a groove in the crag. Continue in the same line to eventually cross the wall (gap), where it turns to cross the edge. Make a steep ascent to the turreted Pikeawassa. The top is a sharp outcrop of grey lichened rock set above the shoulder.

Proceed along Steel Knotts until at the highest cairned top above the descent to Steel End, a path bears off to the left. Follow the path, which zigzags down the shoulder past the two-tiered crags of Birkie Knott, before descending to Lanty Tarn.

Cross the road and pass your starting point. Take the main grassy route straight up the flanks of Hallin Fell. On the shoulder overlooking Ullswater, bear right to reach the 12ft high cairn which marks the summit. Wonderful views along the lake make this climb a prized tourist attraction.

Follow the path descending eastwards, looking directly over Ullswater's last leg towards Pooley Bridge. Continue down through a natural cleft past little craggy outcrops until a distinct path bears off to the right. Follow this back to the road.

Looking along the Martindale Edge from Wether Hill.

6

SOUTHERN FELLS

Coniston Massif CON (21 tops) • Dow Crag Group DOW (15 tops)
Harter Fell Group HAR (11 tops) • Whitfell Group WHI (18 tops)
Black Combe Group BLC (5 tops) • Outlying Eastern Tops OUT (8 tops)

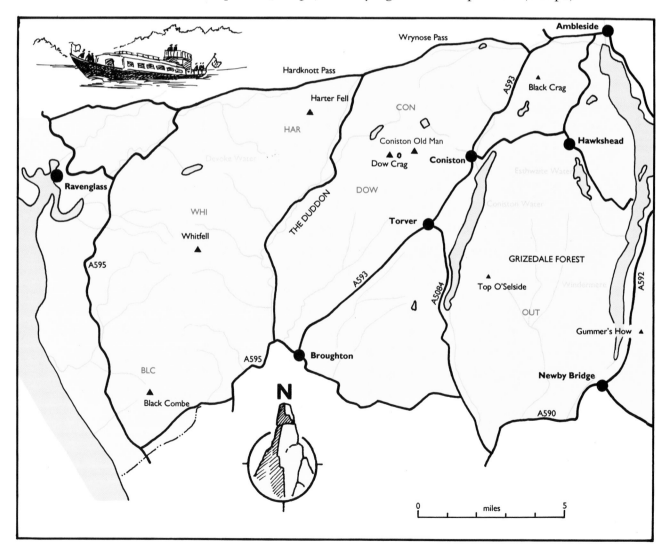

The Southern Fells rise from Eskdale, the Duddon, Little Langdale, Coniston Water and Lake Windermere. The area ranges from forest and lake, to high mountain and seashore. These fells are massive in their diversity and stand united by one underlying quality – each of them offers an unmatched openness of position and expanse of vista.

Stretching the full width of the Lake District National Park, the Southern Fells effectively underpin the entire region. Extending north from Morecambe Bay and the Duddon Estuary, they are separated from other areas by the Old Roman Road linking the west coast port of Ravenglass with Ambleside and Kendal via the mountain passes of Hard Knott and Wrynose. This area is the largest of the six in the book, covering some 280 square miles and comprising six main groups with 74 individual tops.

The greatest upland region of this expansive area lies in its western half, which is effectively split by the Duddon Valley into two chains. The most easterly begins in the north with the Coniston Massif, which rises above Wrynose Pass and the Three Shires Stone before declining southwards as a long shoulder over Dow Crag and Caw. It then crosses the head of Dunnerdale to terminate in Great Stickle at the head of the Duddon Estuary. The western extreme falls from Harter Fell to the west coast over Whitfell, ending with the solo dome of Black Combe.

To the east of this area a number of independent tops provide excellent excursions. These tops rise from long upland ridges which form the great troughs holding Coniston Water and Lake Windermere. They barely lift their heads over the 1000ft contour yet command an expansive view to the higher hills.

It is the higher tops, particularly those of the Coniston Massif, which command the greatest attention. Those to the south and west are less accessible, so they are generally less frequented by walkers. Perfect solitude may still be found here with only the herdwick sheep, red fox, peregrine falcon or raven to accompany you on the heights.

Throughout the area, mining and quarrying activities have been pursued vigorously since before the Romans arrived here. Evidence in the form of spoil heaps and mine shafts still remains, and these features now form an integral and barely obtrusive part of the landscape.

This is an area of great character and much variety. It is forged notably from mountain rhyolite, though Red Eskdale granite may be found around Devoke Water. On the southernmost top, Black Combe, the rock is made up of older Skiddaw slate. Wordsworth wrote of this fell: 'The amplest range of unobstructed prospect may be seen that British ground commands'.

AREA FACT SHEET

THE VALLEY BASES
The Duddon
Camping: Turner Hall at Seathwaite.
Youth Hostels: None.
Inns: The Newfield at Seathwaite.
Bus Services: None.
Eskdale
Camping: Boot, Fisherguard Farm.
Youth Hostel: Eskdale.
Inns: Burnmoor, Woolpack, George IV.
Bus Service: The Mountain Goat Mini Bus.
Great Langdale
Camping: Head of Valley, Baysbrown Farm at Chapel Stile, Neaum Crag above Skelwith Bridge.

Youth Hostels: Elterwater, High Close.
Inns: Old Dungeon Ghyll, Stickle Barn, New Dungeon Ghyll.
Bus Services: Ambleside to Old Dungeon Ghyll.
Little Langdale
Camping: None.
Youth Hostels: None.
Inns: The Three Shires.
Bus Services: The Mountain Goat Mini Bus.
Whicham Valley
Camping: Silecroft.
Youth Hostels: None.
Inns: None.
Bus Services: None.

THE TOWN BASES
Bowness-On-Windermere
Camping: Tower Wood.
Youth Hostel: Windermere.
All other facilities.
Broughton in Furness
Camping: None.
Youth Hostel: None.
Limited facilities.
Coniston
Camping: Coniston Hall.
Youth Hostels: Holly How, Coppermines House.
Limited facilities.

Wetherlam and the Greenburn Horseshoe seen above Little Langdale.

CONISTON MASSIF

·CON·

This the most northerly group in the Southern Fells is also the most mountainous. To the south of the range, Coniston Old Man touches the greatest altitude and is the undisputed king of the region. To the north, standing the furthest forward and offering the most satisfying selection of views, his queen, Wetherlam. When the white snows of winter cap the roof and the east wall stands stark with its steeper rocks still black, this massif appears almost Himalayan in character.

Seen over Windermere Lake or from the Central and Eastern Fells, the Coniston Massif appears as an extensive elevated plateau. Beneath this high roof stands a formidable looking east face. From the east, Wetherlam seems to merge in with the backbone of the group, which runs from Coniston Old Man to the summit of Wrynose Pass. In reality, Wetherlam stands forward, connected by another high shoulder at running perpendicular to the backbone.

Between Coniston Old Man and Wetherlam, a hollowed area is separated further by the ridge which runs down from Black Sails. It includes the tarns of Low Water and Levers Water and the mountain sanctuaries of the Coppermines Valley, the Boulder Valley and Red Dell. To the north of Wetherlam lies the hanging valley of Greenburn. To the east,

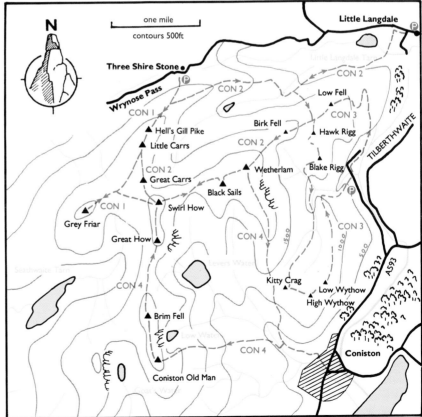

the face of Wetherlam overlooks the Tilberthwaite and Yewdale Fells.

Throughout this area there are mineral mines and slate quarries which date back to the Roman times and beyond. Yet despite these extensive workings of man, the essential character of these fells remains unchanged. Both in terms of unbridled spirit and majesty of form, this is a peerless massif of high hills.

With the advantage of starting from the Three Shires Stone at the summit of Wrynose Pass, Walk CON 1 climbs Wet Side Edge to Swirl Edge. Moving west it visits Grey Friar before making a sweeping return to descend Wet Side Edge to the Three Shires Stone.

Beginning and ending in Little Langdale the Greenburn Horseshoe, Walk CON 2, includes a favourite route up Wetherlam. Moving on to Black Sails it then ascends the notorious Prison Band directly to the summit of Swirl How.

Rapid descent is made down Wet Side Edge before Greenburn Beck is crossed and a straightforward return made along the old mine track.

Behind the craggy rim of the Yewdale and the Tilberthwaite Fells, a table top plateau lies hidden. Beginning at the foot of Tilberthwaite Gill to circumnavigate the plateau, Walk CON 3 includes ten individual tops in a delightful exploratory round. From Great Intake to Kitty Crag there are views of surprising quality.

The Great Round Of Coniston, Walk CON 4, captures the essence of the group and the Southern Fells in general. It includes both Coniston Old Man and Wetherlam which are linked via the high-level crossroads of Swirl How. The route traverses the roof of the massif and includes Brim Fell, for the most part staying above an altitude of 2500ft/760m. Nevertheless, the going throughout is generally straightforward.

The remains of the crashed RCAF Halifax Bomber LL 505.

•CON 1•

CARRS, SWIRL HOW AND GREY FRIAR FROM THE THREE SHIRES STONE

Hell Gill Pike 2172ft/662m
Little Carrs 2270ft/692m
Great Carrs 2575ft/785m
Swirl How 2630ft/802m
Grey Friar 2536ft/773m

Valley Base: Little Langdale, Great Langdale.
Maps: OS OD6, The English Lakes – South West. L90 Penrith & Keswick.
Length: 4.5miles/7.5km.
Ascent: 1740ft/530m.
Approx Time: 3hrs.
Start & Finish: The Three Shires Stone at the summit of Wrynose Pass (NY 277027).
Difficulty: Straightforward and for the most part on well-defined paths. Starting from the summit of Wrynose Pass, an altitude of 1289ft/393m, offers a positive advantage. It should be remembered that this is a high-level route with a reputation for misleading people when the clouds suddenly descend.

Just above the famous Three Shires Stone on the summit of Wrynose, Wet Side Edge rises over Carrs to Swirl How. Within a matter of minutes the tops of the Bowfell Group become your neighbours. This sublime mountain outing has the advantage of instantly placing you in a high and remote environment. Wetherlam and Coniston Old Man soon join the exalted company, and the sheep pastures of Fairfield lead onto the summit of Grey Friar.

A well-worn path rises to the south of the road just beyond the summit rocks of the pass. Although initially steep it levels to contour out across the hillside, with splendid views along Wrynose Bottom and over Hardknott Pass to Harter Fell. From here it steepens suddenly, then it veers left to climb a little cairn on Wet Side Edge. Ahead lies the rugged profile of Great Carrs and Swirl How.

The edge is no more than a steady climb. As it gains an easier shoulder, an

Above Wrynose Pass, Wet Side Edge rises over Carrs to Swirl How.

independent rock island to the right of the path offers a cairned top, Hell Gill Pike, which occupies a commanding position above Wrynose Bottom. The path rises to a rocky niche through the crest of the shoulder. To the left a rocky protuberance marks the top of Little Carrs.

A flat area and a lower hollow separates Little Carrs from Great Carrs above. Falling to the left, a deep gully of breathtaking steepness offers a view to Greenburn Reservoir. Take the path which weaves up the rocky turret to the left (the path leaving the hollow to the right traverses over Wether How in the direction of Grey Friar and will be used in descent). Pass the head of a further gully and walk easily up a slope to the outcrop of white rhyolite crowned by a cairn. This marks the summit of Great Carrs.

Follow the shoulder on its Greenburn edge to the curved, stony-rimmed col known as the Top Of Broad Slack. Prior to reaching it, just to the right lie the sad remains of an aircraft wreckage. The landing gear lies here, with the remainder of the plane scattered down Broad Slack. A cairn and wooden cross mark the site with the following inscription: 'Halifax Bomber, LL 505 – 'S' For Sugar, RCAF, October 22 1944'.

A stony climb levels towards the summit of Swirl How where jagged outcrops of rhyolite resemble the layers of an unfolding pine cone. This is an important high-level crossroads that offers access due south to Coniston Old Man and east to Wetherlam.

Briefly retrace your steps to the col. Make a bee-line west down easy slopes to

the meeting of paths on the grassy pastures of Fairfield, then ascend to the stony top of Grey Friar. Two cairned rock outcrops adorn the summit area. The most south easterly is the higher, while the north westerly offers the finest view.

Return to Fairfield and take the path which leads off to the left (north). Moving easily over Wether How, it rejoins the original path in the hollow beneath the top of Little Carrs. Follow the main path down Wet Side Edge until a knoll is marked by a large cairn. A path to the left falls to another rising from Wrynose. This is a more direct route than that taken in ascent. A closer inspection of the Three Shires Stone reveals that it is limestone and bears only the word 'Lancashire' on its surface. So whatever happened to Westmorland and Cumberland?

WETHERLAM AND THE GREENBURN HORSESHOE FROM LITTLE LANGDALE

Birk Fell Man – Birk Fell 1722ft/525m
Wetherlam 2502ft/762m
Black Sails 2443ft/745m
Swirl How 2630ft/802m
Great Carrs 2575ft/785m
Little Carrs 2270ft/692m

Valley Base: Little Langdale,
Great Langdale.
Maps: OS OD6, The English Lakes –
South West. L90 Penrith & Keswick.
Length: 8.75miles/14km.
Ascent: 3200ft/975m.
Approx Time: 5.5hrs.
Start & Finish: Little Langdale Village,
limited parking by the side of the road
above the telephone kiosk and opposite
the road junction signposted 'Tilberthwaite – Unfit For Cars' (NY 316034). Do
not block the road or any entrances.
Difficulty: Although good paths prevail
this is a long high mountain walk, often
over rough stony ground. The final ascent
of Wetherlam involves a few steepish
rocky sections, possibly just falling into the
category of a very mild scramble.

Overlooking Little Langdale Tarn towards the Greenburn Horseshoe.

Having woken to a view of this round for most of my life, you could justifiably accuse me of bias. In my opinion, these are extraordinary mountains which offer a magnificent expedition. Quietly massive Wetherlam is the prominent hill, while Swirl How, although higher and second only to Coniston Old Man in altitude, stands supplicant behind. Dropping into Greenburn are the steep crags of Carrs broken by a series of deep gullies. This round traverses them all, rising up Wetherlam and finally descending Wet Side Edge, to make a high horseshoe around Greenburn.

Proceed up the main road to a crossroads at the top of the hill. Turn left down the drive to High Birk How Farm. A tremendous view over Little Langdale Tarn and up into Greenburn reveals itself. Take the gate on the right before reaching

the farm. This leads across fields and down to Slater's Bridge. A two-span stone bridge crosses the young River Brathay, one a flat slab of slate and the other a masonry arch reputed to be of Roman origin. Cross the field to a walled track and turn right. Follow the track passing the buildings of first Low and then High Hall Garth. Enter through a gate and cross a little stream, after which the track rises then levels. Ignore a path which forks back up to the left. Just past the head of the tarn, the track to Greenburn branches off left. Follow the track as it rises gently to a stone wall. Walk through the gate then bear left to follow the wall rising up the fellside.

As the going levels near the head of Birk Fell Gill, a rocky knoll rises just right of the wall. Circumnavigate this and climb to a post and wire fence. Bear right

past a stile then go round the corner of the fence. Take the second stile to gain the flanks of Birk Fell. Climb the hillside, first moving to the left and then climb more directly, picking the easiest way to the top of Birk Fell – Birk Fell Man. There are two cairns on two different rock outcrops; both seem of equal altitude.

Continue along the shoulder of Birk-fell Hause, noticing the many different mine levels and spoil heaps to each side. Keep away from any openings though. Both Dry Cove Bottom above Tilberth-waite and Greenburn have been extensively mined for copper. Greenburn takes its name from the green copper colouring of its beck. Hen Crag, buttressing the east face of Wetherlam, lies to the left.

Move right to a natural rock rake/corridor climbing Wetherlam Edge. Nearing the top, a number of options are available

charm. Wetherlam looks tenderly over unspoilt Little Langdale and grandly to the Scafells, the Pennines and across Morecambe Bay.

The path becomes more defined as it crosses the northern flanks of the mountain above Greenburn. Beneath the head of Black Sail make a direct, virtually pathless ascent. Descend to regain the main trod and follow it down into the V to the col of Swirl Hause. The valley to the left falls to Levers Water. Greenburn lies to the right, providing an escape from the horseshoe if necessary.

Up ahead rises Prison Band, aptly named for it is a gruelling ascent to Swirl How, the highest top of the round. From this summit, however, the going is easier and less strenuous. Save for distance, you have cracked the horseshoe. (See CON 1 for further comment on the next section to Wet Side Edge.) Descend to the broad rimmed col, the Top Of Broad Slack. Continue to the cairned rock outcrop on the edge of the precipice which marks the summit of Great Carrs. The path leads down the rim to a hollow, with the top of Little Carrs just to the right. Either follow the edge, with views down into Greenburn or move left to the main path. Both routes lead over a broad shoulder to Wet Side Edge. Plunge rapidly down the edge, until slowed by the steeper and rockier end of the edge known as Rough Crags.

The path bears down to the right and is clear-cut. Beneath the steepest section, follow the broad shoulder before forking down to the right to a stone wall falling to Greenburn Beck. Crossing the beck should not prove difficult. Just above lies the mine track back to Little Langdale.

with a little rocky scrambling of a moderate nature necessary. The going soon levels and the summit cairn on a rocky outcrop is reached. The eye can follow the River Brathay from its source to the head of Windermere Lake, a journey of great

Slater's Bridge, Little Langdale.

•CON 3•

TILBERTHWAITE AND YEWDALE FELLS

Great Intake – Low Fell 1327ft/405m
High Fell 1404ft/428m
Hawk Rigg 1447ft/441m
Haystacks 1381ft/421m
Blake Rigg 1388ft/423m
Kitty Crag 1427ft/435m
Long Crag – Yewdale Fells 1381ft/421m
High Wythow 1345ft/410m
Low Wythow 1220ft/372m
Brackeny Crag 1212ft/370m

Valley Base: Coniston, Little Langdale or Great Langdale.
Maps: OS OD6, The English Lakes – South West. L90 Penrith & Keswick and L96 South Lakeland.
Length: 6.25miles/10km.
Ascent: 1805ft/550m.
Approx Time: 3.75hrs.
Start & Finish: Large car park by the side of the road, beneath the quarries, just before Gill Bridge and Low Tilberthwaite (NY 306010).
Difficulty: Rough and boggy sections, occasionally pathless, but generally of no particular difficulty. Quarry holes and mine shafts of incredible depth abound. Many are unfenced and highly dangerous – stay away from them. Opposite Great Intake, Betsy Crag remains a working quarry – beware of blasting.

This walk makes a circuit of the craggy rim of low level fells above Little Langdale, Tilberthwaite, Yewdale and Coniston. It is an exploration into a forgotten world. Few vantage points look over this upland table, where generations of men once toiled to exploit the earth's natural resources of slate and copper ore. Only one small working quarry remains; the rest, extensively reclaimed by nature, remain as fascinating relics of the past.

Principally however, nestling below the grand auspices of the east face of Wetherlam, this is a walk on which to enjoy the natural world. Craggy top, ancient larch and bracken combine with an airy isolation. From the Low Fell shoulder beneath Great Intake, views over Little Langdale and Blea Tarn to

Great Intake provides a fine viewpoint.

Langdale Pikes could not be bettered; and from Kitty Crag above Coniston extends a vista of quite surprising proportions.

Cross the bridge and proceed along the metal road to High Tilberthwaite Farm. Take the high gate on the left out of the farmyard and follow a rough track, passing through a gate to its summit point. Just beyond, a grassy track loops off to the left, rising gently to a gate and stile in a stone wall.

Above stands an extensively quarried hillside. Take the stile then follow the track to the right, passing an open level on the left. It climbs the toe of the quarry bank and passes a ruined building on the right. To the left, quarry works have created a narrow rift running up the hillside.

Initially keep to the right to round a bank of slate spoil, then cross a low stone wall. Bear left to a built-up level, crossing the rift. In the quarry hole immediately in front (the higher) lies one of the illicit whisky distilling dens of Lanty Slee, the most notorious local whisky manufacturer. Take the path climbing the right edge of the rift for a little way until it is easier to traverse right into a rough stream bed. Move up its right bank. There is no real path here, but climb to reach a boggy area with another slate spoil heap over to the left. Circumnavigate the bog to the right then climb rough heathery ground. Cross rightwards towards the elevated massif of Great Intake and climb its steep flanks at the midway point.

To the right, a long shoulder leads to sharp slatey outcrops from where there are good views. Up to the left lies the final rocky knoll of Great Intake. To climb it, first bear slightly left on a sheep trod. Make a rather awkward rocky step in an exposed position before easier climbing gains the summit cairn.

Descend first right then left, taking care to avoid two craggy outcrops. A hollow, boggy area leads to a stile over the stone wall. Walk round the rocky knoll, then take the first stile over the wire fence. Climb directly past twisted and stunted larch trees to reach the summit and cairn of High Fell.

Continue into the dip beyond, where numerous old stumps of larch were reputedly felled during the First World War, then pass through a crown of larch to gain the open head of Hawk Rigg. The summit lies beyond a little tarn.

A steep descent follows through thick larch. Move slightly left, taking care to avoid the steepest craggy section. Follow a corridor below the aptly named grassy hump of Haystacks. On its top, the most prominent cairn provides a view over the slate quarries to Elter Water.

Head straight down towards Blake Rigg, then rise gently up its grassy shoulder to the final rock outcrops which mark the summit. Return down the shoulder of Blake Rigg until it is possible to head due west across the peat moss to pick up a track rising directly up the edge of Dry

Cove Bottom. Descend the track until a sweeping bend brings the head of the distant Tilberthwaite Gill into sight. At this point bear right above some old mine buildings and past a deep unprotected rift (the fence is ruined – keep away as this hole is very dangerous). Cross the beck just below a pleasant rocky cascade. Bear first left, though keep high above the moss, to find the high miners' track which circumnavigates Yewdale Moss. The high track eventually crosses beneath mine workings to a further track. Continue along this until it drops to cross the stream. Bear slightly right and ascend the grassy slope to the track (an effective short cut). Follow this past a number of old quarry workings on the left and Hole Tarn on the right. Reputedly the silver grey slate from this area adorns the dome of St Paul's Cathedral.

At the highest point of the track move up the grassy flanks to the left. Traverse left to the cairned top of Kitty Crag. Cross the hollow and ascend a grassed-over track, to the long edge of Long Crag. A dished shield of rock adorns the top. Pass a little tarn on the right and ascend High Wythow. The next gentle, rock scattered mound is Low Wythow. Beneath is the collecting basin that feeds White Gill, a lovely cascade of water seen from the Coniston/Ambleside road below.

Head due north. Despite first appearances the way is quite simple and relatively level. There is no path, but with care an easy route can be selected which weaves through the rocky knolls and bracken to Brackeny Crag. This is a fine slab rock outcrop with a number of rowan trees and a holly growing from its eastern flanks. Meanwhile, Yewdale Moss lies to the east and this is our next objective. Descend first north, then west to a distinct grassed track through a natural corridor. Continue west, leaving this track behind, to pick up a well-worn path which circumnavigates the moss on its eastern edge. Follow this until it dips and crosses Crook Beck. Rise to the right along a smaller path which leads down the south bank (true right) of Tilberthwaite Gill. This passes a copper level before turning down Penny Rigg.

After a short exposed section above an elbow in the gill the track improves and leads easily past slate quarries and down to the car park.

GREAT ROUND OF CONISTON

Coniston Old Man 2633ft/803m
Brim Fell 2611ft/796m
Great How 2526ft/770m
Swirl How 2630ft/802m
Black Sails 2443ft/745m
Wetherlam 2502ft/762m

Valley Base: Coniston.
Maps: OS OD6, The English Lakes –
South West. L90 Penrith & Keswick and
L96 South Lakeland.
Length: 7.75miles/12.5km.
Ascent: 3150ft/960m.
Approx Time: 5hrs.
Start & Finish: Limited parking by the
side of the road rising to the Coppermines
Valley track (SD 300979), or in Coniston
Village. Do not block any entrances.
Difficulty: A long high mountain route.
Generally straightforward and over
well-worn paths.

Any walk up Coniston Old Man, the dominant leader of the pack, is something special. Circling the Coniston Fells, the Great Round of Coniston underlines the undefinable character that is unique to the Southern Fells.

From the village, this walk travels through the Coppermines Valley. It follows the quarry tracks first to Low Water then directly to the summit. A long and broad shoulder sweeps north over Brim Fell to Swirl How. Descent of the Prison Band leads to Black Sails and then on to Wetherlam. Beneath, lie the mines and quarries around Low Water, Levers Water, the Coppermines Valley, Boulder Valley and Red Dell.

Beyond the gate, the surfaced road becomes rough and stony. Easy walking leads to the Miners' Bridge across Church Beck. A well-worn path skirts the south side of the beck for a way until, after a stile, it begins to rise to the left. On Crowberry Hows the path joins with the quarry tracks which lead easily to Low Water. It then rises again until a final section of path leads to the summit cairn of Coniston Old Man. This is a powerful position

with views extending to all points of the compass, including Blackpool Tower.

A gentle descent and ascent leads north along the shoulder to the curved top of Brim Fell. Descend again to Levens Hause, the lowest point of the ridge located centrally above Levers Water. En route to Swirl How, you cross Great How. Swirl Band leads gently to the circular beehive cairn which marks the summit of Swirl How.

Descent of the Prison Band is nowhere near so arduous as ascent, nevertheless it is a steep, rough and stony exercise. The path rises to skirt Black Sails and then on to Wetherlam. This is a marvellous vantage point from which to look beyond Coniston and her fells.

A reasonably cairned route leads along an easy shoulder above large cliffs, notably Hen Crag, which is formed by two deep gullies on either side. Take care not to stray too near the edge before connecting with the ridge of Lad Stones. Descend this and finally bear left to find the quarry track rising from the Coppermines Valley. Follow the track, weaving through the quarries to the valley floor.

Coniston Old Man and Brim Fell over the Coppermines Valley.

Caw rises boldly from a sea of cloud, with Black Combe, Buckbarrow and Whitfell in the distance.

DOW CRAG GROUP

·DOW·

From the cathedral-like architecture of Dow Crag, a lengthy shoulder declines to Great Stickle. To the east lie Coniston, Broughton Moor and a collection of secretive and unspoilt valleys which feed the River Lickle. This is an area that once hummed with activity; nowadays only one working quarry, Broughton Moor, remains. To the east lies the elfish beauty of the Duddon Valley, reflecting an air of peace and solitude. From the rocky heights of Dow Crag to the intricate intimacy of the Dunnerdale Fells, this is a region of high contrast.

The shoulder is effectively split into three distinct sections, each covered by the three circular walks described. A high mountain grandeur and sweeping openness stretches from Dow Crag to White Pike, which towers over Caw Moss.

Beyond the moss the shoulder consolidates again to rise in a series of knobbly humps. The hills are collectively known as the Dunnerdale Fells; they stretch over Caw to be divided into two further areas by the valley of Dunnerdale.

Rising from the ancient Walna Scar Road above Coniston, Walk DOW 1 circumnavigates Goatswater to traverse the high shoulder from Dow Crag over Buck and Brown Pike across Walna Scar to White Pike. Finally, it descends from White Maiden to return over High Pike Haw and Torver High Common.

The steep flanks of White Pike rise above Caw Moss before the shoulder again takes shape with a series of knotty outcrops which culminates in the rocky pyramid of Caw. South of Caw, Long Mire cuts into the shoulder almost as if to

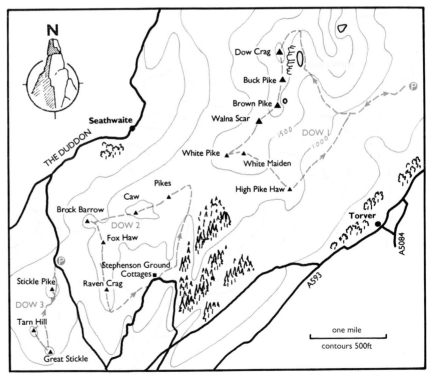

emphasize the latter's independence. Beyond, she rises again with an upland spur running down the east side of the valley of Dunnerdale. Walk DOW 2 rises from and returns to the tiny hamlet of Stephenson Ground. It traces an ancient trackway to the ridge before continuing over Pikes and Caw to cross Long Mire. After visiting the top of Brock Barrow, it then follows the subsidiary ridge over the tops of Fox Haw and Raven's Crag above Dunnerdale.

The most southerly section of the group is marked most distinctively by the plucky, if petite, spire of Stickle Pike. These fells west of the Dunnerdale Valley are easily accessible from Kiln Bank Cross, the start of Walk DOW 3.

◆ DOW 1 ◆

DOW CRAG TO WHITE PIKE SKYLINE

Dow Crag 2554ft/778m
Buck Pike – Seathwaite Fell 2441ft/744m
Brown Pike 2237ft/682m
Walna Scar 2037ft/621m
White Pike 1962ft/598m
White Maiden 1995ft/608m
High Pike Haw 1161ft/354m

Valley Base: Coniston.
Maps: OS OD6, The English Lakes –
South West. L96 South Lakeland.
Length: 7.75miles/12.5km.
Ascent: 2280ft/695m.
Approx Time: 4.5hrs.
Start & Finish: The Walna Scar Road
above Coniston. From the centre of
Coniston a surfaced road rises steeply to
the fell gate marking the start of the
unsurfaced Walna Scar Road. Pass the
gate to find ample parking spaces beside
the track (SD 289970). The road beyond
is rough and used by the heavy plant serving Brossan (Bursting) Stones Quarry,
therefore it is advisable to leave vehicles
at the point described.
Difficulty: A high mountain ridge, rough
and stony in places though generally
straightforward. Torver High Common
may be boggy in places and Torver Beck
must be forded (usually no problem) to
regain the Walna Scar Road.

The high skyline between Dow Crag and White Maiden/White Pike forms the watershed between the Duddon Valley and Coniston. It provides a mountain walk of considerable quality. The summit of Dow Crag is reached after first travers-ing the shore of Goat's Water. A long shoulder falls over Buck Pike and Brown Pike, from where it continues gently over Walna Scar to White Pike before dou-bling back to White Maiden. The route back over High Torver Common, in the shadow of the higher mountains, is spiced with historical landmarks and aban-doned slate quarries. This is a round of quite dramatic mountain scenery and extensive views.

Once an important through route between Coniston and Seathwaite, the Walna Scar Road carried the produce of many slate quarries. Today it provides an excellent high-level start to this walk. Proceed along the metal track until it begins to zigzag steeply up the face of Coniston Old Man to Brossan Stones Quarry (named Bursting Stones on the map). The Walna Scar Road, now an unsurfaced track in a poor state of repair, breaks off to the left. Follow it past tiny Boo Tarn until a path breaks off right,

Dow Crag above Goat's Water.

the wind lifts sheets of water from her surface to shower the surrounding rocks. Climb steeply to the col of Goat's Hause, then bear left to scramble up the final rock outcrop which proudly marks the summit of Dow Crag.

A stony path along a ruined wall leads along the high shoulder towards Buck Pike. To the left lies an unbroken drop over the cliffs. The heads of Great Gully and Easy Gully rise from the depths to break out onto the summit plateau. Neither provides a safe descent for walkers, the first being a climb of some difficulty and the second a dangerous break filled with loose boulders and scree. Continue easily to Buck Pike and finally on to the summit of Brown Pike. The view over the cairn north west to the Scafells is exemplary. Below to the east lies little Blind Tarn, named because there is no visible feed or exit. Nevertheless, on a summer's evening its surface will often be ringed by trout jumping for the fly.

An easy descent leads across the col which marks the summit of the Walna Scar Road. From here, make a gradual ascent to the top of Walna Scar, a long grassy shoulder broken only by the flaggy outcrops of slate. Continue along the shoulder and bear right under White Maiden to the top of White Pike. The lofty top offers an exulted feeling of openness. Steep craggy ground lies below, while beyond stands shapely Caw, the Duddon Estuary, the Whitfell Group and Black Combe.

Head for the rocky top of White Maiden, then descend the shoulder to the left of the wall. Although there is no path, the going is straightforward until the top of Dropping Crag is reached. With care an easy descent route can be selected to enter a secluded little valley beneath the crag. The shoulder meanwhile continues to the unmistakable knobbly dome of High Pike Haw. From its rocks take a high route skirting the bog of High Torver Common where excavations have revealed burial urns from the early Bronze Age.

Cross Ash Gill Beck and follow it past the deep hole of an old slate working. Above the wall, a path leads over Torver Beck and makes a steep ascent to the Walna Scar Road. Retrace this to the start of the walk.

·DOW 2·

A ROUND OF CAW AND THE DUNNERDALE FELLS

Pikes 1539ft/469m
Caw 1735ft/529m
Brock Barrow 1125ft/343m
Fox Haw 1263ft/385m
Raven's Crag 1184ft/361m

Valley Base: Coniston or The Duddon.
Town Base: Broughton in Furness.
Maps: OS OD6, The English Lakes – South West. L96 South Lakeland.
Length: 5.25miles/8.5km.
Ascent: 1675ft/510m.
Approx Time: 3.25hrs.
Start & Finish: A small pull-in opposite Stephenson Ground Cottages (SD 235931), limited to a couple of cars only – do not block the road or any entrances.
Difficulty: The going along the tops is rather rough and undulating with steep, short sections of ascent and descent. Although the route traverses rocky outcrops, fell grass and occasional bracken, ancient trackways or sheep trods prevail and the going is mostly straightforward. Caution should be exercised when descending from Caw, to find the easy gully through the otherwise steep and craggy rocks of Goat Crag.

The sharply pointed craggy outcrop of Caw resembles a mini Matterhorn, particularly when viewed from the lower reaches of The Duddon or the Birker Fell Road. In reality, it rises from a long shoulder which extends beneath White Pike over Pikes to Caw and beyond. It appears as a rough and knobbly ridge of rock outcrop and bracken running between Broughton Moor and The Duddon. Long Mire cuts through the shoulder as does Dunnerdale. Between the two, high ground rises from Brock Barrow above The Duddon. It then extends east over Fox Haw and Raven's Crag before dropping to the table top of The Knotts. The locality was once extensively quarried for slate and mined for copper. Now silent, this beautiful area lies mainly forgotten.

Starting off in front of Stephenson Ground cottages follow the road between

beside a small cairn, to rise steeply up a grassy bank.

Soon, the path joins a rough track and levels to cross The Cove, from where it sweeps around Goat Crag and rises to a fine view over Goat's Water to Dow Crag. This is one of the most impressive cliffs in the Lake District, and a favourite climbers' crag. Centrally at the foot of the precipice notice a tiny blue rectangle. This is the Rescue Stretcher Box.

Continue along the eastern shore of Goat's Water. When tranquil, it appears aqua blue in colour due to the natural copper deposits. When black and furious,

Looking from Caw to Dow Crag.

the stone barns of Stephenson Ground. A gate on the left signposted 'Bridleway Walna Scar' leads to an open track. In the field to the left lie the remains of various stone structures, including a circular wall, perhaps once a kiln used to fire the Coniston Limestone. The track continues along the stone wall and through a small gate onto open fellside. The hillside of thick bracken, a glorious red in autumn, tumbles steeply into the River Lickle below while beyond there is a resplendent view to White Pike.

Traverse the fellside to find deep wheel ruts that have been worn into the rock outcrops. Obviously, this was once a busy highway carrying the heavy produce won from the hills. Pass beneath a little crag through a gap in the wall. After a gill falls over a craggy outcrop to the left, the track begins to rise. At the time of writing, it appeared that some form of archeological excavation was taking place in the bracken to the left. To the right, at the end of the trees, the main beck bears off to cut a deep ravine. Our track rises to the left before it crosses a stream to join a crossroads. Take the path rising to the left.

Where the path levels, Dawson Pike can be seen ahead with two patches of

vivid white quartz. We cross the stream to the left, and climb to find a notch in the first rocky mound. A sudden view northwards appears. Harter Fell, the Scafells, White Pike and The Duddon face of Dow Crag immediately assume prominence. From here, a slight sheep trod can be followed for most of the way. Pass a hollow and a marshy tarn before making an ascent to the three rocky outcrops which mark the summit of Pikes.

Ahead lies Caw, its finger-like trig point standing out distinctively to the right. (It looks noticeably lower than the rocks to the left.) Descend and take a sheep trod which eventually makes a steep and winding ascent of Caw. All around you, stacked slates protrude like razors from the hillside.

Emerging onto the top of Caw it becomes obvious that you are not on a needle point but on a longish rock and grass ridge running east to west. The most easterly rocky tip, which looked the highest from below, can now be seen to be of lesser altitude than the trig point. Notwithstanding this, move on to the trig point and enjoy the fine view.

Descend to the right, following a faint path in the direction of the distant head of

Long Mire. This path finds a narrow, steep but easy rock filled gully through the cliff of Goat Crag that leads safely down to the head of Long Mire. Bear right to join the track and left to cross the stream. Follow the track to its high point then hop the stone wall on the right. A large base stone in the wall forms a sort of stile. Traverse right to an easy ascent through the crag of slate blocks. This leads to a second rocky outcrop, which is the summit of Brock Barrow. An easy climb can be made from the west. Retrace the ascent to regain the track to find another vague grassed-over track which rises from it.

The ridge beyond runs along the length of Dunnerdale, comprising of many different rocky outcrops and grassy humps. The track rises around the first rocky mound to the left. (Those curious to know what the strange object is on top will climb this to find a solar panel with 'Global Seismology Research Group' written on an attached plaque.) Pass through further knolls to regain the path. Continue to the obviously larger summit rise of Fox Haw. A short squat cairn has been skillfully constructed over the sharp-edged summit ridge.

Descend before climbing directly to the next slatey hill. Move down again then make for the cairn on the first and highest top of Raven's Crag. Beyond, a little valley-like hollow leads along the crest to the next lower top which is the last high mound of the shoulder. A path breaks off left and descends to a col crossed by a distinct track. Beyond lies the fine viewpoint of The Knott. Visit this if you have the energy, otherwise bear left immediately, along the track.

Above the buildings of Carter Ground, care should be exercised. Just off the track, hidden in the thick bracken, lies the partially collapsed workings of an ancient copper mine. Keep well away from this as it is completely unfenced and of unknown depth. The track crosses Black Moss Beck before rising to the left slightly away from the wall. Pass the buildings of Jackson Ground to a metal gate, before a barn of modern construction. Walk through the farmyard and down the lane to the surfaced road. Slates resembling gravestones line the road before it rises from the bridge back to the cottages of Stephenson Ground.

•DOW 3•

STICKLE PIKE AND GREAT STICKLE WEST OF DUNNERDALE

Stickle Pike 1231ft/375m
Tarn Hill 1027ft/313m
Great Stickle 1001ft/305m

Valley Base: The Duddon or Coniston.
Town Base: Broughton in Furness.
Maps: OS OD6, The English Lakes –
South West. L96 South Lakeland.
Length: 2.5miles/4km.
Ascent: 705ft/215m.
Approx Time: 1.5hrs.
Start & Finish: Kiln Bank Cross
(SD 214933), ample parking at the summit
of the pass between The Duddon
and Dunnerdale.
Difficulty: A straightforward hill walk,
ideal for a short day or an evening
excursion.

Stickle Pike is a plucky peak rising above Kiln Bank Cross at the head of Dunnerdale with a fine position over Ulpha and the Lower Duddon. Save for her modest elevation (an ascent from the Kiln Bank Cross takes only a few minutes) Stickle Pike would be famous. As it is, she and her sister tops, Tarn Hill and Great Stickle are little frequented.

An ancient grassed track rises from Kiln Bank. Cross past the northern end of Stickle Tarn. This delightful sheet of water bears water lilies and reeds in profusion. Above the tarn leave the track and make a steep climb directly for the summit. A short corridor cleaves the summit rocks. To the left lie slabby, slate-like rocks, while to the right a cairn balances on a higher outcrop. The panorama is excellent, with an uninterrupted view up the Duddon Valley and west across to the Whitfell Group. To the south lies a flatter top that provides a view over Tarn Hill and Great Stickle out across the length of the Duddon Estuary.

Slightly beneath and to the west of the southern end of Stickle Pike, a grassy corridor leads easily down through the steep rocky flanks. Some slate scree at the bottom leads to a good grassed track (the continuation of the original track) which falls through thick bracken to the hollow below. Cross the top of the bog, rise over a slight grassy shoulder, then fall again into a corridor. To the right, the track continues to the summit area of the perfectly named Tarn Hill (the furthest top gives the best view). Descent leads to a level plateau beneath Great Stickle. Move up the flank of the hill to the summit and trig point.

A path bears diagonally down across the flank of Great Stickle. Pass under some small crags and a ruined stone structure to gain the moss which feeds Red Moss Beck. Circumnavigate the bog, then return to the original track and follow this as it rises up the eastern flank of Stickle Pike. Bear right beneath a rock bluff. Rise and cross the small stream of Hare Hall Beck en route to Stickle Tarn. Traverse its eastern shore, or the higher grassy hillocks above for a better view, to regain the grass track. This descends in a short time to the road.

To Stickle Pike on return from Great Stickle.

Harter Fell seen from above Wha House Farm in Eskdale.

HARTER FELL GROUP

•HAR•

Craggy and pyramidal Harter Fell is a gem that shines from all angles – a resplendent fell. For beauty, grace, noble defiance and exposure of summit, she is unsurpassed. To walk her flanks is a pure pleasure, to explore her three rocky tops a privilege.

The Harter Fell Group as a whole lies within a neat triangle. The Ulpha to Eskdale Birker Moor Road forms the base; Eskdale and Hardknott Pass combine to delineate the northern edge; while the Duddon Valley forms the third side. From the Birker Moor Road rises a lonely moss, above which stands the stark stickleback ridge of Birker Fell. Meanwhile a marshy col separates Harter Fell at the head of the triangle.

Birker Fell is a wild and craggy place connected to the Birker Moor Road by a high grassy shoulder. Between the distinct conical tower of Green Crag at the eastern end and Kepple Crag above Eskdale, runs a rough spine of rock. In certain light, when seen in shadow against a brighter background, it resembles the Black Cuillin Ridge. It is relatively seldom visited; there are many hidden qualities waiting to be discovered here.

Walk HAR 1 climbs Harter Fell from

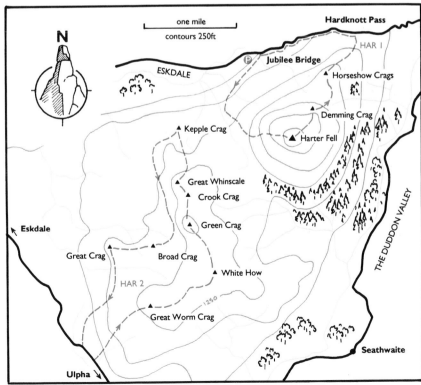

Jubilee Bridge at the foot of Hardknott Pass above Eskdale. It then descends the grassy north shoulder over Demming Crag and Horsehow Crags to the summit of Hardknott Pass. The return down the pass includes Hardknott's Roman Fort, which is regarded by many as the most dramatically sited fort in Britain.

Birker Fell is climbed in Walk HAR 2. This circular outing maximizes the altitude gained by the Birker Moor Road. It passes an ancient circular cairn to climb the exquisitely named Great Worm Crag and then White How. It then tackles the conical head of Green Crag before proceeding along the ridge. Reaching the top of Crook Crag involves a short scramble, though this should not present too much of an obstacle. From Kepple Crag the walk returns beneath the crags, above Low Birker Tarn and Foxbield Moss. This section includes Broad Crag and the impressive little rocky cliff of Great Crag before the track rejoins the road.

◆HAR 1◆

HARTER FELL ROUND

Harter Fell 2141ft/653m
Demming Crag 1722ft/525m
Horsehow Crags 1421ft/433m

Valley Base: Eskdale.
Maps: OS OD6, The English Lakes – South West. L90 Penrith & Keswick, L96 South Lakeland.
Length: 4.5miles/7.5km.
Ascent: 1970ft/600m.
Approx Time: 3.5hrs.
Start & Finish: Car park/pull-off at Jubilee Bridge by the side of the road near the foot of Hardknott Pass (SD 213011) just above the cattle grid.
Difficulty: Straightforward in ascent, very boggy along the shoulder between Harter Fell and Hardknott Pass.

High above the lonely expanse of Birker Moor stands the craggy pyramid of Harter Fell. Her lofty top is jewelled by three rocky fingers which offer marvellous views. The perspectives of the Scafells and the Coniston Group are particularly fine.

This circular walk rises from Jubilee Bridge to ascend the sunny southern flanks of Harter Fell. Time should be set aside for exploration of the three rocky tops before descending along the northern shoulder to the head of Hardknott Pass. (Unfortunately, this shoulder is a boggy affair.) From here, straightforward descent is made down the pass, with the option of visiting the Roman Fort.

Just below the road tumbles Hardknott Gill. Cross it by Jubilee Bridge and climb the steps to find a good track crossing the flanks of the fell. Two kissing gates lead to an open track of solid construction. This rises slowly to offer increasingly better views into Upper Eskdale. Cross Dodknott Gill and walk through a gate in

Along Wrynose Bottom to Harter Fell.

The rocky top of Harter Fell.

ACROSS BIRKER FELL

Great Worm Crag 1400ft/427m
White How – Birker Fell 1457ft/444m
Green Crag 1604ft/489m
Crook Crag 1539ft/469m
Great Whinscale 1394ft/425m
Kepple Crag 1076ft/328m
Broad Crag – Birker Fell 1220ft/372m
Great Crag – Birker Fell 1109m/338m

Valley Base: Eskdale or The Duddon.
Maps: OS OD6, The English Lakes –
South West. L96 South Lakeland.
Length: 7.5miles/12km.
Ascent: 1690ft/515m.
Approx Time: 4hrs.
Start & Finish: By the side of the Ulpha
to Eskdale road over Birker Moor, a couple of hundred yards in the Eskdale direction beyond Winds Gate cattle grid. On
the south west side of the road a Public
Footpath sign points towards the buildings
of Woodend. (SD 184959)
Difficulty: There is no continuous path,
only occasional sections of sheep trod.
Generally the going is over rough fell grass
and quite straightforward though there
are a number of boggy sections. The
ascent to the summit of Crook Crag
presents a mild scramble. Steep crags
abound and caution should be exercised
not to tumble over them.

the stone wall. The track passes through another gate and climbs steadily up the open fellside.

At a cairn on the left, the path bears off to ascend Harter Fell. Take it first through thick bracken then up the open heather clad hillside. The path climbs to the right of some crags and leads easily to the summit of Harter Fell. Turn left up to the trig point situated on the most southerly of the three summit outcrops. The next rock outcrop, the central one, is the highest. If it is too severe a climb from the west, it can by reached by a scramble from the east. The most easterly top can be gained by a scramble from the south.

It might be better to descend the same route as taken on ascent. For those willing to take the rough with the smooth, a path leads north in the direction of Hardknott Pass. Some way down, the domed top of Demming Crag stands to the left. Tra-verse left and ascend to the grass and rock top. From here, there are fine views to the Roman Fort and down Eskdale. Descend the same way and bear down the left bank of the small ravine of Castlehow Beck. Walk over the remains of a ruined wall to regain the main path where it crosses the gill. Leave the main path immediately and sweep back left to a great bog beneath the

craggy face of Demming Crag. Skirt it on the right until a crossing can be made to a stile below a gate over the wire fence. There is no real path here, only rough grass and bog.

Rise leftwards to the rocky top of Horsehow Crags (the outcrop to the left, nearest the edge, feels highest). It looks directly down to Mediobogdvm, offering an extraordinary plan view. Make a boggy trudge back right to find the main path above the forestry fence. (Missing out Horsehow Crags by following the main path right of Demming Crag gives a drier and easier descent.)

The path leads round into a hollow with a pond on the left. A stile climbs a fence, beyond which a track bears left down onto Hardknott Pass on the Eskdale side of its summit. Those true in spirit will keep straight on, maintaining their ascent until the final grassy mound above the summit of the pass is crested. A solitary rock outcrop protrudes from its grassy dome and offers an excellent view along Wrynose Bottom to Wrynose Pass.

Follow the road in descent. To visit the parade ground sited above the fort, take the track bearing off right from the apex of the first hairpin bend (the original Roman road).

Birker Moor stretches east from the high road connecting Ulpha and Eskdale. It is an area of rough upland beyond which stands the stickleback ridge of crags known as Birker Fell. Ulpha Fell connects this ridge to the road. Great Worm Crag, the most accessible point from the road, forms the western end of the shoulder. It is an upland area of independence and character enjoying a surprisingly open aspect with fine views. The rocky knoll of White How marks its eastern end.

This high wilderness area is quiet and chiefly unpathed. It holds many steep crags and only one tree, a solitary rowan. Numerous ancient walls and ruined structures may be observed.

From the road a footpath leads up the true right bank of Freeze Beck and bears left over a short boggy section. The path begins to rise, skirting the eastern flanks of Rough Crag. An easy ascent leads over rough fell grass to a large circular pile of stones, an ancient cairn. Continue directly ahead to climb the final grassy dome of Great Worm Crag. The view is extensive in all directions and particularly fine to Pillar, Scafell and the Coniston Group.

Dipping slightly, proceed along the shoulder towards White How. There is no path here, but the going is easy. A swing left gives access to the nicely proportioned rocky dome of Far Hill. There are actually two rocky knolls here, with the highest point marked by a cairn. At the lowest point of the shoulder, it is necessary to cross a narrow boggy section. Ascend and bear left around a beautiful little crag of white rhyolite to the rocky summit of White How. A distinctive rock table marks the top. From here when the light is in the west, Seathwaite Tarn hangs in the folds of the Coniston Group like a silver thread.

Walk down to the col, which is a little boggy, then ascend along the easiest line towards Green Crag. The intriguingly named Wormshell How stands down to the right. A rocky knoll, a dip and another rise lead to a further rocky turret with a curious black overhanging slab to the right. Left of this an easy grass rake leads up and over a worn slab. A steep ascent to the right leads to a rock outcrop and cairn, with the final tower of Green Crag rising beyond. A path swings up the right then back left to the rocky summit of Green Crag.

Descend due north in the direction of Crook Crag. Although not apparent from above, this is straightforward. Soon the path veers right along a natural grass shelf before descending to the grassy col below. In the middle of the col and left of the path, stands a marker stone – this is the Parish Boundary. From the col there is a view to the Isle Of Man.

Past the col to the left stands The Pike, a conical protuberance ringed by scree. A path continues from here beneath the end of Crook Crag. From below it looks like a formidable rock climb. However, if the ascent is made by first bearing right it proves to be a moderate scramble. Contour round to a short rock groove and scramble up this. A few easy rocky steps

The heathery eastern flanks of Birker Fell.

lead to the top. The actual summit cairn stands on the western end of an elongated rock ridge.

Descend the same way and continue along the path with a large balanced block to the right. Beyond this it is worth climbing up to the top of Great Whinscale, which is miniature in scale though Alpine in appearance. Return to the path by the same route.

After descending slightly, leave the path. Bear right over thick heather and bilberry, aiming for a natural corridor between two rock outcrops. This short section is perhaps the most arduous part of the walk. Beyond the corridor the going becomes easier as Kepple Crag is approached. Pass a crag on the left and rise to the rocky summit of Kepple Crag. This represents the obvious northern end of Birker Fell.

Care must be taken in descent. From the western edge of the summit a way down can be seen to the left. Beware, for a steep crag lies below to the right. (If in doubt retrace the ascent to the head of an

easy corridor which descends along the southern edge of Kepple Crag.) Descend with caution to the heather and bracken beneath the crag. Continue leftwards to a level platform in the slope of the hillside. Pass a small ruined enclosure and rise to a notch in the shoulder. Contour the hillside to the rocky ridge of Great Whinscale standing above to the left. Rise slightly onto the shoulder of the ridge. In the middle of Foxbield Moss stands an interesting rocky island called Fox Bield. Continue to contour the hillside, dropping only

slightly to a boggy area and cairned path rising from below. Skirt above the bogs until you are below Green Crag. Continue to move across to the topmost rocky knoll of Broad Crag.

Proceed easily down the grassy shoulder of Meeting Hill and cross the tiny Rowantree Beck and the low ruined perimeter wall around Great Crag. The distinctive cairned middle finger appears to be the highest point; reaching it directly involves a section of scrambling. An easy ascent, however, can be made from

the far side. The rock outcrop to the north is also cairned though does not appear to be as high. Looking over Birker Moor, Great Crag takes a commanding stance above Birkerthwaite Farm.

Return to cross the ruined wall and strike a contour back over Highfold Beck. Note the rowan tree some 75 yards downstream. The hillside now becomes intermittently boggy. Try to stay as high as possible before skirting beneath Rough Crag to a shoulder which leads back to the road.

The sweeping eastern flank of Whitfell.

WHITFELL GROUP

·WHI·

Extensively swathed in rough fell grass, a range of hills bound the western edge of the Southern Fells. Breaking through this skin a rocky backbone of tops stretches from Corney Fell to Lower Eskdale: Buck Barrow, Whitfell, Stainton Fell, Yoadcastle, Woodend Pike and their satellites fall to desolate Devoke Water, while Rough and Water Crag mark the northern extremity.

Rising virtually from the Irish Sea, the group offers a remarkably open aspect with fine views. Whitfell, the highest top, lies centrally; the Lower Duddon and the Birker Moor Road defines the eastern edge of the group; and to the south the Corney Fell Road cuts across the flanks of Buck Barrow with only Stoneside Hill lying beyond.

The area feels remote and untrodden. Indeed, much of the walking described here is without paths. Although numerous cairns and other ancient relics litter the scene, the overriding interest remains with the wild grandeur and the wonderful mountain vistas.

Walk WHI 1, the Ring of Devoke Water, rises from the Birker Moor Road. It first takes in the gentler granite tops of Rough Crag and Water Crag before contouring out to The Knott. Ascent is then made to the witches finger cairn of White Pike, Woodend Height and Yoadcastle. The return to base includes Seat How, as well as a visit to the granite boathouse on Washfold Point.

Hole House Bridge provides a logical access point for the Whitfell Horseshoe, Walk WHI 2. This includes the ascent of The Pike, Hesk Fell, Yoadcastle and Stainton Pike to reach Whitfell, before a rapid and grassy descent over Bigert leads back to the starting point.

Another feature of the group, the high Corney Fell Road cuts boldly over a bleak wilderness area. Situated at an altitude of 1312ft/400m it is often impassable in winter, blocked by snow, ice or engulfed in thick cloud. With Buck Barrow immediately above and Stoneside Hill beyond it serves to provide easy access onto the southern end of the range. Walk WHI 3 visits Buck Barrow, Great Paddy Crag, Kinmont Buck Barrow, Burn Moor and Plough Fell before returning to the road and continuing to Stoneside Hill.

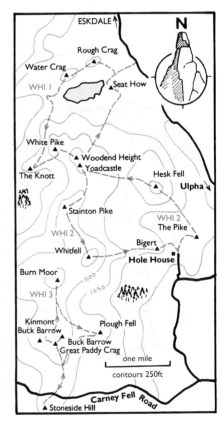

·WHII·

RING OF DEVOKE WATER

Rough Crag – Birker Moor 1047ft/319m
Water Crag 1001ft/305m
The Knott – Stainton Fell 1086ft/331m
White Pike – Birkby Fell 1450ft/442m
Woodend Height 1597ft/487m
Yoadcastle 1621ft/494m
Seat How – Birker Moor 1020ft/311m

Valley Base: Eskdale or The Duddon.
Maps: OS OD6, The English Lakes –
South West. L96 South Lakeland.
Length: 6.25miles/10km.
Ascent: 1900ft/580m.
Approx Time: 3.5hrs.
Start & Finish: Opposite the Devoke
Water junction below the Ulpha to
Eskdale Birker Moor Road, a wide verge
(hard standing) provides parking space
(NY 171797).
Difficulty: There are few sections of
well-defined path though the going, mostly
over rough fell grass is quite straightfor-
ward. Minor boggy sections will be found
at the outfall to Devoke Water and
approaching The Knott.

Open, barren and surrounded by bracken
and craggy fellside, Devoke Water lies at
the northern end of the Whitfell Group.
Surrounding and shielding her are the
hills of Seat How, Rough Crag, Water
Crag and the higher and wilder rocky
peaks of White Pike, Woodend Height
and Yoadcastle. This mountain tarn of
some size, complete with boathouse, fortunately only appears as a name on a signpost to the motorist following the Birker
Moor Road. It is left for the walker to
experience her stark beauty, as there is no
permitted vehicular access along the
track to Washfold Point.

Making an anticlockwise circuit
around the heights surrounding Devoke
Water, this walk contrasts the gentle fells
to the north with the rugged peaks to the
south. Principally, it is a walk on which to
savour the rugged mountain atmosphere.
It is open to the west and presents excellent seascapes, with the view extending
unbroken to the Isle Of Man and the Scottish Hills. Inland the prospect is even
finer, with the Lakeland Fells stretching
out before you in all its splendour.

From the Devoke Water junction, a
rusting signpost points along the track.
With Devoke Water and the distinct tops

of White Pike and Woodend Height
already visible, a vaguely defined path
breaks off right up Rough Crag. The
going levels before finally steepening to
gain the summit plateau. The summit
cairn stands on pink-red granite. Below to
the left a jumble of fissured blocks indicates quarrying activity. (Perhaps stone
for the fine boathouse was extracted
here.) There is a magnificent view to the
Scafells and the Bowfell Group from this
vantage point.

Descend easily into the dip and rise
again towards the summit of Water Crag.
On the final stages, due to a fire in the
heather, numerous circular cairns can be
seen. The first rocky bump encountered
has an in situ cairn. Although surrounded
by rocks of granite the knoll is actually
dark rhyolite. Interestingly, recent OS
information shows that the highest point
lies just to the north. On inspection it will
be revealed that the rock outcrop here is
granite. Somewhere, in the little space
between the two lies the junction of these
two rock types.

Before descending it is useful to
observe the route ahead. Across Devoke
Water on the shoulder rising to White
Pike stands a distinct rock outcrop one

Devoke Water from Seat How.

The Pike above Pike Side Farm.

third of the way up. Use this as a marker point to aim for. It is from here that our route traverses right to pick up The Knott. A path leads down to cross Linbeck Gill falling from Devoke Water. Bear right to a large circular pile of stones and a ruined shelter. A forlorn wooden post also marks the spot.

Bear first left then right (there are numerous clusters of stones here) to pick up the shoulder falling from White Pike. Ascend this to the aforementioned rocky lump. Move right to stand on a pointed, twin-peaked rock outcrop and observe the next objective, The Knott, which is now in view.

Traverse the flanks of the hillside over rock and bracken and descend slightly. Cross a small gill, then ascend to the shoulder plateau extending to The Knott. Unfortunately there is an extensive area of bog which most will cross directly at the expense of damp feet but with the saving of some distance. From here gain the tussocky grass rising to the rock outcrop summit of The Knott.

Marking the top of White Pike the tall, slender cairn, resembling a crooked witch's finger, now beckons. Despite its distant aspect and the rugged rocks standing beneath, the journey is quite straightforward if tackled as described.

From The Knott follow the grassy shoulder rising gently. Notice the many flattened circular piles of stones (cairns). Bear right at the first outcrop to find a natural and well-defined corridor rising easily through the steep ground. At its head bear right to the cairn, precariously balanced on a knife edge. This marks the top of White Pike.

Rise towards Woodend Height, skirting the final craggy outcrops to the left. Finally break through directly to the summit point. A grand cairn stands below the summit to the north. From here the view, which includes Devoke Water, will take your breath away.

Cross the summit and descend slightly to the rock turret of Yoadcastle, which is the imposing highest top on this walk. Gain it by ascending from a small rock walled enclosure then bear right.

Beneath Yoadcastle an easy grassy descent crosses Hall Beck and continues to the base of the fell. With the buildings of Woodend Farm over to the right, an area of soft ground is crossed. A gentle grassy flank, with numerous cairns visible, leads to The Seat. Beyond this stands the rocky knoll of Seat How. Proceed, over a ruined stone wall to ascend the easy eastern flank.

Descend the same way. Take a clockwise circuit around the rocky outcrop before moving down to the track. Those

with energy to spare may care to visit the boathouse and its outbuildings, the latter now sadly ruined.

◆ W H I 2 ◆

HESK FELL, STAINTON PIKE, WHITFELL HORSESHOE

The Pike 1214ft/370m
Hesk Fell 1565ft/477m
Yoadcastle 1621ft/494m
Stainton Pike 1632ft/498m
Whitfell 1881ft/573m
Bigert 1086ft/331m

Valley Base: The Duddon.
Maps: OS OD6, The English Lakes – South West. L96 South Lakeland.
Length: 6.25miles/10km.
Ascent: 2065ft/630m.
Approx Time: 3.5hrs.
Start & Finish: Hole House (SD 181930). Parking is unfortunately extremely restricted. Do not block the road or any gateways. The upper entrance to Hole House offers a wide junction, parking is possible without restricting access but permission should be sought. Possibly permission could be sought to park at Side Pike Farm.
Difficulty: Although chiefly pathless the walking is surprisingly easy going, chiefly over fell grass with only the occasional boggy section.

Encompassing the leader of the group, Whitfell, this walk takes a high horseshoe around the hanging basin of Storthes. The Pike and Bigert stand at the entrance to the horseshoe while the considerable bulk of Hesk Fell, the northern leg, shields much of it from view. Around its head emanate the rocky spires of Yoadcastle and Stainton Pike. This route links them in a logical round which despite its distance is pleasingly mild in execution.

Lying at the open end of the horseshoe, Hole House provides the natural starting point. Opposite stands the sharply defined slopes of The Pike. The surfaced road ends at a gate just over Holehouse Bridge. Follow the Side Pike farm track until, after a short way, a track leads off to the left. Continue along it and then take the gate to the right. Leave the track to follow the blunt nose rising up the open fellside above. Pass the stone remains of an old structure and continue across a ruined wall, then bear right beneath a small craggy outcrop. Another ruined wall rises steeply up the hillside. Follow this until a gap in the wall leads right. Climb to the top of The Pike, which is only slightly higher than the stone wall cresting the summit.

Follow the wall down the shoulder over another, this time ruined, wall. After the shoulder begins to ascend, a wooden gate will be found through the wall. Take it and continue along the other side of the wall until a further gate leads out onto the open fellside.

Proceed straight up the flanks of Hesk Fell without any difficulty. Note the curious stone enclosures built into the hillside at about half height. The angle eases to reveal the extensive flat grass plain which is the summit of Hesk Fell. A few rocks form a poor excuse for a cairn.

Traverse the top and descend easily through tussocky grass and heather to the boggy col of Cockley Moss. On the far side to the left, a ruined stone hut contains a hearth. Perhaps this was once a peat cutters' shelter. Rise directly to a rocky outcrop with a small stone wall in situ, then

bear right to the rocky peak of Yoadcastle.

Descend in the same direction, past the rock outcrop and ascend right, over a number of rocky knolls. Stride a wire fence in the dip beneath Stainton Pike and move up the aesthetic rocky knoll of Stainton Pike.

Strike a line south for Whitfell and cross the wire fence just beyond Hole-house Tarn. As the going begins to steepen a slight path materializes. It leads directly to the substantial beehive cairn standing amid a great circular mass of stones which mark the top of Whitfell. The trig point stands to the east, apparently at a slightly lower elevation. The view is extensive and quite breathtaking.

Proceed east and make a quick descent down the nose of Whitfell to a gate in the wire fence by the ruined stone wall. An ancient track descending diagonally down the fellside merges from the left at this point. Follow it over Bigertmire Pasture before slightly boggy walking leads to a gate in a wire fence. The grass bump beyond this represents the top of Bigert. Take the gap in the ruined wall and descend the open fellside to the left to a track above the beck. Take the gate through the stone wall and follow it. Pass the hazels, heavy with nuts in autumn, to an iron gate and the surfaced road just above Hole House.

· W H I 3 ·

BUCK BARROW ABOVE CORNEY FELL

Great Paddy Crag 1745ft/532m
Buck Barrow 1799ft/549m
Kinmont Buck Barrow 1754ft/535m
Burn Moor 1780ft/543m
Plough Fell 1470ft/448m
Stoneside Hill 1384ft/422m

Valley Base: The Duddon.
Maps: OS OD6, The English Lakes – South West. OS Pathfinder 625, Broughton In Furness. L96 South Lakeland.
Length: 5.5miles/9km.
Ascent: 1100ft/335m
Approx Time: 2.5hrs.
Start & Finish: Parking at the summit of the Corney Fell Road (SD 150896).
Difficulty: Although a section of the walk is pathless the going is straightforward.

The rocky turrets of Buckbarrow and its satellite peaks of Great Paddy Crag and Kinmont Buckbarrow rise like a fairy castle from the grassy slopes of Corney Fell. This is a most distinctive summit area,

Looking to Buck Barrow and Great Paddy Crag from Kinmont Buck Barrow.

To Kinmont Buck Barrow, Great Paddy Crag and Buck Barrow above the Corney Fell Road.

whose angular rock outcrops resemble the remnants of an extinct volcano. Although of a somewhat lesser scale, it is often compared with Scotland's Stac Pollaidh. Forming the southern end of this group, it takes on a desolate and remote stance above the plains of the west coast and the wooded confines of the Lower Duddon Valley. The isolation is broken only by the presence of the Corney Fell Road, which reaches an altitude of 1312ft/ 400m as it runs over the southern perimeter of the group.

A wall rises to the north of the road. To its right lies open fell and an easy grassy track. Take the track, passing the rock outcrops of Peg Crag and Little Paddy Crag until the rocky bastion of Great Paddy Crag looms above. To the right and beyond lie the rock pinnacles and summit dome of Buck Barrow. Bear right around the craggy face of Great Paddy Crag then cut back left, rising easily to the summit rock just above the

ruinous wall. A tiny cairn stands wedged in a triangular rocky niche.

Head directly for the summit cone of Buck Barrow. A central tongue of bouldery scree provides a straightforward means of ascent to reach the cairn standing on a point of rock. Below to the south, above fallen rock debris, are two needles of rock. The adventurous may wish to climb them. Descend the western flank of the cone and proceed to circumnavigate the knoll of Great Paddy Crag. Cross a ruined wall after which it is possible to strike rightwards to a gap in another wall, blocked by a wooden hurdle.

Cross the gap and a make gentle ascent to the rocky summit cone of Kinmont Buck Barrow which rises in shapely fashion above a grassy shoulder. This is another distinct top with a substantial cairn and an unbroken view westwards. To the north stands the great summit cairn of Whitfell. Descend to the north, avoiding the craggy face to the west, then

move right to discover a small wooden gate/hurdle near the end of the stone wall. Climb this and cross a small stream to make boggy progress across the col between Buck Barrow and Burn Moor. Easy ascent leads to the slight rocky protuberance and cairn marking the top of the grassy expanse of Burn Moor. Thankfully for tired walkers the cairn is situated near its eastern edge.

Rapid descent leads to an easy traverse along the 450m contour beneath Buck Barrow Crag to the summit plateau of Plough Fell. A cairn stands on a rock just beyond its eastern rim. Return to the slopes of Buck Barrow to find a high rake leading diagonally up the fellside to Little Paddy Crag. Avoid a boggy spring near its base by traversing above it. From Paddy Crag the track should be followed back to the road. Beyond the road, a grassy shoulder leads to the steep-sided knoll of Stoneside Hill, and this provides a quite logical extension.

Looking south to Black Combe.

BLACK COMBE GROUP

•BLC•

Located on the tip of land between the Irish Sea and the Duddon Estuary, Black Combe stands isolated, exposed and openly independent. Rising like a gigantic beached whale with the sea encircling three points of her compass, Black Combe forms the most southerly top in the Lake District National Park. She is a mountain prominent from afar, offering an expanse of uninterrupted views far outstripping her comparatively meagre altitude.

A small hollow and tarn separate her two tops. From both the vista is famous. Wordsworth said of the view: 'The amplest range of unobstructed prospect may be seen that British ground commands'. Black Combe overlooks a considerable stretch of coastline from the Solway to Morecambe Bay; the Isle Of Man lies to her west and Ireland beyond; the hills of Galloway and distant Snowdonia lay unobscured on a clear day; the Scafells and the heart of Lakeland lie to the north some twelve miles (20km) distant; and to the east lie the Pennines.

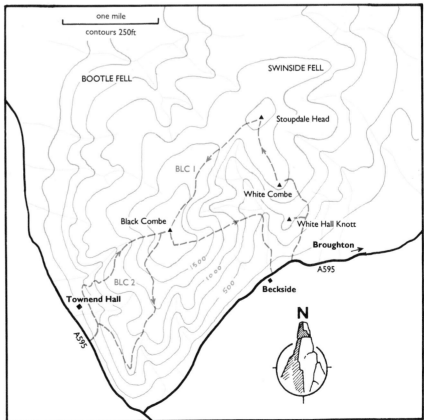

The intriguing Black Combe.

The high Corney Fell Road marks the northern limit of the massif. The A595 running down the west coast and along the Whicham Valley from Duddon Bridge defines its other two sides. From a distance, within this well-defined triangle, Black Combe appears to rise as a smoothly profiled mound of grass and heather. This is a weathered form typical of those hills constructed from the ancient Skiddaw slates. On closer acquaintance, however, there is much to contradict those first impressions.

Gouged from the heart of the moun-tain, a hanging combe is observed. This is actually made up of twin scoops forged in the ice-age which merge and fall into the Whicham Valley. It is these features, Black Combe and White Combe, which give the name to the mountain and her main satellite.

Surrounding this hollow are the tops of White Hall Knott, White Combe, Stoupdale Head and Black Combe. Extending to the southern tip and rearing from bracken covered eastern flanks are a complex of craggy escarpments. Along the narrow western seaboard there are a series of table-top spurs which are unde-tectable from below. Only the northern edge confirms initial impressions. Here the grassy slopes rise in routine manner from the boggy hollow of Black Dub to the long shoulder of Swinside Fell. In addition well-defined, easy graded tracks make the ascent of Black Combe a straightforward affair.

Walk BLC 1 makes a round of the cen-tral combe taking in all the tops of the group. It ascends an ancient track which is deeply grooved into the steep hillside above Fox and Goose Cottages in the

Whicham Valley, before taking the spur along to White Hall Knott. White Combe and the indistinct Stoupdale Head follow before the rim of the basin is traversed to the extensive flats of the summit dome. The summit tarn is skirted to gain the South Top before a direct descent down the shoulder takes you past Whicham Mill to Beckside.

Walk BLC2 first climbs a zigzagging track up the shoulder of Miller Gill above Whitbeck to explore the secrets of the gill. It then emerges directly onto the summit. The descent leads over the South Top and down the grassy track towards Whicham, giving an outstandingly open prospect to the west, south and east. Finally, the route veers west below Townend Knotts, crossing the table-top plateau of Seaness before following an excellent diagonal track to the beech wood south of Townend. Here is an exceptional seascape, which extends along from St Bees Head over Duddon Sands to Walney Island. The ease of walking and the views elevate this descent to classic status.

◆ BLC 1 ◆

CIRQUE OF BLACK COMBE

White Hall Knott 1020ft/311m
White Combe 1361ft/415m
Stoupdale Head 1548ft/472m
Black Combe 1970ft/600m
South Top – Black Combe 1926ft/587m

Valley Base: Whicham.
Town Base: Broughton in Furness.
Maps: OS Pathfinder 625 – Broughton in Furness. L96 South Lakeland.
Length: 5.5miles/9km.
Ascent: 1970ft/600m.
Approx Time: 3.5hrs.
Start & Finish: Car park by the side of the A595 at Beckside (SD 153847).
Difficulty: A straightforward walk over pleasant grassy terrain. The descent is steep but technically easy.

Behind the Fox and Goose Cottages an ancient trackway cuts a deep diagonal rift up the flanks of White Hall Knott. It marks the start of a circuit which takes in all the tops of this group as it traces a high cirque around the scalloped heart of Black Combe. The views are magnificent, the going is generally easy, and the scenic interest is high.

From the car park by Beckside follow the A595 for a short way up the hill, then down towards the Fox and Goose Cottages. Follow a signpost that reads 'Public Footpath White Combe'. Through the gate a muddy trackway is so overhung by hedges on either side that it resembles a dark tunnel. It leads to a further gate, heralding a break in the leafy armour, and on the other side of this stands a large clean boulder of blue agglomerate. The ancient trackway continues to two gates which lead to open, heavily brackened fellside. After a short meander left the track, cut deep into the ground, rises to the right taking a diagonal line up the steep hillside. Now grassed-over, it

Over Sty Knotts to White Hall Knott.

*On the shoulder of White Hall Knott (top) and the cairn marking the
top of White Combe (above).*

shoulder to make the final rise to the table top of White Hall Knott. There is now a commanding view into the very heart of Black Combe.

Return along the shoulder and ascend the trackway. Bear left to the large circular mound of stones and the cairn/shelter which marks the summit of White Combe. From here take a direct though pathless line which provides a gentle ascent to Whitecombe Moss. Bear right to the highest point of the moss. A tiny cairn of quartz rock marks the indistinct top of Stoupdale Head. Depressions which surround this indicate extensive peat cutting operations. Perhaps this was the principal reason for constructing the ancient trackways.

Follow a vague path over Whitecombe Head to traverse the rim of Whitecombe Screes followed by Blackcombe Screes. A pause at the edge of the latter reveals steep broken crags of Skiddaw slate falling to steep scree. This exposed and impressive mountain location is followed by a quick and easy ascent to the broad flat top of Black Combe. From its thin grass surface of playing field evenness and proportion, rises a triangulation point and a large circular shelter cairn. A magnificent open vista stretches extensively in every direction.

To further appreciate the seascape and coastal features, cross the dip holding the summit tarn and continue to the large circular cairn which marks the South Top of Black Combe. The view over the Duddon Estuary to Walney Island and up the West Cumberland coast is now unbroken. An easy descent down the shoulder skirts the rim of the combe before it steepens to gain the plateau of Sty Knotts. This is a little mountain sanctuary ringed by outcrops of black slate and brilliant white quartz. It is worth a pause here before a line is cut down beneath the central craggy outcrop and left to the track along the narrow valley of Whitecombe Beck. The very steep descent, grass with occasional bouldery outcrop, is technically straightforward though there is no definite path and some caution should be exercised.

The track crosses the beck just below a dammed pond which once fed Whicham Mill. Rise slightly to follow the track. The mixed wood plantation on the far side of the stream is carpeted by bluebells in May. Take the stile above the charming cottages of the mill and continue on through Ralliss Farm back to Beckside.

divides in places to offer a dual carriageway route. What ancient traffic was so heavy as to warrant construction of this now forgotten highway? There appears

to be some evidence of mining activity.

Near the shoulder of White Hall Knott take the left and most direct track to the col. Bear left and traverse the grassy

•BLC 2•

BLACK COMBE FROM THE WEST

Black Combe 1970ft/600m
South Top – Black Combe 1926ft/587m

Valley Base: Whicham.
Town Base: Broughton in Furness.
Maps: OS Pathfinder 625 – Broughton in Furness. L96 South Lakeland.
Length: 4.5miles/7.5km.
Ascent: 1855ft/565m.
Approx Time: 2.5hrs.
Start & Finish: Lay-by on the south side of the A595 beneath the wood near Townend (SD 122837).
Difficulty: In ascent the path is a little vague and traverses through thick heather for a short section. Descent is straightforward, on the easiest of grassy tracks.

This ascent from the west moves into the secretive confines of Miller Gill before ascending directly to the summit of Black Combe. The descent, down a pleasantly grassed track of even grade, could hardly provide a greater contrast. This is an interesting way to tackle the dominant western aspect of Black Combe, with the descent of its southern spur, over Townend Knotts and Seaness fully deserving its classic status.

Opposite the lay-by a signpost 'Public Footpath Black Combe' points out the path through the thick bracken. It rises to the left to skirt the hillside above a beech wood and traverses above a wire fence. From the end of the fence it descends slightly into Townend Gill. This is a gill with a craggy north bank which rises in a series of tame steps reminiscent of a landscaped garden. Below stands a fine holly tree and, just discernable through the Scots Pine, a pond above Townend Hall. Cross the gill and descend slightly to a grass track running along the stone wall. Just before reaching the buildings of Whitbeck, a distinct track rises through thick bracken up the south shoulder of Millergill Beck. After a little ascent a large boulder is passed. It is a geological erratic of white granite, so distinctively different to the Skiddaw slates of which Black Combe is composed. The boulder has

been split in half by the explosive force of black powder inserted into eight radial drill holes. One half stands erect, with its mirror image lying prone beneath.

Beyond the boulder the path begins to zigzag and at the first turn a small detour left reveals the fine waterfall in Millergill Beck. The zigzags steepen until at a levelling in the shoulder a vague path traverses left through thick heather. At the first oasis of grass interrupting the heather, the path descends slightly before continuing its horizontal traverse towards Miller Gill where it is no more than a narrow sheep trod. The path does, however, gain the bed of the gill at its widest point. Just above, a rocky outcrop on the north bank shelters the ruins of an old shepherd's hut. From here, the bed of the gill can now be followed. Pieces of aircraft wreckage and three old vaned wheels of curious origin will be found before the gill forks. Take the left fork until its furthest tentacle touches the grassy track from Whicham. Cross the track and climb to the summit shelter enclosing the concrete trig point.

Proceed south past the summit tarn to the cairn marking the South Top of Black Combe, then descend directly to the west to pick up the grassy track. The open airy nature of the descent is quite superb, with fine views to Blackpool Tower.

The track also allows an appreciation that this western flank of Black Combe is not just a grassy dome: there are distinct table-top spurs pointing to the west. There are those to the north and south of Miller Gill, Townend Knotts beyond Townend Gill and finally, Seaness. Descend the main track to the edge of the Seaness table top. This is found just beyond the point where the descent steepens and a spring and stream appears to the left. Cross the table top to the cairns marking the end of Seaness. Beyond lie the five towers and propellers of the Haverigg Wind farm.

Re-cross the plateau to a distinct diagonal track. This leads down the hillside above Throstlerake Crag and beneath White Stones towards the wood below Townend.

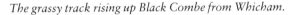

The grassy track rising up Black Combe from Whicham.

Gummer's How from Lakeside.

OUTLYING EASTERN TOPS

•OUT•

To the east of the Coniston Fells lies the greatest tract of low-lying land in the Lake District National Park. Two of Lakelands' largest lakes, Coniston Water and Windermere, are found here. However, the land is far from flat; it actually consists of numerous parallel ridges and troughs running north to south. The troughs hold the lakes and secretive valleys, the ridges consist of rough grazing land. Much of the land is afforested, notably by Grizedale Forest. At first glance there would seem little here to interest the hill walker.

However, on closer examination it will be found that eight tops raise their heads above the 1000ft contour. In doing so they gain a positional advantage which extends their view over this lowly, though lovely, corner of Lakeland to the high hills beyond.

Immediately east of the Coniston Group, Holme Fell and Black Fell stand either side of the upper Yewdale Valley. Walk OUT 1 makes a circuit over them both and includes a diverse range of interest from the spectacular hole of Hodge Close Quarry to the scenic beauty of Tarn Hows. Classic views extend across the head of the two Langdale Valleys down Coniston Water and over the head of Windermere.

Walk OUT 2 rises from the eastern shore of Coniston Water to pass deserted Parkamoor Farm before venturing into Grizedale Forest to conquer Carron Crag. There are no better views of the Coniston Fells than those seen on this walk. Walk OUT 3 contrasts deciduous oak woods with the open tops of Stang Hill, Arnsbarrow Hill and Top O'Selside. This walk would make a delightful and worthwhile afternoon's outing.

Finally east of Windermere, England's largest lake, Walk OUT 4 makes a circuit of Gummer's How by extending the route to top Birch Fell. It is a modest walk, though of surprising quality. It offers a vista of the Southern Fells that stretches from Black Combe to Wetherlam.

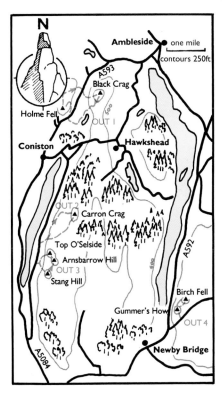

◆ •OUT I• ◆

HOLME FELL AND BLACK FELL – EAST OF THE LANGDALES

Holme Fell 1040ft/317m
Black Crag – Black Fell 1056ft/322m

Valley Base: Coniston, Yewdale.
Maps: OS OD7, The English Lakes –
South East. L90 Penrith & Keswick, L96
South Lakeland.
Length: 6.75miles/11km.
Ascent: 1690ft/515m.
Approx Time: 4hrs.
Start & Finish: Small car park in the
woods by the side of the A593 Ambleside
to Coniston Road at Glen Mary Bridge
(SD 321999).
Difficulty: Straightforward, on paths or
tracks throughout.

The juxtaposition of tree, water and fell make this journey quite superlative, with the most splendid views down the length of Coniston Water. All the mountains at the head of the two Langdale Valleys are arrayed to perfection.

Follow the road to the entrance of Yew Tree Farm. Proceed down the drive over the bridge, then take the track to the right which by-passes the farmyard and skirts Penny House Wood. Immediately beyond the wood pass through a gate and take the path rising to the right. This follows open ground over a hill. Enter Guards Wood above Yew Tree Tarn and continue along the path until the wood thins. Pass a bouldery outcrop and follow a path that begins to climb steeply up to the left to Uskdale Gap. This is the col on the long shoulder of Holme Fell.

A path rises to the left and leads up to the rock slab rib of Ivy Crag. A solid cairn marks the summit. Beyond, two further parallel ribs run in the direction of Coniston Water, with the middle one appearing to be the highest. Below to the west lies a basin of heather and beyond the higher summit outcrop of Holme Fell. Descend into the basin and cross it. Sink into a deep corridor, which is a natural roadway with ancient tracks forking to the left. One carries on through a miniature canyon marked by an interesting standing stone and a hanging rock; the other rises to carry on south beneath the summit knoll. Follow the latter for a short way then climb directly up the knoll by an obvious line of weakness. The summit cairn is placed centrally on the raised plateau.

Descend to the ancient trackway which falls from the corridor and follow it around the side of a boggy hollow. Pass an elegant silver birch to rise to a crest. Do not descend but bear right. Pick a route

A climber in Hodge Close Quarry (right).

through enclosing larch trees, and fall slightly to a stone-walled structure. This was once a dam with an earth core, which has had its filling washed out. The hollow above, now dry, was once a reservoir. The reservoir below still holds water. It supplies the cottages of Holme Ground.

Cross the dam along the top of one of the outside stone walls, avoiding the void in the centre. At the far side the path skirts around to a third and higher pond. This the larger and most scenic, ringed in part by silver birch, is a haven for dragonfly. Follow its shore past the small retaining dam, then break left down the hill past an old quarry to the right. Follow the old track down to a larger track and bear right.

After a gate the large hole of Hodge Close Quarry appears with its extensive banks of slate waste. The path bears right to the right of a wire protective fence. Those wishing to view this extensive hole in the ground should proceed down to the flat bank on its west side.

The path joins a track just above a pond to the left, known as the duck pond. Turn right and follow the track through High Oxenfell Farm after which it becomes a surfaced road. Bear left past Low Oxenfell and continue moving on to a junction and the main A593 Ambleside to Coniston road.

On the far side of the road a track rises through a small but exquisite larch wood before opening out onto fields on the fellside known as Hollin Bank. The open views across to Fairfield and Helvellyn are already impressive. The track skirts the wall, falling slightly to cross a stream before rising again. Climb to the top of the field and take a gate through the stone wall to the left. Pass a large boulder and bear right to join another track. Pass through a further gate with the building of Low Arnside below to the right.

A trig point marks the distant summit of Black Crag which is now visible up to the left. The track continues through another gate, descends slightly then rises alongside a stone wall to the fell gate. Beyond a small knoll with larch trees growing on it, a grassy track bears off left. Cross a low boggy area, with Iron Keld Crag to the right and ascend slightly. The track levels in a short way, with Fairfield dead ahead. A steep path rises up the

View of the Langdales from Black Crag.

grassy bank towards the right to a small cairn. A further vague path leads to the final pull, by a stone wall up the western flank of Black Crag. Throughout 360 degrees the view is superb.

To the north note the stile over the stone wall. Below to the south east, on a little spur, a large circular cairn marks the best viewpoint. There is a view over the head of Lake Windermere to Ambleside, to Wansfell and the hills above Kentmere, and over Hawkshead and Esthwaite Water. Move back west to the shoulder and follow the path down to the edge of a dark conifer plantation. A gate/stile gives access to a rough track descending through Iron Keld Plantation to emerge into an open track. Turn right keeping the fine larch trees to that side. Do not take any gates to the left until, after descending a steep hill, a well-signed gate/stile on the left provides a path to the famous beauty spot of Tarn Hows.

At a junction turn left for the best views across the tarn. The way to the right is shorter. At the bottom of the tarn follow a path down the true right bank of the stream which issues from it. A splendid descent leads through the oak woods. The path leads to a footbridge and back to the car park.

A hide for watching deer on Carron Crag.

•OUT 2•

PARKAMOOR TO CARRON CRAG – EAST OF CONISTON WATER

Carron Crag 1030ft/314m

Valley Base: Coniston.
Maps: OS OD6, The English Lakes – South West. L96 South Lakeland.
Length: 5.5miles/9km.
Ascent: 1215ft/370m.
Approx Time: 3.25hrs.
Start & Finish: Park-A-Moor National Trust car park in the trees above the road running along the eastern side of Coniston Water. (SD 299927)
Difficulty: Sections of the path are rather boggy. Within the forest use of a compass may prove helpful. Following the forestry break, although only for short way, is both rough and arduous.

Surrounded by the dense conifers of Grizedale Forest, the summit rock of Carron Crag stands proud. The approach from Coniston Water, by the rather romantic Parkamoor, provides a splendid walk. Tackled this way only half of the walk is submerged in the pines. The view from the Park over the lake to Coniston Fells is quite superb.

The National Trust car park is named Park-A-Moor on the signpost. A track leaves the back of the parking area to pass a stone barn. Above the gate, a few steps and a stile lead into the oak woods. Follow the track rising up through the wood until at a ruined stone wall the track forks. Take the right branch, which is overgrown and boggy at first, to cross a small stream. Traversing beneath a field the track rises to a gate. Take the stile left of the gate and continue up the field until near the top a stile climbs the wire fence by two old slate gateposts, one standing, one fallen. This joins an old lane.

Although the lane can be followed from the bottom of the field it is best avoided as described for it is extremely boggy. Follow the lane, with a stream on the left, to the unsurfaced track which contours the hillside. This rough track rises from distant High Nibthwaite, providing the only access to Low Parkamoor Farm.

Turn left through the gate and follow the track to the farm. Here you will find a traditional Lakeland farmhouse, totally unspoilt, perched high on the hillside in a perfect location. Continue past the farm to a stile and gate. Turn left and follow the undulating grassy track that weaves its way through boggy hollows and rocky knolls and finally leads up onto the high shoulder of the Park.

A track leads into the forest via a stile and gate. At the time of writing much tree clearance had taken place, allowing an uninterrupted view to the west. The track enters a corridor between high forest fencing and begins to descend. Dead ahead, the top of Carron Crag can be seen (at the time of writing sufficient trees had been felled to allow this). Intercept a main forest road and bear left. In a few hundred yards to the right there is a forestry break. Those wishing to keep their journey to a minimum should cross the ditch and follow it. Those preferring a longer but easier walk may follow the main track for perhaps a kilometre. At a junction it is possible to bear right to gain the track passing the northern end of Carron Crag. (Note, the author accepts no responsibility for those getting lost on this latter option.) It should also be noted that on the OS map, tracks and completely overgrown firebreaks are indistinguishable.

Following the firebreak is not easy, although at the time of writing the trees to the right had all been felled.

Emerge onto a track. Bear left along it, take a right fork and emerge onto an even better track. Turn right and in a little way find a gate and path leading up the north end of Carron Crag.

A summit of character, this rocky whaleback rises above the bracken and heather. It is open here with the trees below. A perched wooden hut observation post straddles the rock and trig point stands at the northern point. Look down from here to observe Grizedale and the Satterthwaite Valley below.

Follow the path down the southern end of the fell to emerge through a gate onto a level track. At the junction bear right and descend slightly into a dip. As the track rises again you reach a further junction. Tracks go left and right but our way lies across the junction. An ancient path rises over the flanks of Mustard Hill.

Levelling, the path again meets a forestry track. Cross this to follow another forest track bearing down the hill in a southerly direction. At the bottom there is a triangular junction. Proceed past the junction and carry on in the same direction for a short way, until a path veers off to the right. Follow this over Farra Grain Gill and through dense conifer to emerge into the blinding light of the open moor at a gate. The boggy track crosses the moor to meet a stone wall, with the ruined buildings of High Parkamoor to the right. Follow the line of the wall to intercept the track serving Low Parkamoor. Beneath lie Coniston Water and the oak woods taken in ascent.

◆OUT 3◆

TOP O'SELSIDE

Stang Hill 1037ft/316m
Arnsbarrow Hill 1056ft/322m
Top O'Selside 1099ft/335m

Valley Base: Coniston.
Maps: OS OD6, The English Lakes – South West. L96 South Lakeland.
Length: 3miles/5km.
Ascent: 1100ft/335m.
Approx Time: 2hrs.
Start & Finish: Nibthwaite National Trust car park in the trees above the road (opposite a field gate) which runs along the eastern side of Coniston Water (SD 296908).
Difficulty: If the Stang Hill and Arnsbarrow Hill section is included the going for a short way is rather arduous involving thick bracken, heather and boggy ground. The problem can be mitigated slightly by avoiding it during the bracken season (May to September inclusive) or completely by missing out these two hills.

Contrasting the oak woods below with fine open views over Coniston Water, Greenodd Sands and Morecambe Bay, this walk is beguiling throughout as it rises through the woods to a high open shoulder which overlooks Bethecar Moor and Arnsbarrow Tarn. However, it must be stated that whilst the distance to reach Stang and Arnsbarrow Hill is short, it involves crossing rather inhospitable terrain. Certainly they occupy good positions but those bent on pure pleasure will be forgiven for passing them to ascend Top O'Selside only.

At the top left corner of the car park an ancient track rises through the magnificent woods of oak, silver birch, sycamore and holly. In a short way an ancient walled lane branches off to the left. Ignore this and rise with the track until it crests a hill and falls slightly to the right. The oaks have now been replaced by a plantation of larch. When the track forks, rise to the left. Exit the wood over a stile into the rough road from the hamlet of High Nibthwaite. Immediately opposite, a curious ruined building has been built into the far bank of the Selside Beck. Turn

left up the road until it makes a sharp bend to the left above the top of the wood. Continue straight on following a small path to the left of the stream. Cross the stream and rise up the brackened hillside to pass the end of a stone-walled field to the right. In a short way join a well-defined path which traverses the hillside.

Those wishing to visit Top O'Selside only should follow it to the left then head directly up the open shoulder to the summit of that hill. Those of stouter constitution and time to spare should bear right along this path which has arisen from High Bethecar. At the closest point to the summit an ascent can be made of Stang Hill. The top is marked by a cairn and occupies a commanding position with an open view to the south.

Cross the heathery divide to the craggy top of Arnsbarrow Hill and descend the shoulder. Circumnavigate little Neile Stove Crag to pass over boggy ground beneath the foot of Arnsbarrow Tarn. Rise up the grassy flanks of Top O'Selside to enter a little corridor, then bear right to climb the heather strewn rocky knoll and its domed summit topped by a cairn. Contrary to first impressions given by the OS

Nibthwaite Wood above Coniston Water.

Top O'Selside above a tranquil Coniston Water.

map, this high shoulder running to the east of Coniston Water is markedly profiled and contains plenty of interest. To the north east a flat table top offers an unbroken view of Arnsbarrow Tarn.

Descend to the west from the summit into a little heathery bowl and exit to the left. An easy and direct descent down the shoulder reaches the point where the footpath from High Bethecar and the rough road from High Nibthwaite intercept. Bear left along the road, passing a walled enclosure above to the left, to the stile that enters the wood. Instead of following the track bear left to a small forgotten path along the bank of the stream. Pass by a series of little waterfalls which are often graced with white fronted dippers. A ruined enclosure to the right is now filled by trees. The path pulls away from the stream slightly and just beyond

•OUT 4•

GUMMER'S HOW – EAST OF WINDERMERE

Gummer's How 1054ft/321m
Birch Fell 1043ft/318m

Town Base: Bowness-On-Windermere.
Maps: OS Pathfinder 626, Broughton in Furness & Newby Bridge. L96 South Lakeland.
Length: 2.5miles/4km.
Ascent: 590ft/180m.
Approx Time: 1.5hrs.
Start & Finish: Large car park above the Newby Bridge to Bowland Bridge road, beneath Astley's Plantation (SD 390877).
Difficulty: A pleasant stroll, though the simplicity of Gummer's How contrasts markedly with the complexities of rougher Birch Fell. A little boggy between Gummer's How and Birch Fell.

Gummer's How stands easily accessible just above the road. On occasions it throngs with the tourist more akin to a summer stroll along Bowness Front. Yet Gummer's How east of Windermere has a unique position. From her heights you can look along the length of England's largest lake, span the entire range of these Southern Fells and look beyond to the Langdale Pikes, Skiddaw, Fairfield, Kentmere Pike and the Pennines. You can also look out across Morecambe Bay and the estuaries of the Kent and the Crake. The view from Gummer's How is her glory. She also has a delightful character.

From the car park ascend the road to the kissing gate on the left. The path is broad and unmistakable. Pass silver birch and ancient larch to rise over polished rock slabs to the stone trig point which marks the summit. For the best view along the lake, walk to the western edge.

From the trig point a path heads north and descends alongside a few larch trees. Bear right and descend east to the edge of a boggy hollow. A small slate quarry lies just to the left near the bottom. Turn left along the edge of the bog. A path, which has been unused for some time judging by the overgrowth of bracken, lies just above. It takes a constructed gateway through a ruined wall, but we turn right to ascend by the wall which rises up the flanks of Birch Fell. After crossing a ruined wall weave through a jumble of larch. Bear left to join a wire fence. This rises over the rocky summit knoll of Birch Fell.

Pick a line through the larch down the southern flank of the fell until it is possible to bear right to the edge of the boggy hollow. A high line can be picked over a series of rocky outcrops which allows a relatively dry crossing. Beyond the hollow, by the corner of the plantation, intercept a good grass path. It follows the edge of the pungent smelling pines until it falls directly down the hill back to the original broad path.

Looking north from Gummer's How.

to the left, observe two flat circular levels; the first has three oaks growing within it. These are charcoal burner levels which have been abandoned, possibly centuries ago. Further along, a track crosses the stream to the left. Join this to return to the car park.

APPENDIX

TOPS IN ORDER OF ALTITUDE (BY GROUP)

WESTERN FELLS
188 tops, 13 groups, 43 walks, 2 supplements

Derwent Water/Thirlmere Fells (DER)
(28 tops, 7 walks)

Name	Altitude (ft/metres)	Map ref
High Raise (High White Stones)	2500/762	NY 281095
Low White Stones	2398/731	NY 282101
Ullscarf	2382/726	NY 292122
Coldbarrow Fell – High Saddle	2215/675	NY 289129
Coldbarrow Fell – Low Saddle	2152/656	NY 288133
Standing Crag	2005/611	NY 296134
High Seat	1995/608	NY 287181
Bleaberry Fell	1935/590	NY 286196
Sergeant's Crag	1873/571	NY 274114
Blea Tarn Fell	1830/558	NY 298143
Lining Crag	1778/542	NY 283112
Eagle Crag	1709/521	NY 276121
High Tove	1689/515	NY 289165
Watendlath Fell	1689/515	NY 289148
Wythburn Fell	1667/508	NY 312125
Shivery Knott	1610/491	NY 289154
Middle Crag	1587/484	NY 288158
Armboth Fell	1570/479	NY 297159
Brown Rigg	1519/463	NY 305146
Raven Crag	1512/461	NY 303187
The Benn	1463/446	NY 302193
Great Crag (Stonethwaite)	1444/440	NY 270147
Castle Crag (Shoulthwaite)	1381/421	NY 300183
Fisher Crag	1381/421	NY 305163
Brund Fell	1363/415	NY 265163
King's How – Grange Fell	1286/392	NY 258166
Walla Crag	1243/379	NY 277213
Great How (Thirlmere)	1100/335	NY 314188

Langdale Fells (LAN)
(22 tops, 5 walks)

Name	Altitude (ft/metres)	Map ref
Harrison Stickle	2414/736	NY 282074
Thunacar Knott	2372/723	NY 279080
Sergeant Man	2414/736	NY 286089
Codale Head	2401/732	NY 289091
Pike O'Stickle	2324/709	NY 274075
Pavey Ark	2288/697	NY 285079
Loft Crag	2238/682	NY 275071
Rossett Pike	2136/651	NY 249076
Thorn Crag	2106/642	NY 280072
Buck Pike (Mickleden)	1988/606	NY 253078
Black Crag (Mickleden)	1929/588	NY 282074
Dead Pike – Steel Fell	1812/553	NY 319111
Tarn Crag	1807/551	NY 303094
Blea Rigg	1776/541	NY 302078
Calf Crag	1762/537	NY 302104
Castle How	1640/500	NY 308076
Gibson Knott	1384/422	NY 317100
Lang How	1358/414	NY 318071
Swinescar Pike	1348/411	NY 313072
Helm Crag	1329/405	NY 326094
Silver How	1294/395	NY 325066
Loughrigg	1101/335	NY 347051

Bowfell Group (BOW)
(20 tops, 4 walks)

Name	Altitude (ft/metres)	Map ref
Bowfell	2960/902	NY 245065
Esk Pike	2903/885	NY 237075
Long Top – Second Crinkle	2816/859	NY 248049
Third Crinkle	2754/840	NY 250050
First Crinkle	2733/833	NY 250046
Fourth Crinkle	2730/832	NY 250051
Gunson Knott – Fifth Crinkle	2674/815	NY 250052
Shelter Crags	2674/815	NY 250053
Pike de Bield	2657/810	NY 236068
Stonesty Pike	2510/765	NY 249041
Little Stand	2428/740	NY 251034
Pike O'Blisco	2313/705	NY 272041
Cold Pike	2300/701	NY 263036
Great Knott	2283/696	NY 260043
High Gait Crags	1877/572	NY 230058
White Stones – The Band	1863/568	NY 261061
Long Crag – Wrynose Fell	1788/545	NY 280040
Blake Rigg (Little Langdale)	1755/535	NY 285039
Brown Howe – Lingmoor Fell	1538/469	NY 303046
Side Pike	1187/362	NY 293054

Borrowdale Fells (BOR)
(12 tops, 2 walks)

Name	Altitude (ft/metres)	Map ref
Allen Crags	2574/785	NY 237086
Glaramara	2568/783	NY 246105
Looking Stead – Glaramara	2543/775	NY 246102
Combe Head	2405/733	NY 250109
Lincomb Head – Glaramara	2365/721	NY 243097
High House – Allen Crags	2244/684	NY 240093
Great Slack – Seathwaite Fell	2073/632	NY 227097
Stonethwaite Fell	2073/632	NY 256114
Rosthwaite Cam – Rosthwaite Fell	2008/612	NY 256118
Seathwaite Fell	1970/601	NY 229102
Thornythwaite Fell	1883/574	NY 245118
Bessyboot – Rosthwaite Fell	1807/550	NY 258125

Eskdale Fells (ESK)
(13 tops, 3 walks)

Name	Altitude (ft/metres)	Map ref
Hard Knott	1803/549	NY 232023
Border End	1713/522	NY 229018
Great How – Eskdale Fell	1713/522	NY 198040
Yew Bank	1637/499	NY 232031
High Scarth	1598/487	NY 215044
Scar Lathing	1440/439	NY 226050
Whinscales – Eskdale Fell	1394/425	NY 199033
Throstlehow Crag	1325/404	NY 227044
Dawsonground Crags	1302/397	NY 204027
Silveryield	1296/395	NY 222039
Whin Crag (Eskdale)	1158/353	NY 200023
Boat How	1105/337	NY 177034
Goat Crag	1024/312	NY 204018

Scafells (SCA)
(8 tops, 4 walks + 1 supplement)

Name	Altitude (ft/metres)	Map ref
Scafell Pike	3210/978	NY 216072
Scafell	3162/964	NY 207065
Ill Crag (Scafell)	3067/935	NY 223074
Broad Crag (Scafell)	3054/931	NY 219076
Great End	2984/910	NY 226084
Lingmell (Wasdale)	2649/807	NY 209082
Pen	2500/762	NY 068221
Slight Side	2499/762	NY 210050

The Screes (SCR)
(4 tops, 2 walks)

Name	Altitude (ft/metres)	Map ref
Illgill Head	1998/609	NY 169049
Whin Rigg (Wasdale)	1755/535	NY 152034
Irton Fell	1296/395	NY 144026
Great Bank	1079/329	NY 144019

Great Gable Group (GRG)
(10 tops, 3 walks)

Name	Altitude (ft/metres)	Map ref
Great Gable	2949/899	NY 211103
Kirk Fell	2630/802	NY 195105
Green Gable	2628/801	NY 215107
North Top – Kirk Fell	2582/787	NY 199107
Brandreth	2344/715	NY 215119
Grey Knotts	2287/697	NY 219126
Fleetwith Pike	2126/648	NY 206141
Base Brown	2120/646	NY 225115
Black Star – Honister Crag	2077/633	NY 213141
Haystacks (Buttermere)	1959/597	NY 193132

Pillar Group (PIL)
(18 tops, 4 walks + 1 supplement)

Name	Altitude (ft/metres)	Map ref
Pillar	2927/892	NY 171121
Scoat Fell	2760/841	NY 160114
Black Crag (Pillar)	2717/828	NY 166116
Red Pike	2709/826	NY 165106
Steeple	2687/819	NY 157117
Haycock	2617/797	NY 145107
Pillar Rock	2560/780	NY 172124
Little Gowder Crag	2405/733	NY 141110
Caw Fell	2288/697	NY 132110
Seatallan	2270/692	NY 140084
Ennerdale Fell	2113/644	NY 123119
South Top – Yewbarrow	2058/628	NY 173085
Looking Stead	2057/627	NY 186118
North Top – Yewbarrow	2021/616	NY 176092
Middle Fell	1908/582	NY 151072
Lingmell (Ennerdale)	1427/435	NY 142130
Glade How	1420/433	NY 134064
Buckbarrow	1388/423	NY 136061

Lank Rigg Group (LAK)
(12 tops, 2 walks)

Name	Altitude (ft/metres)	Map ref
Lank Rigg	1775/541	NY 092120
Crag Fell	1716/523	NY 197144
Whoap	1676/511	NY 099129
Grike	1599/488	NY 085141
Blakeley Raise	1276/389	NY 070135
Kinniside	1230/375	NY 078116
Latter Barrow	1161/354	NY 074055
Swainson Knott	1118/341	NY 080084
Swarth Fell (Kinniside)	1099/335	NY 065120
Stone Pike	1056/322	NY 078078
Burn Edge	1050/320	NY 069126
Ponsonby Fell	1020/311	NY 082071

High Stile Group (HIG)
(13 tops, 2 walks)

Name	Altitude (ft/metres)	Map ref
Grey Crag – High Stile	2648/807	NY 170148
High Stile	2644/806	NY 168148
Red Pike (Buttermere)	2478/755	NY 161154
High Crag (Buttermere)	2442/744	NY 180141
Dodd (Buttermere)	2103/641	NY 164158
Starling Dodd	2077/633	NY 142157
Great Borne	1936/590	NY 124164
Little Dodd (Ennerdale)	1936/562	NY 150155
Herdus	1844/590	NY 118163
Seat	1840/561	NY 186134
Gale Fell	1699/518	NY 134164
Bowness Knott	1093/333	NY 112155
Brown How (Ennerdale)	1056/322	NY 116158

Loweswater Fells (LOW) (21 tops, 4 walks)

Name	Altitude (ft/metres)	Map ref
Blake Fell	1878/573	NY 110197
Carling Knott	1785/544	NY 117203
Gavel Fell	1726/526	NY 117185
Loweswater End – Carling Knott	1703/519	NY 121206
Mellbreak – South Top	1678/512	NY 148185
Hen Comb	1670/509	NY 132181
Mellbreak – North Top	1670/509	NY 143195
High Nook – Gavel Fell	1601/488	NY 120189
Sharp Knott	1581/482	NY 107201
Burnbank Fell	1558/475	NY 110209
High Pen	1558/475	NY 111189
Banna Fell	1496/446	NY 116174
Floutern Cop	1480/451	NY 122174
Knock Murton	1467/447	NY 095191
Low Pen	1427/435	NY 105190
Owsen Fell	1342/409	NY 101209
Godworth	1197/365	NY 101183
Little Dodd (Loweswater)	1188/362	NY 132192
Scale Knott	1109/338	NY 150178
High Hows (Lamplugh)	1027/313	NY 096202
Kelton Fell	1020/311	NY 095181

Fellbarrow Group (FEL) (7 tops, 1 walk)

Name	Altitude (ft/metres)	Map ref
Low Fell	1388/423	NY 137226
Fellbarrow – Mosser Fell	1363/416	NY 132242
Loweswater Fell	1352/412	NY 136223
Sourfoot Fell	1348/411	NY 135233
Smithy Fell	1286/392	NY 133237
Darling Fell	1283/391	NY 128225
Hatteringill Head – Whin Fell	1263/385	NY 133248

NORTH WESTERN FELLS

56 tops, 4 groups, 12 walks

Dale Head Group (DAL) (11 tops, 3 walks)

Name	Altitude (ft/metres)	Map ref
Dale Head	2472/753	NY 223153
Robinson	2418/737	NY 202169
Hindscarth	2385/727	NY 216165
High Spy – Scawdel Fell	2143/653	NY 234162
Maiden Moor	1890/576	NY 237182
High Crags (Newlands)	1736/529	NY 217175
High Snockrigg	1726/526	NY 187169
Red Knott	1483/452	NY 221180
Catbells	1481/451	NY 244198
Scope End	1352/412	NY 224183
Skelgill Bank	1109/338	NY 245206

Grasmoor Group (GRA) (18 tops, 3 walks)

Name	Altitude (ft/metres)	Map ref
Grasmoor	2795/852	NY 175203
Crag Hill	2751/839	NY 193204
Eel Crag	2649/807	NY 190207
Sail	2356/773	NY 198203
Wandhope	2533/772	NY 188197
Thirdgill Head Man	2402/732	NY 184196
Scar Crags	2205/672	NY 207206
Whiteless Pike	2165/660	NY 180190
Causey Pike	2090/637	NY 219209
Ard Crags	1906/581	NY 207198
Outerside	1863/568	NY 211215
Knott Rigg	1824/556	NY 197189
Ill Crag (Newlands)	1791/546	NY 200192
Barrow	1494/455	NY 227218
Stile End	1467/447	NY 221219
Rowling End	1421/433	NY 229207
Lad Hows	1398/426	NY 172193
Rannerdale Knotts	1165/355	NY 167182

Grisedale Pike Group (GRI) (12 tops, 3 walks)

Name	Altitude (ft/metres)	Map ref
Grisedale Pike	2595/791	NY 199226
Hopegill Head	2525/770	NY 186222
Sand Hill	2480/756	NY 187219
Hobcarton Head	2425/739	NY 194220

	Altitude (ft/metres)	Map ref
Whiteside – East Top	2359/719	NY 175221
Whiteside – West Top	2319/707	NY 171220
Gasgale Crags	2306/703	NY 173222
Ladyside Pike	2306/703	NY 185227
Hobcarton End	2080/634	NY 194220
Swinside	1670/509	NY 177239
Dodd (Lorton)	1489/454	NY 169231
Kinn	1227/374	NY 219233

Lord's Seat Group (LOS) (15 tops, 3 walks)

Name	Altitude (ft/metres)	Map ref
Lord's Seat	1811/552	NY 204266
Ullister Hill	1722/525	NY 209260
Whinlatter Top	1722/525	NY 197249
Brown How – Whinlatter	1696/517	NY 191251
Broom Fell	1676/511	NY 194272
Seat How (Thornthwaite)	1627/496	NY 213256
Tarbarrel Moss	1617/493	NY 206253
Barf	1536/468	NY 215268
Graystones	1496/456	NY 178264
Kirk Fell – Lorton	1437/438	NY 173266
Ling Fell	1224/373	NY 180286
Sale Fell	1178/359	NY 194297
Lothwaite	1132/345	NY 203297
Rivings	1099/335	NY 198294
Burthwaite Heights	1043/318	NY 189283

NORTHERN FELLS

58 tops, 3 groups, 14 walks, 1 supplement

Blencathra Group (BLE) (13 tops, 4 walks + 1 supplement)

Name	Altitude (ft/metres)	Map ref
Hallsfell Top – Blencathra	2847/868	NY 323277
Gategill Fell Top – Blencathra	2792/851	NY 318274
Atkinson Pike (Foule Crag) – Blencathra	2772/845	NY 325283
Blease Fell – Blencathra	2638/804	NY 312270
Doddick Fell – Blencathra	2434/742	NY 329277
Bowscale Fell	2305/702	NY 333304
Bannerdale Crags	2240/683	NY 335290
Scales Fell – Blencathra	2238/682	NY 332279
East Top – Bowscale Fell	2185/666	NY 340310
The Tongue	1814/553	NY 344302
Souther Fell	1713/522	NY 355292
Eycott Hill	1132/345	NY 387295
Little Eycott Hill	1099/335	NY 385301

Skiddaw Massif (SKI) (20 tops, 4 walks)

Name	Altitude (ft/metres)	Map ref
High Man – Skiddaw	3053/931	NY 260291
Middle Top – Skiddaw	3044/928	NY 261288
South Top – Skiddaw	3034/925	NY 261285
North Top – Skiddaw	3024/922	NY 261292
Little Man – Skiddaw	2837/865	NY 267278
Broad End	2726/831	NY 261298
Lesser Man – Skiddaw	2674/815	NY 269276
Carl Side	2447/746	NY 255281
Jenkin Hill	2411/735	NY 274275
Long Side	2408/734	NY 249284
Lonscale Fell	2344/715	NY 286271
Lonscale Pike	2306/703	NY 289273
Ullock Pike	2270/692	NY 244288
Sale How	2185/666	NY 276286
Bakestall	2208/673	NY 266307
Hare Crag	1765/538	NY 277299
Cockup	1657/505	NY 259314
Dodd (Skiddaw)	1647/502	NY 244274
Latrigg	1207/368	NY 279247
Watches	1093/333	NY 241304

North O'Skiddaw Group (NOS) (25 tops, 6 walks)

Name	Altitude (ft/metres)	Map ref
Knott	2329/710	NY 296330
Great Calva	2265/690	NY 291312
Carrock Fell	2174/663	NY 342336
High Pike (Caldbeck)	2157/658	NY 319350
Great Sca Fell	2135/651	NY 291339
Little Calva	2106/642	NY 282315
Little Sca Fell	2083/635	NY 290342

	Altitude (ft/metres)	Map ref
Coomb Height	2057/627	NY 311327
Hare Stones	2057/627	NY 315344
Frozen Fell	2050/625	NY 287332
Great Lingy Hill	2021/616	NY 310340
Little Lingy Hill	1998/609	NY 304339
Miton Hill	1991/607	NY 329341
Round Knott	1978/603	NY 334337
Burn Tod	1952/595	NY 283329
Brae Fell	1919/585	NY 289352
Meal Fell	1804/550	NY 283337
Great Cockup	1726/526	NY 273333
Lowthwaite Fell	1670/509	NY 278347
Longlands Fell	1581/482	NY 276354
White Hause	1525/465	NY 272324
Binsey	1466/447	NY 225355
Little Cockup	1296/395	NY 262337
Orthwaite Bank	1142/348	NY 256335
Green How – Aughertree Fell	1053/321	NY 258375

CENTRAL FELLS

66 tops, 4 groups, 16 walks

Great Mell Group (MEL) (7 tops, 2 walks)

Name	Altitude (ft/metres)	Map ref
Great Mell Fell	1762/537	NY 397254
Little Mell Fell	1657/505	NY 423240
Gowbarrow Fell	1579/481	NY 408218
Green Hill – Gowbarrow Fell	1450/442	NY 408214
Great Meldrum	1434/437	NY 415223
Watermillock Fell	1391/424	NY 425233
Little Meldrum	1325/404	NY 422228

Dodds Group (DOD) (25 tops, 6 walks)

Name	Altitude (ft/metres)	Map ref
Great Dodd	2811/857	NY 342206
Stybarrow Dodd	2766/843	NY 343189
White Stones – Green Side	2608/795	NY 353187
Watson's Dodd	2588/789	NY 336196
Little Dodd (St John's Common)	2575/785	NY 337204
Hart Side	2481/756	NY 359198
Randerside	2391/729	NY 349211
Clough Head	2381/726	NY 334226
Birkett Fell	2378/725	NY 365198
Sheffield Pike	2215/675	NY 369182
Calfhow Pike	2175/663	NY 331211
Heron Pike (Glenridding)	2008/612	NY 374178
High Brow	1886/575	NY 368214
Swineside Knott	1814/553	NY 379197
Common Fell	1811/552	NY 383204
Brown Hills	1808/551	NY 378194
Threlkeld Knotts	1686/514	NY 330230
Low How	1631/497	NY 375215
Glenridding Dodd	1450/442	NY 381176
Round How	1270/387	NY 392208
Bracken How	1224/373	NY 393211
Naddle Fell	1171/357	NY 309220
High Rigg	1125/343	NY 307215
Castle Rock	1112/339	NY 322197
Wren Crag	1020/311	NY 316202

Helvellyn Massif (HEL) (10 tops, 3 walks)

Name	Altitude (ft/metres)	Map ref
Helvellyn	3118/950	NY 342151
Lower Man – Helvellyn	3033/925	NY 338155
Nethermost Pike	2922/891	NY 344142
Catstycam	2919/890	NY 348158
High Crag (Grisedale)	2903/885	NY 343137
Raise	2897/883	NY 343174
White Side	2832/863	NY 338167
Dollywaggon Pike	2815/858	NY 346131
Birkhouse Moor	2356/718	NY 364160
Brown Crag	2001/610	NY 328177

Fairfield Group (FAR) (24 tops, 5 walks)

Name	Altitude (ft/metres)	Map ref
Fairfield	2863/873	NY 359118
St Sunday Crag	2758/841	NY 369134
Cofa Pike	2700/823	NY 359121
Hart Crag	2698/822	NY 369112

Dove Crag	2598/792	NY 375105
Gavel Pike	2572/784	NY 373134
Red Screes	2545/776	NY 397088
Great Rigg	2513/766	NY 356104
Seat Sandal	2415/736	NY 344115
High Pike – Scandale Fell	2152/656	NY 374088
Middle Dodd	2146/654	NY 397095
Little Hart Crag – West Top	2091/637	NY 387100
Birks	2040/622	NY 380143
Rydal Fell	2037/621	NY 357087
Heron Pike (Rydal)	2008/612	NY 356083
Gill Crag – Hartsop above How	1870/570	NY 383120
High Hartsop Dodd	1702/519	NY 393108
Gale Crag	1680/512	NY 392124
Low Pike	1667/508	NY 348093
Stone Arthur	1652/504	NY 374078
Wansfell	1597/487	NY 404053
Wansfell Pike	1588/484	NY 394042
Nab Scar	1450/442	NY 356071
Arnison Crag	1422/433	NY 394150

EASTERN FELLS
95 tops, 6 groups, 23 walks

Loadpot Hill Group (LOA) (12 tops, 5 walks)

Name	Altitude (ft/metres)	Map ref
Red Crag	2333/711	NY 450152
Wether Hill	2205/672	NY 456168
Loadpot Hill	2201/671	NY 457181
Low Kop	1877/572	NY 472165
Swarth Fell (Ullswater)	1788/545	NY 454195
Arthur's Pike	1747/532	NY 461207
Bonscale Pike	1718/524	NY 453201
Bampton Fell	1604/489	NY 487165
Four Stones Hill	1362/415	NY 492163
Pinnacle Howe	1257/383	NY 497167
Heughscar Hill	1231/375	NY 488232
Knipe Scar	1122/342	NY 526191

Branstree Group (BRA) (11 tops, 2 walks)

Name	Altitude (ft/metres)	Map ref
Branstree	2339/713	NY 478100
High Howes (Mardale)	2208/673	NY 488103
Selside Pike	2149/655	NY 491112
Brown Howe (Mardale)	1736/529	NY 487122
Hare Shaw	1650/503	NY 498131
Powleys Hill	1526/465	NY 505135
Naddle High Forest	1427/435	NY 492143
Wallow Crag	1421/433	NY 496149
Naddle Low Forest	1398/426	NY 502150
Harper Hills	1375/419	NY 510144
Scalebarrow Knott	1109/338	NY 519152

Shap Fells (SHA) (25 tops, 5 walks)

Name	Altitude (ft/metres)	Map ref
Tarn Crag – Sleddale Fell	2178/664	NY 488078
Grey Crag (Longsleddale)	2093/638	NY 497072
Harrop Pike	2090/637	NY 501078
Great Yarlside	1952/595	NY 522079
Wasdale Pike	1852/565	NY 537085
Great Saddle Crag	1850/564	NY
Ancrow Brow	1816/553	NY 501055
High Wether Howe	1742/531	NY 515109
White Howe (Bannisdale)	1737/530	NY 524042
Borrowdale Head	1734/528	NY 528036
Lord's Seat – High House Fell	1719/524	NY 518066
Little Yarlside	1691/516	NY 532072
Seat Robert	1688/515	NY 527114
Capplebarrow	1681/512	NY 508035
Sleddale Pike	1659/506	NY 536094
Ulthwaite Rigg	1648/502	NY 515093
High House Bank	1625/495	NY 543048
Great Howe (Longsleddale)	1621/494	NY 489064
Long Crag – Bannisdale Fell	1617/493	NY 516052
Robin Hood	1617/493	NY 530059
What Shaw	1593/485	NY 542061
Glede Howe	1562/476	NY 521120
Todd Fell	1314/401	NY 512021
Whiteside Pike	1302/397	NY 521015
Lamb Pasture	1205/367	NY 532021

Kentdale Group (KEN) (6 tops, 3 walks)

Name	Altitude (ft/metres)	Map ref
Sallows	1691/516	NY 433040
Sour Howes	1585/483	NY 428032
Capple Howe	1460/445	NY 432029
Brunt Knott	1400/427	NY 484006
Hollow Moor – Green Quarter Fell	1398/426	NY 469040
Cocklaw Fell	1197/365	NY 481039

High Street Group (HST) (25 tops, 5 walks)

Name	Altitude (ft/metres)	Map ref
High Street	2718/828	NY 441111
High Raise (High Street)	2633/802	NY 448134
Rampsgill Head	2598/792	NY 443128
Thornthwaite Beacon	2572/784	NY 432100
Kidsty Pike	2560/780	NY 448126
Harter Fell (Mardale)	2552/778	NY 460093
Stony Cove Pike	2503/763	NY 418100
Mardale Ill Bell	2496/761	NY 448101
Ill Bell	2483/757	NY 437077
John Bell's Banner – Caudale Moor	2477/755	NY 413101
Low Raise	2474/754	NY 456137
The Knott (High Street)	2423/739	NY 437127
Kentmere Pike	2396/730	NY 466078
Froswick	2360/720	NY 435085
Yoke	2316/706	NY 438067
Gray Crag	2293/699	NY 427119
Little Harter Fell	2234/681	NY 469095
Adam Seat	2185/666	NY 471091
Rough Crag (Riggindale)	2060/628	NY 454112
Goat Scar	2054/626	NY 473069
Hartsop Dodd	2028/618	NY 412118
St Raven's Edge	1946/593	NY 403082
Shipman Knotts	1926/587	NY 473063
Castle Crag (Mardale)	1296/395	NY 469127
Troutbeck Tongue	1194/364	NY 423064

Martindale Group (MAR) (16 tops, 3 walks)

Name	Altitude (ft/metres)	Map ref
Rest Dodd	2283/696	NY 433137
Place Fell	2154/657	NY 406170
The Nab	1890/576	NY 434152
Angletarn Pike – North	1860/567	NY 413148
Angletarn Pike – South	1854/565	NY 414147
Brock Crags	1842/561	NY 417137
The Knight	1778/542	NY 404176
Bleaberry Knott – Birk Fell	1680/512	NY 403183
Beda Head – Beda Fell	1670/509	NY 428170
High Dodd	1644/501	NY 416182
Gowk Hill	1545/471	NY 445167
Brownthwaite Crag	1457/444	NY 443174
Pikeawassa – Steel Knotts	1417/432	NY 440181
Hallin Fell	1273/388	NY 433198
Sleet Fell	1240/378	NY 432189
Low Birk Fell	1224/373	NY 411190

SOUTHERN FELLS
78 tops, 6 groups, 18 walks

Coniston Massif (CON) (21 tops, 4 walks)

Name	Altitude (ft/metres)	Map ref
Coniston Old Man	2633/803	SD 273978
Swirl How	2630/802	NY 273005
Brim Fell	2611/796	NY 271986
Great Carrs	2575/785	NY 270009
Grey Friar	2536/773	NY 260004
Great How – Swirl Band	2526/770	NY 273000
Wetherlam	2502/762	NY 288011
Black Sails	2443/745	NY 283008
Little Carrs	2270/692	NY 270015
Hell Gill Pike	2172/662	NY 269016
Birk Fell Man – Birk Fell	1722/525	NY 296017
Hawk Rigg	1447/441	NY 300015
Kitty Crag	1427/435	SD 295990
High Fell	1404/428	NY 300017
Blake Rigg (Tilberthwaite)	1388/423	NY 301012
Haystacks (Tilberthwaite)	1381/421	NY 301014

Long Crag – Yewdale Fells	1381/421	SD 298990
High Wythow	1345/410	SD 300990
Great Intake – Low Fell	1327/405	NY 303022
Low Wythow	1220/372	SD 303993
Brackeny Crag	1212/370	SD 303998

Dow Crag Group (DOW) (15 tops, 3 walks)

Name	Altitude (ft/metres)	Map ref
Dow Crag	2554/778	SD 263978
Buck Pike – Seathwaite Fell	2441/744	SD 262972
Brown Pike	2237/682	SD 261966
Walna Scar	2037/621	SD 258963
White Maiden	1995/608	SD 254957
White Pike (Seathwaite)	1962/598	SD 249956
Caw	1735/529	SD 230945
Pikes	1539/469	SD 238947
Fox Haw	1263/385	SD 223936
Stickle Pike	1231/375	SD 212928
Raven's Crag	1184/361	SD 224929
High Pike Haw	1161/354	SD 264949
Brock Barrow	1125/343	SD 224929
Tarn Hill	1027/313	SD 210921
Great Stickle	1001/305	SD 212916

Harter Fell Group (HAR) (11 tops, 2 walks)

Name	Altitude (ft/metres)	Map ref
Harter Fell (Eskdale)	2141/653	SD 219997
Demming Crag	1722/525	NY 222002
Green Crag	1604/489	NY 200983
Crook Crag	1539/469	NY 200988
White How – Birker Fell	1457/444	NY 205975
Horseshow Crags	1421/433	NY 224008
Great Worm Crag	1400/427	SD 194969
Great Whinscale	1394/425	SD 198990
Broad Crag – Birker Fell	1220/372	SD 195978
Great Crag – Birker Fell	1109/338	SD 186978
Kepple Crag	1076/328	SD 199999

Whitfell Group (WHI) (18 tops, 3 walks)

Name	Altitude (ft/metres)	Map ref
Whitfell	1881/573	SD 159930
Buck Barrow	1799/549	SD 152910
Burn Moor	1780/543	SD 151924
Kinmont Buck Barrow	1754/535	SD 147910
Great Paddy Crag	1745/532	SD 150909
Stainton Pike	1632/498	SD 153943
Yoadcastle	1621/494	SD 157953
Woodend Height	1597/487	SD 157954
Hesk Fell	1565/477	SD 176947
Plough Fell	1470/448	SD 162912
White Pike – Birkby Fell	1450/442	SD 151956
Stoneside Hill	1384/422	SD 146893
The Pike	1214/370	SD 186934
Bigert	1086/331	SD 176932
The Knott – Stainton Fell	1086/331	SD 144952
Rough Crag (Birker Moor)	1047/319	SD 161978
Seat How (Birker Moor)	1020/311	SD 165971
Water Crag	1001/305	SD 154975

Black Combe Group (BLC) (5 tops, 2 walks)

Name	Altitude (ft/metres)	Map ref
Black Combe	1970/600	SD 135855
South Top – Black Combe	1926/587	SD 136852
Stoupdale Head	1548/472	SD 151874
White Combe	1361/415	SD 155863
White Hall Knott	1020/311	SD 156856

Outlying Eastern Tops (OUT) (8 tops, 4 walks)

Name	Altitude (ft/metres)	Map ref
Top O'Selside	1099/335	SD 309919
Arnsbarrow Hill	1056/322	SD 311911
Black Crag – Black Fell	1056/322	NY 340016
Gummer's How	1054/321	SD 390885
Birch Fell	1043/318	SD 395892
Holme Fell	1040/317	NY 315006
Stang Hill	1037/316	SD 310908
Carron Crag	1030/314	SD 325943

TOPS IN ORDER OF ALTITUDE

Order	Name	Altitude (ft/metres)	Area/Group	Page
1	Scafell Pike	3210/978	W/SCA	56
2	Scafell	3162/964	WSCA	57
3	Helvellyn	3118/950	C/HEL	178
4	Ill Crag (Scafell)	3067/935	W/SCA	56
5	Broad Crag (Scafell)	3054/931	W/SCA	56
6	High Man – Skiddaw	3053/931	N/SKI	144
7	Middle Top – Skiddaw	3044/928	N/SKI	144
8	South Top – Skiddaw	3034/925	N/SKI	144
9	Lower Man – Helvellyn	3033/925	C/HEL	178
10	North Top – Skiddaw	3024/922	N/SKI	144
11	Great End	2984/910	W/SCA	61
12	Bowfell	2960/902	W/BOW	39
13	Great Gable	2949/899	W/GRG	69
14	Pillar	2927/892	W/PIL	76
15	Nethermost Pike	2922/891	C/HEL	181
16	Catstycam	2919/890	C/HEL	179
17	Esk Pike	2903/885	W/BOW	40
17	High Crag (Grisedale)	2903/885	C/HEL	181
19	Raise	2897/883	C/HEL	178
20	Fairfield	2863/873	C/FAR	184
21	Hallsfell Top – Blencathra	2847/868	N/BLE	140
22	Little Man – Skiddaw	2837/865	N/SKI	145
23	White Side	2832/863	C/HEL	178
24	Long Top – Second Crinkle	2816/859	W/BOW	39
25	Dollywaggon Pike	2815/858	C/HEL	181
26	Great Dodd	2811/857	C/DOD	171
27	Grasmoor	2795/852	NW/GRA	118
28	Gategill Fell Top – Blencathra	2792/851	N/BLE	140
29	Atkinson Pike (Foule Crag) – Blencathra	2772/845	N/BLE	141
30	Stybarrow Dodd	2766/843	C/DOD	172
31	Scoat Fell	2760/841	W/PIL	76
32	St Sunday Crag	2758/841	C/FAR	184
33	Third Crinkle	2754/840	W/BOW	39
34	Crag Hill	2751/839	NW/GRA	116
35	First Crinkle	2733/833	W/BOW	39
36	Fourth Crinkle	2730/832	W/BOW	39
37	Broad End	2726/831	N/SKI	148
38	High Street	2718/828	E/HST	225
39	Black Crag (Pillar)	2717/828	W/PIL	76
40	Red Pike	2709/826	W/PIL	76
41	Cofa Pike	2700/823	C/FAR	184
42	Hart Crag	2698/822	C/FAR	184
43	Steeple	2687/819	W/PIL	76
44	Gunson Knott – Fifth Crinkle	2674/815	W/BOW	39
44	Lesser Man – Skiddaw	2674/815	N/SKI	145
44	Shelter Crags	2674/815	W/BOW	39
47	Pike de Bield	2657/810	W/BOW	40
48	Eel Crag	2649/807	NW/GRA	116
48	Lingmell (Wasdale)	2649/807	W/SCA	60
50	Grey Crag – High Stile	2648/807	W/HIG	91
51	High Stile	2644/806	W/HIG	91
52	Blease Fell – Blencathra	2638/804	N/BLE	140
53	Coniston Old Man	2633/803	S/CON	243
54	High Raise (High Street)	2633/802	E/HST	225
55	Kirk Fell	2630/802	W/GRG	71
55	Swirl How	2630/802	S/CON	238
57	Green Gable	2628/801	W/GRG	69
58	Haycock	2617/797	W/PIL	78
59	Brim Fell	2611/796	S/CON	243
60	White Stones – Green Side	2608/795	C/DOD	172
61	Dove Crag	2598/792	C/FAR	186
61	Rampsgill Head	2598/792	E/HST	225
63	Grisedale Pike	2595/791	NW/GRI	122
64	Watson's Dodd	2588/789	C/DOD	172
65	North Top – Kirk Fell	2582/787	W/GRG	71
66	Great Carrs	2575/785	S/CON	238
66	Little Dodd (St John's Common)	2575/785	C/DOD	171
68	Allen Crags	2574/785	W/BOR	46
69	Gavel Pike	2572/784	C/FAR	184
69	Thornthwaite Beacon	2572/784	E/HST	222
71	Glaramara	2568/783	W/BOR	46
72	Kidsty Pike	2560/780	E/HST	227
72	Pillar Rock	2560/780	W/PIL	77
74	Dow Crag	2554/778	S/DOW	246
75	Harter Fell (Mardale)	2552/778	E/HST	222
76	Red Screes	2545/776	C/FAR	185
77	Looking Stead – Glaramara	2543/775	W/BOR	46
78	Grey Friar	2536/773	S/CON	238
78	Sail	2536/773	NW/GRA	116
80	Wandhope	2533/772	NW/GRA	118
81	Great How (Swirl Band)	2526/770	S/CON	243
82	Hopegill Head	2525/770	NW/GRI	124
83	Great Rigg	2513/766	C/FAR	186
84	Stonesty Pike	2510/765	W/BOW	40
85	Stony Cove Pike	2503/763	E/HST	223
86	Wetherlam	2502/762	S/CON	240
87	High Raise (High White Stones)	2500/762	W/DER	22
87	Pen	2500/762	W/SCA	58
89	Slight Side	2499/762	W/SCA	57
90	Mardale Ill Bell	2496/761	E/HST	222
91	Ill Bell	2483/757	E/HST	222
92	Hart Side	2481/756	C/DOD	172
93	Sand Hill	2480/756	NW/GRI	124
94	Red Pike (Buttermere)	2478/755	W/HIG	91
95	John Bell's Banner – Caudale Moor	2477/755	E/HST	223
96	Low Raise	2474/754	E/HST	225
97	Dale Head	2472/753	NW/DAL	111
98	Carl Side	2447/746	N/SKI	148
99	Black Sails	2443/745	S/CON	240
100	High Crag (Buttermere)	2442/744	W/HIG	91
101	Buck Pike – Seathwaite Fell	2441/744	S/DOW	246
102	Doddick Fell – Blencathra	2434/742	N/BLE	140
103	Little Stand	2428/740	W/BOW	40
104	Hobcarton Head	2425/739	NW/GRI	123
105	The Knott (High Street)	2423/739	E/HST	225
106	Robinson	2418/737	NW/DAL	111
107	Seat Sandal	2415/736	C/FAR	187
108	Harrison Stickle	2414/736	W/LAN	32
108	Sergeant Man	2414/736	W/LAN	31
110	Jenkin Hill	2411/735	N/SKI	145
111	Long Side	2408/734	N/SKI	148
112	Combe Head	2405/733	W/BOR	44
112	Little Gowder Crag	2405/733	W/PIL	78
114	Thirdgill Head Man	2402/732	NW/GRA	118
115	Codale Head	2401/732	W/LAN	31
116	Low White Stones	2398/731	W/DER	22
117	Kentmere Pike	2396/730	E/HST	222
118	Randerside	2391/729	C/DOD	171
119	Hindscarth	2385/727	NW/DAL	110
120	Ullscarf	2382/726	W/DER	20
121	Clough Head	2381/726	C/DOD	171
122	Birkett Fell	2378/725	C/DOD	172
123	Thunacar Knott	2372/723	W/LAN	32
124	Lincomb Head – Glaramara	2365/721	W/BOR	46
125	Froswick	2360/720	E/HST	222
126	Whiteside – East Top	2359/719	NW/GRI	124
127	Birkhouse Moor	2356/718	C/HEL	179
128	Brandreth	2344/715	W/GRG	68
128	Lonscale Fell	2344/715	N/SKI	145
130	Branstree	2339/713	E/BRA	203
131	Red Crag	2333/711	E/LOA	197
132	Knott	2329/710	N/NOS	152
133	Pike O'Stickle	2324/709	W/LAN	32
134	Whiteside – West Top	2319/707	NW/GRI	124
135	Yoke	2316/706	E/HST	222
136	Pike O'Blisco	2313/705	W/BOW	37
137	Gasgale Crags	2306/703	NW/GRI	124
137	Ladyside Pike	2306/703	NW/GRI	124
137	Lonscale Pike	2306/703	N/SKI	145
140	Bowscale Fell	2305/702	N/BLE	138
141	Cold Pike	2300/701	W/BOW	37
142	Gray Crag	2293/699	E/HST	225
143	Caw Fell	2288/697	W/PIL	78
143	Pavey Ark	2288/697	W/LAN	32
145	Grey Knotts	2287/697	W/GRG	68
146	Great Knott	2283/696	W/BOW	37
146	Rest Dodd	2283/696	E/MAR	231
148	Little Carrs	2270/692	S/CON	238
148	Seatallan	2270/692	W/PIL	81
148	Ullock Pike	2270/692	N/SKI	148
151	Great Calva	2265/690	N/NOS	154
152	High House – Allen Crags	2244/684	W/BOR	46
153	Bannerdale Crags	2240/683	N/BLE	139
154	Loft Crag	2238/682	W/LAN	32
154	Scales Fell – Blencathra	2238/682	N/BLE	140
156	Brown Pike	2237/682	S/DOW	246
157	Little Harter Fell	2234/681	E/HST	225
158	Coldbarrow Fell – High Saddle	2215/675	W/DER	20
158	Sheffield Pike	2215/675	C/DOD	174
160	Bakestall	2208/673	N/SKI	148
160	High Howes (Mardale)	2208/673	E/BRA	203
162	Scar Crags	2205/672	NW/GRA	116
162	Wether Hill	2205/672	E/LOA	197
164	Loadpot Hill	2201/671	E/LOA	197
165	Adam Seat	2185/666	E/HST	225
165	East Top – Bowscale Fell	2185/666	N/BLE	139
165	See How	2185/666	N/SKI	144
168	Tarn Crag – Sleddale Fell	2178/664	E/SHA	211
169	Calfhow Pike	2175/663	C/DOD	171
170	Carrock Fell	2174/663	N/NOS	152
171	Hell Gill Pike	2172/662	S/CON	238
172	Whiteless Pike	2165/660	NW/GRA	118
173	High Pike (Caldbeck)	2157/658	N/NOS	152
174	Place Fell	2154/657	E/MAR	230
175	Coldbarrow Fell – Low Saddle	2152/656	W/DER	20
175	High Pike – Scandale Fell	2152/656	C/FAR	186
177	Selside Pike	2149/655	E/BRA	203
178	Middle Dodd	2146/654	C/FAR	185
179	High Spy – Scawdel Fell	2143/653	NW/DAL	110
180	Harter Fell (Eskdale)	2141/653	S/HAR	252
181	Rossett Pike	2136/651	W/LAN	32
182	Great Sca Fell	2135/651	N/NOS	155
183	Fleetwith Pike	2126/648	W/GRG	68
184	Base Brown	2120/646	W/GRG	69
185	Ennerdale Fell	2113/644	W/PIL	78
186	Little Calva	2106/642	N/NOS	154
186	Thorn Crag	2106/642	W/LAN	32
188	Dodd (Buttermere)	2103/641	W/HIG	91
189	Grey Crag (Longsleddale)	2093/638	E/SHA	211
190	Little Hart Crag – West Top	2091/637	C/FAR	185
191	Causey Pike	2090/637	NW/GRA	116
191	Harrop Pike	2090/637	E/SHA	211
193	Little Sca Fell	2083/635	N/NOS	155
194	Hobcarton End	2080/634	NW/GRI	122
195	Black Star – Honister Crag	2077/633	W/GRG	68
195	Starling Dodd	2077/633	W/HIG	90
197	Great Slack – Seathwaite Fell	2073/632	W/BOR	46
197	Stonethwaite Fell	2073/632	W/BOR	44
199	Rough Crag (Riggindale)	2060/628	E/HST	227
200	South Top – Yewbarrow	2058/628	W/PIL	80
201	Coomb Height	2057/627	N/NOS	152
201	Hare Stones	2057/627	N/NOS	152
201	Looking Stead	2057/627	W/PIL	76

Order	Name	Altitude (ft/metres)	Area/ Group	Page
204	Goat Scar	2054/626	E/HST	222
205	Frozen Fell	2050/625	N/NOS	155
206	Birks	2040/622	C/FAR	184
207	Rydal Fell	2037/621	C/FAR	186
207	Walna Scar	2037/621	S/DOW	246
209	Hartsop Dodd	2028/618	E/HST	225
210	Great Lingy Hill	2021/616	N/NOS	152
210	North Top – Yewbarrow	2021/616	W/PIL	80
212	Great Borne	2019/616	W/HIG	90
213	Heron Pike (Glenridding)	2008/612	C/DOD	174
213	Heron Pike (Rydal)	2008/612	C/FAR	186
213	Rosthwaite Cam – Rosthwaite Fell	2008/612	W/BOR	44
216	Standing Crag	2005/611	W/DER	20
217	Brown Crag	2001/610	C/HEL	178
218	Illgill Head	1998/609	W/SCR	65
218	Little Lingy Hill	1998/609	N/NOS	152
220	High Seat	1995/608	W/DER	16
220	White Maiden	1995/608	S/DOW	246
222	Miton Hill	1991/607	N/NOS	152
223	Buck Pike (Mickleden)	1988/606	W/LAN	32
224	Round Knott	1978/603	N/NOS	152
225	Black Combe	1970/600	S/BLC	265
225	Seathwaite Fell	1970/601	W/BOR	46
227	White Pike (Seathwaite)	1962/598	S/DOW	246
228	Haystacks (Buttermere)	1959/597	W/GRG	68
229	Burn Tod	1952/595	N/NOS	155
229	Great Yarlside	1952/595	E/SHA	209
231	St Raven's Edge	1946/593	E/HST	223
232	Little Dodd (Ennerdale)	1936/590	W/HIG	90
233	Bleaberry Fell	1935/590	W/DER	16
234	Black Crag (Mickleden)	1929/588	W/LAN	32
235	Black Combe – South Top	1926/587	S/BLC	265
235	Shipman Knotts	1926/587	E/HST	222
235	South Top – Black Combe	1926/587	S/BLC	265
237	Brae Fell	1919/585	N/NOS	156
238	Middle Fell	1908/582	W/PIL	81
239	Ard Crags	1906/581	NW/GRA	118
240	Maiden Moor	1890/576	NW/DAL	110
240	The Nab	1890/576	E/MAR	231
242	High Brow	1886/575	C/DOD	172
243	Thornythwaite Fell	1883/574	W/BOR	44
244	Whitfell	1881/573	S/WHI	259
245	Blake Fell	1878/573	W/LOW	98
246	High Gait Crags	1877/572	W/BOW	40
246	Low Kop	1877/572	E/LOA	197
248	Sergeant's Crag	1873/571	W/DER	22
249	Gill Crag – Hartsop above How	1870/570	C/FAR	184
250	Outerside	1863/568	NW/GRA	116
250	White Stones – The Band	1863/568	W/BOW	39
252	Angletarn Pike – North	1860/567	E/MAR	231
253	Angletarn Pike – South	1854/565	E/MAR	231
254	Wasdale Pike	1852/565	E/SHA	208
255	Great Saddle Crag	1850/564	E/SHA	208
256	Herdus	1844/562	W/HIG	90
257	Brock Crags	1842/561	E/MAR	231
258	Seat	1840/561	W/HIG	91
259	Blea Tarn Fell	1830/558	W/DER	20
260	Knott Rigg	1824/556	NW/GRA	118
261	Ancrow Brow	1816/553	E/SHA	210
262	Swineside Knott	1814/553	C/DOD	172
262	The Tongue	1814/553	N/BLE	138
264	Dead Pike – Steel Fell	1812/553	W/LAN	26
265	Common Fell	1811/552	C/DOD	172
265	Lord's Seat	1811/552	NW/LOS	128
267	Brown Hills	1808/551	C/DOD	172
268	Bessyboot – Rosthwaite Fell	1807/550	W/BOR	44
268	Tarn Crag	1807/551	W/LAN	31
270	Meal Fell	1804/550	N/NOS	155
271	Hard Knott	1803/549	W/ESK	50
272	Buck Barrow	1799/549	S/WHI	260
273	Ill Crag (Newlands)	1791/546	NW/GRA	118
274	Long Crag – Wrynose Fell	1788/545	W/BOW	37
274	Swarth Fell (Ullswater)	1788/545	E/LOA	195
276	Carling Knott	1785/544	W/LOW	98
277	Burn Moor	1780/543	S/WHI	260
278	Lining Crag	1778/542	W/DER	22
278	The Knight	1778/542	E/MAR	230
280	Blea Rigg	1776/541	W/LAN	29
281	Lank Rigg	1775/541	W/LAK	86
282	Hare Crag	1765/538	N/SKI	144
283	Calf Crag	1762/537	W/LAN	26
283	Great Mell Fell	1762/537	C/MEL	164
285	Blake Rigg (Little Langdale)	1755/535	W/BOW	37
285	Whin Rigg (Wasdale)	1755/535	W/SCR	65
287	Kinmont Buck Barrow	1754/535	S/WHI	260
288	Arthur's Pike	1747/532	E/LOA	195
289	Great Paddy Crag	1745/532	S/WHI	260
290	High Wether Howe	1742/531	E/SHA	206
291	White Howe (Bannisdale)	1737/530	E/SHA	210
292	Brown Howe (Mardale)	1736/529	E/BRA	203
292	High Crags (Newlands)	1736/529	NW/DAL	111
294	Caw	1735/529	S/DOW	247
295	Borrowdale Head	1734/528	E/SHA	210
296	Gavel Fell	1726/526	W/LOW	96
296	Great Cockup	1726/526	N/NOS	155
296	High Snockrigg	1726/526	NW/DAL	112
299	Birk Fell Man – Birk Fell	1722/525	S/CON	240
299	Demming Crag	1722/525	S/HAR	252
299	Ullister Hill	1722/525	NW/LOS	128
299	Whinlatter Top	1722/525	NW/LOS	130
303	Lord's Seat – High House Fell	1719/524	E/SHA	209
304	Bonscale Pike	1718/524	E/LOA	195
305	Crag Fell	1716/523	W/LAK	86
306	Border End	1713/522	W/ESK	50
306	Great How – Eskdale Fell	1713/522	W/ESK	52
306	Souther Fell	1713/522	N/BLE	139
309	Eagle Crag	1709/521	W/DER	22
310	Loweswater End – Carling Knott	1703/519	W/LOW	98
311	High Hartsop Dodd	1702/519	C/FAR	485
312	Gale Fell	1699/518	W/HIG	90
313	Brown How – Whinlatter	1696/517	NW/LOS	130
314	Little Yarlside	1691/516	E/SHA	209
314	Sallows	1691/516	E/KEN	218
316	High Tove	1689/515	W/DER	18
316	Watendlath Fell	1689/515	W/DER	18
318	Seat Robert	1688/515	E/SHA	206
319	Threlkeld Knotts	1686/514	C/DOD	171
320	Capplebarrow	1681/512	E/SHA	210
321	Bleaberry Knott – Birk Fell	1680/512	E/MAR	230
321	Gale Crag	1680/512	C/FAR	184
323	Mellbreak – South Top	1678/512	W/LOW	100
324	Broom Fell	1676/511	NW/LOS	130
324	Whoap	1676/511	W/LAK	86
326	Beda Head – Beda Fell	1670/509	E/MAR	231
326	Hen Comb	1670/509	W/LOW	99
326	Lowthwaite Fell	1670/509	N/NOS	156
326	Mellbreak – North Top	1670/509	W/LOW	100
326	Swinside	1670/509	NW/GRI	124
331	Low Pike	1667/508	C/FAR	186
331	Wythburn Fell	1667/508	W/DER	20
333	Sleddale Pike	1659/506	E/SHA	208
334	Cockup	1657/505	N/SKI	148
334	Little Mell Fell	1657/505	C/MEL	165
336	Stone Arthur	1652/504	C/FAR	187
337	Hare Shaw	1650/503	E/BRA	202
338	Ulthwaite Rigg	1648/502	E/SHA	208
339	Dodd (Skiddaw)	1647/502	N/SKI	147
340	High Dodd	1644/501	E/MAR	230
341	Castle How	1640/500	W/LAN	29
342	Yew Bank	1637/499	W/ESK	50
343	Stainton Pike	1632/498	S/WHI	259
344	Low How	1631/497	C/DOD	172
345	Seat How (Thornthwaite)	1627/496	NW/LOS	128
346	High House Bank	1625/495	E/SHA	209
347	Great Howe (Longsleddale)	1621/494	E/SHA	211
347	Yoadcastle	1621/494	S/WHI	258
349	Long Crag – Bannisdale Fell	1617/493	E/SHA	210
349	Robin Hood	1617/493	E/SHA	209
349	Tarbarrel Moss	1617/493	NW/LOS	130
352	Shivery Knott	1610/491	W/DER	18
353	Bampton Fell	1604/489	E/LOA	198
353	Green Crag	1604/489	S/HAR	253
355	High Nook – Gavel Fell	1601/488	W/LOW	96
356	Grike	1599/488	W/LAK	86
357	High Scarth	1598/487	W/ESK	50
358	Wansfell	1597/487	C/FAR	189
358	Woodend Height	1597/487	S/WHI	260
360	What Shaw	1593/485	E/SHA	209
361	Wansfell Pike	1588/484	C/FAR	189
362	Middle Crag	1587/484	W/DER	18
363	Sour Howes	1585/483	E/KEN	218
364	Longlands Fell	1581/482	N/NOS	156
364	Sharp Knott	1581/482	W/LOW	98
366	Gowbarrow Fell	1579/481	C/MEL	165
367	Armboth Fell	1570/479	W/DER	18
368	Hesk Fell	1565/477	S/WHI	259
369	Glede Howe	1562/476	E/SHA	206
370	Burnbank Fell	1558/475	W/LOW	98
370	High Pen	1558/475	W/LOW	96
372	Stoupdale Head	1548/472	S/BLC	265
373	Gowk Hill	1545/471	E/MAR	232
374	Crook Crag	1539/469	S/HAR	253
374	Pikes	1539/469	S/DOW	247
376	Brown Howe – Lingmoor Fell	1538/469	W/BOW	36
377	Barf	1536/468	NW/LOS	128
378	Powleys Hill	1526/465	E/BRA	202
379	White Hause	1525/465	N/NOS	154
380	Brown Rigg	1519/463	W/DER	20
381	Raven Crag	1512/461	W/DER	17
382	Banna Fell	1496/456	W/LOW	96
382	Graystones	1496/456	NW/LOS	130
384	Barrow	1494/455	NW/GRI	124
385	Dodd (Lorton)	1489/454	NW/GRI	124
386	Red Knott	1483/452	NW/DAL	111
387	Catbells	1481/451	NW/DAL	110
388	Floutern Cop	1480/451	W/LOW	96
389	Plough Fell	1470/448	S/WHI	260
390	Knock Murton	1467/447	W/LOW	96
390	Stile End	1467/447	NW/GRA	116
392	Binsey	1466/447	N/NOS	158
393	The Benn	1463/446	W/DER	17
394	Capple Howe	1460/445	E/KEN	218
395	Brownthwaite Crag	1457/444	E/MAR	232
395	White How – Birker Fell	1457/444	S/HAR	253
397	Glenridding Dodd	1450/442	C/DOD	174
397	Green Hill – Gowbarrow Fell	1450/442	C/MEL	165
397	Nab Scar	1450/442	C/FAR	186
397	White Pike – Birkby Fell	1450/442	S/WHI	258
401	Hawk Rigg	1447/441	S/CON	241
402	Great Crag (Stonethwaite)	1444/440	W/DER	21
403	Scar Lathing	1440/439	W/ESK	50
404	Kirk Fell – Lorton	1437/438	NW/LOS	130
405	Great Meldrum	1434/437	C/MEL	165
406	Kitty Crag	1427/435	S/CON	241
406	Lingmell (Ennerdale)	1427/435	W/PIL	78
406	Low Pen	1427/435	W/LOW	96
406	Naddle High Forest	1427/435	E/BRA	202
410	Arnison Crag	1422/433	C/FAR	184
411	Horseshow Crags	1421/433	S/HAR	252
411	Rowling End	1421/433	NW/GRA	116
411	Wallow Crag	1421/433	E/BRA	202
414	Glade How	1420/433	W/PIL	81

Order	Name	Altitude (ft/metres)	Area/ Group	Page
415	Pikeawassa – Steel Knotts	1417/432	E/MAR	232
416	High Fell	1404/428	S/CON	241
417	Brunt Knott	1400/427	E/KEN	216
417	Great Worm Crag	1400/427	S/HAR	253
419	Hollow Moor – Green Quarter Fell	1398/426	E/KEN	216
419	Lad Hows	1398/426	NW/GRA	118
419	Naddle Low Forest	1398/426	E/BRA	202
422	Great Whinscale	1394/425	S/HAR	253
422	Whinscales – Eskdale Fell	1394/425	W/ESK	52
424	Watermillock Fell	1391/424	C/MEL	165
425	Blake Rigg (Tilberthwaite)	1388/423	S/CON	241
425	Buckbarrow	1388/423	W/PIL	81
425	Low Fell	1388/423	W/FEL	104
426	Gibson Knott	1384/422	W/LAN	26
426	Stoneside Hill	1384/422	S/WHI	260
428	Castle Crag (Shoulthwaite)	1381/421	W/DER	17
428	Fisher Crag	1381/421	W/DER	18
428	Haystacks (Tilberthwaite)	1381/421	S/CON	241
428	Long Crag – Yewdale Fells	1381/421	S/CON	241
434	Harper Hills	1375/419	E/BRA	202
435	Brund Fell	1363/415	W/DER	21
435	Fellbarrow – Mosser Fell	1363/416	W/FEL	104
437	Four Stones Hill	1362/415	E/LOA	198
438	White Combe	1361/415	S/BLC	265
439	Lang How	1358/414	W/LAN	29
440	Loweswater Fell	1352/412	W/FEL	104
440	Scope End	1352/412	NW/DAL	110
442	Sourfoot Fell	1348/411	W/FEL	104
442	Swinescar Pike	1348/411	W/LAN	29
444	High Wythow	1345/410	S/CON	241
445	Owsen Fell	1342/409	W/LOW	98
446	Helm Crag	1329/405	W/LAN	26
447	Great Intake – Low Fell	1327/405	S/CON	241
448	Little Meldrum	1325/404	C/MEL	165
448	Throstlehow Crag	1325/404	W/ESK	52
450	Todd Fell	1314/401	E/SHA	210
451	Dawsonground Crags	1302/397	W/ESK	51
451	Whiteside Pike	1302/397	E/SHA	210
453	Castle Crag (Mardale)	1296/395	E/HST	225
453	Irton Fell	1296/395	W/SCR	64
453	Little Cockup	1296/395	N/NOS	155
453	Silverybield	1296/395	W/ESK	50
457	Silver How	1294/395	W/LAN	29
458	King's How – Grange Fell	1286/392	W/DER	21
458	Smithy Fell	1286/392	W/FEL	104
460	Darling Fell	1283/391	W/FEL	104
461	Blakeley Raise	1276/389	W/LAK	86
462	Hallin Fell	1273/388	E/MAR	232
463	Round How	1270/387	C/DOD	173
464	Fox Haw	1263/385	S/DOW	247
464	Hatteringill Head – Whin Fell	1263/385	W/FEL	104
466	Pinnacle Howe	1257/383	E/LOA	198
467	Walla Crag	1243/379	W/DER	16
468	Sleet Fell	1240/378	E/MAR	230
469	Heughstar Hill	1231/375	E/LOA	194
469	Stickle Pike	1231/375	S/DOW	249
471	Kinniside	1230/375	W/LAK	86
472	Kinn	1227/374	NW/GRI	123
473	Bracken How	1224/373	C/DOD	173
473	Ling Fell	1224/373	NW/LOS	131
473	Low Birk Fell	1224/373	E/MAR	230
476	Broad Crag – Birker Fell	1220/372	S/HAR	253
476	Low Wythow	1220/372	S/CON	241
478	The Pike	1214/370	S/WHI	259
479	Brackeny Crag	1212/370	S/CON	241
480	Latrigg	1207/368	N/SKI	145
481	Lamb Pasture	1205/367	E/SHA	210
482	Cocklaw Fell	1197/365	E/KEN	216
482	Godworth	1197/365	W/LOW	96
484	Troutbeck Tongue	1194/364	E/HST	223
485	Little Dodd (Loweswater)	1188/362	W/LOW	99
486	Side Pike	1187/362	W/BOW	36
487	Raven's Crag	1184/361	S/DOW	247
488	Sale Fell	1178/359	NW/LOS	131
489	Naddle Fell	1171/357	C/DOD	168
490	Rannerdale Knotts	1165/355	NW/GRA	118
491	High Pike Haw	1161/354	S/DOW	246
491	Latter Barrow	1161/354	W/LAK	86
493	Whin Crag (Eskdale)	1158/353	W/ESK	51
494	Orthwaite Bank	1142/348	N/NOS	155
495	Eycott Hill	1132/345	N/BLE	136
495	Lothwaite	1132/345	NW/LOS	131
497	Brock Barrow	1125/343	S/DOW	247
497	High Rigg	1125/343	C/DOD	168
499	Knipe Scar	1122/342	E/LOA	199
500	Swainson Knott	1118/341	W/LAK	84
501	Castle Rock	1112/339	C/DOD	169
502	Great Crag – Birker Fell	1109/338	S/HAR	253
502	Scale Knott	1109/338	W/LOW	100
502	Scalebarrow Knott	1109/338	E/BRA	202
502	Skelgill Bank	1109/338	NW/DAL	110
506	Boat How	1105/337	W/ESK	52
507	Loughrigg	1101/335	W/LAN	27
508	Great How (Thirlmere)	1100/335	W/DER	17
509	Little Eycott Hill	1099/335	N/BLE	136
509	Rivings	1099/335	NW/LOS	131
509	Swarth Fell (Kinniside)	1099/335	W/LAK	86
509	Top O'Selside	1099/335	S/OUT	273
513	Bowness Knott	1093/333	W/HIG	90
513	Watches	1093/333	N/SKI	148
515	Bigert	1086/331	S/WHI	259
515	The Knott – Stainton Fell	1086/331	S/WHI	258
517	Great Bank	1079/329	W/SCR	64
518	Kepple Crag	1076/328	S/HAR	253
519	Arnsbarrow Hill	1056/322	S/OUT	273
519	Black Crag – Black Fell	1056/322	S/OUT	270
519	Brown How (Ennerdale)	1056/322	W/HIG	90
519	Stone Pike	1056/322	W/LAK	84
523	Gummer's How	1054/321	S/OUT	275
524	Green How – Aughertree Fell	1053/321	N/NOS	159
525	Burn Edge	1050/320	W/LAK	86
526	Rough Crag (Birker Moor)	1047/319	S/WHI	258
527	Birch Fell	1043/318	S/OUT	275
527	Burthwaite Heights	1043/318	NW/LOS	131
529	Holme Fell	1040/317	S/OUT	270
530	Stang Hill	1037/316	S/OUT	273
531	Carron Crag	1030/314	S/OUT	272
532	High Hows (Lamplugh)	1027/313	W/LOW	98
532	Tarn Hill	1027/313	S/DOW	249
534	Goat Crag	1024/312	W/ESK	51
535	Kelton Fell	1020/311	W/LOW	96
535	Ponsonby Fell	1020/311	W/LAK	84
535	Seat How (Birker Moor)	1020/311	S/WHI	258
535	White Hall Knott	1020/311	S/BLC	265
535	Wren Crag	1020/311	C/DOD	168
540	Great Stickle	1001/305	S/DOW	249
540	Water Crag	1001/305	S/WHI	258

The Scafells from Brown Pike.

TOPS IN ALPHABETICAL ORDER

Name	Altitude (ft/metres)	Order	Area/Group	Page
Adam Seat	2185/666	165	E/HST	225
Allen Crags	2574/785	68	W/BOR	46
Ancrow Brow	1816/553	261	E/SHA	210
Angletarn Pike – North	1860/567	252	E/MAR	231
Angletarn Pike – South	1854/565	253	E/MAR	231
Ard Crags	1906/581	239	NW/GRA	118
Armboth Fell	1570/479	367	W/DER	18
Arnison Crag	1422/433	410	C/FAR	184
Arnsbarrow Hill	1056/322	519	S/OUT	273
Arthur's Pike	1747/532	288	E/LOA	195
Atkinson Pike (Foule Crag) – Blencathra	2772/845	29	N/BLE	141
Aughertree Fell – Green How	1053/321	524	N/NOS	159
Bakestall	2208/673	160	N/SKI	148
Bampton Fell	1604/489	353	E/LOA	198
Banna Fell	1496/456	382	W/LOW	96
Bannerdale Crags	2240/683	153	N/BLE	139
Barf	1536/468	377	NW/LOS	128
Barrow	1494/455	384	NW/GRA	116
Base Brown	2120/646	184	W/GRG	69
Beda Head – Beda Fell	1670/509	326	E/MAR	231
Bessyboot – Rosthwaite Fell	1807/550	268	W/BOR	44
Bigert	1086/331	515	S/WHI	259
Binsey	1466/447	392	N/NOS	158
Birch Fell	1043/318	527	S/OUT	275
Birk Fell Man – Birk Fell	1722/525	299	S/CON	240
Birkett Fell	2378/725	122	C/DOD	172
Birkhouse Moor	2356/718	127	C/HEL	179
Birks	2040/622	204	C/FAR	184
Black Combe	1970/600	225	S/BLC	265
Black Combe – South Top	1926/587	235	S/BLC	265
Black Crag – Black Fell	1056/322	519	S/OUT	270
Black Crag (Mickleden)	1929/588	234	W/LAN	32
Black Crag (Pillar)	2717/828	39	W/PIL	76
Black Sails	2443/745	99	S/CON	240
Black Star – Honister Crag	2077/633	195	W/GRG	68
Blake Fell	1878/573	245	W/LOW	98
Blake Rigg (Little Langdale)	1755/535	285	W/BOW	37
Blake Rigg (Tilberthwaite)	1388/423	425	S/CON	241
Blakeley Raise	1276/389	461	W/LAK	86
Blea Rigg	1776/541	280	W/LAN	29
Blea Tarn Fell	1830/558	259	W/DER	20
Bleaberry Fell	1935/590	233	W/DER	16
Bleaberry Knott – Birk Fell	1680/512	321	E/MAR	230
Blease Fell – Blencathra	2638/804	52	N/BLE	140
Blencathra – Blease Fell	2638/804	52	N/BLE	140
Blencathra – Gategill Fell Top	2792/851	28	N/BLE	140
Blencathra – Scales Fell	2238/682	154	N/BLE	140
Boat How	1105/337	506	W/ESK	52
Bonscale Pike	1718/524	304	E/LOA	195
Border End	1713/522	306	W/ESK	50
Borrowdale Head	1734/528	295	E/SHA	210
Bowfell	2960/902	12	W/BOW	39
Bowness Knott	1093/333	513	W/HIG	90
Bowscale Fell	2305/702	140	N/BLE	138
Bracken How	1224/373	473	C/DOD	173
Brackeny Crag	1212/370	479	S/CON	241
Brae Fell	1919/585	237	N/NOS	156
Brandreth	2344/715	128	W/GRG	68
Branstree	2339/713	130	E/BRA	203
Brim Fell	2611/796	59	S/CON	243
Broad Crag – Birker Fell	1220/372	476	S/HAR	253
Broad Crag (Scafell)	3054/931	5	W/SCA	56
Broad End	2726/831	37	N/SKI	148
Brock Barrow	1125/343	497	S/DOW	247
Brock Crags	1842/561	257	E/MAR	231
Broom Fell	1676/511	324	NW/LOS	130
Brown Crag	2001/610	217	C/HEL	178
Brown Hills	1808/551	267	C/DOD	172
Brown How – Whinlatter	1696/517	313	NW/LOS	130
Brown How (Ennerdale)	1056/322	519	W/HIG	90
Brown Howe – Lingmoor Fell	1538/469	376	W/BOW	36
Brown Howe (Mardale)	1736/529	292	E/BRA	203
Brown Pike	2237/682	156	S/DOW	246
Brown Rigg	1519/463	380	W/DER	20
Brownthwaite Crag	1457/444	395	E/MAR	232
Brund Fell	1363/415	435	W/DER	21
Brunt Knott	1400/427	417	E/KEN	216
Buck Barrow	1799/549	272	S/WHI	260
Buck Pike – Seathwaite Fell	2441/744	101	S/DOW	246
Buck Pike (Mickleden)	1988/606	223	W/LAN	32
Buckbarrow	1388/423	425	W/PIL	81
Burn Edge	1050/320	525	W/LAK	86
Burn Moor	1780/543	277	S/WHI	260
Burn Tod	1952/595	229	N/NOS	155
Burnbank Fell	1558/475	370	W/LOW	98
Burthwaite Heights	1043/318	527	NW/LOS	131
Calf Crag	1762/537	283	W/LAN	26
Calfhow Pike	2175/663	169	C/DOD	171
Capple Howe	1460/445	394	E/KEN	218
Capplebarrow	1681/512	320	E/SHA	210
Carl Side	2447/746	98	N/SKI	148
Carling Knott	1785/544	276	W/LOW	98
Carrock Fell	2174/663	170	N/NOS	152
Carron Crag	1030/314	531	S/OUT	272
Castle Crag (Mardale)	1296/395	453	E/HST	225
Castle Crag (Shoulthwaite)	1381/421	428	W/DER	17
Castle How	1640/500	341	W/LAN	29
Castle Rock	1112/339	501	C/DOD	169
Catbells	1481/451	387	NW/DAL	110
Catstycam	2919/890	16	C/HEL	179
Causey Pike	2090/637	191	NW/GRA	116
Caw	1735/529	294	S/DOW	247
Caw Fell	2288/697	143	W/PIL	78
Clough Head	2381/726	121	C/DOD	171
Cocklaw Fell	1197/365	482	E/KEN	216
Cockup	1657/505	334	N/SKI	148
Codale Head	2401/732	115	W/LAN	31
Cofa Pike	2700/823	41	C/FAR	184
Cold Pike	2300/701	141	W/BOW	37
Coldbarrow Fell – High Saddle	2215/675	158	W/DER	20
Coldbarrow Fell – Low Saddle	2152/656	175	W/DER	20
Combe Head	2405/733	112	W/BOR	44
Common Fell	1811/552	265	C/DOD	172
Coniston Old Man	2633/803	53	S/CON	243
Coomb Height	2057/627	201	N/NOS	152
Crag Fell	1716/523	305	W/LAK	86
Crag Hill	2751/839	34	NW/GRA	116
Crook Crag	1539/469	374	S/HAR	253
Dale Head	2472/753	97	NW/DAL	110
Darling Fell	1283/391	460	W/FEL	104
Dawsonground Crags	1302/397	451	W/ESK	51
Dead Pike – Steel Fell	1812/553	264	W/LAN	26
Demming Crag	1722/525	299	S/HAR	252
Dodd (Buttermere)	2103/641	188	W/HIG	91
Dodd (Lorton)	1489/454	385	NW/GRI	124
Dodd (Skiddaw)	1647/502	339	N/SKI	147
Doddick Fell – Blencathra	2434/742	102	N/BLE	140
Dollywagon Pike	2815/858	25	C/HEL	181
Dove Crag	2598/792	61	C/FAR	186
Dow Crag	2554/778	74	S/DOW	246
Eagle Crag	1709/521	309	W/DER	22
East Top – Bowscale Fell	2185/666	165	N/BLE	139
Eel Crag	2649/807	48	NW/GRA	116
Ennerdale Fell	2113/644	185	W/PIL	78
Esk Pike	2903/885	17	W/BOW	40
Eycott Hill	1132/345	495	N/BLE	136
Fairfield	2863/873	20	C/FAR	184
Fellbarrow – Mosser Fell	1363/416	435	W/FEL	104
First Crinkle	2733/833	35	W/BOW	39
Fisher Crag	1381/421	429	W/DER	18
Fleetwith Pike	2126/648	183	W/GRG	68
Floutern Cop	1480/451	388	W/LOW	96
Four Stones Hill	1362/415	437	E/LOA	198
Fourth Crinkle	2730/832	36	W/BOW	39
Fox Haw	1263/385	464	S/DOW	247
Froswick	2360/720	125	E/HST	222
Frozen Fell	2050/625	205	N/NOS	155
Gale Crag	1680/512	321	C/FAR	184
Gale Fell	1699/518	312	W/HIG	90
Gasgale Crags	2306/703	137	NW/GRI	124
Gategill Fell Top – Blencathra	2792/851	28	N/BLE	140
Gavel Fell	1726/526	296	W/LOW	96
Gavel Pike	2572/784	69	C/FAR	184
Gibson Knott	1384/422	426	W/LAN	26
Gill Crag – Hartsop above How	1870/570	249	C/FAR	184
Glade How	1420/433	414	W/PIL	81
Glaramara	2568/783	71	W/BOR	46
Glede Howe	1562/476	369	E/SHA	206
Glenridding Dodd	1450/442	397	C/DOD	174
Goat Crag	1024/312	534	W/ESK	51
Goat Scar	2054/626	204	E/HST	222
Godworth	1197/365	482	W/LOW	96
Gowbarrow Fell	1579/481	366	C/MEL	165
Gowk Hill	1545/471	373	E/MAR	232
Grange Fell – King's How	1286/392	458	W/DER	21
Grasmoor	2795/852	27	NW/GRA	118
Gray Crag	2293/699	142	E/HST	222
Graystones	1496/456	382	NW/LOS	130
Great Bank	1079/329	517	W/SCR	64
Great Borne	2019/616	212	W/HIG	90
Great Calva	2265/690	151	N/NOS	154
Great Carrs	2575/785	66	S/CON	238
Great Cockup	1726/526	296	N/NOS	155
Great Crag – Birker Fell	1109/338	502	S/HAR	253
Great Crag (Stonethwaite)	1444/440	402	W/DER	21
Great Dodd	2811/857	26	C/DOD	171
Great End	2984/910	11	W/SCA	61
Great Gable	2949/899	13	W/GRG	69
Great How – Eskdale Fell	1713/522	306	W/ESK	52
Great How (Swirl Band)	2526/770	81	S/CON	243
Great How (Thirlmere)	1100/335	508	W/DER	17
Great Howe (Longsleddale)	1621/494	347	E/SHA	211
Great Intake – Low Fell	1327/405	447	S/CON	241
Great Knott	2283/696	146	W/BOW	37
Great Lingy Hill	2021/616	210	N/NOS	152
Great Meldrum	1434/437	405	C/MEL	165
Great Mell Fell	1762/537	283	C/MEL	164
Great Paddy Crag	1745/532	289	S/WHI	260
Great Rigg	2513/766	83	C/FAR	186
Great Saddle Crag	1850/564	255	E/SHA	208
Great Sca Fell	2135/651	182	N/NOS	155
Great Slack – Seathwaite Fell	2073/632	197	W/BOR	46
Great Stickle	1001/305	540	S/DOW	249

PUBLISHER'S ACKNOWLEDGEMENTS

The publishers would like to thank Graham Thompson and Helen Scanlon
for their work on the text, Anne McCarthy for her diligent efforts in shaping
the index, and Ken Vickers and Jeremy Ashcroft for their advice.

INDEX

Entries in **bold** refer to names of walks. Where tops are indexed, page numbers
refer to their first mention in the text, for the walk in which they feature.